LEGISLATORS, LEADERS, AND LAWMAKING

Legislators, Leaders, and Lawmaking

The U.S. House of Representatives
in the Postreform Era

BARBARA SINCLAIR

The Johns Hopkins University Press
Baltimore and London

© 1995 The Johns Hopkins University Press
All rights reserved. Published 1995
Printed in the United States of America on acid-free paper
Johns Hopkins Paperbacks edition, 1998
9 8 7 6 5 4 3 2 1

The Johns Hopkins University Press
2715 North Charles Street
Baltimore, Maryland 21218-4363
The Johns Hopkins Press Ltd., London
www.press.jhu.edu

Library of Congress Cataloging-in-Publication Data will be found
at the end of this book.

A catalog record for this book is available from the British Library.

ISBN 0-8018-5712-0 (pbk.)

For my sisters Julia and Nora

Contents

Tables

Preface, 1998

In 1994 Republicans won control of the House of Representatives for the first time in forty years. How has Republican control affected the legislative process in the House and the functioning of the majority party leadership?

In this book, I argue that the legislative process in the House has changed significantly over the past two decades, that a House majority party leadership that is more active and more central in the legislative process is a key component of the change, and that the contemporary House requires such a leadership to legislate successfully.

I also argue that principal-agent theory offers the best framework for understanding congressional leadership. Congressional leaders are conceptualized as agents of their members; leadership styles and strategies are shaped by members' expectations, which are in turn shaped by the political and institutional context.

The change in party control provides a test of these arguments. Do they hold up with a new majority party? In the Afterword, I discuss Republican majority party leadership in the 104th and 105th Congresses (1995–98), and I contend that the arguments advanced in the body of the book do in fact hold up well. Principal-agent theory explains the leadership of Newt Gingrich and his fellow Republican leaders in the 104th and their somewhat altered leadership in the 105th Congress as well. The strategies Republican leaders use show striking similarities to those developed by their Democratic predecessors. The Republican leaders exerted unusually strong leadership in the heady 104th Congress; but in the 105th, with its much less favorable political climate, they continued as an activist and engaged, if somewhat less aggressive, leadership. To advance their goals, members of the contemporary House need activist leadership, and party leaders as their agents attempt to provide it.

Acknowledgments

Because this study is heavily based on interviews and participant-observation, I owe an immense debt to the many House members, staff aides, and informed observers who gave me some — and in some cases, a lot — of their precious time. They were promised anonymity, so I cannot mention them by name, but I am sincerely grateful. By far my greatest debt is to Representative Jim Wright (D-Tex.) and his staff. They allowed me to observe the leadership operation from the inside in 1978–79 when I was an American Political Science Association Congressional Fellow in the House majority leader's office, and again in 1987–88 in the Speaker's office. I can never truly repay them for that unique opportunity and for their many kindnesses. All unattributed quotations are from interviews I conducted or from my observation.

Steve Smith read the entire manuscript; his suggestions were, as always, perceptive and helpful and much improved the work. Remaining faults are, of course, my responsibility. Many other colleagues have read and commented on parts of the manuscript, often in the form of convention papers. I thank them all.

Francis Carney, Frank Way, and Grace Saltzstein helped me get the time in Washington for research that made this book possible. The Governmental Studies program at the Brookings Institution hosted me for a productive spring; Tom Mann, the staff, and the other fellows also made it an extraordinarily pleasant stay. Henry Tom, my editor, made the process of going from manuscript to book as painless as possible. Shirlee Pigeon did much of the typing with competence and good humor.

The Academic Senate of the University of California, Riverside, supported this research with several intramural grants, and the University of

California did so by granting me a Presidential Chair. The Dirksen Congressional Leadership Research Center also generously provided some financial support.

Some of the material in chapters 4 and 12 first appeared in my article "The Emergence of Strong Leadership in the 1980s House of Representatives," *Journal of Politics* 54 (August 1992): 658–84.

The Leadership Puzzle

An Introduction

In the spring of 1993, reconciliation legislation implementing President Clinton's economic program was approaching consideration on the House floor. Success was critical for the young Clinton administration and for the Democratic party and yet, because the package contained some unpalatable provisions, passage would be difficult. Republicans had made it clear that they would all vote against the plan, so a high level of Democratic support was essential. When "deficit hawk" Democrats expressed strong dissatisfaction with the Ways and Means Committee's provisions concerning entitlement spending, Majority Leader Dick Gephardt (D-Mo.) called the contending parties together and in a series of meetings personally brokered a compromise that assured the deficit hawks' support without losing that of liberals.

The Democratic party leadership then brought the bill to the floor under a rule carefully crafted to maximize the probability of its passage. The rule allowed only a vote on a comprehensive Republican substitute; it barred amendments to delete various unpopular elements of the package — the BTU tax and the tax on Social Security payments to high-income recipients. Many Democrats would have found it very difficult to explain votes against such amendments back home, especially in response to thirty-second attack ads, so allowing such amendments would have confronted Democrats with the unpleasant choice between casting a series of politically dangerous votes and contributing to the picking apart of the package on the floor.

Whip David Bonior (D-Mich.) headed up the vote-mobilization task force, which started work several weeks before the bill got to the floor. Members of the task force and then the top leaders themselves unrelentingly pursued every House Democrat; anyone who might have influence with an undecided or recalcitrant member — state party chairs, governors, union officials, personal friends — were enlisted whenever possible to help in the persuasion effort. The administration was, of course, very much engaged. Cabinet secretaries telephoned and visited Democrats. The president personally called close to sixty members — some of them repeatedly. The Speaker closed floor debate for his party, telling members that "this is a time to stand and deliver; this is a time to justify your election" (Hager and Cloud 1993).

Given the level of effort, Democrats could not fail to understand that how they voted on the bill would affect their future in the House. This vote would count heavily, everyone knew, in the leadership-maintained party-loyalty scores that influence a member's chances of getting a choice committee assignment. As Representative Barney Frank (D-Mass.) said, "Nobody got a pass on this" (ibid.). The pressure was unusually overt: freshmen circulated a petition demanding that any committee or subcommittee chair who voted against the party be stripped of his or her position by the caucus. Within hours, more than eighty Democrats, including several influential committee chairs, had signed.

The vote was close but the bill passed.

★ ★

In early May 1990, President Bush invited the congressional leadership to the White House for budget talks. Huge and rising deficits and major policy differences between Republican presidents and Democratic congressional majorities had made the usual budgetary process increasingly ineffective. In 1987 and in 1989, the congressional party leaders and top-level administration officials had made the key budget decisions in budget summits behind closed doors. With the economy showing signs of slowing, 1990 looked to be an even more difficult year.

The Democratic leaders agreed to begin talks, but they insisted that everything would have to be put on the table and they agreed among themselves that any proposals for higher taxes would have to come from the Republicans. Attempting to shake the high-tax image that Republicans had successfully pinned on them, Democrats were determined to refuse to take the initiative — and the blame — in proposing new taxes. An intense struggle to frame the debate and position themselves favorably followed. Democrats called on the president to exert leadership. The president and congressional Republicans repeatedly asserted that it was up to the Democrats as the majority party in Congress to move first. On June 26 the Democrats' firmness paid off when Bush issued a statement conceding that revenue increases would be necessary.

On September 30, the president and congressional leaders announced that a deal had been reached. Even after Bush's statement in late June, differences over taxes and domestic spending cuts had continued to block progress. Finally, the negotiating group was pared down to include on the congressional side only the top party leaders. The primary barrier to an agreement, Democrats claimed, was Bush's continued insistence on a cut in the capital gains tax without an offsetting income tax rate increase for the wealthy. Media attention increasingly focused on the capital gains issue and on Bush's opposition to any rate increase for the rich. The Democratic leaders refused to give in; nervous Republican congressional leaders, perceiving that Democrats were winning the public relations war on the issue, began to back away from insisting that such a tax change be included in the package. Bush capitulated.

Despite an intense campaign by the Democratic leadership and the president to sell the package, the House rejected it, with majorities of Republicans and Democrats voting in opposition. Many Republicans opposed the package because it included new taxes. Democratic liberals were upset with the big Medicare cuts and the regressive character of the new taxes.

House Democrats moved swiftly to put together their own budget plan. Bush's approval of a package that included new taxes inoculated Democrats against the charge that they alone were high taxers, many Democrats believed; most thought that, in the public exchange over the type of taxes to be levied, Democrats were the clear winners. Ways and Means Democrats, in consultation with the Speaker, put together a package more to the liking of the average Democrat. The bill was brought to the floor under a rule that denied Republicans a vote on their alternative because it cut the deficit by much less than had been agreed to in the summit. The House approved the Democratic reconciliation bill on October 16 by a vote of 227 to 203, with 217 Democrats and 10 Republicans voting for it.

The compromise that emerged from the House-Senate conference included a hike in the tax rate on high-income taxpayers, a proposal Bush had bitterly opposed, and other provisions that indirectly raised the taxes the wealthy would pay; capital gains taxes were not cut. Yet Bush had no real choice but to accept the result; it was that or nothing. And Democrats clearly commanded the high ground in the battle for public opinion.

Throughout the process of putting together a Democratic alternative and then negotiating a conference agreement, the chair of the Ways and Means Committee and the Democratic party leaders kept in contact with their members through frequent caucus meetings, informing them of developments and seeking their advice.

By the time a final conference agreement was reached, the leadership was in the midst of a full-court press aimed at ensuring passage. A vote mobilization task force had been at work; a list of "if-you-really-need-me" votes had been compiled; the Speaker as well as the lower-ranking leaders had made calls to persuade members to vote "yea." At 7:00 A.M. on Saturday, October 28, only hours after final agreement on the five-year, $490-billion deficit-reduction bill was reached, a weary House voted approval. That Saturday afternoon the Senate concurred.

★ ★

In early May 1988, Speaker Jim Wright decided that the House should pass an omnibus drug bill. According to the polls, the issue was the public's top concern during that election year; many House members were introducing bills and offering amendments in response. The Speaker called together the chairs of eleven committees with relevant jurisdiction, discussed with them the reasons for such a bill and its possible contents, and then said he wanted a bipartisan effort. He explained that Majority Leader Tom Foley (D-Wash.) would coordinate the effort and that he hoped a bill could be ready by mid-June.

Foley's task was to monitor the work of all the committees involved, to spot problems and try to work them out, and to push the participants to move quickly and settle their disputes expeditiously. To keep the process as bipartisan as possible, Foley regularly conferred with Minority Leader Bob Michel (R-Ill.). Those issues on which the committees were unable to reach a substantially bipartisan agreement were pushed up to Foley and Michel; which of those issues would be presented to the membership to decide on the floor was determined in negotiations between them. Tom Foley agreed to allow Republicans to offer their top-priority amendments on the floor in return for their limiting the number of such amendments.

By the August recess, the bill was ready for floor consideration and the rule had been adopted by the House; shortly after the recess, the House passed the bill. The end of the session was fast approaching and, if a bill was to be enacted, the myriad of House-Senate differences would have to be resolved quickly. To that end, as soon as the Senate passed its bill late on a Friday afternoon, the House leadership staff got the relevant House and Senate committee staffs together to begin the process. The party leaders had decided to avoid a formal conference if possible. First, staffers in each area were told to try to resolve the minor differences; those the staffers could not settle were pushed up to their bosses, who next attempted to do so. Foley, Michel, and two senators, designated the core negotiating group by the top party leaders, then presided over a marathon meeting to try to work out deals on the issues still outstanding; on each, the relevant members were called in, given a few minutes to present their positions, and pressed to come to an agreement. Finally, the Speaker, the Senate majority leader, and the Senate minority leader joined the core group to work out the final deals. In the wee hours preceding Congress's adjournment, both chambers passed the bill thus negotiated.

★ ⋅★

These stories suggest a House majority-party leadership that is highly active and deeply involved in multiple aspects of the legislative process, one that significantly influences the course of legislation and the probability of legislative success. To the extent that this portrayal of the contemporary majority-party leadership is an accurate one, it presents us with a puzzle. Congressional party leadership strength is generally believed to be a function of the strength of the political parties; vigorous parties with distinctive constituency bases that command the loyalty of most voters, ones that play a significant role in the recruitment and election of candidates, make strong legislative leadership possible (Cooper and Brady 1981; Rohde and Shepsle 1987). As Gary Orren and William Mayer succinctly summarize the common view, "weak electoral parties ensure weak governing parties" (1990, 217). If contemporary American political parties are as weak as conventional wisdom paints them, how could strong congressional leadership have emerged?

According to an argument still prevalent among nonspecialists, weak parties and the reforms of the early 1970s produced a decentralized House inimical to all leadership (see, for example, H. Smith 1988). As a result of party-weakening changes in the party and the electoral systems, members of the House get elected and reelected on their own; they raise their own money, they build their own organizations. Party leaders, institutional or local, can do little to help or hurt their reelection chances. Because party identification in the electorate has weakened so much as a determinant of voter choice in congressional elections, the party's record and the party's national image have little or no impact on members' electoral fates. With the reforms giving even junior members access to significant institutional resources, almost every member is capable of acting as a freelance entrepreneur, furthering his or her own reelection and pursuing his or her own policy agenda. As a consequence, members of a party have no real incentive to work or vote together, party cohesion is low, and leadership is weak and ineffective.

In the mid-1980s, congressional scholars began to notice phenomena at variance with this then widely accepted picture. After 1982, House Democrats' voting cohesion increased significantly; a trend toward more asser-

New Centralization

tive majority-party leadership became more and more evident (see Rohde 1988; Sinclair 1988; S. Smith 1989). By the late 1980s, some had begun to write about a "new centralization" on Capitol Hill (Davidson 1988).

Attempting to explain the increase in the Democrats' party cohesion, David Rohde presented evidence that the electoral constituencies of House Democrats had became more homogeneous since the mid-1960s (1988). As Republicans made inroads in the South and black voters became an important part of southern Democrats' electoral constituencies, the voters electing northern and southern Democrats became more alike demographically and in policy preferences.

Although it is certainly an important part of the answer, this increase in the homogeneity of House Democrats' constituencies does not solve the puzzle completely by any means. House Democrats' electoral constituencies are not so homogeneous as to produce a party membership with identical legislative preferences; members cannot be sure that, on tomorrow's hot issue, the legislative preferences of their constituents will be congruent with those of a majority of their party colleagues and, given the weakening of party identification, members cannot count on party-line voting by those voters who supported them in the last election to assure them of victory in the next. Weak parties external to the legislature give members an incentive to maintain their autonomy within the legislature. If the reformed House provided members with such excellent opportunities to pursue reelection and policy goals as individuals, why strengthen party leaders and thus make it possible for them to constrain members' entrepreneurial activities?

To explain the seeming anomaly of strong congressional party leadership in an era of relatively weak parties is one purpose of this book. More broadly, my aim is to describe and analyze how the current House majority-party leadership functions, to trace its evolution and explain its path. Because Democrats were the majority in the House continuously from 1955 to 1994, this is a study of Democratic party leadership. The focus on party leadership is used as a vantage point for understanding the legislative process in the House and how it has changed in the past several decades.

The analysis is based on the theoretical assumption, much elaborated in the next chapter, that congressional party leaders can best be understood as agents of the membership that chooses them and, therefore, that changes in leadership functioning are best explained as a response to the expectations of members as those expectations are shaped and altered by the institutional and political environment. From this assumption it follows that the functioning of the party leadership can only be understood within the context of an understanding of the functioning of the House as a whole. Consequently, this is also a book about the House and about how the House has changed over the past several decades. Most especially, it is a book about how the legislative process in the House has changed. While stories like those recounted above may be intrinsically fascinating to the political junkie in many of us, our interest in party leadership stems primarily from the potentially critical role the leadership may play in enabling the Congress to perform its core function of lawmaking.

Legislators, Leaders, and Lawmaking

A Principal-Agent Approach

Lawmaking is the central and defining task of a democratic legislature such as the U.S. Congress. A complex enterprise, lawmaking depends for its adequate performance on a number of component tasks being satisfactorily carried out. From the myriad of problems, issues, and policy proposals that someone in the society would like the legislature to address, a manageable subset must be selected for serious consideration. Policies to confront the selected problems must be formulated and legislation crafted. A majority of the chamber must be assembled to approve each piece of legislation. Agenda setting, policy formulation, and vote mobilization are all prerequisites to lawmaking, and each in turn depends on a variety of subsidiary activities.

The time and effort that legislating takes presents the legislature's members with a collective-action problem. Even if every member has an interest in given legislation passing, bearing the costs of carrying out the requisite tasks may be in no member's individual interest. For no member are the benefits likely to be so great that he or she has an incentive to bear the entire cost of producing the legislation alone. Furthermore, legislation is a public or collective good; if legislation a member favors is enacted, that member receives the benefits thereof whether or not he or she contributed to its passage. Consequently, every member has an incentive to take a "free ride," to allow others to bear the costs while that member reaps the benefits without contributing to their production. Since the same calculus holds for all members, none is likely to contribute, the collective good—legislation—will not be produced, and all will, by assumption, be worse off than if each had contributed to the production of the collective good (Olson 1965; Hardin 1982).

Even if legislators are willing to contribute, the problem of coordinating the efforts of many members remains. If each legislator autonomously decides on a course of action, common goals are unlikely to be achieved. Without coordination, some tasks will not be performed, those that are may not be carried out in the proper sequence, and others will be unnecessarily duplicated.

If the members of a legislature have differing legislative preferences, as they frequently do, these problems are exacerbated by the problem of forming and maintaining majority coalitions. A majority of members with reasonably similar or at least nonconflicting preferences must somehow be identified and then convinced to agree on a legislative measure; this coalition must then be held together until the legislation is enacted, often in the face of attempts by those not included to disrupt it and considerable incentives for members in the coalition to defect. And this must occur repeatedly.

Leaders as Agents

Leadership in legislatures can be seen as having been instituted to ameliorate problems of collective action (see Fiorina and Shepsle 1989; Kiewiet and McCubbins 1991; Cox and McCubbins 1993). Like other congressional structures, leadership positions are created to give certain members incentives to carry out necessary tasks that otherwise might not be performed. Within this framework, congressional party leaders are seen as agents of the members who select them and charge them with advancing members' goals, especially (though not exclusively) by facilitating the production of collective goods. Specifically, this approach conceptualizes leaders as agents charged by the party members with the facilitation of lawmaking.

To enable them to carry out the tasks with which they are charged, leaders are given by the members certain powers and resources. Of necessity, these are powers and resources that enable the party leaders to involve themselves in and affect the outcomes of the legislative process. The powers and resources House party leaders possess have, however, varied widely over time, as has the scope and rate of leadership activity. Speakers of the period from 1890 to 1910, for example, possessed enormous powers and employed them to involve themselves actively in all stages of the legislative process, providing necessary coordination but also policy leadership. In contrast, Speakers of the 1950s and 1960s were power- and resource-poor, and confined their activity primarily to the floor stage, coordinating the schedule and attempting modestly to facilitate passage of legislation shaped by autonomous committees.

How can this variation be explained? If leaders are conceptualized as agents of the members, members' expectations shape the functioning of the leadership. Changes in that functioning should then be traceable to changes in what members want or to changes in what, within a given context, members need in order to get what they want. The principal-agent framework thus provides the basis for an understanding of the functioning of the party leadership and its changes. Before the conceptual framework will help us come to grips with the puzzle of leadership in the contemporary House, however, it needs to be formalized and elaborated.

Legislation and the Goals of Members

To overcome collective action problems and make legislating practicable, legislators develop internal rules and structures: they create an institution (see Cooper 1977, 140; Krehbiel 1991, 14). But what sorts of institutional arrangements do they choose? Specifying the character of organizational choices requires assumptions about the goals members seek to advance and some evidence that those goals are linked to the passage of legislation.

What, then, are the goals members pursue? And is the passage of legislation significantly related to the advancement of those goals? The first is predominantly a question about fruitful theoretical assumptions; the second, while primarily an empirical question, hinges on the answers given to the first. Positing members who are single-minded pursuers of reelection, David Mayhew (1974) argues that members as individuals have no real interest in whether legislation passes or not, though he acknowledges that members have a collective interest in Congress functioning on at least a minimal level and thus remaining a player in the national political process.

Here, following Richard Fenno (1978), I will assume that members of the House have some mix of the goals of reelection, good public policy, and influence in the chamber. To those who would argue that reducing the complexity and diversity of goals of the 435 members of the House to only these three is a gross oversimplification, I would reply that this assumption is a necessary and serviceable one. Systematic analysis requires simplifying assumptions; the three goals posited here are relevant to those aspects of members' behavior and congressional functioning in which political scientists are most interested; and the assumption has proven fruitful in past work. To those who contend, conversely, that only the single goal of reelection need be posited, I reply that such oversimplification obscures much that is of interest about Congress. Many policy battles — over aid to the Nicaraguan contras, over foreign aid, over obscenity-related restrictions on National Endowment for the Arts grants, for example — are either totally inexplicable or require bizarre contortions to explain within the one-goal model. Confronted with past federal funding of photographs of sadomasochistic homosexual acts and crucifixes in urine, members who nevertheless work and vote for artistic freedom can in few instances plausibly be seen as motivated solely by reelection concerns. In addition, the reelection-only model lacks the source of dynamism that the potential for conflict among goals and the consequent need to balance goals gives the multigoal model.

Is the passage of legislation significantly related to the advancement of any or all of these goals? Those members for whom good public policy is a prominent goal are dependent on legislation passing for the advancement of that goal. But members solely interested in reelection also have an interest in the passage of legislation. The particularized district benefits that Mayhew and many rational-choice theorists see as so critical for reelection are contained in legislation. Some broader legislative proposals become sufficiently salient that their passage pleases constituents. To the extent that the party's or Congress's record influences voters' decisions, passing legislation becomes important (see Kiewiet and McCubbins 1991; Jacobson 1992b; Cox and McCubbins 1993). The political elites who provide financial and other sorts of campaign aid are likely to be very much interested in legislative results. Finally, for the influence-oriented member, winning is critical; in the legislative context, that usually means legislating successfully. Most members are assumed to pursue all three goals to some extent, and thus to have interests in legislation that stem from each of the three. The legislative preferences of a member are a function of his or her full set of goals.

Organizing to Legislate

If, at least some of the time, the passage of legislation is necessary to advance their goals, members of Congress have an interest in developing and maintaining organizational forms that will allow them to overcome collective action problems and to legislate. Structures and processes for agenda setting, for policy formulation, and for the assembling of majorities are needed. Organizational forms that allow these functions to be carried out involve of necessity the delegation of tasks and of resources for carrying them out to subsets of the membership.

The House long ago decided to organize itself along both party and committee lines. Each of the two structures can be shown to contribute in a distinctive fashion to overcoming the collective-action dilemmas legislators face. Processing a workload of any size and complexity requires a division of labor; a system of standing subject-matter committees divides labor and provides incentives for members to do their work and develop expertise (Fenno 1973; Shepsle 1978, 1989; Krehbiel 1991). Even if the members of a legislature all had the same legislative preferences, some sort of central leadership would nevertheless be required to provide the coordination services needed to funnel through the legislature as a whole the legislation the many committees produce. So long as members are assumed to have heterogeneous legislative preferences, there is an advantage to organizing a subgroup that is large enough to enact legislation but homogeneous in its legislative preferences relative to the membership as a whole. The political party is such a subgroup. Such a group is large enough to have collective-action problems of its own and so to require a leadership structure.

For much of its history, the House has organized itself on the dual bases of party and committee, with committees being charged with primary responsibility for policy formulation in their area of jurisdiction, and the party leadership, the only central leadership in the chamber, being charged with the assembling of majorities and with concomitant tasks of coordination. The distribution of tasks, powers, and resources has, however, varied over time. Furthermore, even these most basic organizational forms are endogenously determined; they are not dictated by the Constitution but are a function of chamber rules, which members could alter.

The internal structure that characterizes the House at a given time can be conceptualized as a particular distribution among party leaders, committee leaders, and rank-and-file members of the capacity to make or participate in the making of legislatively relevant decisions. That capacity can be seen as a function of institutional powers, of institutionally provided resources, and of the leverage over others' behavior these provide an actor possessing them. The distinctions here are among entitlements, specified by rules or customs, to make or participate in the making of certain decisions (that is, authority), resources that may facilitate the exercise of those rights, and influence over the decisions of other actors that may derive from the possession of particular institutional powers and resources.

Overcoming the collective action problems inherent in lawmaking requires that members delegate powers and resources to committees and party leaders. The benefits of such delegation can be great. Party leaders well endowed with powers and resources can significantly facilitate the passage of legislation that furthers the members' policy, reelection, and power goals. They can do so by providing basic coordination services, such as legislative scheduling; by facilitating, through side payments or the coordination of tacit or explicit logrolls, for example, the passage of legislation various subgroups of their membership want; and by policy leadership—that is, using leadership powers and resources aggressively to influence the congressional agenda and the substance of legislative outputs so as to translate broadly shared legislative preferences into law. Such party leaders can also use their legislative powers and resources to provide related (though not directly legislative) collective goods. They can, for example, enhance the party's image — a benefit to all the party's members — by passing legislation but also by other, associated activities (effective public advocacy, for example). Finally, a reasonably well endowed party leadership can provide its members with collective services and selective benefits that facilitate the members' ability to pursue their goals as individuals.

But delegation also carries risks. To be sure, the use of delegated powers and resources may be made contingent on formal, case-by-case member approval; mechanisms for holding agents accountable may make the aggressive or restrained use of delegated powers and resources dependent on contemporaneous member expectations. Yet enabling leaders to facilitate in a significant way the production of legislation requires giving them the authority to make — or (equivalently) the task of making — important legislative decisions directly or giving them the resources and the leverage to influence significantly the actions of those who do have the authority to make those decisions. In a preorganizational legislative "state of nature," the membership as a whole possesses all decision-making authority. By organizing to legislate, rank-and-file members delegate and thus give up, if only contingently, some of their power over decisions.

The Risks of Delegation

Clearly delegation is risky. Agents may use the powers granted them to pursue interests not those of their principals. If the passage of certain legislation furthers a member's goals, the passage of other legislation may have the opposite effect. Certainly legislation contrary to a member's notion of what constitutes good public policy or contrary to the interests or views of a member's constituents adversely affects his or her pursuit of goals. If the legislative preferences of a party's members are highly heterogeneous and noncongruent, the leaders, by promoting the legislative goals of some of the members, are likely to hinder those of others. If leaders are given extensive powers and resources, a member faces the risk that they will be used to facilitate the passage of legislation that hurts rather than helps that member.

Extensive delegation poses a second problem, one relevant to even a homogeneous party membership. Not all strategies for advancing members' goals necessarily rely on collective action or the passage of legislation. Depending on the distribution of powers, resources, and leverage in the House, members may have available a variety of strategies that they as individuals can implement (see Mayhew 1974; Loomis 1988). District-tending activities such as frequent trips home and the full exploitation of the frank are individualist reelection strategies, as is invariably voting in accordance with the wishes of constituents. By participating as individuals in the legislative process, promoting their own agendas and their own policy proposals, members can further any or all of the three posited goals. Entrepreneurial activities such as offering amendments in committee or on the floor or holding subcommittee hearings may yield a payoff in terms of influence, policy, or reelection. The member may establish himself or herself as someone to be reckoned with; he or she may move policy in the desired direction; the member's activities may produce actual district benefits or at least greater district visibility and a more favorable image.

The distribution of the capacity to make or participate in the making of legislatively relevant decisions, or (equivalently) the distribution of powers, resources, and leverage in the House, affects what sorts of individualist strategies are available to members. Certain distributions simply foreclose some strategies; under all, members risk to a greater or lesser degree having leaders use the powers and resources delegated to them in a way that hinders members in advancing their goals through individualist strategies. Both what leaders do themselves and what they prevent members from doing can have this effect. A central leadership that controls the floor schedule can make tending the district through frequent trips home easy or hard for members. Leaders with the power to determine the ground rules under which legislation is considered on the floor may limit the members' right to offer amendments and thus their ability to use legislative participation as a strategy for advancing their goals. Leaders who command great resources may make voting the district a very expensive strategy for some members; pursuing reelection through the individualist strategy of always voting in accordance with district sentiment may, for example, cost members the choice committee assignments they need to achieve their goal of influence.

The Determinants of Institutional Change

How and how much to delegate to agents are highly consequential decisions. Beyond the very broad guidelines set by the dual organizational bases of party and committee, the matter of which tasks, powers, and resources are delegated to certain subgroups and which are retained by the members as individuals has not been settled for all time. Members can change the rules that govern these delegations, and they have, from time to time, done so. They do so, I argue, when an existing set of arrangements no longer serves to advance their goals.

Although members can change existing arrangements, doing so requires collective action; consequently, even after a particular set of arrangements no longer serves to advance the goals of a majority of members, it may persist for a time before the collective-action problems can be overcome. Nevertheless, given the relatively modest size of the group at issue and the benefits to be gained, one would expect that over time members would alter arrangements so they would better serve to advance their goals. Furthermore, because aggressive use of the powers and resources delegated to an agent depends, to some extent, on members' acquiescence, significant change can occur without formal rules being altered.

To understand the delegation of powers and resources to the party leaders at a given time, and especially to understand changes in that set of arrangements over time, one needs an understanding of the costs and benefits to members of differing arrangements and of how those costs and benefits vary with context.

In assessing a change in the delegation of tasks, powers, and resources to the party leaders, a member must weigh against the benefits at least two potential costs of extensive delegation. First, the member must weigh the probability that the collective goods the leaders provide will, in fact, advance rather than hinder the member's goal quest. Unless the members of a party are perfectly homogeneous in their legislative preferences, a member must consider the likelihood that the legislation the leaders choose to advance will not reflect his or her preferences. If the party is highly heterogeneous, then clearly, for any given member, that probability is quite high. Consequently, the more heterogeneous the legislative preferences of the party's members, the higher the costs of a leadership with extensive powers and resources.

Even if their legislative preferences are highly heterogeneous, the members of a party still have an interest in their party leaders providing basic coordination services; the powers and resources leaders need to carry out coordination tasks such as legislative scheduling in a predominantly policy-neutral way are not, however, very great. By a relatively meager delegation of powers and resources, a heterogeneous membership can enable its leaders to provide some basic collective goods necessary to legislating and even equip them to facilitate modestly the members' ability to pursue their goals as individuals without making it possible for the leaders to promote the substantive legislative goals of some of the members at the expense of others. As intraparty homogeneity increases, the costs of policy leadership decrease and its benefits increase: for the typical member, the likelihood that the legislation the leaders seek to enact will be detrimental to the member's goals decreases and the likelihood that it will further those goals increases. Intraparty agreement is never perfect, and policy leadership requires extensive powers and resources. Delegating the considerable powers and resources necessary to enable the party leaders to affect the substance of legislative outputs becomes less risky as the party members' legislative preferences become more homogeneous.

A second cost of extensive delegation arises because leaders with extensive resources are able to constrain members' individualist goal-advancing strategies significantly and will certainly do so to some extent because performing their central task of providing collective goods to the members requires it. Even if the party members are perfectly homogeneous in their legislative preferences, there is always some cost in autonomy of extensive delegation to the leaders.

The question for members then becomes: how much delegation is necessary to secure passage of the legislation members need and want? When members believe a stronger, more assertive party leadership—one with more extensive powers and resources—is likely to make the difference between legislative success and failure, they are most likely to perceive a benefit in increasing leaders' powers and resources. If members do not need the assistance of a well-endowed leadership to pass the legislation they want, or if even a resource-rich leadership is unlikely to effect passage, members are unlikely to see a benefit in a greater delegation of powers and resources to the party leaders. Extant institutional arrangements as a whole, particularly the performance of other agents, and the political context affect the ease or difficulty of passing the legislation members want, and thus the perceived benefits of a well-endowed party leadership.

Since party leaders are not the only agents to whom tasks are delegated, members' judgments about the appropriate extent of delegation to party leaders depends on delegation to other agents and how adequately other agents are perceived as performing. If the legislation members need to advance their goals is being produced, they are unlikely to perceive a need for change. If, for example, committees are able to formulate and pass such legislation without the help of party leaders, members are unlikely to see a benefit in delegating greater powers and resources to those leaders. On the other hand, if committees become incapable of passing their legislation or the legislation they do pass is unsatisfactory, members are likely to look to the possibility of delegating to the leaders power and resources sufficient to enable them to provide the help members need.

The political context also affects the ease or difficulty of passing the legislation members need to advance their goals. The extent to which the president's policy and electoral goals coincide or conflict with those of majority-party members is perhaps the single most important political-context variable. As a president of the other party is likely to have very different legislative preferences, divided control of Congress and the executive branch is likely to increase significantly the difficulty of legislating. Public opinion and especially the political mood as members perceive it, the party ratio in the chamber, and the control of the other chamber may also make passing the legislation members want easy or difficult.

To summarize, a change in the homogeneity of party members' legislative preferences alters the costs and benefits to members of assertive versus restrained party leadership, and consequently may lead members to increase or decrease the powers and resources delegated to party leaders. Changes within the institution or in the political environment that alter the difficulty of enacting the legislation members need to advance their goals may thereby also alter the perceived costs and benefits to members of an assertive or restrained leadership, and thus may lead members to expand or diminish the powers and resources they delegate to their party leaders.

Members base their choices about organizational forms, I contend, on perceived costs and benefits. A proposed change is evaluated in terms of whether it helps or hinders members in advancing their goals. However, since most members have multiple goals, constructing an institution that will allow for the maximization of all of a member's goals simultaneously is unlikely to be possible. Furthermore, uncertainty about the future political context and thus about the impact of particular arrangements is always present to some extent. Consequently, organizational choices involve tough trade-offs. In particular, members confront the most basic trade-off: between extensive delegation to agents so as to facilitate collective action on the one hand and, on the other, an equal distribution of power and resources and consequent high autonomy for members to pursue their goals as individuals.

Given the complexity that multiple goals and uncertainty create, members' assessments of the costs and benefits of various organizational arrangements will almost always lead them to aim for some sort of balance between the extremes. The perceived optimum balance does vary as a function of members' cost-benefit calculus. In the extent of the powers and resources delegated to agents and the extent to which the use of delegated powers is contingent on members' approval, organizational arrangements reflect a past collective judgment about the appropriate balance. In addition, members' current judgments shape their expectations of their leaders. Depending on their notions of the optimal balance, members may expect leaders to use the powers and resources delegated to them aggressively to produce collective goods, especially legislation; or they may expect leaders to use their powers and resources with restraint and avoid putting constraints on members' pursuit of their goals through individualist strategies.

Members' Expectations and Leadership Functioning

Members' expectations of their leaders can be formulated as follows: members of the House expect their party leaders to advance the members' goals of reelection, policy, and influence, especially but not exclusively by facilitating lawmaking, but without imposing unacceptable constraints on members' pursuit of their goals through individualist strategies. The expectation that leaders foster collective action and provide collective goods stands in potential conflict with the expectation that leaders should not unduly constrain members in pursuing their goals through individualist strategies; adequately meeting both requires careful balancing. What members consider the optimal balance will vary over time as a function of the costs and benefits to members of assertive versus restrained central leadership. Those costs and benefits, in turn, are a function of the political and institutional context. The costs and benefits and consequently the optimal balance can vary among members as well as across time, further complicating the leaders' task of meeting members' expectations.

Members may see party leaders as their agents and have certain expectations about the leaders' performance, but why would the leaders be expected to comply? The process by which leaders are selected operates as a key mechanism of accountability (Peabody 1976). Party leaders are directly elected and biennially reelected by the party members. To the extent that leaders value their positions and want to retain them, they have an incentive to try to fulfill members' expectations. Less directly, members "enforce" their wishes through the institutional structure that characterizes the House at a given time. The way in which powers and resources are distributed among party leaders, committees, and rank-and-file members, and the extent and the character of delegation to the leaders, shape and constrain leadership functioning. A given structure reflects a previous collective judgment about the relative costs and benefits of assertive versus restrained leadership. When those costs and benefits change in a major way, members will over time alter institutional arrangements to better conform with their altered expectations.

The conceptualization of party leaders as agents for their members as here elaborated will be used below to explain how the current House majority-party leadership functions, and how and why it developed as it did.

The House and Its Leadership from the 1950s through the 1970s

From feudalism to the atomistic competition of an unregulated market —
this is the way the change in the House from the 1950s through the
reforms of the 1970s is often characterized (see MacNeil 1963; H. Smith
1988). Certainly the prereform and postreform Houses differed radically
in how they distributed the capacity to make or participate in the making
of legislative decisions. As most discussions of the reforms stress, rank-
and-file members gained at the expense of committee leaders. In addition,
the complex of changes during the reform era included a major augmenta-
tion of the powers and resources delegated to the majority-party leaders
and brought about an increase in the scope and rate of leadership activity.

If congressional leaders are best understood as agents of their members,
the explanation for the change in the functioning of the leadership should
hinge on changes in members' expectations — changes resulting from alterations in the costs and benefits to members of extant arrangements.

Party Leadership during the Committee Government Era

"A modern Democratic Speaker," Representative Dick Bolling (D-Mo.)
wrote in the mid-1960s,

> is something like a feudal king — he is first in the land; he receives elaborate
> homage and respect; but he is dependent on the powerful lords, usually
> committee chairmen, who are basically hostile to the objectives of the national
> Democratic party and the Speaker. . . . Rayburn was frequently at odds with
> the committee oligarchs, who rule their own committees with the assured
> arrogance of absolute monarchs. (1965, 70)

1920-1970
Cmt Gov.

The period from approximately 1920 through 1970 can be characterized as an era of committee government in the House of Representatives (see Fenno 1965). The distribution of legislative labor followed familiar outlines, with committees being charged with the formulation of legislation and majority-party leaders with coordination and the assembling of floor majorities. During this period, however, the committees' charge was broadly interpreted, while the leadership's role was narrowly circumscribed. Party leaders were "concerned with the flow of legislation rather than its detailed contents," Randall Ripley reported in the mid-1960s. "Seldom do they take a part in framing legislative language or in initiating legislation. They assume that either the executive branch or the relevant congressional committees will do these jobs" (1967, 6).

Flow / Content

The distribution of powers and resources in the House during this period was consonant with a broad role for committees and their chairs in the legislative process and a narrow role for the party leaders. Particularly after the Reorganization Act of 1946, committee jurisdictions were sufficiently tightly delineated to give the party leaders little leeway in the referral of bills to committee. Rules for bypassing committees were extremely cumbersome. Consequently, the power to propose legislation rested with the committees. To get legislation to the floor, a majority of the members of the committee needed to be persuaded.

Cmt. Chair

Given the enormous powers and resources the committee chair commanded, persuading the committee usually meant first persuading the chair. The chair controlled the committee's agenda, organization, budget, and staff. The chair decided which bills the committee would consider and in what order; the chair determined the committee's subcommittee structure and appointed its subcommittee chairs. Control over budget and staff provided the chair with the resources for maximizing the capacity to shape legislative outcomes that control of the agenda and the committee's organization conferred. Because chairmanships were attained purely on the basis of committee seniority, they were independent positions of influence. Neither the party leaders nor the members had available a practical means for removing a chair. Consequently, in the exercise of their powers, chairs were not constrained by a need to be responsive to any internal party constituency in order to retain their positions.

When committees brought their legislation to the floor, they were aided by the rules. The lack of recorded votes in the Committee of the Whole, where bills are amended, served to deter attempts to alter legislation, and to make attempts that did occur less likely to succeed. The committee chair was aware of how a member voted, while constituents, interest groups, and the media — forces that might dictate a vote contrary to the chair's wishes — seldom were. Given the chair's powers and consequent ability to retaliate, it seldom made sense to challenge the committee.

In contrast to committees and their chairs, the party leaders' powers and resources for influencing the legislative process were relatively meager. The Speaker had the power to appoint members to special and select committees and a variety of commissions, but few of these positions were highly valued. Party leaders exerted considerable influence over the initial assignment of members to standing committees, but the Committee on Committees consisted of Ways and Means Democrats and did not officially even include the party leaders (Masters 1963). Neither the leadership nor any other entity possessed removal power; once a member attained a coveted committee position, that member was considered entitled to hold it for as long as he or she remained in the House.

The task of presiding that the House assigns the Speaker did confer on him some capacity to influence the legislative process.[1] As presiding officer, the Speaker interprets and enforces the chamber's rules. Although rules, precedents, and traditions act as constraints, the position of presiding officer of the House is one of considerable authority.

The party leaders were charged with the scheduling of legislation for floor debate, a task that would potentially bestow considerable leverage, but the leaders' actual control over the flow of legislation to the floor was only partial. The Rules Committee, which grants the special rules under which most major legislation is brought to the floor, was, like other committees, independent of the party leaders; in the late 1930s, it came to be dominated by a conservative coalition of southern Democrats and Republicans. Democratic Speakers of the 1940s, 1950s, and 1960s could not assure consideration on the floor of legislation reported by the substantive committees (Robinson 1963; Oppenheimer 1977). No abundance of resources compensated for the party leaders' meager powers. Staff available to party leaders was minimal. In the late 1950s and early 1960s, Speaker Sam Rayburn (D-Tex.), according to his longtime aide D. B. Hardeman, employed a total of eight people in his leadership and constituency offices combined.

Thus, during the committee government era, legislation was the product of a number of autonomous committees headed by powerful chairs who derived their positions from their seniority on the committees. The chair's great organizational and procedural powers over the committee and structural advantages such as the lack of recorded votes on floor

1. Since certain jobs, such as Speaker and president, have not yet been held by women, I have used "he" when referring to the individuals who have historically occupied those offices.

amendments led to a system of reciprocity or mutual deference among committees that protected most legislation from serious challenge on the floor of the House (Fenno 1973). Committees exercised considerable autonomy in the setting of their legislative agendas as well as in the shaping of legislation, especially during periods of divided control.

Since Franklin Roosevelt's time, when the president and the congressional majority have been of the same party the president has set the majority party's and Congress's policy agenda (Wayne 1978). During the committee government era, when control of Congress and the White House was divided, the majority party's policy agenda consisted of whatever emerged from the autonomous committees. Neither members' expectations nor leaders' powers and resources provided a basis for a strong party leadership role in agenda setting.

The party leaders' role in the policy process was largely restricted to facilitating passage at the floor stage of legislation written by autonomous committees. Party leaders seldom if ever interceded in committee to shape legislation; the chairs' power and norms of deference to committee worked against such involvement.

Even at the floor stage, the role of the leaders was somewhat restricted. Although the Speaker as presiding officer had considerable control over the flow of legislation to and on the floor, the independence of the Rules Committee during this period meant that the party leaders' control over the scheduling of legislation for floor consideration was problematic. Intercommittee reciprocity meant that most committees could expect to pass most of their legislation on the floor without great difficulty; consequently, committees and their chairs did not often require help from the leadership. On the other hand, on those highly controversial issues that were fought out on the floor, the party leaders' meager powers and resources limited the scope and the effectiveness of their coalition-building efforts.

Within the committee government system, rank-and-file members' capacity to participate in the making of legislative decisions was restricted. Committee members were dependent on the chair for their subcommittee assignments, for their current subcommittee chairmanship or their prospects of one in the future, for access to committee staff, and even for the opportunity to participate in committee hearings or the markup of legislation. Rank-and-file members' lack of legislative staff, norms of apprenticeship, and sometimes the autocratic behavior of powerful chairs dampened junior members' participation within committees. Closed committee markups limited the information available to those not on the committee. Their lack of information and staff and their unwillingness to offend powerful committee chairs restricted floor participation by rank-and-file members.

If, as I argue in chapter 2, House members over time shape the chamber's internal structure so that it will facilitate the advancement of their goals, the benefits of the committee government system must have outweighed its costs for a majority of members for some considerable part of its existence. What benefits could the system confer to compensate for the constraints that it placed on rank-and-file members' participation?

These members seem to have gotten two important benefits from the system. First, it enabled them to vote their districts and pay little or no penalty if that meant voting against party majorities. Second, members were given the opportunity to ascend the seniority ladder to committee power secure in the knowledge that no leader or faction could block them. Members who increasingly perceived their electoral fates to be dependent on their own efforts and not on party success or party organization valued independence in voting behavior, especially as the regional split within the Democratic party deepened after World War II (Sinclair 1982). Members increasingly dedicated to House careers valued an automatic mechanism for advancement, especially within the context of a split party (see Polsby 1968). True, the restrictions the system placed on junior members' capacity to participate in the making of legislative decisions imposed costs on those members, but immediate participation was not necessary for reelection. For most members during the 1950s, deferring participation — serving an apprenticeship — in return for eventual automatic advancement was a reasonable trade-off. So too was specialization in return for autonomy, especially since the committee-assignment process tended to put members on those committees most important to their constituencies. So long as the system produced legislation that satisfied a member's policy and reelection goals, the system's benefits outweighed its costs for a majority of members.

In fact, the committee government system did solve the collective-action problem; it enabled the House to produce legislation, though the key coordinating mechanism was intercommittee reciprocity rather than central leadership. The system was effective at producing the sort of legislation — public-works bills and farm legislation — that the majority of members needed for reelection.

After 1946, as a result of the Reorganization Act and the differing electoral safety of northern and southern Democrats, the workings of the seniority system produced a disproportionate number of southern committee chairs. Given the powers of the chairs, the result was a conservative cast to policy. Prior to the 1958 elections, however, a majority of the

House membership was relatively conservative; true programmatic liberals were a minority even within the Democratic party. A precise count of Democrats who perceived the passage of liberal legislation as crucial to advancing their reelection or policy goals is not, of course, possible. However, the list of those who, in early 1957, signed the Liberal Manifesto, a comprehensive program of liberal legislation, provides a serviceable estimate (Kofmehl 1964, 259). These eighty members made up just about one-third of the total Democratic membership of the 85th Congress.

Beginning in the late 1930s, the Democratic party had split along regional lines that became deeper after World War II. Although evident on a number of issues, the split was particularly sharp on social-welfare issues, especially labor legislation (Sinclair 1982). On issues such as housing, aid to education, and the minimum wage, southerners were increasingly conservative and opposed further extensions of the New Deal thrust, while northern Democrats tended to be predominantly though not universally liberal. For much of the period between the end of World War II and the late 1950s, northerners and southerners were fairly evenly balanced in numbers; neither made up a sufficiently large proportion of the House Democratic membership to dominate the party.

The persistent intraparty split clearly affected Democratic members' assessments of the costs and benefits of permissive versus assertive party leadership as it affected their assessments of the costs and benefits of the system as a whole. Party leaders with the powers and resources to engage in true policy leadership would have posed a threat to the policy and reelection goals of a significant segment of the membership. And because, by and large, committees were able to formulate particularistic, constituency-benefit legislation satisfactory to most interested members and pass it on the floor without a great deal of assistance, a majority of the members perceived no need for and thus no benefit to be derived from a more active, assertive leadership.

The leadership strategies of Sam Rayburn, the most highly regarded Speaker of the committee-government era, were clearly tailored to members' expectations of a permissive rather than an assertive central leadership, of a leadership that provided coordination services but seldom engaged in policy formulation (Albert 1990; Cooper and Brady 1981). In the shaping of legislation, he largely deferred to the committees and their powerful chairs. Rayburn might occasionally use his central position to broker agreements among members of the small group of key actors. More frequently, he might petition committee leaders to report out particular legislation, using his longstanding personal relationships with them to produce a favorable response. Because neither membership expectations nor leadership resources provided Rayburn with a basis for directing committees and their chairs, he relied on personal persuasion and made few demands. His demands of rank-and-file members were also sharply limited. In building floor coalitions, he used a highly personal, low-key approach. Members were seldom pressured to vote a given way; rather, Rayburn, who obtained some leverage from the myriad of small favors he performed for members, used personal persuasion and the members' sense of obligation. To dampen intraparty conflict, Rayburn avoided using party mechanisms such as the caucus, which could provide the contending factions with a forum for direct confrontation. Carl Albert (D-Okla.), Rayburn's whip and later the Speaker, summed up Rayburn's approach to leadership and the context to which it was tailored:

> Historically, the elected leadership of Congress had maintained its institutional authority by controlling the Rules Committee and the legislative committees, as well as by using the Democratic caucus to shape party policy. In the 1950s, the Rules Committee had become an independent fiefdom. Only on very important matters could Speaker Rayburn step in to direct a committee chairman's work, and even then his entree was his enormous personal prestige. Sam Rayburn would not cheapen that currency by using it often. The party caucus that other Speakers had used to bind Democrats to a common position had withered to brief biennial assemblies to renominate our leadership team. Mr. Rayburn dared ask no more of it for fear that the party would split wide open. (1990, 231)

The Rayburn strategy — and that followed by his immediate successor, John McCormack (D-Mass.) — was consonant with and well suited to maintaining the committee government system and, as such, met the expectations of those members who benefited from that system. During Rayburn's tenure, such members made up the majority of the party's membership; during McCormack's, the membership changed significantly and its expectations of its leaders also began to change.

The Roots of the Reform Thrust

For a majority of House members, the benefits of the committee government system outweighed the costs, but for junior programmatic liberals the results of that calculus were much less favorable (Bolling 1965; Ferber 1964). The powerful committee chairs were largely conservative southerners; they, not the party leaders or the party as a whole, set the policy agenda and determined the substance of legislation. The chairs thwarted the liberals' policy goals by blocking liberal legislation, and frustrated the liberals' desire to participate meaningfully in the legislative process by the often autocratic way they ran their committees.

During most of the 1950s, liberals were not sufficiently numerous to do anything more than complain. With the 1958 elections, however, the composition of the House Democratic membership began to change. Those elections brought sixty-three new Democrats into the House, fifty-seven of them from the North. The party balance in the chamber changed from 54 percent Democrat in the 85th Congress (1957–58) to 65 percent in the 86th (1959–60).

Despite the big Democratic margins in both chambers, the policy output of the 86th Congress was disappointing to liberals. Many blamed conservative control of the major committees, especially of the Rules Committee, for the meager policy results. Howard Smith (D-Va.), the committee chair, and his bipartisan conservative majority on the Rules Committee had given Speaker Rayburn trouble throughout the congress, refusing to grant rules for legislation liberals wanted brought to the floor or extracting substantive concessions as the price for granting a rule. In a notorious case that became something of a cause célèbre, Smith refused the rule necessary for sending an aid-to-education bill to conference. He thus killed legislation intensely favored by liberals even though both chambers had passed it.

In response to their continued policy impotence in spite of their greatly augmented numbers, liberal Democrats late in the first session of the 86th Congress formed the Democratic Study Group (DSG) (Ferber 1964; Kofmehl 1964). The DSG's initial and ostensible purpose was to provide information and coordination for liberal policy efforts; in fact, it would also play the lead role in efforts to reform the House.

After the election of John Kennedy as president in 1960, the DSG prevailed on Speaker Rayburn to do something about the Rules Committee. Unchecked, the committee might well have prevented the Democratically controlled House from even voting on the major elements of the Democratic president's program. Of the options suggested, Rayburn characteristically chose the one that would do least violence to the committee government system. Instead of purging a disloyal Democratic member, Rayburn decided to pack the committee. After an intense battle, the Speaker prevailed on the floor by a narrow margin (Cummings and Peabody 1969).

During the 1960s, the composition of the Democratic party and of the House continued to change. The Democrats' margin, which had been narrow before 1958, varied between solid and enormous. From 1951 through 1958, Democrats held an average of 52.4 percent of House seats; from 1959 through 1970, they averaged 60.8 percent. As Republicans made inroads in the formerly solid South and Democrats scored successes in previously Republican areas in the North, the Democratic membership became increasingly northern. Members from the core southern states

Table 3.1   Voting Alignments on Domestic Policy in the 1950s, 1960s, and 1970s (% support)

Issue Area	Democrats		Republicans*
	North	South	
Social Welfare			
1953–60	93.5	42.2	32.7
1961–68	95.4	40.4	33.3
1969–76	92.9	50.9	32.8
Civil Liberties			
1953–60	93.9	3.5	64.8
1961–68	76.9	12.0	41.5
1969–76	76.8	24.3	29.3
Government Management of the Economy			
1953–60	91.7	77.1	13.2
1961–68	92.0	69.4	17.3
1969–76	83.1	45.3	24.6

Source: Sinclair 1982.

*Republicans from the South are excluded from mean civil-liberties scores.

(the states of the Old Confederacy, excluding Tennessee) made up 40 percent of the Democratic membership from 1953 to 1958; the proportion dropped to about 33 percent from 1959 to 1964, and to 30 percent during the period from 1965 to 1970.

The ideological differences between northern and southern Democrats not only persisted but intensified as the issue agenda expanded in the 1960s (see Sinclair 1982). Social-welfare issues, which had divided Democrats throughout the postwar years, continued to do so. Southern Democrats were considerably closer to Republicans than to their northern party colleagues in their level of support for social-welfare legislation during the Kennedy-Johnson administration, just as they had been during the Eisenhower administration (see table 3.1). Civil-liberties legislation divided Democrats to an even greater degree, but in the 1940s and 1950s it was a relatively minor part of the congressional agenda. In the late 1950s and the 1960s, civil rights moved to the top of the agenda. The issue of government management of the economy and the nation's resources has historically tended to divide the parties and unite the regional factions within the Democratic party. The emergence of new issues in the latter part of the 1960s strained party unity in this area also. As consumer and environmental legislation began to appear on the active agenda, the support of southern Democrats decreased. In sum, on the full range of domestic issues that were at the forefront of controversy during the 1960s, northern and southern Democrats were at odds.

Despite their increasing numerical dominance of the party, liberal northern Democrats did not control most positions of real power within the chamber. As a result of the seniority system, southerners held a disproportionate share of the committee chairmanships. From the 84th Congress (1955–56), when Democrats regained control of the House, through the 89th Congress (1965–66), members from the core South never held fewer than half the chairmanships of the standing committees, and averaged 55 percent. True northerners (those from states other than the core South or Oklahoma, Kentucky, and Tennessee) held, on average, only 35 percent. By the very late 1960s, southern dominance had abated somewhat; core southerners held 45 percent of the chairmanships during the 90th and 91st Congresses (1967–71) on average, and northerners 50 percent. However, Appropriations, Ways and Means, and Rules, the three most powerful committees, were all chaired by southerners.

Southerners' greater seniority also translated into a disproportionate share of the most attractive subcommittee chairmanships. During the 84th Congress, members from the core South, who made up 40 percent of the Democratic membership, held seven of eleven Appropriations subcommittee chairmanships (64%); by the 91st Congress, when they made up 31 percent of the Democratic membership, they still held five of the thirteen subcommittee chairmanships (38%) — the same number as held by true northerners, who made up almost two-thirds of the party's membership.

Given the starkly differing legislative preferences of the conservative southern committee leaders and the heavily liberal northern rank and file, the committee government system clearly did not serve to advance the goals of the latter. Because of the autonomy of committees and the power of committee leaders, conservatives' control of a disproportionate share of the committee leadership positions biased policy, or so liberals believed. Even the packing of the Rules Committee had not assured the party leadership of firm control over the flow of legislation to the floor. The chair remained powerful and the members independent of the party leadership; when a committee majority opposed legislation the party leadership wanted to bring to the floor, it could still deny a rule.

The rank and file had no real leverage over those with the lion's share of the capacity to make legislative decisions; committee chairs, although nominally agents of the majority party, depended for their positions on neither the rank and file nor the central leadership. On the other hand, the central leaders, whom the rank and file chose and thus could influence, had a restricted role in the legislative process; they provided some coordination services but were precluded from policy leadership.

The policy differences between committee leaders and the rank and file may well have precipitated an increase in autocratic behavior by committee leaders; certainly junior members found the constraints on their participation all the more frustrating because they considered the committees' legislative output unsatisfactory.

The mass of highly significant liberal legislation passed during the mid-1960s demonstrated that, under extraordinary circumstances, internal structural barriers to nonincremental policy change could be overcome (Brady and Sinclair 1984). For a time, liberal dissatisfaction with the system lessened. However, in the late 1960s, in the aftermath of the loss of the overwhelming numbers they had commanded in the mid-1960s and the replacement of a skillful progressive ally with the often hostile Nixon as president, liberals again perceived the committee government system to be a significant barrier to the advancement of their goals.

Party Leadership in the Last Prereform Congress (1969–70)

An examination of the 91st Congress, the last prereform congress, illustrates the restricted scope of leadership activity during the committee government era, the conditions that fostered such a modest role, and the bases for liberal dissatisfaction with the system.

A global generalization about leadership activity in a particular congress inevitably lacks precision, and this makes valid comparisons over time impossible. Independently assessing leadership activity on each of the major pieces of legislation during a congress, in contrast, allows rigorous comparisons with the congresses to be discussed below. Doing so requires that the congressional agenda of major issues be specified. Here the list of major legislation provided in *Congressional Quarterly* (*CQ*), augmented by those measures on which key votes occurred (again according to *CQ*), is used to define the agenda.[2] This produces a list of legislation considered major by expert contemporary observers.

A distinct and important form of leadership activity is agenda setting, a group of activities aimed at highlighting, focusing attention on, and attempting to build pressure toward action on a problem, issue, or policy proposal. As the president is considered the premier governmental agenda

2. For the 91st and the 94th Congresses, the list of major legislation is obtained from the relevant *Congressional Quarterly Almanacs* (*CQA*); for the later congresses, from the periodic listings in the *Congressional Quarterly Weekly Reports* (*CQWR*). A very few items, on which there was no House action, that did not reach the floor in the Senate and were not items on either the president's or the leadership's agenda were deleted.

setter in the American political system, House party leadership agenda setting must be assessed relative to presidential agenda setting (Light 1982; Peterson 1990). There are standard forums used by presidents for agenda setting, the State of the Union address being the most important. Majority-party leaders also have available forums that routinely receive considerable press coverage and that, therefore, they will favor for agenda-setting activities. The president's agenda is here defined as those items mentioned in the State of the Union address or its equivalent and in special messages of some prominence.[3] Majority-party leadership agenda setting, if it occurs, will become manifest in the Speaker's speech upon being elected to the office of Speaker at the beginning of a congress, the party's reply to the president's State of the Union address, the leaders' reply to special presidential addresses, or major news conferences.

Of the fifty items on the agenda of the 91st Congress, almost half (48%) were from the president's agenda.[4] Draft reform, postal reform, welfare reform, and extension of the surtax were among the Nixon proposals to which Congress gave agenda space. In the 91st Congress, agenda setting by the Democratic House leadership was minimal at best. "The Speaker's philosophy, according to his friends, is that the Democrats' role under the Nixon Presidency should be to keep the Kennedy and Johnson programs from being stripped by the Republicans" (CQWR, January 9, 1970, 85). In his speech upon being elected Speaker, McCormack proposed no agenda and, in fact, made no references to issues. In response to the three-way 1968 presidential election contest, McCormack and Minority Leader Gerald Ford (R-Mich.), on January 7, 1969, jointly endorsed reform of the electoral college. Only this could be remotely considered agenda setting.

If the leaders played a negligible role in setting the congressional agenda, how active were they in other aspects of the legislative process within the House? Leaders' involvement may take a variety of forms: the leaders may involve themselves in the shaping of legislation, in the structuring through procedure of floor choices, in vote mobilization, or in other aspects of legislative strategy. In order to make comparisons over time possible, summary measures based on these modes of activity but not attempting to make fine distinctions among them are constructed. The

3. Routine administration requests for reauthorization of legislation without major changes do not qualify the items for presidential agenda status.

4. The president's agenda and that of the House Democratic leadership sometimes contain items in common. In the 94th Congress, energy legislation was on both agendas. The "Other" category, where used, is mutually exclusive of the other two. Although entrepreneurs often do attempt to use the president's agenda items to further their own agendas, such piggybacking attempts are not included in the "Other" category.

first measure, intended to distinguish some involvement from none, is based on answers to the following questions: (1) Was the bill a part of the leadership's agenda? (2) Did the Speaker or the majority leader advocate passage during floor debate? (3) Did *Congressional Quarterly's* account report the leaders as being involved? If any one of the answers is yes, the leadership is considered to have been involved. A second, more refined measure distinguishes major from minor involvement on the basis of the mode or modes of involvement reported by *Congressional Quarterly.* Four modes are distinguished: (a) the leaders use their control over scheduling, special rules, or some other procedure to advantage the legislation; (b) the leaders are involved in an effort to mobilize floor votes; (c) the leaders are centrally involved in some other aspect of legislative strategy; or (d) the leaders participate in shaping the content of the legislation by talking or negotiating with or among the committee or committees or with the Senate or with the president. Major leadership involvement is defined as engaging in (d), shaping legislation, or in any two of the other activities (e.g., 1, 2, a, b, c).[5]

The House majority-party leadership was involved in fewer than half (46%) of the items on the congressional agenda in the 91st Congress; on only 28 percent of the items was leadership involvement major. In a number of cases, the leaders did use their scheduling powers to aid legislation. On draft-reform legislation, the major battle was over the rule, with liberals trying to open up the closed rule to allow amendments aimed at broad-scale draft reform. The Democratic leaders, working with their Republican counterparts, suddenly postponed the vote because, as Republican Whip Les Arends of Illinois said, "We thought we'd be stronger in the morning" (CQA 1969, 350). Similarly, the leaders postponed consideration of the antipoverty program reauthorization for ten days to give proponents time to mobilize against an amendment that would turn the program over to the states. Either the Speaker or the majority leader spoke on the floor in a number of instances. Both spoke against further cuts in foreign aid during consideration of the foreign-aid authorization bill in 1969; Majority Leader Carl Albert urged the House to override Nixon's veto of the Hill-Burton bill, while both urged an override of the Housing and Urban Development appropriations bill veto.

5. Since the measures rely fairly heavily on CQ's accounts, one might ask whether the findings of increased leadership involvement are simply a function of more thorough coverage by CQ. Available evidence indicates that this is not the case. From the 91st through the 100th Congress, there is no significant increase in total number of pages in CQWR. In a regression equation of total pages for a congress as a function of time (coded 0 for the 91st, 2 for the 92nd, etc.), the unstandardized regression coefficient is 11.2, t = .45, r2 = .02. The correlation between total pages and total index references to the Speaker and majority leader is .11.

In a limited number of cases, the leaders' role was major: they were involved in negotiating a compromise with Nixon on education funding in the Labor–Health, Education, and Welfare appropriations bill; McCormack led vote mobilization on the Voting Rights Act extension after the committee's initial floor defeat; Albert was deeply involved in negotiating the terms of the resolution that led to the seating of Adam Clayton Powell (D-N.Y.). Yet, compared to later leaders, the McCormack-Albert team's involvement was neither frequent nor broad in scope. With the exception of matters affecting the chamber itself, involvement tended to be restricted to the floor stage of the legislative process, it often seems to have been stimulated by trouble on the floor, and it seldom addressed the substance of legislation.

The party leaders' involvement was restricted, but the committees by and large did not need much help. The major and often controversial measures that make up the congressional agenda as here defined were subject to a mean of only 1.5 amendments decided by teller or roll-call vote, and only 0.4 such amendments per bill were adopted.

Because amendments can vary so much in importance, all amendments adopted were examined, as were other votes (e.g., on recommittal, passage, or conference report). A committee was judged to have clearly won on the floor if its legislation passed without the acceptance of any major amendments.[6] By this tough standard, the committee clearly won on the floor on 70 percent of the measures on the congressional agenda; it clearly lost on only 13 percent.

A foreign-trade bill illustrates the power of some committee chairs to prevail on the floor. The Ways and Means Committee brought the bill to the floor under a closed rule. However, many members wanted an opportunity to amend the bill and a majority defeated the previous question on the rule, thus allowing them to offer another, less restrictive rule for floor consideration. Yet rather than acceding, the chair of the Ways and Means Committee, Wilbur Mills (D-Ark.), asserting that his committee had instructed him to have the bill considered only under a closed rule, threatened to pull the bill off the floor if the vote were not reversed. Enough of those members who had hoped to amend the legislation but wanted a bill

---

6. CQ's opinion, the content of the amendment, and the extent to which the committee fought the amendment were the bases of judgment. There were few borderline cases; which amendments are key is almost always clear because all relevant actors are agreed. Consequently, coding clear losses is also straightforward; they occur when key votes—on major substitutes, killer amendments, recommittal, passage, and so forth—are lost. Not all cases fall into the clear win or the clear loss category; a committee may defeat some but not all major amendments. Such cases were placed into intermediate categories, which are, however, less reliable and are not reported here.

even more changed their votes, a closed rule was adopted, and the bill passed the House as written by the committee.

The chair's power and the system of intercommittee reciprocity were not the only bases for committee success. Although control of Congress and the presidency was divided, committee majorities frequently agreed with the president and thus were spared a formidable opponent. On almost half (47%) of the classifiable agenda items, the president and the committee agreed; on only 40 percent were they directly at odds.

The frequency of agreement reflects to some extent the murky ideology of the Nixon administration; for example, welfare reform, a core item on the president's agenda, elicited agreement from the committee of jurisdiction but was opposed by both liberals and conservatives. More important, however, was the ideological split within the Democratic party. Frequently conservative Democrats combined with Republicans on the committee to report a bill satisfactory to the president but much less so to the liberal wing of the Democratic party.

The Democratic membership's ideological heterogeneity manifested itself,[7] in the late 1960s and early 1970s, in a startlingly high rate of disagreement between the reporting committee and liberals.[8] Of the items that reached the floor and on which there was some conflict, fully one-third provoked such disagreement. The issues involved ranged from food-stamp reform to pollution control to emergency home-financing legislation to the depletion allowance to Vietnam-related matters. During the 91st Congress, floor coalitions were seldom partisan; of the agenda items that reached the floor, only 13 percent evoked partisan alignments, while 53 percent split northern and southern Democrats.

Intercommittee reciprocity seemed to work better for conservative-dominated committees than for predominantly liberal ones. Certainly in the 91st Congress conservative committees were more successful on the floor than liberal ones were. Of the six instances in which committees were "rolled" on the floor (that is, where the committee clearly lost), five involved the generally liberal committees of Education and Labor, Banking, and Judiciary. In the sixth case, Ways and Means was defeated on the floor on the question of indexing Social Security payments; Mills never-

---

7. Here and throughout the book, ideological heterogeneity and homogeneity are used as synonyms for legislative-preference heterogeneity and homogeneity. A member's legislative preferences, it should be remembered, are assumed to be a function of his or her full set of goals — e.g., reelection as well as policy (and also, though less often relevant, influence).

8. I rely on the account in CQ. CQ's reports of liberal opposition to a committee-reported bill are usually corroborated by roll-call evidence, but sometimes liberals were not able to force a recorded vote.

theless prevented the provision from becoming law in that congress by refusing to go to conference. In one instance — extension of the Voting Rights Act — the party leaders helped the committee pull out a floor victory after the conference committee had reversed the damage done during initial House floor consideration. In the other cases, however, the leaders were either not involved or not successful. Thus even when they controlled a committee, liberals did not derive the same benefits from the committee government system that more conservative members did.

While committee majorities and committee chairs did not, by and large, need party leaders' help to advance their goals through lawmaking, and consequently saw little benefit in strong leadership, the liberals who made up the bulk of the reform forces were less favorably situated and did need help in passing the legislation that would advance their goals.

The Dimensions of Reform

Northern liberals' policy dissatisfaction provided the initial impetus for and a continuing driving force behind the reform movement. Dissatisfaction with the meager opportunities the system allowed for rank-and-file participation in the legislative process also fueled the reforms and extended their appeal beyond programmatic liberals. The liberals saw the two problems as interrelated. As the junior liberal Democrats saw it, the seniority-based committee government system gave disproportionate decision-making power to an unrepresentative and unaccountable cadre of conservative southerners, and deprived more numerous but junior liberals of their fair share of influence; the result was, in their view, public policy that was not responsive to the preferences of a party majority.

To use my terminology rather than theirs, the reformers were dissatisfied with the way in which the committee government system distributed the capacity to make legislative decisions among the members and their various agents, and with the system's lack of mechanisms for assuring the responsiveness and accountability of agents to the members.

To remedy these problems, the reformers believed, it was necessary to distribute the capacity to participate in the making of legislative decisions more broadly, make those to whom legislative powers were delegated — especially committees and their chairs — accountable, and enhance the capacity of the party's only central agent, the party leadership, to advance the party majority's legislative objectives.

The reforms instituted between 1969 and 1976 displayed a mix of these thrusts (see Dodd and Oppenheimer 1977; Sheppard 1985; Ornstein 1975). The requirement that committee chairs and the chairs of subcommittees of the Appropriations Committee win majority approval in the

Democratic Caucus was intended to make them responsive to the party
majority, which was now clearly a liberal majority. A provision for regular
meetings of the Democratic Caucus provided a forum in which rank-and-
file members could inform Democratic committee contingents of their
views, and a few instances in which the caucus instructed committees put
committees on notice that they had better listen to strongly held caucus
sentiments.

The desire for better policy and greater responsiveness also underlay
the shifting of the committee-assignment function from Ways and Means
to the new Steering and Policy Committee, which the Speaker chairs and a
number of whose members the Speaker appoints. Ways and Means Democrats were seen as too conservative and not accountable to the party. The
Steering and Policy Committee was designed to be both representative and
responsive, its membership a combination of members elected from regional groups, elected party leaders, and leadership appointees.

Granting the Speaker the power to nominate all Democratic members
and the chair of the Rules Committee, subject only to ratification by the
caucus, was clearly intended to give the leadership true control over the
scheduling of legislation for the floor. By making Rules Committee Democrats dependent on the Speaker for their positions on the committee, reformers made the committee an arm of the leadership. At the same time
they reserved for the caucus the power of confirming the Speaker's nominees, and wrote into caucus rules a procedure by which the caucus can
instruct the Rules Committee on the character of rules.

A series of rules changes, some principally aimed at expanding participation opportunities, others also motivated by policy concerns, had
the effect of increasing opportunities and incentives for participation in
committee and on the floor. In an effort to spread positions of influence,
members were limited to chairing no more than one subcommittee each.
The subcommittee bill of rights removed from committee chairs the power
to appoint subcommittee chairs and gave it to the Democratic caucus of
the committee (that is, the Democratic members of the committee); it
guaranteed subcommittees automatic referral of legislation and adequate
budgets and staff. The supply of resources—most importantly, staff—
available to Congress and its members was expanded and distributed
much more broadly among members. The institution of the recorded teller
vote in the Committee of the Whole changed the dynamics of the floor
stage, increasing the incentives for offering amendments and often for
opposing the committee's position. "Sunshine reforms" opened up most
committee markups and conference committee meetings to the media and
the public, allowing members to use those forums for grandstanding as
well as for policy entrepreneurship.

The reformers' dissatisfaction with the legislative process of the committee government era extended beyond the conservative cast of the policy it tended to produce to its inability in key areas to produce coherent policy at all. In the budget area, committee autonomy resulted in the various spending and taxing decisions being made independently without any in-chamber coordination (Fenno 1966; Schick 1980). As a result, over the course of the twentieth century, budgetary power had shifted to the executive branch. President Nixon's attempt to expand radically the power of the executive by claiming an unrestricted power to impound — or not spend — congressionally appropriated funds convinced many members not usually associated with the reform forces that a congressional response was necessary, and in 1974 the Budget and Impoundment Control Act became law. The act set up a mechanism by which Congress could make decisions about the overall level of spending, taxes, and the deficit, as well as about spending priorities. As such, it was a potentially centralizing mechanism and could become a powerful tool in the hands of the leaders.

By mid-decade, the committee government system was dead and a very different House was in the process of emerging. Committee chairs' powers and control over scarce resources had been severely curtailed; the bases of committee autonomy had been undermined. The reforms significantly enhanced the powers and resources available to the party leaders for facilitating the passage of legislation. At the same time, however, rank-and-file members' capacity for pursuing their goals through individualist strategies was also greatly increased. An examination of the 94th Congress, the first in which the reforms were fully in place, allows an assessment of the immediate impact of the reforms on the legislative process in the House.

The House and Party Leadership in the Immediate Postreform Era

In the 1974 elections, fought in the midst of a recession and in the aftermath of Watergate, Democrats made a net gain of 49 seats and won a total of 295 seats in the House. The class of 1974 — seventy-five strong — provided the votes in the Democratic Caucus to pass the final round of rules changes that collectively constitute the reforms and, using new procedures, to depose three committee chairs. When three extremely senior members, all southerners, two of them conservatives, were voted out of committee chairmanships they had held for years, all committee chairs were put on notice: responsiveness to the caucus was a prerequisite to retaining their positions.

Strengthened by their large electoral gains and facing a president weakened by his unelected status and his unpopular pardon of Richard Nixon, House Democrats, especially liberals, believed the 94th Congress offered ✓ them an unusually favorable opportunity for advancing their policy goals. These members were unwilling to allow the party's agenda to be determined by the decisions of the various committees acting independently and without coordination. Under pressure from such members, Speaker Albert played an aggressive agenda-setting role. In late 1974, he appointed a task force to draft an economic recovery program. The president took this effort sufficiently seriously that, on January 13, the day the task force's report was released, Ford gave a televised speech on economic and energy policy to try to preempt the Democratic program. In Albert's speech upon being elected Speaker on January 14, and in his televised response to Ford's January 15 State of the Union address, he talked in some detail about the Democratic agenda of energy and economic stimulus programs.

The Democratic leadership's agenda constituted 17 percent of the forty-eight measures on the congressional agenda in the 94th Congress, while President Ford's agenda accounted for 23 percent. Clearly Ford's political weakness precluded his dominating the agenda as Nixon had during the 91st Congress, and the House Democratic leaders took advantage of that weakness to play a prominent role in setting the agenda.

The Democratic leaders were considerably more active on the congressional agenda in the 94th Congress than their counterparts in the 91st Congress had been. The Albert-O'Neill team involved itself with 60 percent of the agenda items — up from 46 percent in the 91st Congress; on 40 percent of the measures, leaders' involvement was major, compared to 28 percent in the earlier congress. In addition to the measures on its own agenda, which primarily addressed issues of energy and economic stimulus, the leadership was active on a wide variety of other issues ranging from tax legislation to a congressional pay raise, from budget resolutions to lobbying reforms to aid to New York City.

All four fights over budget resolutions elicited major involvement on the part of the leaders. In the House, the budget process was highly partisan from its inception, and Budget Committee Democrats needed the help of party leaders in passing their resolutions (Ellwood and Thurber 1981). In 1976, on the first budget resolution, for example, the leaders were involved in the crafting of floor amendments deemed necessary to produce a majority for passage, and directed a major mobilization effort to marshal a floor majority.

Thus, in response to the expectations of a sizable majority of the members, the House Democratic leadership played an aggressive role in setting the agenda and increased its involvement in the legislative process. How-

ever, despite the expanded resources that reforms had granted party leaders, the ideological heterogeneity of the party and the members' desire to
participate more fully in the legislative process that had, in part, fueled the
reform movement presented the leaders with problems they could not
surmount in the 94th Congress.

HR 6860, an energy bill, provides a good example of these problems.
The Arab oil embargo of 1973–74 had put energy conservation at the top
of everyone's agenda. Ford sent Congress a multipart energy package in
January 1975; its conservation strategy was based on higher energy prices.
Leadership-appointed Democratic task forces in the House and Senate
had been at work, and they unveiled a Democratic plan on February 27.
Ways and Means Democrats then came up with their own plan, but only
with great difficulty. On a vote of nineteen to sixteen, the committee
reported out a bill that oil-state conservatives and Republicans opposed
and liberals considered not tough enough.

Ways and Means had traditionally brought its bills to the floor under a
closed rule; during the 91st Congress, for example, five of the measures on
the congressional agenda were reported by Ways and Means, and all —
including welfare-reform and foreign-trade legislation — were protected
from floor amendments by closed rules. Reformers, in a move aimed specifically at Ways and Means, established a procedure by which the Rules
Committee could be instructed by caucus vote to allow amendments. On
HR 6860, Ways and Means did not even ask for a closed rule; the rule it
requested and was granted was basically an open one.

Originally having scheduled the bill for floor action in May, the party
leaders postponed consideration after a deluge of amendments indicated
the level of opposition. When the bill was brought up in June, twenty-one
noncommittee amendments were offered. Amendments came from both
ends of the ideological spectrum and from the perspectives of a variety of
interests. Six amendments passed, including the Stark amendment, which
deleted the twenty-cent gas tax that constituted the heart of the bill. Democrats were badly split on many of the amendments, but on the Stark
amendment not even a majority of northern Democrats supported the
committee. Although the bill subsequently passed the House, the amending process had emasculated the bill and it never became law. Thus, on a
core item of the Democratic leadership's agenda, the Democratic membership splintered. The reforms facilitated the public expression of, and
thereby perhaps amplified, the party's ideological heterogeneity.

The reforms did make committees and their chairs more responsive to
the predominantly liberal Democratic Caucus. The frequency of disagreement between the reporting committee and liberals fell from 33 percent in
the 91st Congress to 14 percent in the 94th. And, by increasing the respon-

siveness of the chairs, the reforms strengthened the leadership's hand. Sidney Waldman quotes a contemporary leadership staffer as saying, "The three chairmen being thrown out has affected the willingness of chairmen to cooperate with the leadership. In 1973 when we voted on them, they didn't get the message. They took the positive vote as continuing support for them. In 1975, when three were deposed, they got the message. That was important" (1978, 12). The conservative chair of the Appropriations Committee, told that Speaker Albert intended to have Steering and Policy pass a resolution urging Appropriations to report funding for emergency jobs, replied, "Let's avoid that. . . . I'll do it. I'll do whatever you want" (ibid., 17). George Mahon (D-Tex.), the committee chair, not only got the bill reported out of his committee but actively worked to pass it and to override Ford's veto.

The new relationships created by the reforms appear to have changed the behavior of the leaders as well. In the 91st Congress, when the leaders involved themselves with measures that split the reporting committee and liberals, they took sides, supporting the committee and opposing the liberals. By and large, this was not an ideological response by the leaders; they also supported liberal committees against their conservative foes on the floor. Rather, the leaders appear to have interpreted their role as entailing support, tacit or active, for all committee-reported legislation, whatever its ideological hue; to a considerable extent, they saw themselves primarily as agents of the committees. Given the lack of an active caucus to serve as a counterweight to committees as enunciators of party policy positions, that reading of members' expectations was, from the perspective of leaders interested in keeping their leadership positions, the least risky one. In the 94th Congress, with the caucus active and expecting responsiveness from its party as well as its committee leaders, the party leadership's role on measures that divided the reporting committee and liberals changed. Rather than automatically supporting the committee, the leaders tended to act as mediators or damage controllers. On other measures as well, the leaders were occasionally willing to take on a committee, as they had not been in the 91st Congress. The party leaders, for example, refused to schedule a food-stamp reform bill, thereby protecting the many freshman Democratic members who did not want to vote on the legislation, especially not on the issue of food stamps for strikers. The leaders believed that, in the wake of the Hayes sex-payroll scandal, refurbishing the image of the party and the chamber required passage of a meaningful reform package; Albert pushed through a leadership-designed package even though doing so required pressuring the House Administration Committee, which lost power under the plan.

While the new responsiveness to the caucus of committee chairs and

committees gave the leaders increased leverage, the legislative consequences of members' desires to participate more extensively made the
leaders' task of facilitating the passage of legislation by fostering collective
action much more difficult and often overwhelmed the effect of the new
leverage. Democrats were no longer willing to allow Ways and Means to
bring its legislation to the floor under closed rules. In addition to the
energy bill, two major tax bills were considered under rules allowing floor
votes on some amendments. The leaders may have obtained control of the
Rules Committee, but they could not use that control to protect legislation
on the floor with restrictive rules. They had every reason to expect the
members to refuse to acquiesce in such use of the leaders' new resources.
In fact, the only item on the congressional agenda brought to the floor
under a closed rule was the leadership-supported resolution to strip the
House Administration Committee of its control over members' perqui-
sites.

Increased participation by rank-and-file members took a number of
forms, the easiest to document and the most problematic for the party
leadership being the increase in amending activity on the floor. As a result
of the reforms, incentives for offering floor amendments increased and the
costs of doing so decreased. The number of floor amendments decided on
a teller or recorded vote rose from 55 in 1955–56 to 107 in 1969–70; with
the institution of the recorded teller, it jumped to 195 in 1971–72 and,
with electronic voting, jumped again to 351 in 1973–74 (S. Smith 1989,
33). During the 94th Congress (1975–76), 372 such amendments were
offered on the floor and, during the 95th Congress, that number reached
439.

The major legislation constituting the congressional agenda as here
defined shows the impact of this change in floor behavior. From the prereform 91st Congress to the reformed 94th Congress, the mean number of
amendments decided on a teller or recorded vote to items on the congressional agenda more than tripled, from 1.5 to 5.3; the mean number of
amendments per measure adopted increased more than fourfold, from 0.4
to 1.8. The increase in amending activity made legislation more vulnerable
to change on the floor. The success of committees in passing their legislation intact decreased. During the prereform 91st Congress, the committee
of origin had clearly won on the floor on 70 percent of the measures that
reached the floor; in the reformed 94th Congress, the committee won on
57 percent. Yet given the larger Democratic margin in the 94th Congress
and the weakened president, Democratic committee contingents might
reasonably have expected to increase their floor success.

The continuing deep North-South split within the Democratic party
exacerbated the problems created by increased floor participation. Only

28 percent of the measures on the congressional agenda evoked partisan alignments on the House floor, while on 40 percent, northern and southern Democrats split. As a result, despite its huge Democratic membership, the 94th Congress was a legislative disappointment to Democrats. Committees were successful on balance in enacting legislation in their preferred form on fewer than half (48%) of the items on the congressional agenda, compared to 57 percent in the 91st Congress.[9] The Democratic agenda proposed by the party leaders did not fare well. The leaders clearly prevailed on the floor on only half the items, and won on balance on final disposition on half.

Even when Democrats were in substantial agreement, legislative success often proved elusive. On those measures pitting two-thirds or more of the House Democrats against the president, the oversized Democratic membership produced a high rate of floor success; the Democrats' position clearly prevailed on 83 percent of such measures.[10] The Democrats' win rate on final disposition was, however, much lower; they won on balance on only 44 percent of the measures. Ford made extensive use of the veto, and Democrats were seldom able to maintain sufficient cohesion to override.

Such meager legislative results from a congress in which Democrats seemed so favorably situated led to intense criticism of the majority-party leadership. Speaker Albert was pilloried for not being sufficiently active and assertive (see Waldman 1978; CQWR, June 28, 1975, 1332–33). From the leaders' point of view, however, the problem was a lack of willingness to follow. As a senior staffer said, "People . . . want leadership for the other guys, the guys who don't agree with them. They want the leadership to get those who defect from the positions they desire, but they don't want to be told what to do" (Waldman 1978, 3).

The continued ideological split within the Democratic party greatly

9. On the basis of the CQ account, a judgment was made as to whether the committee and, where relevant, the president and House Democrats as a group had on balance won or lost on final disposition. This judgment is often somewhat more subjective than the classification concerning winning and losing on the floor, where votes provide an important guide. Because most major legislation that is enacted involves some compromise after committee consideration — most frequently in conference — the classification of winning on balance is considerably less demanding than the classification of winning on the floor, and simply requires that the committee (or the president or House Democrats) achieve a favorable compromise. Where a measure involved a clear-cut conflict between two sides and the result appeared to be an even compromise, the measure is placed into a middle, no-clear-winner category.

10. For a measure to be included in this category, the president must have a clear, publicly stated position, two-thirds or more of the House Democrats must vote together on all important roll calls on the measure, and the president's position and that of House Democrats must be directly opposed.

hindered the party leaders in their attempt to satisfy the liberal majority's legislative objectives. For southern Democrats, reelection needs and policy preferences frequently dictated behavior inimical to their liberal colleagues' legislative goals. As a result of the reforms, such members in their capacity as committee leaders did have to be responsive to the sentiments of party majorities; in their capacity as ordinary members voting on the floor, they were under no such injunction.

The Democratic party was too ideologically heterogeneous to make successful policy leadership possible. Although liberals constituted a substantial majority of the membership, a sizable minority of the party had legislative preferences not merely different from but at odds with those of the majority on a broad array of key issues. Successful policy leadership requires that legislative preferences be broadly shared over a range of issues within the party, a condition that did not hold in the mid- and late 1970s.

Furthermore, the leaders' difficulties were by no means caused only by a conservative minority faction. Many of the northern Democrats who had supported changes that would strengthen the party leadership and claimed to want policy leadership nevertheless did not act in a way that allowed the leaders fully to exploit their new powers and resources. Having multiplied opportunities and incentives for rank-and-file participation, the reforms exacerbated the collective-action problem inherent in the passing of legislation. The new resources granted leaders were not sufficient to make it possible for leaders to coerce the members into behaving cooperatively; legislative success consequently required that members as individuals be willing to compromise and to exercise restraint. Success frequently depended on a large proportion of northerners being willing to eschew exploiting readily available participation opportunities, since the leaders could not count on many southern votes. Yet many northern Democrats were unwilling to forgo the immediate payoffs of freelance policy entrepreneurship for the more distant and less certain payoff of policy results. The former could be obtained through individual activity, through the offering of floor amendments for example, while the latter required collective action and, given the ideological split among Democrats and a hostile president, was less certain.

The Democratic leaders of the 94th Congress believed that, while the members did want them to secure the passage of legislation by facilitating collective action, those members were unwilling to accept significant constraints on their newly acquired opportunities to participate broadly in the legislative process. Thus, although the reforms had bestowed new powers on the party leaders, they did not perceive a willingness on the part of the members to sanction the aggressive use of those powers. The behavior of members during that congress—especially the high rate of amending activity—seemed to support the priority members placed on being free to pursue their goals through individualist strategies. However, the widespread dissatisfaction with Congress's policy output suggested that many members were not willing simply to sacrifice legislative results. The reformers had believed that rules changes could produce a House more likely to further both their policy goals and their desire to participate. The 94th Congress demonstrated that advancing both goals simultaneously was more problematic than the reformers had anticipated.

Thus, by the mid-1970s, a new House of Representatives had emerged, one that confronted its members and their leaders with new problems. The core problem the postreform House presented was how to induce the collective action necessary to secure passage of the legislation members wanted without constraining too much members' opportunities to participate broadly in the legislative process. In the 1980s, House Democrats would have to grapple with the problem in a political environment much more hostile to their policy, reelection, and influence goals.

4

The Emergence of Activist Leadership in the House of Representatives

The House of the early 1990s was very different from the immediate postreform House, yet no major formal institutional restructuring had taken place since the reform era. The 1980s saw the emergence of a House majority-party leadership that was highly active and deeply involved in multiple aspects of the legislative process, one that significantly influenced the course of legislation and the probability of legislative success. The emergence of strong leadership, I argue, is a consequence of a change in members' expectations driven by changes in the institutional and political context that altered the costs and benefits to members of such leadership. As leadership assistance became increasingly necessary to passing the legislation members needed to advance their goals, and as House Democrats' ideological heterogeneity decreased, they came to expect their leaders to use aggressively the powers and resources the 1970s reforms had granted them to facilitate the production of collective goods, especially legislation.

Documenting the Emergence of Activist Majority-Party Leadership

To demonstrate rigorously that the 1980s saw the emergence of a House majority-party leadership substantially more active and more consequential in the legislative process than its post–World War II predecessors, that the contemporary majority-party leadership is, by twentieth-century standards, a strong leadership, terms must be defined in ways that lend themselves to measurement, and data must be gathered over time. To that purpose, one House majority-party leadership will be defined as stronger than another if it was more active in organizing the party and the chamber, in setting the House agenda, and in the internal legislative process, and if its legislative activity had an impact on legislative outcomes.

Although ideally one would like to be able to compare all the leaderships of the post–World War II era, gathering the enormous amount of data required would be too big a task. Therefore, I have employed a comparative statics research design. Four congresses were chosen so as to maximize analytic leverage in terms of the variables posited as important in the explanation to be offered and in some plausible alternative explanations. A fifth congress was then added as a check and to provide recent data. The 100th Congress (1987–88) is the congress that, by general agreement, first clearly showed the full emergence of strong leadership. A prominent alternative explanation attributes strong, successful leadership in the 100th Congress solely to the particular circumstances of that congress—especially to the lame-duck, weakened character of the president under conditions of divided control. That hypothesis can be tested by comparing party leadership in the 100th Congress with leadership in a congress comparable to it on those attributes. The most recent such congress is the 94th (1975–76). Although not a lame duck, Ford was weakened by the Watergate scandal, his unelected status, and the Democratic congressional landslide of 1974. Control of Congress and the presidency was divided, and had been since 1969. Democratic congressional strength was significantly greater in the 94th Congress than in the 100th, and Ford was probably weaker than Reagan; thus if presidential strength and opposition-party numbers in Congress are the key variables, the majority-party leadership should have been at least as active and as decisive in the 94th Congress as in the 100th. The 91st Congress (1969–70) was chosen because it was a prereform congress and the first of the Nixon-Ford presidency; the 97th was selected because it was the first of the Reagan presidency. By comparing the 91st and the 97th with the 94th and the 100th, which are the last congresses of those presidencies, the effects of the president's political strength and of the stage of the presidency can be assessed. As the 91st was a prereform congress and the 94th was the first in which the reforms were fully in place, comparisons of the four congresses allow some inferences about the effects of the reforms. The impact of the political environment of the 1980s can be gauged by comparing the two congresses of the 1970s with the two of the 1980s. The 101st Congress (1989–90), the first Bush congress, continues the series of first congresses under conditions of divided control, but provides variation in the identity of the chief executive and of the Speaker; it allows us to ascertain whether strong leadership in the 100th Congress was primarily a function of the

Table 4.1   The Party Leadership's Enlarged Role in Organizing Party and
Chamber

	Congress				
Entity	91st (1969–70)	94th (1975–76)	97th (1981–82)	100th (1987–88)	101st (1989–90)
Rules Committee	$\frac{0}{15}$	$\frac{11}{16}$	$\frac{11}{16}$	$\frac{9}{13}$	$\frac{9}{13}$
Committee on Committees	$\frac{0}{15}$	$\frac{8/2}{24}$	$\frac{8/3}{29}$	$\frac{8/4}{31}$	$\frac{8/4}{31}$
Whip System	$\frac{2}{21}$	$\frac{5}{25}$	$\frac{21}{44}$	$\frac{59}{81}$	$\frac{84}{103}$

Note: Top figure is number of leadership appointees; figure to right, if any, is number of members who are ex officio from the leadership; bottom figure is total size.

personality of a particular Speaker or a response to a president who was both a hard-line conservative and adept at using the media.[1]

Organizing Party and Chamber

The expansion of the Democratic party leadership's role in organizing party and chamber that occurred during the 1970s and the 1980s as part of and in response to the reforms was briefly described in chapter 3 and will be discussed at length in chapters 5–8. The leadership's enlarged role is evidenced by the change in the leaders' powers to appoint members to three key entities — the Rules Committee, the Democratic Committee on Committees, and the whip system (see table 4.1).

Setting the Agenda

The majority-party leadership became substantially more active in agenda setting during this period (see table 4.2). Clearly the congressional leadership's level of activity depends also on whether the president is at the beginning or the end of his tenure. The majority-party leadership accounted for only 2 percent of the items on the congressional agenda of major measures in the 91st Congress, the first of Nixon's presidency; it accounted for 9 percent in the 97th, Reagan's first, and for 12 percent in the 101st, Bush's first. In the 94th Congress, the last of the Nixon-Ford presidency, the Democratic party leadership accounted for 17 percent of the agenda items; in the 100th, the last of the Reagan presidency, it ac-

1. Democratic strength in the congresses was as follows: 91st Congress, 243 House, 58 Senate; 94th Congress, 291 House, 61 Senate; 97th Congress, 243 House, 46 Senate; 100th Congress, 258 House, 55 Senate; 101st Congress, 260 House, 55 Senate.

Table 4.2   The Leadership's Expanded Agenda-Setting Role (% of agenda items)

	Congress				
	Nixon/Ford		Reagan		Bush
Agenda Setter	91st (1969–70)	94th (1975–76)	97th (1981–82)	100th (1987–88)	101st (1989–90)
President	48	23	44	23	18
Leadership	2	17	9	33	12
Other	34	35	16	23	na
N	50	48	45	40	50

counted for 33 percent of them. In the 100th Congress, the Democratic leaders actually played a considerably more prominent agenda-setting role than the president did.

The Increase in Leadership Involvement

Party leaders may become more actively involved in the internal legislative process by increasing their role in the shaping of legislation, in the structuring through procedure of floor choices, in vote mobilization, or in other aspects of legislative strategy. Contemporary party leaders appear to be substantially more involved than their predecessors in all these ways; however, constructing valid measures of the incidence of each of these activities over the five congresses seems overambitious, given the data available. Instead, I have constructed summary and presumably more robust measures of leadership involvement in the major items constituting the congressional agenda, as defined in chapter 3. The first measure distinguishes some leadership involvement from no involvement; a second, more refined measure distinguishes major from minor involvement.

Leadership involvement increased steadily and significantly over the first four congresses; although somewhat lower in the 101st Congress than in the 100th, it was nevertheless high compared to the earlier congresses (see table 4.3). House majority-party leaders were involved in fewer than half the items on the congressional agenda in the 91st Congress; they were involved in 83 percent in the 100th and in 68 percent in the 101st. Major involvement increased even more. In 1969–70, party leaders played a major role as defined above in only 28 percent of the legislation on the congressional agenda; in 1987–88, they played such a role in 60 percent of that legislation, and in 1989–90, in 54 percent. Thus, systematic data substantiate that the House majority-party leadership has

Table 4.3   The Increase in Leadership Involvement on the Congressional Agenda (% of agenda items)

Leadership Involvement	Congress				
	91st (1969–70)	94th (1975–76)	97th (1981–82)	100th (1987–88)	101st (1989–90)
Some	46	60	67	83	68
Major	28	40	38	60	54
N	50	48	45	40	50

become more active in organizing the party and the chamber, in setting the House agenda, and in the internal legislative process.[2]

Explaining the Emergence of Strong Party Leadership

I have argued that the balance between benefits and costs to members should determine leadership strength. When the benefits of strong leadership are perceived as significantly outweighing the costs for a substantial majority, members should be more willing to grant their leaders additional resources or to allow their leaders to exploit fully the resources they already possess. Conversely, when the costs are perceived as greater than the benefits, party leadership strength should decrease. During the period under study, I contend, changes in the institution and the political environment increased the benefits and decreased the costs of stronger leadership and led to a change in members' expectations of their leaders.

By the mid-1970s, reforms had transformed the legislative process in the House. Increased participation by rank-and-file members at both the committee stage and the floor stage, the growing attractiveness of the freelance entrepreneurial style, and large numbers of inexperienced subcommittee chairs multiplied the number of significant actors and radically increased uncertainty. Legislation became more vulnerable to attack on the floor of the chamber. By the end of the 1970s, many Democrats had become concerned about some of the unexpected consequences of the reforms. When, as a result of the weakening of committees and the wide-open amending process, legislation was severely altered on the floor, the policy cost could be high (S. Smith 1989). Democratic committee contingents, Democratic committee leaders, and the Democratic members needed help passing their legislation, and began to look to the party leadership for that help (Sinclair 1983).

2. A demonstration that leadership activity translates into legislative success will be undertaken in chap. 12.

The open, participatory process that the reforms established became even more legislatively problematic within the context of the 1980s political environment (ibid.; Sinclair 1985). With the 1980 election of Ronald Reagan, House Democrats faced a conservative, confrontational president who threatened all their goals. Aided by a widespread perception of a policy mandate and a Republican Senate, Reagan was a formidable opponent. The president's political strength and the deep policy divisions between Reagan and House Democrats made the 97th Congress a very difficult one for those Democrats and their leadership. The series of damaging losses — especially on the budget resolution, the reconciliation bill making major spending cuts, and the tax-cut bill — that the House Democrats and their leadership sustained in 1981 led to intense criticism of the leadership as weak and ineffective, but also to demands for more aggressive leadership. Even after the mandate perception faded, continued Republican control of the Senate and the large and growing budget deficits made the passage of legislation favored by Democrats difficult.

The 1970s and 1980s also witnessed a change in the structure of legislation that contributed to majority-party members' greater need for the sort of assistance that only the party leadership can provide. Increased jurisdictional conflicts among committees and the House's inability to realign jurisdictions created a need for an outside arbiter when committee leaders could not agree. The multiple-referral rule, stipulating that legislation be referred to all committees with jurisdiction, was instituted in 1975; it formalized the Speaker's role and gave the Speaker new powers to set reporting deadlines for legislation referred to more than one committee.

In the 1980s, deep policy divisions between President Reagan and House Democrats resulted in much more frequent employment of omnibus measures as well. The major battles came to revolve around budget resolutions, reconciliation bills, and other omnibus measures concerning basic priorities. Because of the number and magnitude of issues and sometimes also the number of committees involved in omnibus measures, putting together and passing such legislation often required negotiation and coordination activities beyond the capacity of committee leaders. Furthermore, on such high-stakes, broadly encompassing measures, committee leaders lacked the legitimacy to speak for the membership as a whole. Thus as omnibus measures became more prominent on the congressional agenda, the need for leadership involvement increased.

In the 1970s and early 1980s, then, the potential benefits of stronger leadership grew as institutional changes and changes in the political environment increased the Democratic members' and Democratic committee contingents' need for help in advancing their goals through legislation. Leadership activity did increase in the mid-1970s and early 1980s, but the full development of strong leadership, I contend, depended on a decline in the costs of strong leadership, and particularly on a decrease in the ideological heterogeneity of the Democratic party.

In fact, during this period, the costs of strong leadership declined as the effective ideological heterogeneity of the Democratic membership declined and as the political environment made the freelance, Lone Ranger sort of policy entrepreneurship prevalent in the 1970s much less feasible. The change in southern politics that the civil-rights movement and the Voting Rights Act set off had, by the early 1980s, resulted in a less conservative southern Democratic House contingent. As African Americans became able to vote and as more and more whites voted Republican, those Democrats who won House seats in the South were likely to be dependent on African American votes. The supportive electoral coalitions of southern Democrats began to look more similar to those of their northern party colleagues (Rohde 1991). Continuing members shifted their voting behavior and, as seats became vacant, the character of the newly elected membership changed. The political environment of the 1980s narrowed the feasible policy space; expensive new social programs were ruled out by the deficit. This constraint on the nature of the policy proposals that could seriously be considered also contributed to the Democrats' growing ideological homogeneity, which became particularly evident after 1982.

After the 1982 elections, the voting cohesion of House Democrats began to increase; in the late 1980s and early 1990s, it reached levels unprecedented in the post–World War II era. For the period from 1951 through 1970, House Democrats' average party-unity score was 78 percent; this fell to 74 percent for the period from 1971 through 1982. After the 1982 elections, the scores began rising, and averaged 86 percent for the period from 1983 through 1992. During that period, the proportion of party votes (that is, roll calls on which a majority of Democrats voted against a majority of Republicans) also increased, averaging 56 percent compared with 37 percent during the period from 1971 through 1982 (ibid.; CQA, annual volumes; see also Powell 1991, especially table 1).

Much of this increase in Democratic cohesion was the result of increased party support by southern Democrats. From 1985 through 1992, southern Democrats supported the party position on 78 percent of partisan roll calls, while the average support of northern Democrats was 90 percent. Compare that modest twelve-point difference with an average difference between the two groups of about thirty-eight points for the period from 1965 through 1976 and twenty-four points for the period from 1977 through 1984 (Rohde 1988; CQA, annual volumes).

During the 1980s, a more homogeneous Democratic membership, confronted with an institutional and political environment that made it extremely difficult to pass the legislation necessary for the advancement of its reelection, policy, and power goals, turned to its party leadership for help. Democratic committee contingents, Democratic committee leaders, and the Democratic membership often required assistance in putting together a satisfactory legislative package and in mobilizing the votes to pass it on the floor. The reformers of the 1970s had given their leaders new powers and resources that, aggressively used, could significantly increase the probability of legislative success. In the immediate postreform period, Democrats had been unwilling to allow their leaders to employ those new resources expansively. Now, faced with a much more difficult legislative context, members were not only willing to allow their leaders to use aggressively those powers and resources to help pass the legislation the members wanted, but insisted that they do so. With the range of legislative preferences broadly shared within the party having grown substantially, members now increasingly demanded true policy leadership.

The Changing Costs and Benefits of Strong Leadership: Hypotheses

The complex historical explanation offered above cannot be rigorously tested in toto. A number of key component parts can, however, be substantiated. The following changes that increased the benefits of strong leadership because they increased majority-party members' need for help in passing legislation were hypothesized:

1. Legislation became more vulnerable to attack and change on the House floor in the 1970s in the wake of the reforms.
2. The structure of conflict changed during the period under study, with deep policy divisions between the president and House Democrats becoming more frequent in the 1980s.
3. The structure of legislation changed as multiply referred bills and omnibus measures increased in frequency.

The following changes that decreased the costs of strong leadership were hypothesized:

4. The ideological heterogeneity of the House Democratic membership decreased in the 1980s.
5. Opportunities for legislative entrepreneurship decreased in the 1980s.

The next several sections will substantiate that these changes did, in fact, occur. The trends are clearly evident on the major legislation that constitutes the congressional agenda as here defined. I will thus have demonstrated that the changes and the increase in leadership activity documented earlier occurred together. My argument is that these changes, through their impact on members' assessments of the costs and benefits of strong leadership, account for the increase in leadership activity. To bolster that argument, the relationship between leadership involvement and its costs and benefits as hypothesized above will then be examined cross-sectionally. If, within a congress, the leadership is more frequently involved when the benefits to members are greatest (when members most need help because, for example, the president opposes the legislation) and when the costs to members are lowest (when Democrats are united, for example), then my argument about the causal relationship over time is strengthened.

Increased Floor Vulnerability of Legislation in the 1970s

That legislation became more vulnerable to attack and change on the House floor in the 1970s in the wake of the reforms has been most thoroughly documented by Steven Smith (1989, 31). He shows that over the sixteen-year period from 1955 to 1972, amendments offered on the floor of the House approximately doubled from about 400 to about 800 per congress; the number then abruptly jumped to 1,425 in the next congress (the 93rd Congress, 1973–74), and remained high in the 94th and 95th Congresses, peaking at 1,688 in 1977–78. The number of amendments then began to decline; it stood at about 1,000 in the 99th Congress (1985–86). Amendments decided by teller or recorded vote display the same trend, increasing from 55 in the mid-1950s (the 84th Congress) to 107 in the early 1970s (the 91st). With the institution of the recorded teller vote in the 92nd Congress, they jumped to 195 and, with the switch to electronic voting, shot up to 351 in the 93rd. The number of such amendments peaked at 439 in 1977–78, and has declined since (ibid.).

This change in amending activity on the floor is clearly evident on the major legislation that makes up the congressional agenda as here defined. In the prereform 91st Congress, those measures that reached the floor were subject, on average, to 1.5 amendments decided by a teller or recorded vote, and, on average, 0.4 amendments per bill were adopted. By the reformed 94th Congress, the mean number of amendments offered per measure had more than tripled, to 5.3, and the mean number adopted more than quadrupled, to 1.8 per measure (see also ibid., 18–19). Amendments decided on a recorded vote can vary considerably in significance, from killer amendments and major substitutes altering the thrust of the legislation entirely on the one hand to those having little policy impact on the other. To provide a more refined assessment of the impact of amending activity on the committees' success on the floor, all the amendments to a measure that were adopted were examined, as were other votes on the measure, such as votes on recommittal, passage, and the conference report. A committee was judged to have clearly won on the floor if its legislation passed without the acceptance of any major amendments.[3] From the prereform 91st Congress to the reformed 94th Congress, the success rate for committees on the floor declined from 70 percent to 57 percent. Yet given that the president was weaker in the latter congress and the Democratic seat margin in the House much larger, committees might have expected their floor success to increase. Clearly, then, legislation did become more vulnerable on the floor, and committee majorities found it more and more difficult to pass their legislation intact.

The Changing Structure of Conflict and Its Consequences for Legislative Success

To demonstrate that frequent, deep policy divisions between the president and House Democrats distinguish the 1980s from the previous decade, measures on the congressional agenda were classified with regard to whether or not they clearly pitted the president against the preponderance of House Democrats. For a measure to be coded as doing so, the president must have had a clear, publicly stated position, two-thirds or more of the House Democrats must have voted together on all important roll calls on the measure, and the president's position and that of House Democrats must have been directly opposed.

A major change occurred in the structure of conflict between the early 1970s and the late 1980s, with the frequency of battles pitting House Democrats against the president increasing from only 18 percent of congressional agenda items in the 91st Congress to 61 percent in the 100th (see table 4.4). When Bush replaced Reagan in the 101st Congress, the frequency dropped, but only to 53 percent. During the 1980s and early 1990s, then, House Democrats often found themselves in direct opposition to the president, whose party also controlled the Senate from 1981 to 1986. The result in the 97th Congress was a low legislative success rate for Democratic committee contingents and for the Democratic membership. Committee majorities won, on balance, on final disposition on 48 percent of the measures on the congressional agenda in the 97th Congress, compared with 57 percent in the 91st and 70 percent in the 100th.[4] The 97th Congress's winning proportion of 48 percent is not very different from the 49 percent in the 94th; however, the stakes were considerably higher in the 97th Congress than in the 94th. President Reagan's program, which domi-

3. CQ's judgment, the content of the amendment, and the extent to which the committee fought the amendment were the bases of judgment. See chap. 3, note 6, for more detail.

4. On the basis of the CQ account, a judgment was made about whether the committee and, where relevant, the president and House Democrats as a group had on balance won or lost on final disposition. See chap. 3, note 9, for more detail.

Table 4.4 The Changing Structure of Conflict: Increase in Policy Battles Pitting President against Two-Thirds or More of House Democrats

Congress	Percentage of Items that Got to Floor
91st (1969–70)	18
94th (1975–76)	42
97th (1981–82)	47
100th (1987–88)	61
101st (1989–90)	53

nated the congressional agenda, represented significant policy change in a direction strongly opposed by a majority of Democrats. In fact, the committees' success rate when the committee and the president disagreed was much lower in the 97th than in any of the other congresses — 22 percent versus between 46 and 65 percent. In the 97th Congress, on measures pitting House Democrats against the president, Democrats won on final disposition only 28 percent of the time. (See tables 12.1 and 12.2 and the accompanying discussion for a further analysis of win rates.) In the early 1980s, then, Democrats were having great difficulty not only in passing legislation that would advance their goals but even in blocking legislation inimical to them.

The Changing Structure of Legislation: Multiple Referral and Omnibus Bills

Multiple referral of legislation and omnibus measures were hypothesized to stimulate leadership involvement. Both types of measures have become more prominent on the congressional agenda. The multiple-referral rule went into effect in 1975, and, in the 94th Congress, about 6 percent of the measures on the congressional agenda as here defined were multiply referred; this grew to 12 percent in the 97th Congress, to 28 percent in the 100th, and to 32 percent in the 101st. Thus, multiply referred legislation came to constitute a significant proportion of the congressional agenda of major legislation.

The political climate of the 1980s, I argue, led to the domination of the agenda by omnibus measures, especially ones addressing basic questions about priorities. Institutional change — the budget process instituted in the mid-1970s — fed into and provided one of the vehicles for this development. Budget resolutions are, by definition, omnibus measures that involve decisions about priorities.

In the 91st Congress, no item on the congressional agenda could remotely qualify as omnibus. In the 94th, only the four budget resolutions (the first and second each year) did. In the two congresses of the 1980s, by contrast, 20 percent of the agenda items were omnibus measures, and these included much of the most important legislation of those congresses — budget resolutions, reconciliation bills, full-year continuing resolutions (e.g., omnibus appropriations bills). In the 101st Congress, omnibus measures made up only 8 percent of the agenda but included some of the most important legislation of the congress.

In the 1970s and early 1980s, then, the potential benefits of stronger leadership grew as institutional changes and changes in the political environment increased the Democratic members' and the Democratic committee contingents' need for help in passing legislation that would advance their goals.

The Declining Costs of Strong Leadership: Decreasing Ideological Heterogeneity and Entrepreneurship Opportunities

Leadership activity did increase in the mid-1970s and early 1980s, as I have shown, but the full development of strong leadership depended on a decline in the costs of strong leadership. Specifically, the ideological heterogeneity of the Democratic party in the 1970s retarded the development of strong leadership, while the party's growing homogeneity in the 1980s made that development possible.

Voting was more partisan and House Democrats were more cohesive on party votes in the late 1980s and early 1990s than at any time in the previous four decades. This change is clearly evident on the major legislation here under consideration. The ideological heterogeneity of the Democratic party in the early 1970s manifested itself in frequent disagreements between a committee majority and Democratic liberals. Of all the agenda items that reached the House floor and elicited some conflict in the 91st Congress, fully 33 percent saw liberal Democrats in opposition to the committee majority's position. This declined to a mean of 16 percent in the 94th and 97th Congresses and a mean of 10 percent in the 100th and 101st Congresses.[5]

In the 91st Congress, over half the measures on the congressional agenda divided northern from southern Democrats on the House floor (see table 4.5).[6] A major change occurred during the congresses under study. Over time, floor coalitions were increasingly likely to be partisan

5. I rely on the account in CQ. CQ's reports of liberal opposition to a committee-reported bill are usually corroborated by roll-call evidence, but sometimes liberals were not able to force a recorded vote.

6. A measure was classified as evoking a partisan floor coalition if all major roll calls saw a majority of northern Democrats and a majority of southern Democrats vote together and against a majority of Republicans.

Table 4.5   The Changing Character of Floor Coalitions (% of agenda items)

	Congress				
Coalition Structure	91st (1969–70)	94th (1975–76)	97th (1981–82)	100th (1987–88)	101st (1989–90)
Party	13	28	30	61	45
North/South Dem. split	53	40	28	11	15
Party-North/South split mix	2	21	18	14	6
Crosscutting	7	5	8	11	19
Universalistic (90% + or voice)	22	7	15	5	15
N	45	43	40	38	47

and decreasingly likely to be characterized by a split between northern and southern Democrats.

The political climate of the 1980s, House members report, constricted opportunities for policy entrepreneurship (see, for example, Price 1989, 424–26). The data on agenda setting provide some evidence that this perception has, in fact, influenced members' behavior. The agenda-setting process in U.S. national politics involves many players in addition to the president and the majority-party leadership. Based on *Congressional Quarterly*'s account, there are cases in which some other identifiable individual or group — most frequently one or a group of liberal entrepreneurs, or a group such as labor — are the primary agenda setters. Thus measured, the agenda-setting role of identifiable individuals or groups other than the president or the leadership was smaller in the 1980s than in the 1970s, accounting for an average of 20 percent of major legislation in the congresses of the 1980s compared with 35 percent in the 1970s.[7]

The impact of large deficits can be seen in the character of the legislation successfully placed on the congressional agenda by identifiable individuals or groups in the 100th Congress. Although in all but two cases the agenda setter was in the liberal camp (broadly defined), only one of the bills in question cost money. Only the legislation providing an apology and reparations to Japanese Americans interned during World War II entailed a significant cost to the government. By implication, the deficit depressed entrepreneurial activity.

When the environment precludes freelance entrepreneurship, when

7. For more detail on the coding, see chap. 3, note 4.

Table 4.6   Leadership Involvement by Type of Measure (% of agenda items)

	Congress				
Type	91st (1969–70)	94th (1975–76)	97th (1981–82)	100th (1987–88)	101st (1989–90)
Omnibus	—	100	100	100	100
Multiply referred	—	100	60	82	88
Other	46	54	58	77	53
% omnibus and/or multiply referred	0	14	31	45	40

policy battles between Democratic committee contingents and significant groups within the party are rare rather than standard, when major legislation most frequently splits Democrats from Republicans rather than northern from southern Democrats, the potential costs of strong leadership to House Democrats have clearly decreased.

Patterns of Leadership Involvement

If variations in the costs and benefits to members of strong leadership determine variations in the rate of leadership activity over time, such variations across measures should be related to the cross-sectional pattern of leadership involvement. That is, the likelihood of party leaders' involvement should be greatest when the members most need help and when the costs of the leaders' providing such help are lowest for members of the majority party and for the leaders themselves.

Because the passage of omnibus and multiply referred legislation may require negotiation and coordination activities beyond the capacity of committee leaders, the party leaders should be involved more frequently on such bills than on other legislation. In fact, omnibus measures appear to demand leadership involvement; the leaders were active on every omnibus measure in the congresses under study (see table 4.6). Generally, multiply referred legislation is more likely to draw leadership involvement than singly referred, nonomnibus legislation.[8] The increase in multiply referred and omnibus measures has contributed to the change in the leaders' role. It does not completely explain the increase in leadership activity, however. Even among singly referred, nonomnibus measures, leaders' involvement has increased.

8. Because multiple referrals and omnibus measures were strictly defined, there is little overlap. Thus, although reconciliation legislation typically involves large numbers of committees, it is not technically multiply referred. The omnibus trade bill in the 100th Congress, which involved eleven committees, is a multiply referred omnibus bill.

Table 4.7   Leadership Involvement and the Structure of Conflict

% of Items in which Leadership Was Involved	Congress				
	91st (1969–70)	94th (1975–76)	97th (1981–82)	100th (1987–88)	101st (1989–90)
When committee/ president disagree	40	65	74	87	82
All other measures	49	53	59	67	53
When committee/ liberals agree	69	52	70	96	73
When committee/ liberals disagree	50	50	67	0	58
On partisan measures	83	92	75	91	76
On North/South Dem. split	54	47	82	50	86
On president vs. House Dem. measures	75	72	72	96	79
All other measures	40	53	63	65	62

The structure of conflict on a measure is a major determinant of the need for leadership help and of the costs of its provision. Democratic committee leaders and committee contingents are more likely to need leadership help to pass their legislation when the committee and the president disagree than otherwise, since the president can be a tough opponent. In fact, in every congress except the 91st, the leaders were substantially more likely to involve themselves when committee Democrats faced a hostile president (see table 4.7).

The costs of the leaders' involvement to party subgroups and to the leadership itself are higher when the party membership is split and lower when it is united. Yet an intraparty split increases the difficulty of passing legislation, and consequently the proponents' need for help. Under certain circumstances, the party leaders will be forced to involve themselves despite the membership being badly split (see Sinclair 1983, especially 127–28, 190–213). However, on balance, one would expect the costs of involvement to outweigh the benefits when the membership is badly split and, consequently, one would expect deep intraparty splits to depress the likelihood of leaders' involvement.

In all five congresses, the leaders were more likely to involve themselves when the committee and liberal Democrats agreed than when they disagreed, although the differences were sometimes small; in three of the five congresses, leaders were more likely to get involved on partisan measures than on those that split the party along North-South lines. The 97th Congress illustrates the circumstances under which the party leaders become actively involved despite a severe split among the members. Many of the measures at issue in 1981–82 — the first budget resolution (Gramm-Latta I), for example — were so important to the preponderance of the Democratic membership that the leaders had to involve themselves despite the costs of doing so in terms of their relations with southern Democrats.

Leadership involvement can take varied forms, some more expensive than others in terms of the leadership's relations with party subgroups. The figures in table 4.7 for leadership involvement when the committee and liberal Democrats disagree hide an interesting trend in type of leadership activity. In the prereform 91st Congress, when the leaders involved themselves they supported the committee, even though in these instances that meant taking sides against an appreciable subgroup in the party. In the later congresses, in contrast, leaders' involvement more frequently took the form of mediation and damage-control activities.

Measures that pit the president against the bulk of House Democrats combine high benefits with low costs, and consequently should elicit a high rate of leadership involvement. In practice, leadership involvement is consistently and considerably higher on such measures than on others (see table 4.7). Regression analysis (and probit as well) shows that the best predictors of leadership involvement are whether the measure is omnibus or multiply referred and whether the measure pits the preponderance of House Democrats against the president.[9] Thus, cross-sectionally as well as longitudinally, leadership involvement is associated with circumstances in which members need help to pass legislation and the costs to party subgroups of the leaders' providing that help are relatively low.

9. The ordinal character of the dependent variable "leadership involvement" (coded 0 for none, 1 for some, 2 for major involvement) makes the use of regression somewhat suspect. The regression coefficients, unstandardized and standardized, and the values of t are as follows:

	B	Beta	t
Omnibus	.93	.33	5.4
MR	.41	.16	2.7
Dem. vs. Pres.	.47	.26	4.4

The adjusted R^2 = .20

A probit analysis with involvement dichotomized as major vs. none or minor produced very similar results. The same variables (with Omnibus and MR combined into one variable) are the best predictors and are significant at better than the 0.001 level.

X

★   ★

Systematic analysis of five carefully selected congresses thus shows that the 1980s did indeed see the emergence of an activist majority-party leadership in the House, and that this phenomenon is related to changes in the institutional and political context that altered the costs and benefits to members of such leadership. The summary measures of leadership involvement used, however, reveal relatively little about the character of leadership activity, and even less about how leaders have managed to become so much more actively involved in the legislative process without encroaching to an unacceptable extent on members' pursuit of their goals through individualist strategies. Those are the tasks of the chapters that follow.

5

Leadership in a Changing Environment

Tasks, Resources, and Strategies

At bottom I think the membership expects the leadership to formulate policies that are good politics for them and which they perceive to be good policy for the country. They also expect the House to be run rationally. Some kind of schedule that they can understand. Some consideration for their own personal needs.

[Members want the leaders to] organize the legislative business and schedule and activities in a way that minimizes inconvenience, maximizes political opportunity and success, and generally brings about strong public reactions that are positive toward the party and to the individual members. To make their life as easy as possible, and be legislatively successful as often as possible.

[Members expect the leaders] to lead. Not only to be sensitive to the mood of the American public but to the fact that districts are different. To be sensitive to family concerns so we don't have a lot of night sessions. . . . To be sensitive and not bring up votes if they are difficult and the bill is not going to become law.

[Members] want [the leaders] to lead, to stake out a program. [Members] want it to be adopted; they want it to be something of which they can be proud. They want [the leaders] to protect them in some circumstances from highly controversial votes. . . . They want to have a predictable schedule.

[Members expect the leadership] on substantive issues to have a clear message as to what the Democratic party stands for and have that reflected in legislation. To schedule and generally run the House efficiently.

[Members expect the leaders] to implement a program that is acceptable to the majority of the caucus and the country, that improves our image as a party and that cares about the needs of the country. . . . To make sure the House runs well in terms of scheduling of time.

When asked what members expect of their leaders, members and leaders respond in similar terms. (The second, fourth, and sixth quotations are from leaders; the first, third, and fifth are from members.) Both see leaders as agents of their members and see facilitating the passage of legislation as a key leadership task. In addition, both leaders and followers identified a second facet of the job of the leadership: although the phrases they used varied, all of them spoke of an expectation that leaders facilitate when possible and certainly that they not hinder their members' pursuit of their goals through individualist strategies — that, for example, members not be forced to take tough votes unnecessarily, and that scheduling be sensitive to the members' needs for predictability and for time in the district.

If members simply expected their leaders to ensure the passage of legislation most Democrats unequivocally favored, the leaders' task would be a relatively easy one. To be sure, converting widespread support for general principles into firm backing for a specific proposal can be a complex enterprise. Yet members expect their leaders to do more than merely work to pass legislation that has broad support within the party. They also expect leaders to facilitate the passage of legislation that is important for electoral or policy reasons to a significant segment of the membership, at least so long as it does not impose direct and significant costs on another segment; in fact, they now often expect the leaders to find a way out of such conflicts. In addition, they expect leaders to pass legislation necessary to protect, and when possible enhance, the reputation of the party membership collectively. Doing so entails ensuring that legislation important to particular segments of the party is publicly defensible; it also requires effectively communicating the party's legislative accomplishments to the public. Since Democrats are the majority party, it also entails passing legislation necessary to maintain the House's reputation as a functioning legislature. This may mean, and in recent years not infrequently has meant, engineering passage of legislation that provides little in the way of electoral or policy benefits to most Democrats individually or even collectively, yet that must be passed to avoid an enormous cost to the party collectively. Legislation to increase the debt limit is the quintessential example, but in recent years other budget-related legislation has often been characterized by a similar configuration of payoffs; the House and its majority party receive little credit for passing such legislation but, were they to fail, the blame heaped on them would be immense and the impact on the party's image devastating. And not only do members expect their leaders to produce these collective goods, they expect them to do so without imposing too high a cost on them as individuals.

The Development of Leadership Offices

The Speaker, the majority leader, and the majority whip form the core of the majority-party leadership in the modern House of Representatives. Of these offices, the only one mentioned in the Constitution and the only one that is an office of the House is the speakership. In Article I, the Constitution provides that "the House of Representatives shall choose their Speaker and other officers." Because the Constitutional Convention did not debate the nature of the office, we do not know what the framers envisioned. Mary Follett argues persuasively that the Speaker was intended to be a political leader, not simply an impartial moderator (1974, 25–26). The early Speakers, according to Follett, were "keen guardians of party interest" but not "real party leaders" (ibid., 69). Henry Clay, who served six terms as Speaker between 1811 and 1825, was the leader of his party and established the position of Speaker as a legislative leader (ibid., 71). "As a presiding officer Clay from the first showed that he considered himself not the umpire but the leader of the House: his object was clearly and expressly to govern the House as far as possible. . . . He made no attempt to disguise the fact that he was a political officer" (ibid., 71–72). Most of the Speakers between 1825 and the Civil War did interpret the office as a political one, but not all were leaders of their parties or factions. The political turmoil surrounding the slavery issue frequently made choosing a Speaker difficult, with the consequence that "second-rate men" or "tools in the hands of the real leaders" were sometimes chosen (ibid., 96). Since the Civil War, the Speaker has been considered, and has almost always in fact been, the leader of his party in the House.

The positions of majority floor leader and whip were partisan, formally as well as actually, from their inception. During the nineteenth century, the chair of the Ways and Means Committee was usually considered the majority floor leader because his committee handled so much of the major legislation. Occasionally the Speaker chose a trusted lieutenant or his leading intraparty rival to serve as majority leader. Sereno Payne in 1899 became the first officially designated majority leader and at the same time chair of the Ways and Means Committee. The offices remained joined until 1919, when they were separated, and the majority leader now gives up his committee positions upon assuming the party office (Ripley 1967, 24–25; Galloway 1961, 107–8).

The hard-fought party battles of the late nineteenth century led to the formal creation of the position of whip (Ripley 1967, 30–36). Speaker Reed appointed the first whip in 1897 to help him keep track of his party members' whereabouts at the time of significant votes. Although they were sometimes important assistants to higher party officers, the whips in both parties were only sporadically active until the 1930s. It was in response to Franklin Roosevelt's ambitious legislative program that both parties in the 1930s developed whip organizations of some complexity.

Leadership Selection

The full membership of the House formally elects the Speaker. In reality, each of the two party contingents selects a nominee for Speaker at the beginning of each congress, and the majority party's candidate is elected by a straight party-line vote. The Democratic Caucus, the organization of all House Democrats, selects its candidate for Speaker at the organizing caucus meetings in December of election years. No incumbent Speaker has been denied renomination while his party remained in the majority. Usually, sitting Speakers face no opposition within their parties and are routinely renominated. Since the 1930s, Democrats have elevated their majority leaders to the speakership when that office became vacant as a result of retirement or death (see table 5.1; see also Peabody 1976).

As party officers, the majority leader and the whip are chosen solely by the members of their own party. Both are now elected at the December organizational caucus meetings. Democratic majority leaders frequently have previously served as whip, but that pattern of succession is not so firmly established as that from majority leader to Speaker. Of recent majority leaders, neither Jim Wright nor Dick Gephardt moved up from whip. Wright had served as one of several appointed deputy whips; Gephardt had been active in leadership vote-mobilization efforts and had held the elective position of caucus chair. Until 1987, the whip was appointed, nominally by the majority leader, but actually by the Speaker. Those who favored continuing the old selection process argued that by appointing the whip, the Speaker could assure himself of a loyal lieutenant and balance the leadership team as necessary. The ultimately successful proponents of election argued that since frequently the whip did move up the leadership ladder, members should choose who mounted the first step.

In recent years, campaigns for open leadership offices have become increasingly intense and elaborate. In 1976, when Thomas P. "Tip" O'Neill (D-Mass.) moved up to Speaker, a spirited four-way contest for the majority leadership developed. John McFall (D-Calif.), the whip, was tainted with scandal and was knocked out in the first round of voting. On the final ballot, Jim Wright defeated Phil Burton (D-Calif.) by one vote (Oppenheimer and Peabody 1977). The first whip election saw Tony Coelho (D-Calif.) mount an early-starting and highly sophisticated campaign

Table 5.1   The House Majority-Party Leadership, 1955–94

Year	Speaker	Majority Leader	Whip
1955	Sam Rayburn,[1] TX	John McCormack, MA	Carl Albert, OK
1962	John McCormack,[4] MA	Carl Albert, OK	Hale Boggs, LA
1971	Carl Albert,[4] OK	Hale Boggs,[1] LA	Thomas P. (Tip) O'Neill, MA
1973		Thomas P. (Tip) O'Neill, MA	John McFall,[2] CA
1977	Thomas P. (Tip) O'Neill,[4] MA	Jim Wright, TX	John Brademas,[3] IN
1981			Thomas Foley, WA
1987	Jim Wright,[4] TX	Thomas Foley, WA	Tony Coelho,[4] CA
1989	Thomas Foley, WA	Richard Gephardt, MO	William H. Gray III,[4] PA
1991			David Bonior, MI

Note: Reason for leaving position, if not to move up:
[1] death
[2] lost leadership race
[3] lost election
[4] retired from House

and defeat several formidable challengers (Brown and Peabody 1987). Gephardt, Bill Gray (D-Pa.), and Bonior all won their positions in contested elections (Brown and Peabody 1992). Even in those cases where no challenger emerged, as when Wright succeeded O'Neill as Speaker, considerable campaigns to obtain pledges of support and scare away challenges were mounted.

Challenges to sitting leaders have been rare, yet the membership must formally confirm the leaders every two years. Even when an incumbent leader is unchallenged, the formal process of an election in the Democratic Caucus is played out almost in its entirety. Nominating and seconding speeches are made, with the leaders choosing the speakers with great care to show broad appeal across the party's membership. The only concession to the lack of a challenge is that the vote will be by acclamation.

Current selection processes, as well as the offices' historical development, make the leaders agents of their party's members. Even the Speaker, who is an officer of the House and is formally chosen by its entire membership, is party leader first. It is his fellow partisans who really choose him and who could remove him; the biennial caucus reconfirmation process and the procedural ease with which a challenge can be mounted serve to remind a Speaker of his dependence on the members of his party. It is their expectations that he must be most concerned to satisfy.

During the past half-century, Democrats have chosen as their leaders members with considerable seniority and ones who ideologically are within the broad mainstream of the party. They have usually chosen a regionally balanced team, including one member from each of the two historically important regions. When, as in the early 1970s, movement up the leadership ladder resulted in the two top positions being held by southerners, the Speaker used his appointive powers to balance the team, adding Tip O'Neill, a liberal northerner, as whip (see table 5.1).

Thomas S. Foley of Washington was elected Speaker in June 1989 when Jim Wright was forced to leave the office and the House under an ethics cloud. Foley was first elected to the House as a part of the big 1964 class and, like many in that class, defeated an incumbent Republican. Unlike many of his classmates, he held his seat even though as a rural western Washington district it was not natural Democratic territory; several times during his career, his electoral margin was narrow. An active advocate of reform, Foley became chair of the Agriculture Committee in 1975 when the caucus deposed three sitting chairs. Foley served two terms as chair of the Democratic Caucus before O'Neill chose him as whip in 1981.

Dick Gephardt, from St. Louis, was first elected to the House in 1976 and quickly became active in the leadership's legislative efforts. He served as caucus chair from 1985 to 1988, and mounted a credible race for the 1988 Democratic presidential nomination before being elected majority leader. When Bill Gray decided to leave the House in mid-1991, David Bonior, who represented a blue-collar area near Detroit, succeeded him as whip. First elected in 1976, Bonior was appointed to the Rules Committee in 1981, became a deputy whip in 1985, and was named chief deputy whip by Speaker Jim Wright in 1987.

This leadership team was similar to its predecessors in that it was reasonably representative ideologically of the party membership; Bonior was a liberal, and Foley and Gephardt were moderate liberals. The team was somewhat less senior than its predecessors, and was clearly atypical in that none of the top three leaders was a southerner. Given the decline in the proportion of southerners and the transformation of the whip position from an appointive to an elective one, regional balance is no longer assured. Gephardt's opponent in the race for majority leader based his campaign largely on the need for regional balance, and one of Gray's opponents in the whip race made the same argument, yet both lost handily. Neither of the southern candidates had solid southern support. Although these results suggest a decline, regional loyalties and identification have certainly not disappeared. Speaker Foley responded to southerners' demands for inclusion by appointing a southerner as one of the chief deputy whips (see chap. 6).

Leadership Tasks, Powers, and Resources

The Speaker is both leader of the House and leader of its majority party. From each position derive certain tasks the Speaker is expected to perform. As formal leader of the House, he is expected not just to preside over floor sessions but to oversee the legislative process, especially at the floor stage, ensuring that it functions smoothly and fairly. As leader of the majority party, he is expected to facilitate the passage of the legislation his members want. Because the Speaker is selected by a partisan majority, the partisan facet of the position takes precedence. The tasks that have devolved upon the Speaker by virtue of his being the presiding officer and leader of the House provide the Speaker with powers that, within certain limits, can be used to perform the tasks expected of him as party leader.

Within the legislative context, powers can be defined as entitlements, specified by rules or customs, to make or participate in the making of certain decisions. Rules or customs that allot tasks, therefore, at the same time distribute powers. Inherent in the tasks traditionally assigned to the Speaker and the leaders collectively are powers that can be used to facilitate the passage of legislation important to their members. New powers and resources acquired by the leadership during the reform era provide additional tools. Yet some of the potentially most potent leadership tools depend directly on members' acquiescence for their effectiveness; and, while member constraints have lessened in recent years, leaders must still avoid using their powers in ways that infringe too much on members' ability to pursue their goals through individualist strategies.

As the chamber's constitutionally designated presiding officer, the Speaker either presides over the House himself or appoints the presiding officer. Despite the accretion of rules, precedents, and traditions that act as constraints, the position of presiding officer of the House is a powerful one. As former House parliamentarian Floyd Riddick has pointed out, "Tradition and unwritten law require that the Speaker apply the rules of the House consistently, yet in the twilight zone a large area exists where he may exercise great discrimination and where he has many opportunities to apply the rules to his party's advantage" (*Congressional Quarterly's Guide to the Congress* 1971, 129).

In light of this discretion, the choice of appropriate presiding officers to act in the Speaker's stead can influence outcomes, and only majority-party members are selected. When the Speaker finds it necessary to appoint a Speaker pro tempore he goes down the leadership hierarchy, asking the majority leader first, then the whip, and so on. By custom, the Speaker never presides over the Committee of the Whole. Since it is in the Committee of the Whole that bills are amended, great care goes into the selection of the presiding officer when important bills are scheduled.

A parliamentarian and two assistant parliamentarians aid the Speaker in discharging his duties as presiding officer. The office of parliamentarian is nonpartisan in the sense that a change in party control of the chamber does not necessarily lead to a change in personnel. The parliamentarians advise the committees and individual members of both parties as well as the majority-party leaders. Nevertheless, the parliamentarians owe their first duty to the Speaker; their job is to help him accomplish his aims within the rules. Since the House rules are immensely complicated, the Speaker's access to the parliamentarians' expertise becomes itself an important resource.

The parliamentarian also assists the Speaker in selecting members to preside over the Committee of the Whole. Lists of members, arranged by the type of bill under consideration when they presided, are maintained. When a controversial bill is scheduled, the parliamentarian will often present the Speaker with a list of recommendations from which to make his choice. Political factors are kept in mind: "We don't want a chairman who will have to make a ruling which is politically embarrassing to himself." The choice of presiding officer is most crucial when a bill is both controversial and new in approach. According to a participant, "There are five or six outstanding presiding officers and the Speaker tries to use those on the really tough bills — those on which there are no precedents." On minor bills, the Speaker often selects junior members to preside. In this way, the Speaker singles out a member and gives him or her some visibility in the chamber. As Speaker Tip O'Neill explained, members "get pride out of the prestige of handling the Committee of the Whole, being named the Speaker of the day" (Malbin 1977, 942). Under certain circumstances, that honor will be especially valued. Alerted that the parents of a junior member were in Washington for the first time since their son's election, Speaker Wright made sure the parents had an opportunity to see their son presiding over the House.

The Speaker can replace the presiding officer at any time. In late September 1980, the House was involved in routine business and a junior member was in the chair. In a surprise move, the Republicans made use of an obscure rule that allows any member of the Rules Committee to call up a resolution cleared by the committee seven days after it has been reported. The resolution called up contained a waiver of the Budget Act, so that if the previous question were to be defeated, as Republicans were urging, the Senate budget resolution could have been offered as a germane amendment. The purpose of the maneuver was to embarrass the Democrats during the election period. As soon as Republican Rules Committee member Trent Lott of Mississippi made the motion, the presiding junior member was replaced by Dan Rostenkowski (D-Ill.), then chief deputy whip and an experienced presiding officer.

Among his limited powers, the presiding officer has some discretion regarding the length of recorded votes. Before the installation of the electronic voting system, roll-call votes ordinarily took thirty minutes, and this time could easily be stretched to an hour. Electronic voting has reduced but not eliminated the leeway. Members must be given fifteen minutes to vote, but the presiding officer can declare the vote over as soon as the fifteen minutes have expired — or allow some extra time. In the spring of 1979 a bill raising the debt limit came up for a vote. The bill had already failed once, and a major effort had been mounted to pass it on the second try. As time ran out, the leadership was ahead by two votes. O'Neill's gavel fell instantly. Members were not given the opportunity, as they often are, to change their votes. Conversely, in a situation where the leadership position is trailing, the presiding officer may allow a vote to go on considerably beyond the fifteen minutes to give the leaders time to switch some votes. In 1987, when the fifteen minutes ran out on passage of the extremely important reconciliation bill and the bill was behind by one vote, Speaker Jim Wright held the vote open for ten additional minutes, until a member willing to change his vote could be located (see Barry 1989, 467–74).

The 1987 use of the presiding officer's discretion produced enormous Republican outrage, although numerous earlier instances had not. Made increasingly irrelevant by the Democrats' higher cohesion and their more forceful leadership in the mid-1980s, Republicans responded to having a rare victory snatched from them by protesting loudly and mounting a media campaign aimed at painting the Democratic leadership as dictatorial. Although the majority-party leaders have little direct incentive to respond to minority-party wishes, being perceived as fair is important to the party's image, and a deeply disgruntled minority can make the majority's life difficult. Consequently, the likely negative response of the minority must be weighed against any benefits in the aggressive use of the presiding officer's discretion.

In general, rulings of the chair (that is, the presiding officer) can be appealed to the chamber's membership. In the House, unlike the Senate, such appeals are rare and, when they do occur, the pressures on majority-party members to support the leadership are intense (see Murray 1990,

17–18; Sinclair 1983, 91–92). Nevertheless, that such an appeal can be made constrains the Speaker to some extent. In making a ruling, he must consider the likelihood of such an appeal, and, if not the likelihood of its success, at least the costs of defeating it.

The majority-party leadership has long been charged with the task of scheduling legislation for floor debate. Many elements of the task are highly institutionalized, but mostly not in a way that limits the leaders' discretion (see Sinclair 1983, 42–47). Floor scheduling is an indispensable coordination service that the leaders perform for the House as a whole. The power to decide whether and when legislation comes to the floor and the related power to be able to pull a bill off the floor if it runs into trouble can also be used to facilitate the passage of legislation majority-party members want as well as to block legislation they oppose. During most of the committee government era, the party leaders' scheduling powers were limited by their lack of control over the Rules Committee, with which they share those powers. Then and now, the use of those powers is constrained by the need for members' acquiescence. To bring legislation to the floor under a rule requires a majority vote; to bring it to the floor under the suspension procedure requires a two-thirds vote (see Oleszek 1984).

The Speaker, through the appointments he was charged with making, traditionally played a major role in organizing the chamber and the party. The immense appointive powers of the speakership in the nineteenth and early twentieth centuries were, however, stripped away in the revolt against Speaker Joseph Cannon (R-Ill.) in 1910–11. The task of appointing all members and chairs of committees was taken from the Speaker and given to the House as a whole, where it immediately devolved upon party committees. The Speaker was left with the task of appointing the members of select and special committees, of various commissions, and of conference committees. During the committee government era, committee chairs actually chose conferees. Commissions and select committees seldom make decisions of such importance that the Speaker, through his ability to shape their membership, has the opportunity to shape major decisions about legislation. Nevertheless, these appointments can be useful to the Speaker. Some are desirable to members because they constitute a significant element of a member's individualist strategies for advancing his or her goals. An appointment to a select committee may, for example, provide a member with a forum for taking part in debate on an issue in which that member has a policy interest, or for showing concern about a problem of particular importance to the member's constituency, or both. By a skillful deployment of the selective benefits he controls, the Speaker can increase the probability of members' being willing to engage in the collective action necessary to enact legislation. Favors received and favors anticipated encourage members to exhibit cooperative behavior.

During the committee government era, the Democratic party's top leaders — the Speaker and the majority leader when the party was in the majority — were not formally members of the party committee that assigned Democratic representatives to standing committees. Although they certainly influenced committee assignments, their influence was indirect (Masters 1963). The reforms of the 1970s greatly expanded the leaders' formal powers in the committee assignment process. The Steering and Policy Committee to which that task is now entrusted is chaired by the Speaker; the majority leader, the majority whip, and the four chief deputy whips are members ex officio, as are the chair and vice chair of the Democratic Caucus and the chair of the Democratic Congressional Campaign Committee (DCCC); the Speaker appoints about a third of the remaining members. Potentially, the leaders can use their larger role in the assigning of members to committees to shape committees, or they can use choice assignments as selective benefits, or both. Because decisions about committee assignments are so centrally important to representatives' careers, the expansion of leadership powers potentially is highly significant; for the same reason, members' expectations constrain leaders' use of these powers. Because members care so much about these decisions, leaders must be particularly sensitive about balancing criteria derived from the dictates of collective action and those derived from the facilitation of members' individualist strategies.

The single most important new power the Speaker was given during the reform era was the right to nominate the Democratic members and the chair of the Rules Committee, subject only to ratification by the Democratic Caucus. Caucus rules make clear that this is a responsibility the Speaker is to discharge anew at the beginning of every congress and, thus, that members of the Rules Committee have no property right to their positions. Consequently, Democratic members of the Rules Committee are dependent on the Speaker for their positions, and the committee has become an arm of the leadership. Control of the Rules Committee gives the leadership true control over floor scheduling, a control it lacked when the committee was independent and sometimes simply refused rules for legislation the leaders wanted to bring to the floor. In addition, because the rule under which a bill is brought to the floor sets the conditions for floor consideration, control of the Rules Committee can be used to structure the choices members face on the floor. Complex and often restrictive rules — ones that restrict the amendments that may be offered, for example — have become central to leadership strategy. Although probably the single most powerful tool in the leadership's arsenal, complex rules must be approved by a majority vote, and thus their use is immediately constrained by what a majority will accept.

The Speaker has always referred bills to committee, but the 1946 Reorganization Act to a large extent made this task a mechanical one. New rules governing the referral of legislation that the House adopted during the 1970s conferred new powers on the Speaker (see Collie and Cooper 1989; Davidson and Oleszek 1992). When the House adopted multiple referral, it gave the Speaker the power to set time limits on committees for reporting the bill out. The current rule specifies that the Speaker can set a reporting deadline for any committee on any legislation. Members' expectations do not, however, support such broad use of the power. In practice, deadlines are routinely set on committees other than the first when legislation is sequentially referred to several committees. Reporting deadlines force committees to act or lose their jurisdiction, and thus prevent them from using delay to kill legislation or from extracting an exorbitant price for reporting it.

During the reform era and in the succeeding years, the leaders gained resources that enhanced their capacity to exploit their powers, old and new, to the limit set by members' expectations. Because of the labor-intensive character of the legislative enterprise, staff is the premier resource; in this period, leadership staffs grew significantly. (On staffs, see Fox and Hammond 1977.) Like any other member, each leader may hire up to eighteen full-time and four part-time employees. In addition, in the early 1990s, specifically designated leadership staff aides totaled approximately eighty-nine for House Democrats. The Speaker employed about twenty-four aides in his speakership offices and another twelve at the Steering and Policy Committee; the majority leader had twenty-three employees on his leadership payroll; the majority whip, thirteen; the chief deputy whips, six; and the Democratic Caucus, eleven.[1]

Professional staff aides to the leaders perform a variety of functions, information gathering being perhaps the most central. They serve, as one said, "as the eyes and ears" of the leaders. "Our job," said another, is "to make sure the leadership is not surprised." The effective use of the powers the leaders command so as to facilitate the passage of legislation clearly requires information. Within the postreform House, with its wider participation, sufficient information is harder to come by; staff information-gathering activities are critical. Beyond that, staff aides perform a range of activities on the leaders' behalf ranging from seeing that business flows

1. These figures are averages of those reported in the Report of the Clerk of the House for the first quarters of 1990, 1991, and 1992.

smoothly on the House floor to negotiating on legislation to dealing with the media. Staffers greatly extend the range of matters in which the leaders can involve themselves.

Leaders must delegate a variety of often delicate tasks to their staffers if they are to involve themselves as broadly and deeply in the legislative process as their members expect them to. They can do so with reasonable confidence because these aides serve at the leaders' pleasure and often have worked for their principals for years. The moderate size of the staffs and the feedback on staff behavior leaders receive from other sources also work to assure that staff aides serve as faithful agents of the leaders.

In a variety of ways, the reforms of the 1970s gave the leaders new influence or leverage in the legislative process. The rules subjecting committee chairs to a confirmation vote in the Democratic Caucus require them to be responsive to the party leadership to the extent that it represents the members' wishes. The institution of multiple referral of legislation, and the decline in committee autonomy that it and the other 1970s reforms brought about, provided an opening for greater leadership involvement in the prefloor and postfloor legislative process.

The extent to which these and other rules changes create leverage for the leaders, and the extent to which party leaders can use their powers and resources aggressively, depend, however, on members' expectations.

A Changing Context and Changing Expectations

As chief of the chamber's majority party, the Speaker and the leadership collectively are charged with facilitating lawmaking. That charge can, however, be broadly or narrowly conceived. Members may expect the leadership to concentrate on coordinating activities and on helping members pursue their goals through individualist strategies. With regard to facilitating the passage of specific legislation, members may simply expect the leaders to assist committees that need help in passing their bills when they reach the floor. Thus, they may expect the leaders to schedule committee-approved legislation for floor consideration expeditiously, and with some eye toward strategic advantage; to employ the presiding officer's discretion to the advantage of such legislation; and, when necessary, to mobilize votes for passage. At the other extreme, members may expect their party leaders to take a major role in setting the congressional agenda, thereby assuring that it reflects the needs and preferences of the party membership; to be actively engaged in shepherding key legislation through the prefloor legislative process to ensure that it emerges in timely fashion and reflects, in its substance, the members' views and the party's needs; and to orchestrate floor strategy and vote-mobilization efforts.

Both the level and the character of the activity members expect of their party leaders vary, I argued earlier, with changes in the perceived costs and benefits to members of assertive, activist leadership versus more permissive, restrained leadership, and those costs and benefits are a function of the institutional and political context. A much more activist leadership emerged in the 1980s. The 1970s reforms and the adverse political climate of the 1980s created a context in which passing the legislation Democrats needed to advance their goals required leadership involvement early in the legislative process, long before the legislation reached the floor; it required party leaders to become centrally involved in the planning of strategy and the orchestration of the floor effort; and it demanded such involvement in a considerable number of legislative battles. The Democratic members' declining ideological heterogeneity meant an increase in the range of legislative preferences broadly shared within the party. With a change in the costs and benefits of assertive leadership came a change in members' expectations.

During the 1980s, then, members' expectations of their party leaders changed; House Democrats came to expect more activist, aggressive leadership, an expectation that continued into the 1990s. However, members also still expected their leaders to facilitate when possible and certainly not to hinder unduly members' pursuit of their goals through individualist strategies. Members' ideal point has shifted, but successful leadership is still a balancing act.

Leadership Strategies

Developing strategies that allow them to supply the collective goods the members want while at the same time helping where possible (and certainly not hindering) members in the pursuit of their goals through individualist strategies is the challenge the party leaders face. Because the desired balance between the two thrusts is a function of context and thus may vary over time, appropriate leadership strategies may also change over time.

In the immediate postreform period, party leaders confronted a membership that wanted and needed help in passing legislation, but members who as individuals were unwilling to accept significant constraints on their newly acquired opportunities to advance their goals through individualist means. Party leaders operated within a legislative system made much less predictable by greater openness and an increase in the number of significant actors. These factors shaped the strategies Speaker Tip O'Neill and Majority Leader Jim Wright developed in the late 1970s. As members' expectations changed during the 1980s in response to an altered political environment, the leaders adjusted their strategies accordingly.

The provision of selective benefits — favors — to members has been a central leadership strategy, probably throughout the history of the House and certainly during this century. Leaders' discretionary control over "goods" useful to members in the pursuit of their goals by individualist means can be employed so as to enhance the probability of cooperative behavior. Members' knowledge that leaders can help them get a desired committee assignment, raise campaign funds, or have a locally important project included in a bill gives leaders' requests for cooperative behavior added weight. For the party leaders in the immediate postreform era, helping members individually was an important tactic. Because it involved placing no constraints on members' behavior, it was a strategy compatible with members' expectations. And the reforms had to some extent increased the selective benefits at the leaders' command.

In addition, the O'Neill-Wright leadership team emphasized much more than its predecessors had the provision of services to the members collectively. Legislative scheduling was carried out with much greater attention to members' needs for predictability and time in the district. The whip system began to distribute a wide array of information, including timely and easily digestible summaries of the legislation up for floor consideration. Such services are collective goods that aid members in advancing their goals through individualist strategies. In providing such services, the leaders were responding directly to their members' expectations and thereby contributing to a favorable climate. Additionally, by making it possible for members to tend their districts more efficiently, such services may have given members greater leeway to pursue goals other than reelection (Fenno 1978). However, since by definition no member can be deprived of the benefits of a collective good, the leaders' provision of such goods does not translate directly into incentives for members to cooperate.

In response to the central conundrum of the 1970s House of Representatives — the uncertainty created by high participation, which threatened the legislation members wanted, and yet the unwillingness of members to curb their participation even to increase the probability of legislative success — the O'Neill-Wright leadership team developed the strategy of inclusion. The strategy dictates drawing into the leadership's orbit and including in leadership efforts as many Democrats as possible. Implementation of the strategy has entailed the expansion and use of formal leadership structures and the development of new processes. As it evolved, the strategy reshaped the whip system and the process of vote mobilization (see chaps. 7 and 10, and Dodd 1979). In the early 1970s, the whip system was a small organization with about twenty members, most of them elected by regional groups of Democrats. By the mid-1980s, it had become a large and elaborate organization, including about 40 percent of the Democratic House members. Most of the whips are now appointed by the leaders. In the 1970s, Speaker O'Neill began entrusting vote-mobilization efforts on particularly important bills to specially designated task forces. For each task force, the Speaker chose a chair, usually a well-regarded junior member of the committee of origin, and the chair and the leaders, often through senior staff aides, attempted to enlist in the effort a broadly representative group with ties to all segments of the party. Membership on the committee of origin was not a prerequisite to task-force participation; only a willingness to work for passage was essential. In the early 1980s, the responsibility for staffing the task forces shifted from the Steering and Policy Committee to the whip system. As the number of task forces increased and the standard vote-mobilization process came to revolve around task forces, the procedure for constituting task forces changed. Instead of special invitations to selected Democrats, most task forces recruited their members by issuing a broadly based general invitation to Democrats.

The strategy of inclusion, especially as it manifested itself in the task-force device, made it possible, in the late 1970s, for the O'Neill-Wright team to satisfy to a reasonable extent the members' potentially conflicting expectations. Task forces gave the core leaders the help they badly needed in the unpredictable environment of the immediate postreform House. By increasing the number of people working in an organized way to pass the bill at issue, a task force increased the probability of legislative success. Task forces also gave a large number and broad variety of Democrats, especially junior Democrats, an opportunity to participate meaningfully in the legislative process, but in a way that contributed to rather than detracted from the leaders' efforts to pass legislation that a broad party majority wanted or needed. At a time when members were unwilling to countenance leadership constraints on their autonomy, task-force work was sufficiently attractive that many members freely chose to participate.

In the more difficult political climate of the 1980s, Democrats became willing to accept some constraints on their autonomy, particularly limitations on the offering of floor amendments. The price in terms of policy of maintaining the wide-open, participatory process of the immediate postreform era had proved to be too high. But with floor participation more restricted, the value to members of task-force participation increased. Task forces provided Democrats with the opportunity to become significantly involved in legislation they cared about, even if they were junior members or not on the committee of origin — an opportunity that was seldom available on the House floor.

As members traded some of their autonomy for an increased probability of legislative success, the strategy of inclusion in its various forms became, if anything, more important. Democrats still wanted to participate meaningfully in the legislative process; with some arenas closed off, especially to junior members and to those not on the committees, the value of other routes to participation increased. In addition, members wanted access to the leaders and a sense that they could directly influence a leadership that is highly consequential in the legislative process.

Structuring through procedure the choices members face so as to advantage one's preferred position is the quintessential legislative strategy. The highly complex and relatively restrictive rules under which the House operates make this potentially a powerful strategy for increasing the probability of legislative success. The 1970s reforms granted the party leaders some additional and highly significant powers for structuring choices. Most importantly, control over the Rules Committee gave the Speaker true control over the flow of legislation to the floor and provided him with a tool that was both strong and flexible for structuring members' floor choices.

In the immediate postreform period, Democrats were unwilling to allow their leaders to use these powers aggressively. Intent on exploiting fully the new opportunities to participate that reforms had opened up to rank-and-file members, Democrats would not countenance leadership-imposed restrictions on their freedom of action. Since the use of special rules to structure choices usually entails restrictions on amendments, Democrats' insistence that they be at liberty to offer any germane amendment on the House floor severely limited the leaders' use of this strategy. Even had the leaders been willing to endanger their own positions by proposing constraints on participation unacceptable to members, they could not have mustered the majority vote needed to pass each special rule.

In the mid- and late 1970s, Democrats learned that a wide-open amending process was a two-edged sword; while it offered them new opportunities for freelance policy entrepreneurship, those opportunities came at a high price. Republicans — and Democrats' own dissident party colleagues — became adept at drafting amendments that confronted Democrats with an unpalatable choice, pitting their policy preferences against their reelection needs. Legislation written by committees that were now quite representative of the party membership was picked apart on the floor. Debate often dragged on and on, disrupting schedules and wearing members out.

By the late 1970s, many Democrats had become concerned about the costs of the wide-open floor amending process that the reforms had established, and a number of them began urging the leadership to use restrictive special rules to bring some order and predictability to floor consideration (see Bach and Smith 1988, 41). Within the much more hostile political climate of the 1980s, most Democrats became convinced that the costs of an unrestricted amending process were too high.

The leaders responded to the members' changing expectations and needs by increasing their use of rules to structure choices. Whereas in the mid-1970s, most major legislation was considered under a simple open rule, by the late 1980s most was brought to the floor under a restrictive rule.

Although on its face the strategy of structuring choices by using restrictive rules seems coercive, the leaders generally use it in such a way that it contributes to the reconciliation of the members' expectation that aggressive action will be taken to pass legislation the members want with their potentially conflicting expectation that the leaders will be sensitive to members' individual needs. Since adoption of a rule requires the approval of a majority of House members and thus usually a much larger proportion of Democrats, members must acquiesce in having their choices constrained. They do so because most of the time the leaders have skillfully crafted the rule so that approval furthers, on balance, most members' goals. Frequently, the leaders attempt to provide cover for members to enable them to vote their policy preferences without paying too high a reelection price. Sometimes the rule makes possible the passage of a bill that all members know must be enacted but that is unpalatable on both policy and reelection grounds. And if a significant group of Democrats needs a vote on an amendment for constituency reasons, the leaders will provide the opportunity, though they will structure the choice so as to minimize the policy damage.

Carefully crafted and often restrictive special rules are important tools the leaders use to structure choices, but they are not the only ones. Shaping the character of the legislative vehicle that comes to the floor or making sure members have the opportunity to cast a symbolically important vote are other forms of this strategy. Changes in the legislative process in the 1970s and the adverse political climate of the 1980s and early 1990s diminished the capacity of committees to pass their legislation on the floor intact. Increasingly often, Democratic committee contingents needed help from the party leadership. Providing the necessary assistance has drawn the leaders more deeply into the prefloor legislative process. To the extent that the leaders take a hand in shaping the character of the vehicle that comes to the floor, they are involved in making decisions about the substance of legislation. Democratic committee contingents and Democratic committee leaders countenance such leadership activity because it is aimed at, and is necessary to, passage of the committee's legislation, because the party leaders in their dealings with the committee represent the sentiments of the Democratic membership, or both. Party leaders do not simply impose their decisions on the committee; they almost always work with committee Democrats to shape a legislative vehicle that structures members' choices so as to increase the probability of legislative success. The strategy of inclusion thus makes the decline in autonomy easier for committee Democrats to accept.

The strategy of "going public" was thrust on Democratic party leaders by changes in the expectations of the members. Since at least Franklin Roosevelt's time, presidents have attempted through the mass media to influence elite and mass perceptions so as to shape the political agenda and the images of the parties. In the early 1980s, Reagan's media skills, in combination with the political climate, allowed the president to dominate political discourse. Reagan used that dominance to control the policy agenda and to propagate a highly negative image of the Democratic party. Unable as individuals to counter this threat to their policy, power, and reelection goals, Democrats expected their leaders to take on the task.

Unlike rank-and-file House members, party leaders have considerable access to the national media. In fact, in the aftermath of the Republican takeover of the Senate, the press anointed Speaker O'Neill the chief Democratic spokesperson. However, because House party leadership had been defined as quintessentially an insider job, the leaders of the 1980s and 1990s had to invent the means for carrying out their members' mandate. Structures and tactics had to be developed, tried out, and refined—a continuing process.

Although members want their leaders to act as spokespeople, they do not thereby commit themselves to silence or to an automatic echo of their leaders' messages. The means party leaders develop for influencing national political discourse cannot be predicated on their being the congressional party's single voice. Lacking both the means and the will to impose uniformity on members who value their autonomy of expression, the leaders rely on tactics that encourage voluntary accord. Such tactics will frequently fail to produce a single clear message, and a cacophony of voices obviously dilutes the impact of the message the leaders are attempting to convey. Yet members' expectations limit the tactics available to the leaders to persuasion-based ones.

Changes in the institutional structure of the House and in its political environment have altered the problems majority-party members face in advancing their goals, and so have shaped and changed those members' expectations of their leadership. In response, party leaders have attempted to develop strategies for meeting their members' altered needs and expectations. House Democrats came to expect their leaders to act aggressively to facilitate the passage of legislation broadly supported by Democrats but to do so without unduly constraining members' advancement of their goals through individualist strategies. These potentially conflicting imperatives have shaped leadership strategies; their mark is evident in the mix of strategies and in the way in which those strategies are implemented.

Depicting the operation of current leadership strategies in practice and showing how that operation is affected by the changing expectations of members and by the continuing imperative of balancing potentially conflicting expectations are major tasks of the chapters that follow. Because, responding to members' expectations, the majority-party leaders are now deeply involved in all stages of the legislative process, the following chapters can also be read as an analysis of the legislative process in the contemporary House.

Organization, Communication, and Accountability

The strategies party leaders have developed for meeting their members' expectations depend heavily on a set of party and House organizations — the Democratic Steering and Policy Committee, the whip system, the caucus, the Rules Committee, and the inner circle of the leadership itself — that provide them with information, resources, and assistance. The reforms of the 1970s created, restructured, or changed the functioning of these organizational entities, and leaders' and members' adaptation to the postreform environment of the late 1970s and to the 1980s climate of adversity resulted in further alterations in how these entities operated. Their current structure and functioning have been shaped by the leaders' need for help, by the members' desire for leadership accountability, and by members' and leaders' needs for information.

Consider the expanded leadership inner circle, the Steering and Policy Committee, and the Democratic Caucus. For an agency relationship to work to the satisfaction of both principals and agents, principals must have means of holding their agents accountable and agents must have means of meeting their principals' expectations. These three entities are instrumental in providing those means. Clearly, information is essential. Leaders must be able to find out what members want; members must to able to find out what leaders are doing. In a collectivity as large as the House, satisfactory communication depends on organization. These organizational units are among those that support such communication. To ensure accountability, members do not, however, rely solely on ex post information or their power to vote their leaders out of their positions. Members attempt to ensure leadership accountability by insisting that key organs be representative and accessible. These entities also provide the leaders with resources for and assistance in meeting the members' expectations.

The Expanded Leadership Inner Circle

Members' changing expectations of their leaders have led to an expansion of the leadership inner circle. In the 1940s and into the 1950s, the inner circle consisted of just the Speaker and the majority leader; by the early 1970s, it had expanded, but only to include the whip as a full-fledged member. By the 1990s, the chair and vice chair of the Democratic Caucus and the four chief deputy whips had been added to the inner circle. In the 103rd Congress the leadership inner circle consisted of Speaker Thomas Foley of Washington, Majority Leader Dick Gephardt of Missouri, Majority Whip David Bonior of Michigan, Chief Deputy Whips Butler Derrick of South Carolina, Barbara Kennelly of Connecticut, John Lewis of Georgia, and Bill Richardson of New Mexico, Caucus Chair Steny Hoyer of Maryland, and Caucus Vice Chair Vic Fazio of California.

The inner circle is not a formally designated group. It consists of those members who regularly attend leadership meetings. Since the Speaker determines who is invited to most such meetings, he controls who belongs to the inner circle. The composition of the group can thus vary depending on a particular Speaker's leadership style. Yet all recent Speakers have needed assistance to sustain the high level of legislative activity their members expect, and the expansionary trend has been evident during all recent speakerships.

Members regard the party leaders as their agents and expect the leaders to be accessible and accountable. The traditional emphasis on a geographically balanced leadership team has its roots in these expectations; southerners, for example, believed that having a fellow southerner in the leadership would ensure that their voices would be heard and their interests protected. In recent years, as the leadership has become more central in the legislative process, members' demands for access and accountability through the inclusion of a representative in the inner circle have grown. Since such demands have meshed well with the leaders' need for assistance, the Speaker has complied. In 1987, rust-belt liberals were concerned about an all-western leadership team; Jim Wright, the new Speaker, appointed David Bonior of Michigan chief deputy whip and included him in the inner circle. In the summer of 1991, when Bonior replaced Bill Gray as whip, African Americans, women, and southerners all expressed dissatisfaction about their exclusion from the leadership team. Speaker Foley responded by asking the caucus to split the chief deputy whip position into three, and appointing John Lewis, an African American, Barbara Kennelly, and Butler Derrick of South Carolina to the new positions. In 1992, a fourth chief deputy whip position was created, and Foley appointed Bill Richardson of New Mexico, a Latino, to the position. These members have also been incorporated into the inner circle.

The Division of Labor

The division of labor among members of the inner circle is in part institutionalized and in part a function of the interests of particular leaders and of the wishes of the Speaker, who, as the majority party's top leader, oversees and is responsible for the entire leadership enterprise.

As the highest-ranked leader, the Speaker bears a special responsibility to represent the chamber and the majority party in interactions with the other key institutional actors, the president and the Senate. The president dictates the frequency and the subject matter of presidential contact with the House majority-party leadership. Formal meetings at the White House and less formal contacts by telephone and through intermediaries tend to be more frequent when the president and the House majority are of the same party and less so when control is split. During the Reagan and Bush years, White House meetings were infrequent even by the standards of divided control, and were almost completely devoted to foreign affairs. President Clinton, in contrast, meets with the Speaker and other House leaders often and on the full range of issues.

The Speaker and the Senate majority leader together determine the character of interchamber leadership relationships. Since Democrats regained control of the Senate in the 1986 elections, contact between the two leaderships has been much more frequent and intensive than in the past. In 1987 the leaderships began to meet for breakfast every other week, with the Speaker and the Senate majority leader alternating as host; in the late 1980s, formal meetings began to be held once a week. Special, often impromptu meetings and phone calls are frequent at the level of the leaders and nearly continuous at the staff level. Coordination of the congressional schedule and of the party's message is most often the objective of regular meetings; special meetings frequently address specific legislation.

The "broad purposes [of the job of majority leader] are to determine the scheduling of legislation, to participate in organized efforts to advance that legislation and to provide support for efforts to develop Democratic majorities in the House to pass it, and to be a spokesman for the party," a recent occupant of that position explained. "It is marked very strongly by those sorts of duplicative powers of the Speaker. . . . The Speaker does everything that the majority leader does and so the majority leader has the job of doing it with the assistance and guidance and support of the Speaker." Majority Leader Dick Gephardt outlined the post's duties in similar terms:

> The Majority Leader has prime responsibility for the day-to-day working of the House, the schedule, working with the committees to keep an eye out for what bills are coming, getting them scheduled, getting the work of the House done, making the place function correctly. [But] you are also compelled to try to articulate to the outside world what Democrats are for, what Democrats are fighting for, what Democrats are doing. (Madison 1990, 2906)

Certain aspects of the majority leader's job have become institutionalized. The office is charged with the routine tasks of scheduling legislation for floor consideration. This was an extremely complex assignment in the 1970s, when the amount of legislation coming out of the committees far exceeded available floor time, but scheduling became easier as environmental constraints such as the big deficits dampened legislative activism and thus the volume of legislation (see Sinclair 1983). The majority leader is also responsible for guarding the floor—that is, making sure that business flows smoothly and that opponents do not disrupt the legislative process, through surprise parliamentary maneuvers or other means.

Although the majority leader gives up his committee assignments upon being elected, he serves as the Speaker-designated majority-party representative on both the House Budget Committee and the Intelligence Committee. Since its inception in 1974, the budget process has often been at the center of controversy, and the majority leader's position on the Budget Committee has often placed him in the midst of leadership efforts to negotiate and pass acceptable budget resolutions. The centrality of the majority leader in such efforts, as in others, is, however, ultimately determined by the Speaker.

In contrast to the majority leader's job, that of the whip is more clearly delineated. He runs the whip organization, which is charged with the gathering and dissemination of information and with vote mobilization. Bill Gray, whip from 1989 to 1991, likened the job to that of Chief Engineer Montgomery Scott of the *Starship Enterprise*. "Remember how he is always telling the bridge that there isn't enough power and the engines are overheating? That's my job. Get the power up, keep the engines cool and remind the bridge from time to time of the limits of the ship" (Dirksen Congressional Center 1991, 8). The whip system's organization and processes have become increasingly institutionalized; how frequently and when to employ that system are ultimately decisions the Speaker makes.

The other leadership positions are newer and their tasks less clearly defined. To be sure, caucus rules specify that the chair of the Democratic

Caucus presides over caucus meetings and administers caucus affairs. But beyond these broad charges, the caucus chair's duties and his position in the leadership are fluid, a function of his own proclivities and the Speaker's wishes. This is even more the case for the caucus vice chair, a position previously designated as secretary of the caucus. Other than performing the duties of the caucus chair when the chair is unable to do so, the caucus vice chair has no specified duties. In the 102nd and 103rd Congresses, Vic Fazio, the caucus vice chair, also served as chair of the DCCC. The chief deputy whips are expected to aid the whip in major vote-mobilization efforts. The job, one explained, "is to get the votes, to sell the program and, if we find that we don't have enough votes, to find out what it takes to get the votes."

Leaders, even more than ordinary members of Congress, are perforce generalists. Given the still-modest size of even the expanded inner circle, the fluid and ill-defined division of labor among the leaders facilitates the handling of a legislative workload of considerable size and immense scope. When an intensive vote-mobilization effort on top-priority legislation is underway, everyone is expected to pitch in. Otherwise each leader, in addition to carrying out whatever duties are associated with his or her position, takes on various nonroutine leadership tasks as his or her own interests and the Speaker's wishes dictate. Any special talents, interests, connections, and other institutional positions such as committee assignments that members bring to the leadership, as well as the composition of the workload, may affect the division of labor within the leadership inner circle.

Because of his longstanding interest in and activism on Central American issues, David Bonior routinely took the lead in the frequent battles on aid to the Nicaraguan contras during the Reagan administration. As a member of the Ways and Means Committee, Barbara Kennelly was particularly active on tax issues, leading the vote-gathering task force on Clinton's reconciliation bill in 1993, for example. Committee assignments and a special political adeptness made Vic Fazio the lead person on congressional ethics reform and other delicate internal issues; he chaired the Appropriations Subcommittee on the Legislative Branch and served on the Ethics Committee. Fazio's prominent role on freedom-of-choice issues, on the other hand, derived from personal interest. Although he held a tangentially related committee assignment, Steny Hoyer's activism on the AIDS issue was primarily dictated by personal interest.

Information Gathering

Integral to all the leadership positions is information gathering. If leaders are to act as faithful agents and satisfy the members' expectations, they need ways of finding out what members want and means of obtaining the information required for fulfilling those expectations. Members need information on what leaders have done if they are to hold them accountable. Clearly, a two-way flow of information is a prerequisite to a satisfactory relationship between leaders and members. All who belong to the inner circle contribute to that flow.

"They're another set of eyes and ears," was a senior leadership aide's first response to a question about the job of the new chief deputy whips. Each leader, together with his or her staff, constitutes an information-gathering enterprise. Each has a somewhat different set of legislatively relevant actors, both inside and outside the chamber, with whom regular contact is maintained and from whom information is gleaned. From the point of view of the members, each provides a potential point of access, a conduit for members' views to enter leadership deliberations, as well as a source of information about leadership plans and activities. Both leaders' and members' interests dictate a leadership diverse enough to pick up a representative sampling of members' views.

Essentially all of the leaders' leadership-related activities produce legislatively relevant information as a by-product. The liaison duties that the Speaker in particular performs provide him with valuable information about the president's and the Senate leadership's preferences and plans. The majority leader's scheduling tasks and the whip's operation produce innumerable bits of information about individual members' and committees' preferences, problems, and plans. All the leaders are asked for favors by members, and each request conveys information that may prove useful later.

The speaking leaders do on their members' behalf provides a particularly useful form of information. All the top leaders are asked by members to speak to groups of constituents in Washington and in the members' districts. Most often a visit to the district entails attendance at a fundraiser for the member. All the top leaders travel extensively; Jim Wright estimates that when he became Speaker he had spoken for two hundred then-sitting members, and he continued such activity during his speakership. Such a visit is a valued selective benefit leaders can bestow on their members; bringing in the Speaker or another top leader is likely to raise a member's status with his politically active constituents and, since the top leaders are good draws, the member is also likely to raise more money. The leaders, in addition to gaining some leverage with members thus benefited, also obtain the sort of information about the member's constituency and political situation not available in Washington, information invaluable in efforts at persuasion. Having a good sense of when a member can be pushed to vote the party position and when a particular vote would, in fact, pose a reelection problem helps leaders satisfy members' expectations for legislation without imposing too high a cost.

Members of the inner circle share information through a variety of often quite informal means. Every day that the House is in session, a short leadership meeting precedes the Speaker's press conference. Meetings of the entire inner circle to discuss major upcoming issues take place about twice a week; such a get-together now occurs regularly on Thursday mornings before the whip meetings. All members of the inner circle attend the weekly whip meetings; most are also regular participants in the daily message meetings (see chap. 11). The chief deputy whips have offices in the same Capitol corridor as the whip, making contact among them almost continuous. Senior staff aides and often the leaders themselves spend time on the floor during roll calls and touch base there. In addition, the Speaker calls special meetings when necessary.

Intraleadership Agreement and Disagreement

A relatively large and diverse inner leadership circle facilitates information gathering but raises the probability of intraleadership policy disagreements. The increase in Democratic party cohesion that occurred in the 1980s and leadership selection processes militate against frequent, crippling disagreements. Top leaders choose some members of the inner circle and keep the need for smooth working relationships in mind. Thus, when Speaker Foley decided to appoint a southerner as a chief deputy whip, he chose Butler Derrick, a moderate and a proven party loyalist, rather than a more conservative or maverick representative from that region. The selection of leaders by election of the full membership tends to produce leaders who are in the party's mainstream, especially in a period of considerable ideological cohesiveness.

Nevertheless, disagreements among the leaders do occur. Personal policy views or reelection needs may place a member of the inner circle at odds with his or her colleagues in the leadership. In such instances, the leader in question simply does not participate in leadership efforts. A member of the inner circle explained how he had handled such an instance: "I let everybody know early where I stood. And I didn't work against the Speaker's position and they didn't work me." So long as this occurs only occasionally, it causes little problem; everyone recognizes that leaders, like rank-and-file members, must win reelection. However, as one leader said, "The expectation is that when you are in doubt you will go with the leadership." And were a member of the inner circle to find himself or herself at odds with the other members frequently, that leader's position would become untenable.

Legislation implementing the North American Free Trade Agreement

(NAFTA) tested the leadership's ability to cope with a deep policy split. It was, in fact, a case in which the leaders faced conflicting expectations: the expectation that they would advance the legislative preferences of the majority of their members clashed with the expectation that they would support the policy priorities of a president of their own party. Whip David Bonior and Majority Leader Dick Gephardt opposed NAFTA; Speaker Tom Foley supported it. President Clinton had endorsed the pact during the campaign and mounted a vigorous fight for its approval. In leading the battle against NAFTA, which he had opposed long before Clinton's election, Bonior represented the majority of House Democrats, especially those from rust-belt districts like his own. Foley's support was consistent with his own long-held views on free trade, and with the expectation that congressional leaders of the president's party would support his major initiatives. To contain the long-range damage the split might do to the leadership team, the participants followed certain tacit ground rules. Bonior did not employ the official whip apparatus in his campaign. Speaker Foley and Majority Leader Gephardt kept their own participation low-key and carefully refrained from the sort of heated rhetoric that would make reconciliation after the fight difficult.

Although an intraparty fight on such a prominent issue inevitably leaves some residual problems, the leaders in this case seem to have contained the damage by waging the fight carefully. The alternatives — a united leadership either working against the strongly held preferences of a majority of its members or opposing a still-new Democratic president — probably would have been more costly.

The Steering and Policy Committee

When reformers in the early 1970s set up the Democratic Steering and Policy Committee and then gave it the function of assigning members to committees, they intended it to be a centralizing entity, one that would increase the party leadership's clout; they also intended it to be accessible and accountable to the membership. To a considerable extent, their aims have been met.

Development, Composition, and Accountability

House Democrats first created a steering committee in 1933. Although it continued in existence until 1956, it never played a significant role in setting party policy. Sam Rayburn was Speaker during much of this period, and his leadership style was highly personal. The committee's final chair explained its lack of function: "Mr. Sam decided what will be done"

(Ripley 1967, 47). In 1962, at the behest of liberals, the committee was reestablished, but again it was simply a paper entity, seldom meeting and having no legislative or political impact (ibid.). In 1973 the old committee was replaced with a new Steering and Policy Committee, which in late 1974 was made the committee on committees, assuring it a role of real significance. The committee was also intended to provide a forum for political and legislative discussion and, to some extent, for setting party policy.

Initially, the committee consisted of twenty-four members: the Speaker (who served as chair), the majority leader (vice chair), the caucus chair (second vice chair), and the majority whip as ex officio members, twelve members elected from different geographical areas, and eight members appointed by the Speaker. Late in 1980 the secretary of the caucus and the chairs of the four most important committees (Appropriations, Budget, Rules, and Ways and Means) joined the committee as ex officio members. The chair of the DCCC and the chief deputy whip were added, first as nonvoting members, later as full members. When the chief deputy whip position was split into three positions in 1991 and then a fourth chief deputy whip was added in 1992, all were made ex officio members of the Steering and Policy Committee. In the 102nd Congress, the Speaker was temporarily granted a ninth appointment because Vic Fazio, as caucus vice chair and chair of the DCCC, held two of the positions with ex officio membership. To allow for appointment of two freshmen from the large 103rd Congress class, the rule was rewritten to give the Speaker the power to appoint as many as ten members. In the 103rd Congress (1993–94), the committee had thirty-five members: thirteen ex officio (because Fazio still held two slots), twelve regionally elected, and ten appointed by the Speaker. Appointed and elected members may serve no more than two consecutive full terms.

Through a mix of regionally elected, appointed, and ex officio members, reformers hoped to strike a balance among a number of not necessarily congruent concerns. The regional members were expected to represent the subgroup that elected them, to provide access for and be accountable to those members. The Speaker was expected to use his appointments in part to assure the representativeness of the committee by appointing members from subgroups not otherwise included. Thus, the Speaker's appointees have usually included a woman, an African American, and a freshman representative. Making the Speaker chair, including other top leaders as ex officio members, and giving the Speaker appointive powers were acts clearly intended to give the leadership — and the sort of party-based criteria the leadership was expected to emphasize — significant influence on the committee's decisions. The growth over time in the leaders' presence on the committee has further increased their potential for influencing committee decisions.

Speakers use their appointments to balance the committee along a number of dimensions. Foley in the 103rd Congress chose two freshman representatives and one other very junior member — one an African American, one a woman, and the third a Latino; one from the South, one from the Northwest, and the third from the Southwest. He also included John Dingell (D-Mich.), chair of the Energy and Commerce Committee, by far the most important House committee without ex officio representation on the Steering and Policy Committee; another committee chair, a Latino from Texas; and several other key players, most notably David Obey (D-Wis.) and John Murtha (D-Pa.). While seeking representativeness, Speakers also choose people on whose loyalty they can rely. Two of Foley's 103rd Congress appointees were from his home state of Washington, and several others were close to him.

Because the Steering and Policy Committee makes decisions of major importance to members, the Speaker's appointive powers provide him with a resource of real worth. These appointments are selective benefits members truly value. When Bob Clement of Tennessee was appointed to the committee, his office sent out a press release informing his constituents of how he had been singled out: "Clement, the only freshman appointed to the committee, will play a significant role as a liaison to newly-elected freshmen members of the House of Representatives, as well as other members including those from the Southeastern United States." Making the most of the selective benefit at his disposal, Speaker Wright provided Clement's office with a glowing statement, which was used in full in the press release: "'During his first year as a member of Congress Bob Clement has demonstrated dedication to his responsibilities and an ability to communicate with his colleagues that is vital in this important position,' said Wright. 'I am confident he will display the same dedication and a sense of fairness as a member of the Steering and Policy Committee'" (December 6, 1988).

Committee Assignments

By far the most important decisions the Steering and Policy Committee makes are those on the assignment of Democrats to standing committees. For members, committee-assignment decisions are among the most crucial of their House lives. The committees they serve on determine the issues on which they will spend most of their time and shape the strategies they have available for advancing their reelection, policy, and power goals (see Fenno 1973). The membership composition of committees strongly influences the character of their policy outputs and, consequently, is important to all those members whose policy or reelection goals are thereby affected. Thus members care not only about their own committee assignments but also, to widely varying extents, about the makeup of other committees.

For both members and leaders, committee assignments raise the question of the appropriate balance between individual and collective concerns in its starkest form. To what extent should assignments be made so as to further members' ability to advance their goals by individualist strategies? To what extent should they be made so as to further the membership's collective interest in a satisfactory legislative product? Considered from the leaders' perspective, to what extent should leaders use their influence in the process to do favors for members and to satisfy concerns about distributive fairness? To what extent should the leaders attempt to shape committee memberships so that the legislation they report will be satisfactory to House Democrats as a group?

Throughout the period between the November elections and the time committee assignments are made (early December to mid-January), freshman representatives and those continuing members who wish to change assignments make their preferences known to members of the Steering and Policy Committee. All such Democrats must communicate with their regional representatives; many also visit or write the leaders. As the Democratic Study Group advises new members:

> Members-elect should discuss their committee assignment preferences with their regional representative on the Steering & Policy Committee, with the Democratic leadership, with the dean of their state delegation, and with other Members from their state. Committee assignment requests should then be communicated to the Steering & Policy Committee staff, which prepares a list of all requests for the committee prior to its first meeting . . . and to the Member's regional representative, who has responsibility for placing the Member's name in nomination for assignment to the committees he or she has selected.

When the Steering and Policy Committee meets to make committee assignments, members sit around large tables set up in a U-shape with the party leaders at the end. The most sought-after committees are taken up first, because once assignments to them are made, slots on other committees open up. Ways and Means and Appropriations Committee vacancies are filled first, often in December during the organizing caucuses. Budget and Commerce Committee vacancies are usually considered next. When nominations are opened, the regional representatives make their nominations first, followed by the other members. The representatives usually say a few words about their nominees, whose names are written on a blackboard. Voting is by secret ballot.

A complex voting system by which only one nominee is selected on a given ballot was instituted in 1979. On each ballot, members must vote for the number of nominees that matches the number of slots still to be filled. To win, a nominee must receive both a majority and more votes than any other nominee. If on a given ballot two nominees receive a majority and are tied, the next ballot serves as a runoff between the two. Thus the number of ballots required to fill all the vacancies on a committee is equal to or greater than the number of vacancies. In 1979, for example, ten ballots were required to fill five Ways and Means Committee vacancies. Although the procedure is cumbersome, it allows the selectors "to get a look at the ideological and geographical makeup of the committee" at each stage. It was this feature that led to its adoption.

The Steering and Policy Committee was designed to ensure that a variety of criteria would be brought into play in the committee-assignment process. The elected members are charged with protecting the interests of the Democrats in their geographical zones, and many of the other members feel a similar responsibility. A deputy whip said, "Now [on committee assignments] you become a little more parochial because your state delegation has a right to have a fair representation on the committees. Nobody quarrels with that. . . . It's part of the game."

The leaders themselves pursue a number of not always complementary goals in the committee-assignment process. In keeping with tradition and its own service orientation, the leadership attempts to accommodate members by giving them assignments they have requested (see Gertzog 1976; Shepsle 1978). The leaders place a great deal of importance on putting together a slate the membership at large considers fair, where fairness is defined not solely but predominantly in terms of regional representativeness. Each of the leaders also tries to obtain good assignments for the members from his or her own state. A leader's success in obtaining good assignments for his or her state colleagues fortifies the leader's reputation because there is an expectation within the Washington community that he or she will do so and because appearing powerful is an important component of influence. When Jim McDermott, a junior member from the Speaker's home state of Washington, received a coveted Ways and Means Committee seat in December 1990, this was interpreted as signaling a more aggressive stance on the part of Tom Foley at the beginning of his first full congress as Speaker (see Hook 1990a).

The leaders also attempt to shape committees, especially those most important to the leadership, through the assignment process. "We tried to put reasonable people on the [important] committees," a leader explained. "Some members who wanted new assignments didn't get what they wanted. Members who never go with the leadership — never help out. It's not only [the other leaders] and I who did this. The other Steering and Policy members — the elected ones — feel the same way."

The nominating speeches as well as the letters that members requesting assignments send to the leaders indicate which arguments members believe most effective. For the majority of the committees, the most frequently mentioned argument in the nominating speeches is that the member needs the position because of his or her political situation. "Public Works is very important to his district; it's what he wants; it will keep the district firmly Democratic," said one nominator succinctly. "___ took the seat from a Republican and this assignment is critical to him," another claimed. "If he lost it, we would probably lose the seat."

That the nominee's region is underrepresented on the committee of choice and thus deserves the slot appears to be the second most frequent argument. Because representation in Congress is geographical, fairness in the committee-assignment process tends to be defined in terms of geographical representativeness. States and regions protect "their seats" on committees, and arguments about a region or state "deserving" a position are frequent.

For positions on the Appropriations, Ways and Means, and Budget Committees, similar arguments are made but party loyalty is more strongly emphasized. In recent years, that emphasis has become increasingly pronounced and has spread to being an important criterion for decisions on other choice policy committees such as Commerce and Armed Services as well. Of the process in 1979 one participant said, "Generally, loyalty to the leadership and to the principles of the Democratic party was stressed much more than in the past — certainly more than four years ago. Members seem to have realized that this would be the case. The letters sent to the leadership asking for support for committee positions tended to stress loyalty explicitly." During the 1979 deliberations several leaders brought in indexes of party loyalty, and at the request of members these were written on the blackboard next to the nominees' names. Loyalty scores entered into the voting again in 1981.

Participants questioned in the late 1970s and early 1980s agreed that party loyalty was considered in the making of assignments, especially to the key committees. "While the leadership was reluctant to put together a slate for the important committees out of fear that they would end up making angry more than they satisfy, there was, I think, more consideration of party loyalty than had been the case, at least in the previous congress," one participant reported. Another indicated that loyalty could be a tie-breaking factor:

> The skillfulness of the zone representative is very important. Whether the applicant's region is properly represented on the committee, the applicant's popularity, his reputation, is very important. Within that, in the last year or two, there's been a lot more attention to the applicant's faithfulness to party positions. Whenever there's a tough contest, people will bring up the level of party support.

Some members nevertheless believed that not enough emphasis was placed on party loyalty. "Loyalty is considered, but not enough," one member said. "Some people who take chances to stick with the leadership aren't getting rewarded." Another complained that the impact of specific assignments on the reliability of the committee as a whole was not sufficiently considered: "I think it's very important that you look at the structure of the committee. . . . We really ought to have a committee that represents all segments of thinking *and,* if you're running the House, you ought to have a committee that in a pinch is going to end up on your side of the ledger. That isn't done at all."

By the late 1980s and early 1990s, the importance of party loyalty had increased significantly. The party leaders computed party-support scores for members based on their own selection of key votes. In nominating speeches for exclusive committees, the nominee's party loyalty in voting and his or her efforts on behalf of party causes are prominently mentioned. "__ voted 97 percent with the leadership," one nomination began. This nominee to the Appropriations Committee had "taken some tough votes," had helped the DCCC with fund-raising despite still having a campaign debt, and "was a team player." Another candidate was presented as having "over 90 percent support for the leadership. He has been very active on [whip] task forces, he represents a good Democratic district and is a team player." About a third, the nominator said, "He comes from a conservative district but votes with the leadership a good part of the time. He's shown himself to be courageous."

For committees below the top ranks of the exclusive committees, party loyalty is mentioned increasingly often. A nominating speech for an Armed Services Committee vacancy illustrates the variety of considerations that members believe relevant:

> There's no member from [our state] on Armed Services, although there are many military installations — many in B's [the nominee's] district. B has 20 years in the Army reserves. He wanted the appointment originally but C [another member from the state] applied and B deferred. C is now supporting

him. B has taken some courageous positions in standing with the leadership on some tough votes.

Given the number of ex officio and Speaker-appointed members on the Steering and Policy Committee, the leaders can determine any specific committee assignment. With the increase in the early 1990s in ex officio leadership members, the Speaker gained "operating control" of the committee, as a leadership staffer phrased it. On assignments that they care about, recent Speakers often arranged matters so that, by the time the meeting was held, their candidates were known to have majority support and no actual vote among contending candidates took place. By making his preferences known and assuring that his choice commanded a majority before the meeting, the Speaker avoided the uncertainties of a secret ballot and the unsuccessful candidates and their nominators avoided the embarrassment of losing.

In such cases, other candidates may still be nominated but their candidacies withdrawn before a vote takes place; alternatively, a Steering and Policy Committee member may bring up some other member's interest in the committee less formally. These are attempts to stake a claim to a future position on the committee. As a primary criterion, seniority does not rank high, but, other things being equal, members who have paid their dues, who have waited their turn, are considered to have claims superior to those of more junior members or members without a longstanding expression of interest.

The Speaker's "operating control" of the Steering and Policy Committee does not free him to ignore considerations other than party loyalty. Regional balance particularly must be maintained if the leaders are to satisfy members' expectations. And regional considerations can conflict with considerations of party loyalty. Speakers have increasingly often developed leadership slates of candidates for the major committees. By putting together a slate — a process that involves considerable consultation and bargaining — the leaders can more easily attain a satisfactory balance among the multiple objectives they attempt to satisfy in the assignment process. It is the "operating control" of the Steering and Policy Committee that makes such slating possible.

When other considerations dictate the choice for an important assignment of someone who has not demonstrated substantial party loyalty, promises of support are frequently extracted from the nominee. In 1979 one such member received the assignment he had requested only after he promised the Steering and Policy Committee that he would support the leadership when his support was needed and that he certainly would not be a party to bottling up legislation in committee. In 1981, however, despite strong opposition from a number of Steering and Policy Committee members, Phil Gramm, a very conservative Texan, was placed on the Budget Committee. Gramm had promised to support the Budget Committee's position on the House floor, and Majority Leader Jim Wright had vigorously supported him for the slot. It was a "victory" Wright was to regret bitterly. Not only did Gramm vote against the committee majority on the floor, he also cosponsored the Republican substitutes to the budget resolution and the reconciliation bill. Gramm was taken off the Budget Committee at the end of the congress and then switched parties (Sinclair 1983, 91–92, 192). While the Gramm debacle taught the leaders that members do not always keep their promises, it taught members that, unless one is willing and able to switch parties, the cost of such behavior could be high.

Recent Speakers have regularly talked with members aspiring to positions on key committees before they are nominated, and have made their expectations known. "We don't demand ironclad conformity but don't want to give it to someone who is not reliable, who has no sense of obligation to the caucus," one explained. Before making assignments to the Ways and Means Committee in late 1992, both the party leaders and the committee chair quizzed applicants on a number of the touchy issues the committee would face in the early years of the Clinton administration (Zuckman 1992b, 3788).

In one recent instance, the Speaker engineered the candidate's coming to him with promises of good behavior. An exclusive committee position opened up and everyone agreed that a southern delegation deserved the slot, but even though the delegation-supported candidate was more supportive of party positions than most of his state colleagues, his level of support was not high. The Speaker, on a southern tour for the DCCC, mentioned to some people that although he liked and thought highly of the candidate, he was unsure whether the candidate's district would allow him to be "a good enough Democrat. We need a team player, someone who will be with us when we really need him," the Speaker explained. When a leadership staffer who knew the district said it would allow the candidate to be loyal, the Speaker replied that he knew that, that talking in terms of the district was simply a polite way of making his point. "I want him to come to me and tell me he will be a team player," the Speaker explained. The member in question got the message, he voluntarily pledged to be reliable, and he received the position. In the Steering and Policy Committee meeting where the assignment was made, both his relatively low party support and his conversation with the Speaker were discussed.

Occasionally circumstances allow the Speaker to attain a number of objectives through a single assignment. In late 1988, when two Appropriations Committee vacancies opened up, Speaker Wright obtained one of the positions for Jim Chapman, a junior member from Texas. He thus engineered a choice assignment for a member of his state delegation, one that would help ensure Chapman's reelection in a tough district. In addition, the Speaker discharged a debt to Chapman, who had changed his vote on a difficult and highly visible issue and had thereby given the Speaker an important floor victory. Finally, and at least equally important, he sent a message to the Democratic members that taking a tough vote to support the party position would be rewarded.

Data on which committees members request and which they actually receive provide the best basis for judging how well the various aims of members and leaders are met. Such data are available for the 96th Congress. Accommodating members' requests was one goal that was largely achieved. Of the forty-two freshman representatives, thirty-seven (88%) received at least one of their requested committees; twenty-nine (69%) received a requested exclusive or major committee assignment, and of these twenty-five (59.5%) received their first or only choice. Returning members who requested either a change in assignments or an additional committee assignment fared less well. Of the forty-two incumbent members who made such requests, fifteen (35.7%) were accommodated. The committees continuing members requested account for their lower success rate: thirty-seven requests were for Budget, Appropriations, or Ways and Means Committee assignments. Of the twenty freshman requests for these three committees, seven (35%) were granted. In order to accommodate nominees, sometimes the size of a committee is increased — something only the majority party can do. At the beginning of the 96th Congress, for example, three members told the Speaker that an assignment to the Public Works Committee was crucial to their political survival, and he agreed to create the necessary new slots.

Freshman representatives, members and observers agree, are much better treated than they once were. Speaker O'Neill often told of an incident that occurred when he was a freshman in the 83rd Congress (1953–54). One of his classmates, John Moss of California, received only one assignment, and it was to the District of Columbia Committee. Moss no doubt was horrified when the Sacramento papers headlined the story "Moss Elected to D.C. City Council." The other freshmen, O'Neill said, did not fare much better. Caucus rules and members' expectations now require that freshman representatives receive decent committee assignments.

In the 1980s and 1990s, however, these members seldom received assignments on the most sought-after and most sensitive committees, as they had in the immediate postreform era. From 1982 through 1992, only one freshman representative won assignment to the Appropriations Committee; none was assigned to Ways and Means, and only two to Budget. Members of the Steering and Policy Committee prefer to have the information a House record provides before making such consequential appointments. The sheer size of the 103rd Congress freshman class forced an exception to the rule, but only a small one; of the sixty-three freshmen Democrats, one won appointment to Appropriations, one to Ways and Means, and two to Budget. The newly elected representatives placed on the exclusive committees were carefully chosen. For example, Carrie Meek of Florida, who won the Appropriations Committee seat, was a veteran legislator from a safe Democratic district who, by her campaign for the position, showed herself to be an adept inside politician. "She's viewed as somebody who has paid her dues and is a team player and has a lot of potential," a member of the Steering and Policy Committee said (Zuckman 1992b, 3786).

Even in the late 1970s, party loyalty was given considerable weight in making assignments to the Budget, Appropriations, and Ways and Means Committees, data show. In 1979, for example, nineteen incumbent members requested the Budget Committee. The mean party-unity score of those assigned was 81.8 percent; of those passed over, the mean score was 72.8 percent.[1] The four Steering and Policy Committee choices of incumbent members for the Appropriations Committee had a mean party-unity score of 65.9 percent, while the mean score of the five requesters not assigned was 54.4 percent. Ways and Means Committee assignments were the exception in the 96th Congress. The three incumbents selected by the Steering and Policy Committee as a group scored slightly lower than the six who were not selected (65% versus 68.9%). A conflict among leadership goals accounts for this deviation from the pattern. Two of the nominees had high party-support scores (a mean of 84%); the third, Sam Hall of Texas, had a very low score (26.8%). Despite opposition from some in the inner leadership circle, the majority leader believed he had to support his state colleague, and he prevailed in the Steering and Policy Committee. In the Democratic Caucus, however, Hall was defeated by a much more supportive southerner.

Although similar data for a more recent congress are not available, other evidence does support the increased importance of party loyalty. The mean party-unity score in the congress before appointment of the sixteen returning members who received Appropriations Committee slots during the 98th through 102nd Congresses (1983–92) was 87 percent,

---

1. Ninety-fifth Congress CQ party-unity scores, adjusted to disregard absences, were used.

and only two of the sixteen scored more than two points below the mean for all Democrats in the congress. Ways and Means Committee appointees averaged 86 percent party-unity scores, and only three of eleven scored below the Democratic mean. For the Budget Committee, the mean score was 85 percent, and ten of thirty-nine appointees scored more than a point below the mean for all Democrats. Because of the unusually large number of vacancies, assignments to the key committees in the 103rd Congress provide a particularly good test of the importance of party loyalty. The eleven continuing members newly assigned to the Appropriations Committee had a mean party-unity score in the previous congress of 92 percent; the lowest scorer who received an assignment, a southerner, had voted with his party 83 percent of the time. The nine continuing members who received Ways and Means Committee assignments had averaged 89 percent on the party-unity index; the two who had scored below the party mean of 86 percent—both southerners—had scores in the mid-70s. On the Budget Committee, with its rotating membership, the Steering and Policy Committee relaxed the standard, but only a little; five of the twelve newly assigned members had scored below the party average in the previous congress, though only one, Bill Orton of Utah, was among the party's least reliable supporters, with a score of 59 percent, and the mean score of all the new members was 85 percent.

Thus, most of the members who land spots on these desirable committees are loyalists. A senior leadership staffer spoke matter-of-factly about the current Speaker using "objective criteria" in the making of assignments to the choice committees: region and a member's record on leadership votes. Members know that these are the criteria, he explained. "If they're not helping out [on leadership votes], they shouldn't be surprised" when they do not get the coveted assignments.

Members believe that their voting records make a difference. Everyone knows about the support scores the leaders maintain. "[The leadership] was watching and so we who were interested in Appropriations did watch our votes at the end of the 101st, feeling that might make a difference, that we could screw things up if we didn't watch out," a member explained. Furthermore, members believe party support should make a difference. When, early in Foley's speakership, two choice positions went to members who, though generally loyal, had defected on an important leadership vote, "there was a lot of grumbling by members."

Particular committee-assignment decisions continue to raise questions about the appropriate balance between individual and collective concerns, but the increase in party voting cohesion has eased the tension. The concerns are less frequently in conflict, and therefore striking a satisfactory balance is easier than it used to be.

Other Steering and Policy Functions

In addition to its committee-assignment function, the Steering and Policy Committee is, according to caucus rules, "vested with authority to report ... resolutions regarding party policy, legislative priorities, scheduling of matters for House or Caucus action, and other matters as appropriate to further Democratic programs and policies" (Preamble and Rules of the Democratic Caucus, January 9, 1991, 15). To this end, caucus rules require the committee to meet at least once a month while the House is in session.

Despite its charge, the Steering and Policy Committee has never functioned as a true steering and policymaking body on any sort of continuing basis. Its membership is not quite right for that purpose; on any given issue, the key people, who will almost always include members of the House committee of origin, may not be on the Steering and Policy Committee. On the one hand, it is too large to respond quickly to changing strategic circumstances. On the other, if the leaders need to assess the members' reactions to a policy proposal or a strategic move, more inclusive forums are readily available.

Speaker O'Neill, in the late 1970s and early 1980s, used the committee as a forum for outside speakers of note, as had Speaker Albert before him. During the Carter presidency, high-level administration officials would brief the committee on upcoming issues. Influential people from the private sector — the head of the AFL-CIO, for example, or members of the Business Roundtable — would appear for an informal exchange. The inexorable time pressure under which members, especially senior members, work resulted in attendance at such meetings often being poor. In the mid-1980s, the Committee on Party Effectiveness of the caucus began to take on this function, and the Steering and Policy Committee gave it up. With the advent of a Democratic administration, however, the Steering and Policy Committee again began serving as a point of contact between House Democrats and the administration, with high-ranking officials briefing the committee periodically on presidential initiatives.

Also under O'Neill, the committee began endorsing legislation. The leadership seeks endorsements of legislation central to the party program. "We do not cheapen the Steering and Policy endorsement by putting it on everything. In fact, we don't use it unless we're trying to demonstrate that we really mean it," a member of the committee explained. "The only policy there is, is that you don't do it unless it's important. And I'd say also probably you don't do it unless there's at least some concern about getting it through." No Speaker has been refused an endorsement he requested of the committee. Voting is usually by voice, and members who disagree with the leadership's position keep quiet. ("They just slink off into darkness," a member reported.) As a result, endorsements can be reported as unanimous. That an endorsement does not necessarily signify a true intraparty consensus seems to lessen its impact; nevertheless, members believe the endorsements have an effect. They serve as a signal to members of the importance their leaders place on the bill, and the vote is likely, members believe, to be included in leadership party-support indexes.

Although it is not a true policymaking body, the committee at its monthly meetings does serve as a forum for discussion and information exchange. Staff aides try to schedule the required meetings so that there is some business — the filling of an interim committee vacancy, the assignment to committees of a new member elected in a special election, an endorsement, or, every four years, the nomination of superdelegates to the party convention. Whenever members get together, they talk, and not just about the items on the formal agenda. When the group includes the entire party leadership and the chairs of four key committees, the information swapped can be of considerable value. When the group is as broadly representative as the Steering and Policy Committee, information disseminated at a meeting soon reaches the entire Democratic membership. The Steering and Policy Committee, then, in the words of a close observer, is "one more tool by which the leadership gets the word out and the word back. It's another communication tool." As such, it is useful both to the leadership and to the members who serve on the committee.

During the organizing caucuses for the 103rd Congress, House Democrats created a Working Group on Policy Development, the purpose of which is "to assist the Leadership, the Steering and Policy Committee, the individual committees and the Caucus in the establishment and implementation of a consensus policy agenda" (caucus rule 43E). Although the demand for appointment to the group was high and Speaker Foley's thirty-one appointees included eight committee chairs and a number of midlevel and senior activists, the group got off to a slow start in the early period of the Clinton administration. Created in response to the perceived need for a more explicit Democratic agenda during a period of divided control, the Working Group's role has been less clear with Democrats controlling the White House.

The Democratic Caucus

The Democratic Caucus, according to a recent chair, is "a forum for discussion and participation in debate over major issues facing Congress, a place where steam can be let off, differences aired, information disseminated." The Democratic Caucus, the organization of all House Democrats, is an instrument members can use for communicating among themselves, for communicating with and sending messages to their party leadership, and for holding their leaders accountable. The leaders, too, can use the caucus for communicating with their members. The top leaders are very much aware of the caucus's multifaceted character. As one leader expressed it:

> The Caucus ought to serve as a safety valve and a sounding board. Members can get a caucus if fifty request it. It should serve as a brake on the arbitrary exercise of power by the leadership. We know if we schedule unpopular legislation that members would rather not vote on, they could call a caucus and ask us not to do it. Sometimes a caucus serves the purpose of venting frustrations and expressing displeasure at a situation that is not fully understood and gives the leadership the opportunity to answer questions. It's similar to the British question period. The leadership, the committee chairmen, can be questioned.

Organizing the Party and the House

The Democratic Caucus meets in early December of election years to organize itself and, so long as Democrats constitute the House majority, to make decisions about the organization of the House. The caucus elects party leaders, votes on the Steering and Policy Committee's nominees for committee positions, and debates and votes on proposed changes in caucus and House rules.

The caucus convenes for its initial meeting of a congress at noon in the House chamber; its first order of business is the election of a chair. Rules specify that the chair of the caucus may serve no more than two consecutive terms, so a real contest occurs at least every other congress. In an order determined by lot, the candidates are nominated and then seconded by four members. Members vote by secret ballot. After the votes have been tallied, the outgoing caucus chair announces the results and hands the gavel over to the newly elected chair.

The caucus then proceeds to select its nominee for Speaker and to elect the floor leader, whip, and vice chair of the caucus. Even if there is no contest, nominating and seconding speeches are made. As each of these officers is chosen, he or she briefly addresses the caucus. The Speaker-designate, as the party's top leader, is expected to speak at somewhat greater length and can, if he so chooses, use this forum for outlining an agenda for the upcoming Congress. The Speaker-designate announces his choices for chief deputy whips and for chair of the DCCC. Although the rules specify that the latter is to be nominated by the DCCC, he or she is actually the Speaker's choice. The caucus must, however, ratify that choice.

This biennial process serves to remind leaders that they are agents of their members, and that members have readily available means for holding them accountable. Leaders use the process to signal their members about their leadership style. In particular, by their choices of nominators and seconders, leaders communicate their commitment to inclusiveness and the breadth of their ties to the various segments of the party. In 1988, for example, the typical nominating contingent included a very senior member, usually the dean of the nominee's delegation; a much more junior one, often a first termer; a member from the South, often a fairly conservative one; a woman; and an African American. And the Speaker's nominators were just as diverse as those for the caucus vice chair. When the majority leader has speaking for him both Sonny Montgomery (D-Miss.), an old-style conservative southern Democrat, and John Lewis, an African American who made his name in the civil-rights movement, when Bill Gray, an African American from Philadelphia, has seconding his nomination for caucus chair Charlie Stenholm, an activist conservative from rural Texas, those leaders are signaling their commitment to an inclusive style of leadership.

For a member of modest seniority, being asked to make a seconding speech is a valuable favor a leader can bestow. It singles out a member as someone to watch. In 1988, when Louise Slaughter (D-N.Y.) at the beginning of her second term appeared as a seconder for three of the party leaders and for the Budget Committee chair, she was marked as a rising star. (Speaker Foley named her to the Rules Committee in 1989, and in 1991 she was chosen to chair the caucus Committee on Organization, Study, and Review.)

The caucus elects the chair of the Budget Committee following a process similar to that used for the election of party leaders. Nominations are made from the floor; nominees need not be members of the Budget Committee, which, unlike most committees, has a rotating membership. Thus Leon Panetta (D-Calif.), who was elected chair in December 1988, was not then a member of the committee, though he had in the past served on it. In this case, the real contest was over long before the organizing caucus met. Panetta had amassed sufficient support that his two opponents conceded him victory. But the process was played out almost in its entirety. Panetta's set of nominators, like those of the party leaders, sent signals about the sort of Budget Committee chair he intended to be. His being nominated by Majority Leader Tom Foley indicated that he had the leadership's full confidence, a prerequisite to a successful budget process. By including among his seconders Charlie Stenholm, one of the most conservative House Democrats, and Ron Dellums (D-Calif.), one of the most liberal, he signaled his understanding of the diversity of the party and his willingness to work with the full spectrum of the membership.

Other committee chairs are subject to a ratification vote of the caucus, but are nominated elsewhere. The Speaker or Speaker-designate nominates a member to serve as chair of the Rules Committee. The Steering and Policy Committee nominates the chairs of the other standing committees. Although caucus rules specifically state that "such nominations need not necessarily follow seniority," up to 1991 all initial nominations did, in fact, do so. In late 1992, the Steering and Policy Committee passed over the ailing Jamie Whitten (D-Miss.), Appropriations Committee chair since 1979, and nominated instead William Natcher (D-Ky.), the next most senior member. However, when in 1994 a successor to Natcher had to be selected, the Steering and Policy Committee chose David Obey over Neal Smith (D-Iowa), who on the basis of seniority was next in line. A large majority of Steering and Policy Committee members decided Obey's aggressive leadership style and his skill at promoting party priorities outweighed the dictates of the seniority rule. The caucus agreed by ratifying the choice handily.

Chair nominees are subject to a secret-ballot vote in the caucus during the organizing period. On a long paper ballot with all those nominated by the Steering and Policy Committee listed, members can mark approval or disapproval of each. Should a nominee be rejected by a majority of those voting, the Steering and Policy Committee is charged with reporting a new nomination within five days. When that nomination comes to the caucus, additional nominations may be made from the floor.

Reformers used this process in 1975 soon after it was instituted to depose three committee chairs, thereby signaling all chairs that it was no mere formality. Since then, three members have lost their chairmanships and one had a very close call. Melvin Price (D-Ill.), who lost the chairmanship of the Armed Services Committee in 1985, Glen Anderson (D-Calif.), who was voted out of the Public Works Committee chairmanship in late 1990, and Frank Annunzio (D-Ill.), who the same year lost his position as chair of the House Administration Committee, were perceived by many members as incompetent committee leaders due in large part to their advanced age. In the first and last cases, policy position and party image also motivated the revolts. Price was seen as too unquestioning a supporter of the military and as not capable of representing the Democratic position in debates with the administration on the issues of arms control, weapons systems, and military spending that were so prominent during the 1980s. Many Democrats did not want a member tainted with the savings and loan scandal representing them in the battle over campaign-reform legislation that the House Administration Committee would report. Commenting on the events of 1990, David Obey, a senior Democrat and an activist, remarked, "It sends a message to all chairmen that they have to be more responsive. What this demonstrates is that people don't want to have to work around chairmen. They want to be able to work through them" (Hook 1990b, 4059).

Les Aspin's close call in 1987 probably served as the most forceful reminder to chairs that they are, indeed, agents of the Democratic Caucus and could lose their positions if they are perceived as unfaithful in that trust. Aspin (D-Wis.), who in 1985 succeeded Price even though he was less senior than six other committee Democrats, was rejected by the caucus on the initial ratification vote in January 1987. A considerable proportion of Democrats believed he had reneged on policy promises he had made two years earlier. In the end, Aspin won the chairmanship again in a four-person contest. He certainly interpreted the experience as a warning and promised to be more responsive, "more open [and] more up front" (Calmes 1987, 139).

Subcommittee chairs of the Appropriations Committee and, beginning with the 103rd Congress, those of the Ways and Means Committee must also win a secret-ballot confirmation vote in the caucus. In addition, the caucus must approve all committee assignments made by the Steering and Policy Committee on a committee-by-committee basis. Caucus members may—and occasionally do—nominate additional candidates for Budget Committee positions and for vacancies on the Appropriations and Ways and Means Committees.

At the beginning of the 103rd Congress, the Democratic Caucus approved a new rule whereby the Steering and Policy Committee or fifty members can request a vote of the caucus to remove the chair of a committee or subcommittee at any time during a congress.

The caucus thus not only has final authority for the selection of party and committee leaders and the distribution of committee assignments but also has the means in caucus procedure for exercising that authority. The formal selection and confirmation processes during the organizational caucuses every two years remind both sets of leaders that they are, in fact, agents of the caucus, and that the caucus has readily available means for holding them accountable.

The Caucus as Forum and Policy Player

During the committee government era, the caucus never met after the organizational session at the beginning of a congress. Liberal Democrats in the late 1960s seized on the caucus as the primary device through which to reform the House. In 1969 they persuaded Speaker McCormack to accept a rule requiring monthly caucus meetings. Most of the far-reaching rules changes adopted during the 1970s were proposed by a committee of the caucus.

Some liberal Democrats wanted to use the caucus as an instrument of policy as well. They argued that, on selected issues of overriding importance, the caucus should take positions and, when necessary, instruct committees. In 1972, the caucus directed the Foreign Affairs Committee to report out legislation ending U.S. military involvement in Southeast Asia. The committee complied, but the resolution failed in the House. In the following few years, several other policy resolutions won caucus approval. Concern about undermining the committee system, as well as these efforts' limited success in actually effecting policy change, led to their decline.

CYCLES AND TRENDS IN CAUCUS ACTIVISM

Since the mid-1970s, the level of caucus activity has varied, depending partly on leadership views, but more fundamentally on members' need for the sort of inclusive forum the caucus provides. O'Neill was leery of the caucus during his first few years as Speaker and preferred that it be quiescent. A senior leadership aide of that era said, "The caucus is too unpredictable. For making policy, there's Steering and Policy. Most members don't want any more meetings anyway. They've elected members to Steering and Policy." Asked in the late 1970s about leaders' use of the caucus, a staffer replied, "You've got other tools so much more effective. You get into caucus and you get some sort of a resolution—then you've got a problem of how to get around the resolution, when maybe the resolution wasn't a very good idea in the first place. The leadership almost never uses the caucus to get something done."

Some participants in the late 1970s believed the leaders could make greater use of the caucus. "The caucus itself is a power for the leadership that it never uses," one said. "I don't know why it doesn't—to get a party position hammered out, for ventilating the issues." There also were members who wanted to see the caucus assume new functions. One expressed his view this way:

> I believe the caucus can be expanded as an information and communication mechanism for the House so that we don't feel threatened about going there. Too many members now don't show up at the caucus because they are afraid that if they go there and there's a quorum, some fool thing will occur. Well, you know, we need to break out of that. Democrats need to communicate with each other better around here, and express our differences. We need a better mechanism within the caucus for sharing our diversity of opinions rather than running away from our diversities out of fear that if we were to get together and have a quorum that some horrible resolution would come out that we wouldn't like.

During the Carter administration the leaders preferred not to use the caucus because they believed it to be unpredictable, because they feared it might limit their flexibility on important matters, and because they believed superior instruments were available to them. Some members believed the caucus should play a greater role, and some suggested alternative roles, but there existed no groundswell for a more active role.

The 1980 elections changed both members' and leaders' views of the role of the caucus. The Democratic House members who returned to Washington in January 1981 were demoralized by the election results, worried about the future, and badly split on both policy and strategy. Leaders and members alike perceived the need for an inclusive forum to discuss such matters. Although Steering and Policy Committee and whip meetings offered a number of members the opportunity to discuss party strategy with the leadership, this was a debate in which all members wanted to participate. A senior staffer explained:

> We now have obviously a different party in the White House. And there's a greater need for Democrats to meet on a regular basis — one, to plan responses to announced administration programs, and two, and probably more important to most of these guys, to plot survival tactics. With the margin being reduced so greatly and with the possibilities existent that we may not have a margin at all a year from November, there's a much larger concern coming from the individual members to be thinking like Democrats as opposed to be thinking of themselves; in other words, they know there's no way that they can stay chairman of such and such a subcommittee by themselves. So there's a greater need to sort of work out things collectively to preserve the majority and I think obviously a much greater awareness of this.

Gillis Long (D-La.), the newly elected caucus chair, had run on a platform of revitalizing the caucus. "One of his themes at the time was the need for greater communication, to bring things out into an open forum much more than they were in the past, and he's been very effective at doing that," a leadership staffer said. The caucus was more active in 1981 than it had been in the previous four years. After the organizational meetings at the beginning of the congress, eleven meetings were held in the first half of the 1981 session; during the period from 1977 to 1980 nonorganizational caucus meetings had averaged slightly fewer than ten per session. More indicative of the increased activity is the number of meetings that attracted a quorum. Of the thirty-nine meetings called during the 95th and 96th Congresses, only five achieved a quorum, while seven of the first eleven meetings in 1981 attracted a quorum (Malbin 1981). Since the early 1980s, the level of caucus activity has remained fairly high, though it continues to vary with members' felt need for the sort of inclusive forum the caucus provides. Crisis periods during which the direction the party should take is hotly debated provide a special incentive to hold meetings.

CAUCUS AS INCLUSIVE FORUM

Rules specify that the caucus meets monthly and upon petition of fifty members. The meetings themselves vary greatly; some are pro forma with no business whatsoever; others are desultory affairs attended by a handful of members; still others attract a modest number of intensely interested Democrats; and some are gatherings of almost the entire Democratic membership for the exchange of information and debate on issues of deep concern to all. During the 102nd Congress, the full caucus met forty-four times; eleven of those meetings dealt exclusively with organizational matters, most frequently the ratification of the Steering and Policy Committee's assignment decisions; one was held to hear presidential candidate Bill Clinton. The other thirty-two meetings were primarily devoted to policy discussions.

Caucuses are called sometimes to discuss general party policy and sometimes to talk about specific legislation. During the 102nd Congress, for example, caucus meetings were called to discuss HR 1, the civil-rights bill, HR 5, the Fairness in the Workplace Act of 1991, HR 6, the banking bill, the National Energy Efficiency Act, and the budget resolutions, among other specific measures. At other meetings, health-care policy and issues of economic growth and tax fairness were broadly discussed. The caucus met twice, once in late 1991 and once in early 1992, to consider the Persian Gulf crisis and the party's response to it; the House bank scandal and the leadership's plan for reforming the administration of the House occasioned several meetings.

If specific legislation is at issue, the meeting of the caucus begins with a progress report by the committee chair; he or she then answers questions from the floor. A general discussion follows in which members bring up other matters. Committee leaders can use the caucus to explain the politics and the substance of legislation, sometimes in blunter terms than they might use in a public forum. In the spring of 1988, before bringing a civil-rights bill to the floor of the House, Judiciary Committee leaders and other closely involved members urged their fellow Democrats to support the legislation despite the language concerning abortion added to the bill in the Senate. "I'm not happy about the Danforth language," the task-force chair said. "All of us on the pro-choice side have heard from groups we ordinarily are associated with and, while they are not happy about the language, they support the bill and won't try to change it." An African American committee leader reported, "All the legitimate civil-rights groups are satisfied." And a woman member said, "The pro-choice groups are not going to count this vote against you."

Because budget resolutions have frequently presented enormous political and policy problems for House Democrats, the Budget Committee chair and the party leadership often use the caucus to outline the situation to their members and to get feedback. Budget summits have made such a forum even more necessary. In a November 1987 caucus meeting, for example, the leaders reported on the ongoing summit negotiations — their initial difficulties and their current status:

> What the administration means by revenues and spending cuts are not the same as what we meant. That led to much confusion at the beginning. . . . They've been very wide-ranging talks. The Senate Republicans are closer to us than the House Republicans. There's some difference between House and Senate Democrats, mostly on defense spending. Most of the plans have had some bipartisan support. . . . We're not quite there but the outlines of the deal are $2.6 billion in discretionary spending cuts below the Gramm-Rudman baseline — that includes some foreign aid — $5.0 billion from defense, $4.0 billion from entitlements, $9.0 billion from taxes, $1.0 billion from users' fees, and $5.0 in asset sales, for a total of $30 billion — which meets the Gramm-Rudman target without the asset sales.

Members asked about the substance and the politics of the emerging deal. ("What does it mean for sequestration [the imposition of automatic across-the-board spending cuts]?" "What are the implications for meeting next year's Gramm-Rudman targets?" "What's happened to our tax bill? Is it being ignored?" "What's the economic downside [of the agreement]?" "Will we [the House] have to act first on postponing the Gramm-Rudman date? We bit the bullet on the tax bill, we shouldn't have to on this.") The leaders reassured the members on substance ("Social Security is off the table, though we talked about COLAs [cost-of-living allowances]; [we agreed on] no COLA cuts in the end") and on politics ("[the vote to delay the Gramm-Rudman date] is not a heavy vote. It will pass the Senate only if it's blessed by the president and the leaders of both parties. Then it's not a rough, difficult vote"). To members whose expectations were unrealistic, the leaders responded bluntly. Complaining that "we walked the plank by voting for taxes," a member in effect argued that the summit agreement should incorporate the House tax provisions without alteration. "We can't force the Senate to take our bill or the president to sign it," a leader said pointedly. "Under normal procedure, we would expect to have to compromise in conference." He continued, "There's no option other than a summit agreement or sequestration. The question is which is better. I believe the agreement is going to be substantially better than sequestration."

The leaders tried to reassure members about the process. In outlining the components of the tentative agreement, the leader emphasized that the contents of the $9 billion in taxes called for "will require negotiations between Ways and Means, Finance, and the administration. We are *not* trying to write a tax bill — or an appropriations bill." Asked by a senior member of the Ways and Means Committee, "If agreement is reached, is it the leadership's intention to go to conference?" a leader replied:

> Basically yes. The Senate will take the budget agreement and made it an amendment to our reconciliation bill. They will send it over here and we'll request a conference in ordinary course. The administration would like the package to be accepted in toto without change. However, this summit group is not a legislative body. It can only recommend. [The agreement] can only be implemented by the regular legislative committees through the regular legislative process. As to broad outlines, it will have a certain legitimacy. But the committees could ignore it.

"The summit is similar to the Budget Committee in that it will set a target, it won't tell committees how to reach the targets," another leader said.

The leaders used the caucus to begin the job of selling the package to their members. "Ronald Reagan said he wouldn't raise taxes or cut defense. If he signs on to this agreement, he'll have reversed himself on both," a negotiator pointed out. "When we get an agreement, I hope you'll support it." Said another, "We must break the notion that no taxes are possible. Otherwise Democrats face a future where all the programs we're for will be squeezed between debt service and entitlements."

In 1987–88, Speaker Jim Wright employed numerous caucus meetings to keep the members informed on his contra-aid strategy, which many believed was too risky. Those meetings also provided members with an opportunity to let off steam, and that provided the leaders with information on members' sentiments.

According to a leadership aide, the caucus is especially useful for getting a sense of where the members stand when the issue is still too amorphous to do a whip count.

> Yes, you really can have a real discussion in a caucus. You wouldn't think with 170 members or so that would be possible, but basically a member will speak for two or three minutes. The members on each side organize themselves so they have to kind of think through their arguments, divide them up and the like. We seldom have a vote. We don't even very often have a show of hands, but at the end of a caucus you get a really good idea of the strength of the various positions and this is sort of one of the reasons why a caucus is very useful when it is just too early and things are too amorphous to count. You can test out two or three things, or proposals, or variations, very quickly in the

caucus and get an idea of how they will fly. Now of course when things jell a little more, a whip count gives you a much better, more accurate, reading.

In late 1990, after House Democrats and Republicans defeated a bipartisan budget summit agreement worked out by their leaders, the chair of the Ways and Means Committee and the party leadership used a series of caucus meetings to guide them in working out a package that the great majority of Democrats could support. "There were eight caucus meetings in October and November, and going from a period when people were all over the map, we ended up united," a participant explained. He continued:

> On the tax bill [in 1992] it worked that way as well. People were all over the lot to start with, but Dick Gephardt kept reiterating the need for middle-class tax relief, and over a period of time we did get a consensus. We had a series of meetings and Rostenkowski participated in every one of them, and he participated enthusiastically and you know that he is not really so much in favor of caucus meetings. He thinks it is usually a waste of time, but he saw that it really was producing a consensus. And I think that is an important function of the caucus on the big national issues, to aid in developing a kind of coherent — if not a single — position among Democrats.

Caucus meetings provide members with a forum for sending messages, including policy messages, to their party and committee leaders. Although the caucus seldom passes policy resolutions and has not instructed committees in recent years, strongly held and strongly expressed policy views of members do influence party and committee leaders. Those leaders know, as a top party leader said, "In the ultimate, the caucus can establish party policy. It could be used to instruct the leadership to support a given position or instruct a committee."

CAUCUS AS POLICY SEMINAR

As the congressional workload has increased and the pace of congressional life has quickened, opportunities to reflect on issues in some depth and with a longer-range time horizon have shrunk. Opportunities to discuss with colleagues political and policy problems in a broad context have diminished even further. Whip meetings and sessions of the caucus, as valuable as they are, tend to focus on the pressing issues of the day and are too short to allow in-depth exploration of issues.

In response to the problems facing House Democrats after the 1980 elections and also to this chronic problem, the party leadership convened an issues conference in early 1981. Over a three-day period, members discussed among themselves and with knowledgeable invited guests what the Democratic party should stand for and what policies it should pursue

(Baker 1983, 22). The second Democratic issues conference, held in early 1983, concentrated on formulating a Democratic strategy to deal with the recession.

Now held annually, the issues conference is a caucus event to which all House Democrats are invited. The organizers — the caucus chair and staff, with the Speaker providing general oversight — have sited the conference in fairly secluded, resortlike settings, most frequently the Greenbriar Resort in West Virginia. Members bring their families and spend three days getting to know each other better and discussing issues in a way that the normal jam-packed congressional schedule does not allow.

Since the leaders can set the agenda for the issues conference, they can use the conference to educate the members on difficult issues. In 1992, for example, economic growth and health care were the issues emphasized. On health care, particularly, the Democratic leaders wanted to be sure their members understood the magnitude of the problem and the difficulty of the choices. By "walking members through the choices" they would have to make in reforming health-care policy, the leaders expected to educate members enough to keep them from pushing for quick action before a consensus had jelled, and hoped to contribute to the formation of a consensus.

Caucus chair Gillis Long wanted to see the caucus "undertake a long-term role as a vehicle for policy discussions and recommendations" (ibid., 23). At the first issues conference, he called for "the establishment of balanced task forces to develop policy proposals" (ibid., 22). With the support of the Speaker and the majority leader, Long in the 97th Congress appointed a caucus task force and charged it with working out a statement of Democratic economic principles. Long also appointed a Committee on Party Effectiveness. With an ideologically and geographically diverse membership of thirty-three, the committee served as the first forum for the discussion of the task force's statement. The committee approved the draft of the statement, which was then endorsed by the Steering and Policy Committee and, on April 8, 1981, adopted by the caucus. The economic-policy statement was "not very strong," a participant conceded, "but we did get everyone to agree, which was a major accomplishment." In September 1981, work began on six more policy statements on the topics of crime, housing, long-term economic policy, the environment, women's issues, and small business. In September 1982, the task forces issued their report under the title "Rebuilding the Road to Opportunity," soon dubbed the Yellow Brick Road because of its bright yellow cover.

During every congress since the 97th, the caucus has engaged in a similar enterprise. Task forces produce policy statements on a range of topics, and a report is issued. In presidential election years, the report is a

ORGANIZATION, COMMUNICATION, AND ACCOUNTABILITY   113

recommendation to the Democratic Platform Committee. Assessing the impact these reports and the process that produced them have had on policy is not easy. Although they certainly provide information on caucus preferences to other committee decision makers and to the party leaders, the reports have not become recognized as authoritative statements of party policy within the House. Their most likely influence is through the process that produced them. When a broad group of members — junior and senior, liberal and moderate, from the committee and those just interested in the subject matter — works through an issue together and comes up with a position all can support, the process is likely to influence those who took part. "It teaches them what they agree on," a staffer contended. "And that they agree on a lot more than they disagree, which is something they sometimes lose sight of."

These caucus task forces provide a large number of Democrats with another forum for participating in the policy process. In the 100th Congress, fourteen task forces, chaired by twenty-six members, produced reports on issues ranging across the whole spectrum, from the environment to drugs, from national security to the family. Each of these task forces involved a number of members. The task force on the Strategic Defense Initiative (SDI), for example, consisted of twenty-four members, including key members of the Armed Services and Appropriations Committees, as well as more junior members and those with an interest in the issue but no relevant committee position.

During the 1980s, the Committee on Party Effectiveness provided the organizational framework within which these task forces operated. The committee itself began as a disparate group of Democrats that Long brought together in the wake of the 1980 election disaster to discuss the future of the party. Over the years, membership grew and then meetings were opened to any Democrat. In the 102nd Congress, the de facto situation was regularized and the committee now includes the entire caucus. At the same time, the status of the issue task forces was changed; they are no longer task forces of the committee but rather of the caucus directly.

Since the mid-1980s, the bimonthly lunch meetings of the Committee on Party Effectiveness have usually focused on specific upcoming legislation, on a broader policy problem, or, less frequently, on external political matters. A bill's supporters sometimes use the forum the committee provides to educate their colleagues as well as to argue for their positions. In 1988, for example, Ron Dellums and Howard Wolpe (D-Mich.) explained the complex provisions of their antiapartheid legislation. Meetings that focus on less immediate policy questions feature outside experts as guests. Political developments sometimes become the topic; in 1988, for example, Dukakis's senior campaign staff appeared several times to report on the campaign and to ask for help. Although it is less important than it was in the early and mid-1980s, when it served as a forum for debates on the Democratic party's direction, the Committee on Party Effectiveness continues to provide members with one more site for discussion and information exchange.

Caucus as Rule Maker

The caucus Committee on Organization, Study, and Review (OSR) considers proposed changes in caucus and House rules and makes recommendations to the caucus on them during the organizational period. It is this committee that the reformers used to formulate and implement the revolutionary caucus rules changes in the early and mid-1970s.

Appointed by the chair of the caucus, OSR generally consists of twenty to thirty members. Recent OSR chairs have been members of the Rules Committee. Martin Frost of Texas, a young activist with close ties to Jim Wright, served as chair from 1981 through 1990. Louise Slaughter became chair in 1991. Although roughly representative of House Democrats in terms of geography and seniority, the OSR membership is heavily weighted toward activist members with a special interest in internal process matters. In the 102nd Congress, for example, it included seven members of the Rules Committee, the chair of the House Administration Committee, two of the chief deputy whips (the five top party leaders are ex officio members), David Price (D-N.C.), the only congressional scholar in Congress, and activists such as David Obey, Mike Synar (D-Okla.), and Pat Williams (D-Mont.).

OSR holds a series of meetings in the months before the organizational caucuses. Any Democrat can bring a proposal to the committee. After extensive discussion, a list of proposals to be submitted to the caucus is agreed upon. OSR recommendations, both positive and negative, usually prevail in the caucus. The caucus seldom turns down a recommended change or approves a change the committee opposes. OSR's success is not, however, an indicator of independent power. The committee's recommendations are assumed to carry the imprimatur of the party leadership. Although chosen by the chair of the caucus, the chair of OSR is assumed to have been approved by the Speaker. All the changes OSR recommends are also assumed to have been cleared with the leadership. Furthermore, behind-the-scenes bargaining may well precede the unveiling of OSR recommendations, and sometimes rules changes proposed by the committee are altered before a caucus vote because of members' opposition.

OSR provides members with an official yet easily accessible and quite informal forum where they can bring their ideas and get a hearing. OSR serves the leadership as an instrument for promoting desired rules changes and for discouraging those it opposes. The chair of OSR and its other members can bear the brunt of arguing against and voting down proposals the leaders believe unwise. When the leaders want a particular change, especially a potentially controversial one, OSR can begin the process of educating members. And the leaders can use OSR to launch trial balloons; should substantial opposition arise, the proposal, which would never have been formally labeled as the leadership's, can be quietly withdrawn.

The committee's success reflects its own and the leadership's sensitivity to members' sentiments as well as members' willingness, in many cases, to defer to the leaders' greater interest in and knowledge of party and especially chamber rules. House rules changes approved by the caucus are included in the resolution setting out the rules of the House for the Congress. Because this resolution is adopted on a party-line vote, the leadership's strong influence on OSR recommendations and caucus decisions translates into a significant impact on House rules. For example, during the 102nd Congress, Republicans frequently used a House rule giving a motion involving the privileges of the House immediate floor access to disrupt the schedule and embarrass Democrats. The rules package brought to the floor and adopted at the beginning of the 103rd Congress gave the Speaker new powers over the floor consideration of such motions. The leaders' influence over rules, however, exists only so long as they use it in a manner satisfactory to their members, as it is contingent on the support of members in OSR and the caucus and on the House floor. During the organizing caucuses, each proposed change in caucus or House rules is considered and voted on separately, giving Democrats an opportunity to vote down changes supported by the leaders if they so choose. As long as the leaders are sensitive to members' sentiments and act as their faithful agents, this influence over rules is an important leadership resource.

★ ★

Members' expectations for a more activist but also more open and accountable leadership are manifest in the development and current functioning of the leadership inner circle, the Steering and Policy Committee, and the Democratic Caucus. Each of these entities provides the leadership with resources or assistance for meeting the members' demands, and each serves to link members and leaders in such a way as to enhance accountability.

Information and Inclusion

The Whip System

The room on the third floor of the Capitol is sizable but looks smaller because it is crowded. Men and a few women — Democratic members of the House — sit on chairs set close together in narrow rows balancing coffee, doughnuts, and copies of the tentative floor schedule for the next week; staff aides stand at the back of the room, which, however contains the only door, making entry difficult for latecomers. In the front of the room, on an ill-assorted collection of chairs, sit the party leaders — the Speaker, majority leader, whip, caucus chair, and vice chair.

The Majority Leader: Today we recess and then reconvene to hear [the prime minister of Australia]. Then we do the Fair Housing Amendments. This is really a triumph for the committee, for Don Edwards [the subcommittee chair]. We now have a bill supported by the Leadership Conference on Civil Rights *and* the National Realtors!

(cheers and laughter)
He reads the next week's floor schedule.

By the end of next week, we'll have finished all appropriations bills.

(cheers)

A Deputy Whip and Appropriations Committee Member: It's the first time since 1971 we've passed all the appropriations bills!
The Speaker: Thanks to the Appropriations Committee for working overtime. Thanks to you all. You're making the House look good.

On Fair Housing, it was great to get everyone on board. The Republicans give us a lot of trouble but when we can, it's good to get them on board. I plead with you to come to [the Australian prime minister's address]. Byrd didn't attend the function for him yesterday on the Senate side and this was played very big in the Australian press. Australia is a very good ally and friend. So come or send a distinguished-looking male aide.

(boos, hoots, and lots of ribbing)
After several minutes, when the sound level decreased enough to allow him to be heard:

The Whip: I want to thank [two whips] who chaired the ___ task force and [two other whips] who chaired the ___ task force. You did a great job. Thanks to [the subcommittee chair, also a whip] for his handling of the bill.

On fair housing, this is the first time the disability community is involved. That's a major landmark.

A Committee Member: The McCollum amendment decreases the number of units for the disabled.

He briefly explained the content of this Republican amendment expected to be offered on the floor.

Let's beat it and beat it bad!

The Whip: The Senate expects to pass plant closing today.

(cheers)

They think they got the sixty-sixth vote yesterday. If they got that, they expect to get more. Then we'll pass it here and send it to the president.

A member brought up an amendment for a "drug-free workplace" that Republican Bob Walker of Pennsylvania had been attempting to add to all appropriations bills, and a lively discussion ensued. Members grumbled about being put on the spot on an amendment they considered unworkable but hard to justify opposing.

A Whip: If we think it's a good idea, we shouldn't give Republicans the credit. I hope on ___, we don't.

An Appropriations Subcommittee Chair: The Walker amendment is no longer part of the ___ appropriations bill.

(cheers)

The Whip: ___ is working on a drug-free environment amendment that will cover everything. It's coming along well. Everything is under control.

A typical whip meeting, as this depiction shows, is boisterous, contentious, and fun. As it also suggests, whip meetings and the whip system of which they are the most visible activity serve some serious purposes for members and leaders. Less obvious perhaps is the relationship between the former and the latter; the huge, seemingly unwieldy number of whips, which contributes to the boisterousness, also makes the system more capable of serving leaders' and members' needs.

The whip system performs two primary functions: it serves as a central conduit for information between leaders and members and it plays a key role in the vote-mobilization process. The leaders' need for help, the members' desire for access and accountability, and the need of both leaders and members for information — the same forces that influenced the entities discussed in chapter 6 — have shaped the system's evolution since the early 1970s and influence its current functioning. The strategy of inclusion finds its fullest expression in the contemporary whip system, enabling leaders to get the help they need while simultaneously providing members with opportunities to participate in the legislative process.

Evolution of the Whip System

A whip system in the Democratic party consisting of a chief whip and a number of assistant whips first arose in the early 1930s. Each of the assistant whips was chosen by and was responsible for the members of one geographical area or zone — New England, for example. In the 1950s, Speaker Sam Rayburn, who preferred a very informal leadership style, made little use of the whip system or even of the chief whip. Carl Albert, who became majority whip in 1955, was assigned so few responsibilities that his aide got bored and asked for a transfer to the district office. As one senior staffer notes, "Rayburn ran the whole thing out of his back pocket." And when the position of deputy whip was created in 1955 for Hale Boggs (D-La.), who had wanted to be whip, a senior aide explained, "Boggs's consolation prize was the deputy whip [position]. No staff, no nothing, just a paper job. But Albert didn't have anything to do, so Boggs had double nothing to do."

As Speaker during the 1960s, John McCormack made more use of the whip system than Rayburn had, although by later standards the level of activity was not impressive (Ripley 1969, 212). To a large extent the White House liaison staff performed the vote-counting function during the Kennedy and Johnson administrations.

In the 1970s the whip system expanded as the number of whips appointed by the leadership increased. The deputy whip position was divided into two positions in 1970. In 1972 the position of chief deputy whip was created, and the number of deputy whips grew to three. Three new appointive positions, called at-large whips, were added in 1975. Women, blacks, and freshman representatives were demanding inclusion in the whip system, and these new positions were created in response to those demands (Dodd 1979, 31). When Tip O'Neill became Speaker in 1977, he increased the number of at-large whips to ten. In 1981 a fourth deputy whip position was created, and the number of at-large whips rose to fifteen. The title "task-force chairman" was created for Dick Gephardt in the mid-1980s. During the 1980s and early 1990s, the number of deputy and at-large whips continued to grow and, in 1991 and 1992, the chief deputy whip position was split into three and then four positions to accommodate women, African Americans, southerners, and Latinos, who were clamoring for inclusion in the top ranks of the leadership.

In summary, a whip system that consisted of twenty-one members in the 91st Congress (1969–70) expanded to forty-four by the 97th (1981–82), to eighty-one by the 100th Congress (1987–88), and to ninety-four by the 103rd Congress (1993–94). In 1993, the whip system consisted of the whip, four chief deputy whips, eleven deputy whips, a floor whip, an ex officio whip, two task-force chairs, fifty-six at-large whips, and eighteen zone whips. "The next step is to rent RFK Stadium for the whip meetings," a longtime deputy whip joked. Except for the majority whip, who, like the Speaker and the majority leader, is elected by the full Democratic Caucus, and the zone whips, who are elected by regional groups of members, the whips are appointed by the top leaders.

The contemporary whip system is highly diverse, including members from all segments of the party. Northerners and southerners, conservatives and moderates as well as liberals, women, African Americans, Latinos, and Asians are all represented. Junior members — including, in the 103rd Congress, eight freshmen — are a part of the system, but so are very senior members; in the 103rd Congress, seven committee chairs served as appointive whips.

The leadership's need for help in a changing environment fueled the whip system's expansion (Dodd 1979). The initial impetus came from the Democratic loss of the White House in 1968, which deprived the House leadership of services previously provided by the administration liaison staffs. The unpredictability of the immediate postreform House environment and the adverse political climate of the 1980s increased the demands for legislative assistance that members placed on their leaders and made meeting those expectations difficult for the leadership. In the 1960s the zone whips were charged with both obtaining vote counts and persuading their colleagues to support the leadership position (Ripley 1969, 199). Yet because they were chosen by the members of their zones, their loyalty to the party was sometimes minimal. The leaders needed a loyal group of assistants to aid in persuasion efforts, and they appointed whips to get that help.

As the leadership became more active and more central in the legislative process, members became increasingly eager for access to the leaders and for inclusion in their orbit. Democrats increasingly sought to become part of the whip system and, since the number of regionally elected whips is fixed, they asked to be appointed by the leaders. Democrats who had served the maximum two consecutive terms as zone whip that caucus rules allow often requested an appointed slot. Thus members' desires for inclusion also contributed to the expansion.

The Whip Meetings

Asked the ideal size of the whip system, a senior whip staffer smiled and replied, "Oh, about 262" — then the size of the Democratic House membership. Because information exchange is one of the system's central functions, its seemingly unwieldy size is actually an advantage. The weekly whip meetings are a key mechanism for information exchange and, because of the number and diversity of the whips, provide both leaders and members with a reasonably accurate sense of Democratic sentiment on the issues of the day.

The whips meet at 9:00 A.M. every Thursday morning that the House is in session. The meetings outgrew the largest room in the whip's suite and now are held in a sizable meeting room on the third floor of the Capitol. When Hale Boggs initiated whip meetings during the 1960s, neither the Speaker nor the majority leader attended. Now all of the top leaders participate faithfully. Whip meetings have priority for all the leaders; very occasionally a leader will miss a meeting because he or she is out of town, but almost never because another meeting is considered more important. Although there are always absences among rank-and-file whips, attendance tends to be high.

The whip, who presides, first calls on the majority leader, who briefly discusses the legislative schedule for the remainder of the week and then announces the schedule for the following week. He may comment on some of the legislation, informing members of particularly important substantive or strategic aspects. The Speaker and then the whip make any announcements they have. These statements are often interrupted by questions from the floor, and are followed by general discussion.

Leaders use the meetings to inform their members about a wide range of matters. Explaining a relatively rare Monday session, Majority Leader Foley said, "We will try to go to conference on the debt limit on Monday. So we need to be in for that. That's one reason for having votes on Monday." They may report on meetings with administration officials or with Senate leaders. In the fall of 1987, for example, Speaker Wright briefed the whips on his meetings with White House Chief of Staff Howard Baker and Secretary of State James Baker about a possible budget summit. "I said the president needs to be on board; they said they could get him on board." The leaders may explain the status of conference negotiations between House and Senate. "We're making very fast progress on the debt limit. You can expect a vote next week. The Senate made a new offer that looks good. [A key Republican] praised it," a leader told the whips in the fall of 1987. The leaders may bring in polling data to raise morale generally or to bolster a course of action they advocate. In the spring and summer of 1987, for example, Speaker Wright used poll numbers to argue for a progressive tax increase. In 1988, when Democratic chances of retaking the White House looked favorable, those poll results were frequently mentioned.

The leaders' most frequent subject is legislation and the legislative process in the House. The leaders talk about substantive and strategic aspects that they believe their members need to understand. These are almost always instrumental communications: the leaders hope to persuade as well as to inform. Discussing a tax bill reported by the Ways and Means Committee, a leader said, "It's a very good, fair bill that puts no burden on those with low or middle income. It's a bill we can defend and support wholeheartedly. And the alternative is sequestration." At another meeting, a leader explained why any amendment requiring doctors to report AIDS cases to their state health departments was "pernicious. Health professionals say it will drive it underground." Informing and exhorting members, a leader began a whip meeting by saying,

> The Japanese reparations bill is up today. We scheduled it to coincide with Constitution Day. The Lungren amendment is the critical vote — it strikes the authorization. There are about sixty thousand survivors; if it reaches the courts, it will be much more expensive. The bill is long overdue. I plead with every member of the whip organization to do everything they can on this bill.

Another leader added, "It's very important. It's a civil-rights matter. It redresses a grievous wrong."

On potentially difficult votes, leaders emphasize the groups supporting their position. Thus, members were told that all the major medical groups — which were listed — agreed with the leaders in opposing a series of amendments to the AIDS bill. Both the Leadership Conference on Civil Rights and the National Realtors Association supported the fair-housing amendments, members were told in the summer of 1988.

Material that provides persuasive arguments for and thus can be fashioned into explanations for tough votes is brought to members' attention. Copies of Op-Ed pieces, "Dear Colleague" letters, editorials (especially if in prestigious or unexpected newspapers), or letters by experts or prominent political actors may be handed out. The leaders, for example, distributed an Op-Ed piece by then-governor Bill Clinton endorsing the welfare-reform bill as that legislation approached the floor. As the veto override vote on the Civil Rights Restoration Act drew near, a letter signed by the leaders of a number of major religious organizations was given

prominent play. Conservative judge Robert Bork's opposition to a constitutional amendment requiring a balanced budget, expressed in a letter to
Speaker Tom Foley, was highlighted during the fight to defeat such an
amendment.

Unexpected or unusual parliamentary moves will be explained. On
April 1, 1988, members were warned that Republicans would move to
recommit to conference the agreement on the trade bill and that, if they
succeeded, all provisions would be open to revision. This is the usual
procedure, the leaders explained; the minority just usually does not take
advantage of the opportunity to offer a motion to recommit at this stage.
"Anyone who has anything in the trade bill they really care about damn
better vote against the motion to recommit," a leader said forcefully.

The meetings give the leaders an opportunity to alert their members to
late-breaking developments or important votes that might confuse them.
In late 1987, the leaders warned the members that passage of a motion to
extend the Iran-Contra Committee for the remainder of the congress was
essential; a great deal of material had been requested from the administration and had not yet been delivered. The committee needed to be in existence to accept the material. The motion was on the schedule for later that
day and, because negotiations with the Republicans had broken down,
they could be expected to oppose it. The leaders also explained the unusual rule under which the resolution would be brought to the floor.

In the spring of 1988, the leaders talked to the members about a resolution urging the Supreme Court to review a lower-court decision that went
against Representative Don Sundquist (R-Tenn.). Because Sundquist was
not particularly popular with Democrats, the leaders feared that the members might cast a gut vote against the resolution. They explained that the
case involved an important principle of congressional privilege.

Either at the leaders' behest or on their own initiative, whips also use
the meetings to inform their fellow members of progress on legislation of
general interest, explain floor strategy, and ask for support. "On the hate-
mail bill coming up today," a liberal Judiciary Committee member explained, "you should all know that we are supporting the Swindall substitute to the Gekas amendment. The Gekas amendment is very broad and
very objectionable. The Swindall substitute makes it much less objectionable." The information was important because most Democrats considered Swindall as right-wing as Gekas, and might not have understood the
differences between the two amendments.

Do not accept the Senate's version of legislation on dealing with the
U.S. Embassy building in Moscow, a member of the Foreign Affairs Committee urged. "It contravenes all sorts of treaties and agreements. It's
totally irresponsible." A member warned his colleagues against an amend-

ment to a labor bill that would be offered by a liberal Republican whom some Democrats might be inclined to support. It is too complex to explain here, he said. "Read the excellent 'Dear Colleague' by Dave Obey. Call me if you have more questions." Urging members not to sign a discharge petition to force a balanced-budget constitutional amendment onto the House floor, one of the whips working on the issue said, "The leadership asks you to sign the legislation, not the petition, if you feel you must for constituency reasons. [A discharge petition is] an irresponsible way to handle such a major issue."

Sometimes a whip will urge his or her colleagues to take other sorts of action. In 1991 the chair of the Ways and Means Committee was resisting his subcommittee chair's pleas to report legislation extending unemployment compensation. Although both were whips, the subcommittee chair took advantage of the chair's absence from a whip meeting to urge those who wanted the legislation to let the chair know forcefully. Rostenkowski was claiming that no one other than the subcommittee chair seemed really to care.

Occasionally members will remind their fellow whips of past help received. "This is a different and weaker version," a strong supporter of legislation regarding plant-closing notification said to his southern colleagues. "It's not such a difficult vote. Sometimes there's legislation that's important to one section of the country. The textile bill was a difficult vote for me. The rust-belt fellows need this [legislation]. We need your help." A southeasterner replied, "I'm grateful for what you did. This is a tough vote for me but I'm not going to vote against [plant-closing notification provisions]. I urge [other members of] the textile caucus to do the same. We'll need to come back to you for help and unless we help you, we don't deserve aid."

The leaders sometimes ask the whips for information on current developments. For example, the leaders had heard that Republicans intended to offer a motion to instruct the conferees when the motion to go to conference on the welfare-reform bill was made. The majority leader informed the whips to expect that vote later that day and then said, "We don't know what it contains. If anyone does, let us know." One whip did.

The concerns members express in the meetings and the requests they make of the leadership also provide valuable information to the leaders. Some information is specific to a particular legislative battle and helps the leaders make sound strategy. "If you come from a district like mine," a whip warned the leaders, "nothing means anything in the trade bill if [the] plant closing [notification requirement] is taken out." Discussing the Democratic package of humanitarian aid to the contras, a southern whip asked, "When will we know what will be in the package?" He referred to a

Washington Post story contending that the package might include the lifting of sanctions on Nicaragua. "That would be a big problem for me." Another whip concurred. "We in the southeast are really getting beat up on this issue. . . . If the package can be designed to help us we'd appreciate it." Expressing concern about a gasohol tax provision in the reconciliation bill, a midwestern member said, "That needs to be worked out. It's serious for a number of us."

Members make all sorts of requests related to scheduling. They ask that bills that confront them with tough votes not be brought to the floor unless the Senate guarantees to consider the legislation. Some perpetually ask that no votes be scheduled for Mondays or Fridays, and gripe when they are. Conversely, one whip wanted assurance that there would be recorded votes on the Tuesday of her state's primary election. She was justifying staying in Washington rather than returning home on the basis of there being votes. During a discussion of an upcoming Department of Defense authorization bill, legislation notorious for consuming floor time, a whip said, "I sure hope Rules will not allow 240-plus amendments." His plea was seconded by a buzz of agreement from the other whips.

The meetings sometimes serve as a forum for the expression of members' frustrations. Annoyed about being kept in session by the Senate's slowness in finishing necessary business and by a budget compromise he disliked, a whip exploded, "Things need to change around here next year. We've capitulated to the Senate on everything; I'm tired of that. You [the leaders] have done a great job; we've worked hard, but we don't get any credit." A leader suggested the whip sponsor a constitutional amendment to abolish the Senate, and everyone cheered. Another whip told of reading in the *Washington Post* that several Republican members had district projects in the continuing resolution. "If they don't give us any votes, if they make us bite the bullet and pass it on our own, I don't think they should get any goodies," the whip said, to cheers. "I haven't complained about the schedule all year, so this is my chance," another whip said. "We have some 75 to 80 percent popular issues—like parental leave. Some of you have problems with those and the leadership has listened to your very vocal complaints and hasn't scheduled them. Those of us who have problems with things like the drug bill—with the death penalty, with user accountability—should scream about it next year."

The most frequent source of frustration during the years of divided control was the Republican president and his ability to shape national political discourse and thereby shape policy; the most frequent debate in whip meetings concerned how to counter the president and cast the Democratic party and its policy proposals in a favorable light. Both Reagan and Bush, Democrats believe, played politically adept but totally irresponsible games with the budget. A discussion in mid-1987 about revising the Gramm-Rudman balanced-budget law to comply with a Supreme Court decision revolved around fears of increasing executive discretion on the one hand and the desire to force the president to make hard choices on the other. The "hard OMB [Office of Management and Budget] trigger" for setting off automatic spending cuts would force the president to negotiate seriously with Democrats, some members claimed. "That's wishful thinking," others retorted. "Nothing will make him act responsibly on this." "Beware of the OMB trigger," an Appropriations Committee member argued. "It's hard to realize how much leeway OMB will really have unless you've served on Budget or Appropriations. . . . And the president can say he was opposed to sequestration — and the horrendous cuts — but was forced into them by the Democrats. He still has the only megaphone in town." A leader concurred: "If you pass the hard trigger, sequestration will happen and Reagan will impose his priorities and blame it on us."

A discussion of the budget resolution in the spring of 1989 led to the following exchange:

> *Budget Chair:* I want to thank the task force [for passing the rule]. Today you get to consider a series of alternatives. I think we can make the case that the Budget Committee's is the only one [that is at all reasonable and can pass].
>
> He then described the alternatives allowed by the rule.
>
> I know some argue that a crisis would be better as a strategy than this budget resolution. A crisis, if it happens, should be the president's responsibility.
>
> *Member A:* I congratulated Leon on doing the best he could. I'm disappointed that Marty Russo's amendment was not made in order. It draws the lines between us and the Republicans in a politically advantageous way and we need to do that.
>
> *A Leader:* We are trying to get the message out that they [Republicans] have been in charge for the last eight years. The disasters — savings and loans, housing scandals — are theirs. They are trying to blame them on everyone else. We shouldn't let them get away with it. Committee and subcommittee chairs, if you are holding hearings on some of those things, let us know. Henry Gonzalez is having hearings next week on how that great housing expert Jim Watts got $300 thou of housing money for making one phone call.
>
> He mentioned several others who were planning hearings and talked about highlighting these issues in a series of one-minute speeches on the House floor.
>
> *Member B:* The one-minutes are fine in terms of drawing lines between the parties but I'd like to know how the decision was made to not allow the Russo amendments on catastrophic or the Durbin amendment or the AuCoin amendment on drugs. We're really hit on at home on catastrophic. Why did

the leadership allow the Kasich amendment and not these others? They [Republicans] put us on record on the freeze and we don't put them on record on anything. The leadership needs to loosen up on amendments, allow debate and decisions on the floor.

A Leader: Recent practice — not just this year — has been to not have single transfer amendments on the budget resolution. We could, of course, change that. But it could be very time consuming; there could be a very large number of amendments.

Member C: Since the subject has been opened up — no loyal Democrat on the Budget Committee got to offer an amendment while some of these others didn't even present their proposals to the Budget Committee and yet they get floor votes. Why does Dannemeyer get an amendment every year? There's a provision for a kook amendment and he gets it?

A Leader: Republicans use their amendments about as ineffectively as possible. If the Republican leader and the Republican committee leaders vote against the amendment, it can hardly put us on the spot.

Member A: We're the majority and I know we have to act responsibly. But there should still be ways of drawing lines, of making political points.

A Committee Leader: The budget resolution probably isn't the place. But appropriations bills are coming up. We should plan now for some amendments — they should be under the control of the leadership so they can control what happens. Use those amendments for drawing lines, for putting Republicans on the spot.

Member D: The Republicans are going to give us all kinds of opportunities to trash the Constitution on drugs. Why couldn't we do AuCoin [transferring money from Star Wars to drug wars]? It's a good issue; it's easy to explain.

Member E: We're still losing the battle with young people.

He presented some figures on party identification among the young.

We need to show them there is a difference between the parties.

A Leader: The problem is there isn't a consensus within the party on these things. We're not drawing any very effective lines if half the Democrats don't vote for the amendment. The amendment splits the Democrats.

Another Leader: The problem is we were forced into the budget talks by circumstances. . . . So we're quarrelling among ourselves, fighting over the scraps, pitting good projects and programs against each other. . . . Leon basically did a good job under a lousy set of circumstances.

The opportunity whip meetings give members to convey their concerns to their leaders on the whole spectrum of issues, to question them, to confront them and require them to justify their decisions, is valued by members; it is a major payoff of being a whip. The meetings give members a shot at influencing their leaders and a basis for assessing whether the leadership is, in fact, acting as a faithful agent.

For leaders, the meetings provide information on the wishes and moods of the members and an opportunity to explain their decisions to a cross-section of the membership. The meetings also serve as a safety valve. For the energetic and goal-driven, legislative life almost always involves frustrations; certainly during the period of divided control and constraining deficits, the frustrations were often major. By providing a forum sanctioned by the leadership for the airing of frustrations, the meetings may defuse dissatisfaction or, at least, direct it away from the leadership.

Although the meetings do serve as a forum for the venting of members' complaints and sometimes for intense debates over party policy, their mood is usually one of camaraderie. Members go to the meetings in part because, by and large, they are fun. The atmosphere often has a sort of fraternity flavor to it; members joke and laugh, boo and cheer. Announcing that the Juvenile Justice and Delinquency Prevention Act amendments would be on the schedule for the following week, the majority leader commented that it was a widely supported bill. "Even the [Republican] administration supports it," he said. "What's wrong with it?" several members asked simultaneously, and everyone laughed. An Appropriations Subcommittee chair reported that his conference report should not take long on the floor, though there were several points in disagreement. To his statement that Dingell, the chair of the Energy and Commerce Committee and a notoriously aggressive guardian of his committee's turf, was concerned about one of these because of a jurisdictional question, a number of whips responded "OH, NO!" in mock astonishment. The majority leader congratulated Leon Panetta on his fiftieth birthday to cheers and said the soon-to-be-elected Budget Committee chair did not look fifty. "After he's been Budget Committee chairman for a year, he will!" a whip exclaimed. Amid the laughter that greeted this statement, a voice boomed out, "He'll look like Mel Price!" (a frail octogenarian).

The leaders are always generous in their praise, singling out for recognition members who as whip task-force chairs successfully steered legislation to passage, or those who appeared on TV or had an Op-Ed piece published. In addition, they thank members collectively for taking a tough vote and for helping pass needed legislation.

Most whips say they enjoy the meetings but also perceive more concrete benefits from being whips. "It's good fun, and you find out a lot of useful information. That's the main reason why I go, for my own benefit," said one. He continued, "I find out what is on the schedule, who is lining up and how, and I get to know other people that way and I get a working relationship with Coelho and to some extent Foley and Wright. And in addition to that you get to know [senior leadership floor staff] and the other people that work with the organization, so it gives you good insight and a working understanding of how things get passed around here."

Another whip explained, "It is clearly of some value in terms of the access to the leadership and being in the network of activities so that you know what is happening earlier. . . . There have been a number of instances where I have learned of things in time to have an influence that I may not have learned about quite so promptly [otherwise] and where the time frame would have been too short to have influenced events." A member who served as whip during his first term believes the opportunity to get to know the leaders and many members paid off in a variety of ways, most notably in terms of good committee assignments. "I enjoy the whip meetings more than anything else I do," a very senior Democrat said, "because I get the feel of how the Congress feels, which is how the country feels."

"The most important commodity around a legislative body is information," a whip explained succinctly. He, like a number of other whips, disseminates the information he picks up at the meetings in a formal way. Immediately after a meeting, his staff puts together a whip notice that includes the schedule and other "hot items" that were discussed at the meeting. Most zone whips make up and distribute to their zone members some sort of information sheet. The whip quoted above himself hands out his whip notice during the second roll call of the day. "When things go to my office, I often don't see them; they get lost in the crush," he explained. "That's why I hand it out." Key information that emerges out of a whip meeting thus spreads quickly to the entire Democratic membership.

Taking a Whip Count

Conducting whip counts constitutes a second and more formal facet of the whip system's information function. Whip polls are conducted to determine the voting intentions of House Democrats on major legislation. The initial count provides the information necessary for an effectively targeted persuasion effort. "A whip count is never really completed," a participant explained. "It's a rolling process of turning names over, of counting and persuading. A process, not an event." That process has now been divided into two distinct phases: the initial count, which is conducted by the zone whips, and the process of refining the count and of persuasion, which is carried out by a whip task force.

The division initially arose out of the problem created by the doubtful loyalty of some of the zone whips. The heavy workload contributed to its continuation. The uncertainty of the 1970s House environment with its large number of floor votes made it necessary to conduct whip polls more frequently. Randall Ripley reports that seventeen completed polls were conducted in 1962 and 1963 (1969, 212). Fifty-three were taken during the 93rd Congress (1973–74) (Dodd 1979, 39). According to the chief staffer in the whip's office, approximately eighty polls were conducted during the 95th Congress (1977–78) and about the same number were taken during the 96th Congress (1979–80). In the 1980s the leadership found ways of reducing the number of roll-call votes, but the leaders' increasingly active role in the legislative process necessitates an active whip system. In the late 1980s and early 1990s, about seventy task forces operated per congress; each entailed one and sometimes more than one whip count.

Both the Speaker and the committee chair must sign off before a whip count will be taken. However, because counts are done so frequently, the process has become routinized. The whip and his senior staff know what needs to be counted. If the committee chair has not requested a count, the whip will prod the chair. The whip will then clear the count with the senior staff of the Speaker.

The whip system will never refuse a chair's request for a count. However, if a chair asks for a count the leaders believe is unnecessary, the effort will be pro forma. "If the chairman comes in and says I want a whip count, we'll do a whip count," a recent whip explained. "We've done that a number of times without following through with anything else." The whip must always be concerned about overstraining the system.

Once a decision to count a bill has been made, the question or questions to ask must be determined. To be useful, the whip poll must ask about members' voting intentions on the most difficult votes, which may be on the rule, on amendments or a substitute, on recommittal, or on passage. Because they know most about the legislation, Democratic committee leaders and their staffs are instrumental in making those decisions. The floor manager and his top committee aides work closely with the whip and his senior floor staff.

Committee leaders not infrequently want the whip system to count a number of votes; the leaders and their staffs, always aware of the system's limits, are determined to keep the number of questions to a minimum. One senior staff aide expressed the consensus: "We have committee chairmen saying, count this for us and count that. If you did it their way, you'd be counting ten things. Well, you just can't do that. If you want to count a bill, really three questions is max and you're much better off with two, and you're still better off with one."

When the decision on what to ask has been made, an experienced staffer in the whip's office writes the question or questions. "To get an accurate count, you have to have a good question," a senior staffer explained. "How the question is phrased is important, so that we don't give people an out."

Questions are always worded so that "yes" is the position supported by the leadership. As a result, informing members of the leadership's position is a by-product of a whip poll. A count also signals to Democrats a certain level of leadership interest. This, according to one key staffer, is why some floor managers push for a seemingly unnecessary count: "Sometimes a chairman wants us to do a whip count simply because that communicates to members that the leadership is interested in the bill."

The whip's office clears the wording of the questions with the floor manager, the Speaker's office, and the majority leader's office. Then the question or questions are faxed to the offices of the zone whips. They are accompanied by explanatory material; if the issue or the procedure is complex, that material may run to three or four pages.

Zone-whip counts are conducted by staff aides. No longer does anyone involved even pretend otherwise. "If you're lucky, it's AA [administrative aide] to AA and, if you're not, it's intern to intern," a senior whip's staffer said wryly. In the zone-whip offices surveyed, a specific staffer is designated to carry out that task and usually develops a regular contact person in the office of each zone member. The designated staffer in the zone whip's office calls the office of each of the zone's members, asks the specified questions of the staff contact person, and provides explanatory background as needed. The contact person in the zone member's office may answer the questions himself or herself—basing the responses on their member's past record—or may check with the member. A senior whip's staffer estimated that perhaps half the time the report is based on actually checking with the member. If the contact person does not feel comfortable about answering for the member and cannot ask the member within the time allotted for the poll, he or she tends to report the member as undecided. When the zone whip's staffer has answers from all zone members or the allotted time has run out, he or she calls or faxes the results to the whip's office.

In most cases, the time allotted is short. "The norm" for a count "is one day turnaround," a whip's aide said. "I would say a third of the counts are less than that." Occasionally, the time limit is two hours or even "as soon as possible," zone-whip staffers report. Whips' staff aides are aware they are making severe demands on these zone-whip staffers; they are grateful for their hard work and try to make them feel they are part of the effort. The whip cannot, however, ease the task of the zone whips by giving them more time because of the nature of the enterprise. "The counts are strategically designed in terms of what we are asking about," a participant explained. "You can't count a bill much ahead because you don't know what the hell is really going to happen. By the time you figure out what is really happening, you need to go."

The result of the initial poll is a division of Democrats into support categories: yes, leaning yes, undecided, leaning no, no, absent, and not contacted. The whip's staff puts the zone whips' results into the computer as they come into the office. When initial counts are conducted under severe time constraints, the number of Democrats reported as undecided or not contacted tends to be high. Increasingly, when time is very short, the whip system works from an alternative estimate of members' voting intentions.

Evolution of the Vote-Mobilization Effort

In the 1960s, the Speaker, the majority leader, the whip, the deputy whip, the White House and departmental liaison officials, and the relevant committee chairs carried most of the burden of mobilizing the votes needed to pass major legislation (Ripley 1967, 73–75, 127–38). They were sometimes assisted by committee supporters of the bill and by loyal zone whips.

When the Democrats lost the presidency in 1968, Democratic House leaders also lost White House assistance in vote mobilization. That, combined with the impact of the reforms on the legislative process in the House, put demands on the leaders with regard to vote mobilization that they could not meet. The appointment of increasing numbers of at-large whips to aid in persuasion efforts was one response. By the mid1970s, appointive whips and then other interested members were being drawn into vote-mobilization efforts on a fairly frequent basis. Then, in 1977, Speaker O'Neill began using specially appointed task forces to carry out vote mobilization on legislation considered centrally important and difficult. According to a senior O'Neill aide, the new leadership had narrowly lost an important bill early in 1977, a loss O'Neill attributed to lack of organization. The Speaker's response was the task force, an ad hoc group charged with passage of a specific bill.

The task-force device proved to have some real benefits for both leaders and members. Task forces gave leaders badly needed help; they provided members, especially junior members, with opportunities to participate meaningfully in the legislative process. In the late 1970s, Speaker O'Neill used Steering and Policy Committee aides, who are directly responsible to the Speaker, to staff task forces. During those years, task forces were employed only on the most important legislation. As a contemporary staffer expressed the decision rule, "They should be used only on significant legislation that is clearly part of the Democratic party program." Fourteen task forces operated during the 95th and 96th Congresses (1977–80). (For a detailed discussion, see Sinclair 1983, 138–46.)

In the early 1980s, new whip Tom Foley brought task forces into the whip system. The appointive whips were used more often and staffing was provided by the whip's office. In 1987, when Tony Coelho became whip, he instituted a streamlined procedure that has since become institutionalized. All leadership vote-mobilization efforts are now task-force efforts. With rare exceptions, the decision to conduct a whip count is also a decision to have a task force. A chair or two or more cochairs are chosen first. Almost always one is from the committee; the other is often but not always from the whip system. Then, in most cases, an invitation to participate is sent to all the whips and to the Democrats on the committee or committees of origin. The notice informs them of the time and place of the first task-force meeting and invites them to attend. Whoever shows up constitutes the task force. Occasionally, on legislation of extreme political delicacy — a congressional pay raise, for example — task-force members will be selected and invited individually, but the great majority are general-invitation task forces.

The task force usually works from the zone-whip count; it is responsible both for refining the count and for persuading sufficient members to pass the legislation intact. (For a full discussion, see chap. 10.) Task-force efforts vary enormously in scope and intensiveness, depending on the time available and the difficulty of the task assigned. But, whether the task is defeating a Republican floor amendment offered unexpectedly or passing a major bill on which the committee and the leadership have been working for months, the use of a task force has become standard operating procedure.

The task-force device has persisted and developed in this fashion because it benefits both leaders and members. Task forces give leaders badly needed help; as they presently function, they make it possible for the leadership to involve itself in a large number of legislative battles. Conducting several full-scale vote-mobilization efforts simultaneously — as now often occurs during the busiest periods — becomes feasible.

Task forces broaden the opportunities available, particularly for junior members, to participate meaningfully in the legislative process on issues that interest them. Serving on task forces "has been useful in at least three ways," David Price, an unusually reflective junior member, explained:

> First, it has let me help mobilize support for measures that I thought were important. . . . Second, it has made me a partner, albeit a junior one, in leadership undertakings. This can be intrinsically satisfying and it can also bring other rewards. Those of us [seeking assignment to the Appropriations Committee] joked about what a coincidence it was that we so often found ourselves on the whip's task forces. Finally, it has brought me into discussions of floor strategy and the last-minute alterations needed to maximize votes on various bills. (Price 1992, 80)

From the inception of task forces, junior Democrats have been dispropor-
tionately likely to serve as members (see Sinclair 1983, 146). That pattern
continues today. Asked what sorts of members are most likely to be active
on task forces, a leadership staffer replied, "That's easy. Those who have
been here two years but not yet eight years." After an initial term of
adjusting to the House and the district demands of the job, still too junior
to have assumed substantial committee responsibility, many members
seek opportunities to participate in the House. Task-force efforts provide
such opportunities.

Tip O'Neill believed that giving a large number and a wide variety of
Democrats "a piece of the action," but under the aegis of the leadership,
and thus giving them a stake in the leadership's success, would make those
members more responsive to the leadership generally. Work on a task
force was thought to be especially likely to influence junior members, to
teach them the value of joint action under the aegis of the party. Studies
indicate that he was correct; working on a task force did seem to lead to an
increase in party voting (Garand and Clayton 1986). Although the Democratic membership is less ideologically heterogeneous now than it was in
the late 1970s, the leadership still benefits when members understand the
problems of coalition building and the value of joint action.

Information Services

As a service to members, the majority whip's office disseminates a variety
of legislatively and politically relevant information. The floor schedule for
the following week is hand-carried to every Democrat's office by 3:00 P.M.
Friday. Sometime on Friday, a whip packet containing copies of all scheduled bills that have been printed is delivered to all offices.

In 1973 John McFall, the newly appointed whip, initiated the whip
advisory, a one-page summary of the content and legislative history of and
amendments expected to be offered to a bill scheduled for floor action. An
advisory was prepared for every scheduled bill, resolution, and conference
report. In the mid-1980s, the whip's staff stopped doing advisories for the
large number of minor bills considered under suspension of the rules.
Now an advisory is prepared for all legislation of some importance, which
is usually defined as legislation considered under a rule from the Rules
Committee.

Over time, a routine procedure for preparing advisories has developed.
When the schedule for the following week has been determined — usually
by Thursday morning — the whip's staffer in charge calls the committee of
origin of each bill and asks for a summary of the legislation. He reviews it

for clarity and length. Since committee staffs sometimes provide a too-technical or too-long summary, he may have to rewrite the committee's draft. The advisory should include "what people want to know" about the bill. Any changes are faxed to the committee for review and approval. As a staffer explained, "You must have the advisory in a form agreed to by the committee. You can't have the committee chairman disown it on the floor. The committee has got to be 'on board.'"

The advisories are considered by the whip's staff to be factual, not persuasive, communications. Their credibility depends on a relatively evenhanded, objective presentation of the material. Nevertheless, the advisories, as they are prepared under the aegis of the leaders, certainly do not slight material favorable to the party position. The advisory for HR 3090, the Family Planning Amendments of 1991, indicated that the bill authorized $195 million for fiscal year 1992, increasing significantly to $237 million in fiscal year 1996, but also pointed out that "these increases take into account the fact that Title Ten has received virtually no funding increases over the last seven years because it has not been reauthorized during that period" (April 30, 1992).

The whip's office periodically prepares and disseminates other information that it believes will be of use to the members. Issue papers containing analyses of complicated and controversial issues are distributed periodically. Before recesses and adjournments, the whip's office sends every Democrat a package of materials to use when speaking in his or her district. These "recess packets" include a legislative checklist of the achievements of the congress, various whip issue papers that discuss selected issues and accomplishments in more detail, and speech cards that summarize the major points of the issue papers.

Most of the expansion of information services took place in the 1970s, and staffers in the whip's office during that period explained it as a response to the growing independence of House members in the 1970s. Members, no longer willing to follow blindly the lead of the committee majority, insisted on knowing the details of issues on which they were voting. Members have long since come to take their leaders' provision of these information services as a matter of course. By doing so, leaders facilitate the members' pursuit of their goals through individualist strategies as their members expect them to do. In addition, leaders gain a modicum of control over the information that shapes the members' decisions.

★ ★

As a collector and disseminator of information and as a vote mobilizer, the whip system is a key mechanism through which the party leaders meet members' expectations that they facilitate the passage of legislation important to the members. The system's inclusive structure and style of operation offer members opportunities to participate in the legislative process to compensate for the constraints on individualist goal-seeking strategies required to engineer the passage of legislation. By embodying the strategy of inclusion, the whip system facilitates the balancing act that successful contemporary leadership demands.

Structuring Choices

The Rules Committee

Not long after the stock market crash in the fall of 1987, during a period of intense concern about the deficit, welfare-reform legislation was ready for consideration on the floor of the House. The Ways and Means Committee, which had primary jurisdiction over the legislation, wanted a closed rule. A significant number of Democrats, however, thought the bill too expensive and wanted to amend it on the floor. The leadership determined that a closed rule would not pass. Discussion centered on an amendment Tom Carper (D-Del.) wanted to offer. Letting him do so, the leaders believed, would doom the bill because enough Democrats would join all the Republicans to pass the amendment. Adoption of the amendment, which made draconian cuts in the program, would alienate most strong supporters of welfare reform, and they would join most Republicans to defeat the bill on final passage.

The leadership decided to bar the Carper amendment but to allow an amendment by Mike Andrews (D-Tex.) that also cut the program but not by so much as to alienate the original bill's strong supporters. With this solution, those Democrats who wanted to demonstrate their fiscal responsibility were given a vote to trim the program. The rule, Andrews's amendment, and the bill all passed with relative ease.

Structuring choices through the use of procedural devices is the quintessential legislative strategy. House leaders have available a variety of means for structuring choices so as to advantage the outcome their members favor. In recent years, the Rules Committee has become by far the most important leadership instrument for structuring choices, and doing so by way of special rules has become a central leadership strategy.

Effective leadership use of this powerful tool is, however, dependent on the approval of the membership; every rule must be able to command a majority in the House. Thus, in the construction of rules, leaders must weigh facilitating the passage of legislation that their members collectively desire against not unduly interfering with members' pursuit of their goals through individualist strategies. Successful leadership requires striking a balance that members consider satisfactory.

The Rules Committee–Party Leadership Relationship

The Rules Committee is a House, not a party, organ. Nevertheless, members perceive it to be, in the common phrase, an "arm of the leadership." As its chair, Joe Moakley (D-Mass.), said, "This is the Speaker's committee" (Phillips 1989, 14).

In the past century the relationship between the party leadership and the Rules Committee has come almost full circle (*History of the Committee on Rules* 1983). Speakers in the latter part of the nineteenth century developed the Rules Committee into a powerful instrument for controlling the flow of legislation to the floor. During that period the committee, then chaired by the Speaker, began to make use of special orders or rules that permitted legislation to be taken up out of order and governed the amount of debate time and, sometimes, the number of amendments allowed. These rules soon became the primary route by which major legislation reached the floor.

Joseph Cannon as Speaker used the Rules Committee to thwart the legislative aims of progressives within his own party. When in 1910 insurgent Republicans and Democrats combined to strip the Speaker of what they believed to be arbitrary powers, they removed him from the Rules Committee. Without the Speaker as a member, the committee became a potential base of influence independent of the party leadership. From the late 1930s until 1961 the committee was dominated by a bipartisan conservative majority and was often at odds with the Democratic leadership, sometimes blocking legislation desired by the leaders and a majority of Democrats and frequently extracting substantive concessions as the price for granting a rule. The Speaker was forced to bargain with the committee, but his resources for doing so were limited. Thus the leadership's control over floor scheduling, perhaps its most powerful tool, was incomplete during this period (Robinson 1963).

When John Kennedy was elected president in 1960, Speaker Rayburn decided the Rules Committee had to be reined in, for if it was not the Kennedy program would be doomed from the beginning. He proposed enlarging the committee by three members and, after a bitter fight, the House approved the so-called packing of the Rules Committee by a vote of 217 to 212. Even though Rayburn in effect chose the new Democratic members of the Rules Committee, the leadership majority was often shaky. The very conservative Howard Smith remained chair through 1966, and given the powers of that position, conservatives were still able to make trouble for the party leaders. After Smith was defeated in the 1966 primary the equally conservative William Colmer (D-Miss.) became chair. Colmer, however, was forced to accept written rules for the committee that limited his power. As Democratic positions on the committee opened up, Speakers used their informal influence over these appointments to make the committee more reliable. By the early 1970s the Rules Committee was no longer an independent obstructionist force; it generally gave the leadership what it wanted (Oppenheimer 1981a).

At the beginning of the 94th Congress the Democratic Caucus passed a major rules change that solidified the Speaker's control over the committee. The Speaker was empowered to name the chair and all Democratic Rules Committee members, his appointments subject only to ratification by the caucus. Furthermore, the Speaker's nominating powers were to apply to incumbent as well as new members; he could remove Democratic members from the committee. Although Speakers have not chosen to, and in the foreseeable future probably will not, strike anyone from the committee, they have both guarded and used with great care their prerogative of naming new members. When Andrew Young (D-Ga.) left the committee at the beginning of the 95th Congress, O'Neill named Shirley Chisholm (D-N.Y.) to replace him, even though southerners laid claim to the position on the basis of geography. At the beginning of the 96th Congress, when the California Democratic delegation attempted to select the Californian to go on the committee, O'Neill stated publicly that he considered state delegation endorsements of potential Rules Committee nominees illegitimate and would consider such endorsements a strike against the member so endorsed (Speaker's press conference, January 18, 1979). He pointedly chose a different Californian. Thus O'Neill, who had served on the committee during the period when it was independent of the leadership, not only made sure that the members appointed were people on whom he could depend, but also guarded against the development of norms constricting the Speaker's discretion.

Subsequent Speakers have been equally careful to assure themselves of true control of the Rules Committee. All recent Speakers have talked with potential appointees and made their expectations completely clear. "When Tip asked me to go on the Rules Committee," a committee Democrat recounted, "he said to me, '___, now if you take this, I expect you to support me on the committee and, if every once in a while you can't, to make sure it doesn't influence the outcome on the committee.'" As this member added, "The kind of people appointed to Rules are the kind that are not going to have trouble supporting the leadership." The members appointed to the committee by O'Neill, Wright, and Foley on average scored 87 percent on the party-unity index in the congress before their appointment, and only two scored below 85 percent.

Before reappointing the Democratic members of the Rules Committee at the beginning of a new congress, Speakers generally meet with them as a group; although it is not necessarily overt, the message conveyed at these meetings is that Democrats serve on the committee at the pleasure of the Speaker. The process of reappointment is then carried out in full, whether or not any truly new members are to be appointed: the Speaker formally communicates his choices to the Steering and Policy Committee at a meeting and later to the caucus, and the caucus votes on the Speaker's choice for chair.

From Directing Traffic to Structuring Choices

During the committee government era, the Rules Committee was often likened to a "traffic cop," determining which bills proceeded to the floor and which were stopped. It exercised little discretion with regard to the form of the rules it granted. Now the form a rule will take is a major decision and, not infrequently, rules are constructed so as to structure floor choices to the benefit of the majority party.

The Trend toward Complex and Restrictive Rules

Through the late 1960s, most legislation was considered under simple open rules that allowed all germane amendments. The exceptions were revenue bills from the Ways and Means Committee, which were considered under closed rules prohibiting all but committee-offered amendments. During the 91st Congress (1969–70), for example, 80 percent of the measures identified earlier as major legislation were brought to the floor under simple open rules; 16 percent — primarily bills from the Ways and Means Committee — were considered under closed rules; only two measures came to the floor under rules more complex than simple open or simple closed rules.

In the mid- and late 1970s, most ordinary legislation was still considered under open rules. The preponderance of open rules did begin to decline in the late 1970s and early 1980s, and then dropped sharply from the mid-1980s through the early 1990s (see table 8.1).[1] In the 101st Con-

---

1. The decrease in the number of rules over time evident in table 8.1 seems to be a result of the increased use of omnibus legislative vehicles where previously several separate bills

Table 8.1   The Trend in Open vs. Restrictive Rules, 1977–92

Congress	Total Rules Granted[a]	% Open	% Restrictive[b]
95th (1977–78)	211	85	15
96th (1979–80)	214	75	25
97th (1981–82)	120	75	25
98th (1983–84)	155	68	32
99th (1985–86)	115	57	43
100th (1987–88)	123	54	46
101st (1989–90)	104	45	55
102nd (1991–92)	109	34	66

Source: Compiled by Donald Wolfensberger, Minority Counsel, Committee on Rules, from *Rules Committee Calendars* and *Surveys of Activities.*

[a]Rules for initial consideration of legislation, except rules on appropriations bills that only waive points of order.

[b]Restrictive rules are those that limit the number of amendments that can be offered and include so-called modified open and modified closed as well as completely closed rules and rules providing for consideration in the House as opposed to the Committee of the Whole.

gress (1989–90) for the first time fewer than half the rules for initial consideration of legislation were open rules.

When only major legislation as defined earlier is considered, the change is even more dramatic (see table 8.2).[2] The proportion of open rules declined from 80 percent in the 91st Congress (1969–70) to about 25 percent in the 100th and 101st Congresses (1987–90). The frequency of the use of closed rules, which bar all amendments, has not increased. The big change is in the frequency of the use of complex rules, which now usually have restrictive features of some sort, most often restrictions on the amendments that can be offered.

The two rules in the 91st Congress that fell into neither of the traditional categories but had more complex provisions were expansive rules; they allowed amendments or substitutes — in both cases ones supported by the president — to be offered that would not otherwise have been in order under House rules. In the 94th Congress, the first in which the reforms were fully in place, almost 80 percent of the measures were con-

---

would have been used, and of a large increase in the use of the suspension procedure. In the 95th Congress (1977–8), 38% of all measures passed were considered under suspension; in the 102nd Congress (1991–92), 52% of all bills passed were considered under suspension.

2. In the 1980s, appropriations bills were increasingly brought to the floor under rules, so, for purposes of comparability, an appropriations bill that makes the list of major legislation that is brought to the floor without a rule is coded as having been considered under a simple open rule.

Table 8.2   The Changing Character of Rules on Major Measures

| Congress | Total Measures | Measures Considered under Rules* | % Considered Under | |
			Complex or Closed Rules	Closed Rules
91st (1969–70)	50	44	20	16
94th (1975–76)	48	42	21	2
97th (1981–82)	45	35	45	11
100th (1987–88)	40	34	77	9
101st (1989–90)	50	37	72	13

*Appropriations bills are included and, if not considered under a rule, are coded as having been considered under a simple open rule (see chap. 8, n. 2).

sidered under simple open rules — no real change from the prereform congress for which data are available. However, only one measure was brought to the floor under a closed rule; measures that would have been considered under a closed rule in the past — tax measures from the Ways and Means Committee — were being brought to the floor under restrictive but not totally closed rules. New procedures and processes — multiple referral and the budget process — dictated the employment of several other complex but nonrestrictive rules.

The frequency of the use of simple open rules dropped steeply between the 94th Congress (1975–76) and the 97th Congress (1981–82), and again between the 97th and the 100th and 101st Congresses (1987–90). By the late 1980s, three-quarters of major measures were considered under complex or closed rules. Closed rules made something of a comeback after almost disappearing in the 94th Congress, but they are still relatively rarely used. The big increase is in complex but not closed rules and, from the 97th Congress on, almost all the complex rules to a lesser or greater extent have restricted the amendments that may be offered. The typical rule of the 1990s is a complex, restrictive rule.

Contemporary Rules: Determinants and Characteristics

A rule always specifies the amount of time allowed for general debate and who is to control that time. In addition, a rule may waive points of order, may restrict amendments in a variety of ways, and may include other special provisions to govern consideration of the legislation on the floor.

A number of institutional and political developments during the 1970s and 1980s contributed to the trend toward complex and restrictive rules (see Bach and Smith 1988; S. Smith 1989). In addition to the well-known explosion of amending activity on the House floor in the wake of the

1970s reforms, the increase in omnibus bills and in the use of multiple referral and the problems the House confronted in complying with all of its own complicated rules made increasingly complex special rules for floor consideration necessary.

If a bill in some way contravenes a rule of the House, it can be knocked off the floor by one member making a point of order against it. A special rule can protect such a bill by waiving such points of order. Appropriations bills, which are privileged and thus do not need rules to get to the floor, are increasingly being considered under rules because they need a waiver of the House rule prohibiting appropriations for a program not yet authorized. In the 1980s and early 1990s policy disagreements between Congress and the president made reauthorization of some programs impossible; congressional majorities favored continued funding of such programs — Legal Services, for example — and the money was included in appropriations bills. The budget process as it has been elaborated over time — with the Gramm-Rudman requirements, for example — added another complex set of rules that sometimes need to be waived.

When a bill is referred to several committees, setting the ground rules for floor consideration can present a host of complicated and delicate problems (Bach and Smith 1988, 18–23). Not only must debate time be divided but, when two or more committees have reported different provisions on a given matter, which committee's language will constitute the base text and how other committees' versions will be considered must be determined. The first rule for the consideration of the 1992 energy bill, which had been referred to nine committees, split five hours of general debate among the committees, with the Energy and Commerce Committee receiving one hour and the other eight being allotted a half-hour each. The committees having worked out as many of the conflicts among themselves as they could, the Rules Committee decided in the remaining cases which committee's version would go into the base bill that would serve as the original bill for the purpose of amendment on the floor. Other committees were given the opportunity to offer their language as amendments on the floor. The rule limited the amendments that would be in order to those listed in the Rules Committee's report, set debate time for each amendment, ranging from five to twenty minutes per side, and specified that those amendments "shall not be subject to amendment except as specified in the report" (*Congressional Record,* May 20, 1992, H 3462). And this rule governed consideration of only the first seven titles of the bill. The energy bill was so substantively and parliamentarily complicated that the remainder was considered under a second rule, which again limited the amendments that could be offered and permitted the chair of the Energy and Commerce Committee "to offer amendments en bloc consisting of the text of amendments printed in the report and germane modifications" (*Congressional Record,* May 21, 1992, H 3705).

Democrats' growing disenchantment with the political and policy consequences of the huge number of amendments offered on the floor in the immediate postreform years contributed to the increased use of rules that restrict amendments. So too has the growing frequency in the 1980s and 1990s of omnibus bills. Bills such as continuing resolutions, which are omnibus appropriations bills that may fund the entire government, or reconciliation bills, which change law often across the whole spectrum of government activity, are so broad in their scope that almost any conceivable amendment would be germane. The omnibus drug bills of this period have been almost as broad. Consideration of such legislation under an open rule would likely require weeks of floor time, and the results would be highly unpredictable.

Rules that restrict amendments may allow all amendments that were submitted to the Rules Committee or printed in the *Congressional Record* by a certain date, or they may make in order only a subset of the amendments that House members would like to offer. A restrictive rule may allow only a few amendments or it may allow a specific but long list of amendments. Such rules either entirely prohibit second-degree amendments (that is, amendments to amendments) or they make in order only specific second-degree amendments.

Some rules make in order only one or a small number of comprehensive substitutes for the base legislation. In the 1970s, budget resolutions were considered under open rules and multitudes of highly specific if not picayune amendments were regularly offered. In 1979, for example, more than fifty amendments to the budget resolution were offered, and floor consideration took nine days (Sinclair 1983, 180). Since 1980, tighter rules have been used and, for a number of years, only entire substitutes have been allowed. The standard procedure has been to give Republicans two substitutes and the Black Caucus a substitute, and perhaps to allow one or two other Democrats to offer substitutes. The budget resolution is supposed to be a macroinstrument, the argument goes, so microamendments — transferring a few hundred million dollars from Star Wars to the war on drugs or vice versa, for example — are not appropriate. Major, ideologically charged legislation addressing social-welfare and civil-rights issues is also often considered under tight rules that let members choose among major alternatives.

In contrast, some restrictive rules allow large numbers of amendments to be offered. Rules for the consideration of defense-authorization bills in recent years have been of that sort. In 1987, for example, the rule allowed about two hundred amendments — approximately half of those that members had requested. The rule also set time limits for various amendments and specified, or gave the committee chair the discretion to specify, the order in which the amendments were to be considered. The large drug bills of the late 1980s and early 1990s were also brought to the floor under rules that made in order a large but still limited number of amendments.

As they have evolved over recent years, special rules are powerful devices that can be used to focus attention and debate on the critical choices, to save time and prevent obstruction and delay, and sometimes to structure the choices members confront on the floor so as to advantage some outcomes over others. "Our function is to focus the debate and the actual votes on the items of major controversy," a Rules Committee Democrat said.

> To get rid of the extraneous matters and to focus attention on the major amendments so that the members can decide, and to structure that in such a way, both in terms of time limitations and in terms of limiting the number of amendments, so that you cannot have a de facto filibuster in the House of Representatives by members exercising their right to offer an amendment and to speak for five minutes on anything.

Their fellow Democrats expect them to perform these functions. As a senior staffer said, "The committees like the predictability that structured rules give. Members like the regularity of process. There are some who like the wide-open amending process, but most prefer the certainties and knowing when things will happen and when they will be over."

When the rule gives members a choice among comprehensive substitutes but bars votes on narrow amendments, it focuses the debate on alternative approaches, on the big choices rather than the picky details. Major legislation is increasingly considered under such rules; tax bills, budget resolutions, civil-rights bills, and social-welfare legislation on issues such as parental leave, minimum wage, and childcare have in recent years been brought to the floor under rules structured in this fashion.

Legislation that is the product of a number of committees often could not be considered on the floor without highly structured rules. Ordinary House procedure has no way of addressing multiple versions of a provision where no version has precedence — which is often the situation when a bill has been multiply referred. The rule for the energy bill discussed earlier illustrates how a rule can impose order on an otherwise chaotic situation.

Rules that restrict amendments and waive points of order save time and prevent obstructionism. Most House members have little patience with protracted floor consideration; when any but the most important legislation is on the floor for more than two or three days, members begin to complain. The amending marathons of the mid-1970s are still brought up by members as horrible examples and as justifications for tight rules. Because of its size, the House requires restrictive procedures if it is to function, and when a minority employs procedures to delay, the majority often demands that its leadership respond through the use of tighter special rules. In 1991, for example, James Traficant, a maverick Democrat from Ohio, miffed that a provision he favored had been excluded from an appropriations bill, began to raise points of order against sections of the bill for funding programs that had not yet been authorized. Republicans, seizing an opportunity to embarrass the majority party, jumped in to do the same, and much of the bill was knocked out. At the behest of the Democratic members, the Rules Committee responded by reporting rules for appropriations bills with much more extensive waivers.

How Rules Structure Floor Choices

Members want focused debate and an efficient use of time, but even more they want policy results and want them secured at minimum cost to themselves as individuals. Democrats increasingly expect their leaders to use rules to structure choices to accomplish these ends. Any restrictions on amendments, even simply the requirement that amendments be submitted to the Rules Committee several days prior to being offered on the floor, help the bill's proponents by reducing uncertainty. Proponents can focus their efforts and plan their strategy more efficiently; opponents lose the element of surprise.

In addition to reducing uncertainty, carefully crafted rules can structure choices so as to advantage a particular outcome. They usually do so by structuring choices in a way that allows or forces members to choose on the basis of that goal which dictates the vote leading to the structurer's desired outcome. Most frequently, the Democratic leaders try to structure choices so that the members can base their votes on their notions of good public policy. Conversely, their Republican opponents attempt to confront Democrats with votes that make them choose between policy concerns and furthering their reelection prospects.

The case of welfare-reform legislation that began this chapter illustrates this kind of strategic situation and how a rule can be used to structure choices. Most Democrats — enough to constitute a clear majority of the House — favored passing a welfare-reform bill; they believed it constituted good public policy. Many, however, believed that, for reelection reasons, they had to go on record as favoring a reduction in the costs of the program. By allowing a vote on the moderate Andrews amendment but barring one on the draconian Carper amendment, the rule gave those members who needed it the opportunity to demonstrate fiscal responsibility and also assured that legislation most Democrats favored would be enacted.

The 1991 civil-rights bill, the product of an excruciatingly difficult process of compromise aimed at building a coalition sufficiently large to override an expected veto, was brought to the floor under a rule that strictly limited amendments. The leadership's compromise version, a Republican-administration version, and a liberal–Black Caucus version were made in order as substitutes to the original bill. Women members were not allowed to offer an amendment to lift the cap on punitive damages to women who could prove their employers had intentionally discriminated, and Republicans were denied a motion to recommit with instructions (which would have provided another means of amending the bill). The amendment to lift the cap would have confronted many Democrats with an extremely unpalatable choice: their strong supporters favored the amendment fervently, they themselves believed it just, but its adoption would extinguish the bill's chances of becoming law because it would drive away need Republican votes on passage. The strategic problem was how to structure floor choices so that Democrats would not be confronted with a choice between, on the one hand, having to explain a strategic vote to the bill's and their own strongest supporters and, on the other, casting a sincere vote that would endanger the bill. The leaders barred this amendment but allowed the much stronger Black Caucus substitute, thus giving liberals who needed to show their purity on the issue the opportunity to do so, but making the choice to oppose the alternative easier for most Democrats. Republicans were given a substitute but were denied a motion to recommit with instructions, to prevent them having a "second bite of the apple," as a senior staffer expressed it. The leaders feared Republicans would come up with some alternative provision, possibly even the lifting of the cap, that would unravel the compromise. If Republicans could come up with something that an appreciable number of Democrats would have real difficulty voting against, they might sink the bill despite strong House support for it.

The rule for the reconciliation bill implementing Clinton's economic program in 1993 allowed only a vote on a comprehensive Republican substitute; amendments to delete various unpopular elements of the package — the BTU tax and the tax on high-income recipients' Social Security payments — were not made in order. Passage was crucial for the young Clinton administration and for the Democratic party, but the constraints imposed by the huge deficit and the need to reduce it made putting and holding together a package extremely difficult. The rule was intended to focus debate on the broad philosophical differences between the two parties' approaches to the problem of reducing the deficit and to protect

Democrats from having to cast a series of excruciatingly tough votes. Many Democrats would have found it difficult back home to explain votes against amendments striking unpopular taxing provisions, especially in response to thirty-second attack ads; allowing such amendments would have confronted Democrats with the unpalatable choice between casting a series of politically dangerous votes or contributing to the picking apart on the floor of the carefully constructed compromise, the passage of which, most believed, was crucial to the future of the country and their party. This rule also denied the minority a motion to recommit with instructions because, like amendments, that would have allowed Republicans to force a vote on the least popular provisions of the package.

Although they are still relatively rare, rules limiting or denying the minority the right to offer a motion to recommit with instructions have increased in recent years. From 1977 through 1984, on average, fewer than four rules per congress were of this sort (Wolfensberger 1992); in the period from 1985 through 1992, in contrast, the average was about seventeen per congress. Republicans object, often in inflammatory language, to such restrictions for the same reasons the Democratic leaders find them so useful. The motion to recommit with instructions gives the minority flexibility and the element of surprise. The movers need not decide on the substance of the motion until just before they make it and, whenever they decide, they can keep it secret until the last moment. Consequently, the bill's supporters cannot plan a response.

Republicans' bitter complaints and the frequent partisan floor battles over rules are an indicator of how important the decision on the character of the rule is. Republicans claim that restrictive rules unfairly curtail their opportunities to participate meaningfully in the legislative process. Democrats respond that Republicans want open rules so as to play irresponsible political games, and that their aim is not to participate seriously in making policy but to find opportunities for putting Democrats on the spot and for unraveling carefully thought-out compromises reached at the prefloor stage where the actual shaping of legislation should take place. In fact, rules are never neutral in their effect (Krehbiel 1988); any rule — whether open or closed or somewhere in between — advantages some outcomes over others. The majority-party leadership will structure rules so as to advantage the outcome its party members favor rather than that favored by the opposition party.

At the most basic level, legislative leaders of all sorts attempt to make it easy for members to vote for their own most preferred outcome and hard to vote for alternatives they oppose. What members find difficult to vote for or against depends heavily on their reelection calculus. A vote that lends itself to ready exploitation by an opponent, one that is too difficult to explain to one's constituents, is, most members believe, one better not cast (see Kingdon 1973). Both the character of a member's constituency and the political climate determine which votes are better avoided. For any given district, there are issues that are always dangerous; a vote for gun control is a high-risk vote in many rural districts. There are also votes that take on this character only within a given political climate; the votes on the welfare-reform bill were problematic because of the widespread worry about the deficit and the economy.

How the political environment influences the strategy of structuring choices, and the limits of that strategy, are well illustrated by probably the most famous of all complex rules — that for the 1981 reconciliation bill — and the one for its 1980 predecessor.

In 1980 President Carter and the Democratic leadership agreed that the sudden huge increase in the inflation rate required a strong legislative response. The budget would have to be cut, they concluded, and this would require reductions in a number of popular programs. The cuts were incorporated in a reconciliation bill, which for the first time had been ordered by the first budget resolution.

The strategic situation dictated bringing the bill to the floor under a highly restrictive rule. An open rule permitting any and all amendments, the participants agreed, would doom the bill. Members would find the pressure to restore various cuts irresistible, and little of the legislative savings so painfully achieved would survive. "If you give them a free choice, there's no way that they'll ever vote for savings," a senior Budget Committee Democrat explained. "The pressures around here on the school-lunch subsidies and on the postal subsidies were unreal, and if they had had a straight up-or-down vote on either one of those, we would never have voted to cut them. But when you're able to package it into a savings package, they're not going to go home and say they voted against saving six and a half billion dollars." The rule's victory — albeit on a close vote — assured the bill of easy passage.

In 1981, Ronald Reagan and his Republican House supporters confronted a similar strategic situation in attempting to pass the new president's program of massive domestic spending cuts over the opposition of the Democratic House leadership. Although the Democratic leadership controlled the Rules Committee, the premier institutional tool for structuring choices, Reagan dominated the national political debate and that enabled him to prevail. Reagan and his congressional supporters wanted one vote on the president's package of cuts — a single vote that they could portray as a vote against wasteful federal spending and for the popular president's program to fix the ailing economy. The Democratic leaders, who believed many of the cuts went much too far, wanted to force votes on a number of the specific components of the Reagan package; members would be faced with voting for or against a number of popular federal programs — school lunches and student loans, federal housing programs, cost-of-living allowances for military pensioners.

Both sides agreed that the way in which the rule structured choices was the crucial decision and would determine the outcome. Under the leadership's direction, the Rules Committee reported a rule for consideration of the Democratic reconciliation bill that would allow the Reagan plan to be offered as a series of specific cutting amendments. These amendments could contain only cuts; no restorations that could serve as sweeteners would be allowed (see Sinclair 1983, 206). To get the rule of their choice, House Republicans needed to defeat the previous question on the rule proposed by the Rules Committee; they could then propose a rule that specified an up-or-down vote on the Reagan package as a whole. Effectively using the president's great media access, Reagan raised the visibility of a usually obscure procedural vote, making it a test of support for himself and his program. Enough Democrats defected and joined all the Republicans to defeat the previous question and pass the Republican rule, and that assured passage of Reagan's package of cuts.

Rules have become even more flexible and powerful tools for structuring choices with the development in recent years of some entirely new parliamentary devices. A "king-of-the-hill" provision in a rule specifies that a series of amendments or substitutes are to be voted on seriatim, with the last one that receives a majority prevailing. This device makes possible a direct vote on each of several alternatives; in ordinary parliamentary procedure, if an amendment or substitute receives a majority, no vote on the original (unamended) version of the legislation ever occurs. Clearly, when this procedure is employed, the amendment or substitute voted on last is advantaged. The procedure also makes it possible for members to vote for more than one version, which is sometimes politically beneficial. Because it does allow a vote on each version whatever the results of prior roll calls, members often consider it fairer than ordinary parliamentary procedure.

Budget resolutions are often considered under a king-of-the-hill rule. Members are thus guaranteed a vote on each of the substitute versions of the resolution made in order by the rule. The House Budget Committee version is always placed in the advantageous last position. The rule for the civil-rights bill discussed earlier specified that the substitutes were to be offered in a specific order under the king-of-the-hill procedure. The rule gave liberals a vote on their much stronger version but put that substitute first in line. Having cast a vote in favor of the tough bill civil-rights activists favored, these members later could support the leadership compromise. The rule next gave House Republicans and the Bush administration a vote on their preferred version. It put the Democratic compromise last, in the advantaged position.

Another new device — a self-executing rule — provides that when a rule is adopted by the House, the accompanying bill is automatically amended to incorporate the text of an amendment either set forth or referenced in the rule. The procedure provides a parliamentarily simple way of inserting last-minute corrections or compromises into a bill. In 1993, after the reconciliation bill implementing President Clinton's economic program was reported from committee, the leadership, in order to amass the votes needed to pass the bill, worked out a compromise on entitlements with conservative Democrats. The language was incorporated into the legislation by a self-executing provision in the rule. This device also sometimes provides strategic opportunities. The rule for the final 1987 continuing resolution, for example, carried a self-executing amendment denying members of Congress a pay raise. Earlier legislation had included a provision that could be interpreted as giving members a pay raise. Given the political climate, members were loath to vote for that bill, and did so only after the leadership promised them a quick vote to kill the pay raise. By using the self-executing device, the leaders gave the members an extra incentive to vote for the continuing resolution rule, and put Republicans who opposed it in an embarrassing position. Republicans had been attacking Democrats as voting to raise their own pay during a period of economic turmoil. Now they were confronted with a vote that could be portrayed in similar fashion: if they voted against the rule, they were voting for a pay raise.

The Rule-Crafting Process

The rule-crafting process starts formally when the chair of a legislative committee writes the Rules Committee requesting a hearing and outlining the sort of rule he wants. The chair may have already talked informally to acquaintances on the Rules Committee and "filled them in." Committee staff aides may call Rules Committee staffers and, depending on the character of the legislation at issue, the Rules Committee staff may have been monitoring the bill's progress.

The legislation that comes to the Rules Committee varies considerably in its visibility, and so does the amount of information committee members have before they specifically focus on it. According to a senior committee staffer: "One-fifth is so important that you know a lot about it. Two-fifths — you know a little about; you read the magazines, *CQ,* you talk to people. Two-fifths — you know very little."

The Rules Committee's agenda is effectively set by the party leadership. The party leaders decide on the floor schedule, they inform the Rules Committee chair, and the chair determines the committee's agenda accordingly. The leaders need rules to bring most major legislation to the floor, but neither the members of the Rules Committee nor the party leaders want rules granted far ahead of floor action. As a Rules Committee staffer explained:

> We don't want to grant a rule certainly not before a couple of weeks before it's ready to come to the floor. The reasons for that are that if you grant a rule early, say a month before the bill is scheduled, something may come up, like someone may have an amendment that they want to offer, and that way you'll have to go back and redo it. So, if you wait to grant the rule until about time for the legislation to actually get to the floor, there will be no need to revisit it. The other reason is that after seven days, any member can call up a rule, and that means that the Republicans can do that and while they can't do a lot of harm, they can cause some trouble by calling a rule up.

Communication between the Rules Committee and the party leaders is constant and takes place at all levels — senior staffers, members, and top leaders. The committee's chief staffer is in nearly continuous contact with the Speaker's and the majority leader's senior floor aides. (The Rules Committee's offices and hearing room are in the Capitol a short walk away from the offices of the party leaders.) Often there is at least one person who is a member of both the committee and the core leadership group and thus serves as an information conduit between them. In the early 1990s, both David Bonior and Butler Derrick did so. Members of the committee and the leadership see each other on the floor of the House and at various meetings. A large proportion of Rules Committee Democrats are whips — in the 103rd Congress, all but two — and attend the weekly whip meetings. The Speaker and the chair of the Rules Committee can easily confer on the floor of the House, and occasionally the Speaker asks the chair and sometimes the other committee Democrats to his office to talk. "The leadership offices are an important source of information, especially on the political aspects" of bills, for Rules Committee Democrats, a committee aide explained. And Rules Committee Democrats, who are themselves quite central in the House information network, in turn provide information to party leaders.

After the decision to schedule a bill has been made, a majority member of the Rules Committee will often announce on the House floor that all members desiring to offer amendments to the legislation must submit their amendments to the Rules Committee or, occasionally, have them printed in the *Congressional Record* by a certain date. Only when the committee expects to grant a totally open rule is this procedure not followed.

The decision on the character of the rule will almost always have been made before the formal meeting of the Rules Committee. "Usually the rule has been drafted before the formal meeting," a staffer said. "There are very few decisions actually made during the course of those formal meetings." A half-hour before a scheduled Rules Committee hearing, committee Democrats meet in the chair's office just off the hearing room. The issues involved in the business of the day are discussed and "in 90 to 95 percent of the cases, that is where the rule is decided." An extremely contentious issue will require more discussion. "If it's something very controversial," a staffer explained, "it may be discussed, say, on a Tuesday for when the meeting on the rule will be on a Wednesday or it may be discussed over the course of the day as things develop or very rarely a special meeting of the Democratic caucus [of the Committee] may be held." On bills with many amendments, such as the defense-authorization bill, Rules Committee staff aides will work with the staff of the committee of origin to "classify the amendments in some coherent fashion and then present the information" to Rules Committee members. "On DOD [Department of Defense] there were several meetings to decide which amendments to allow," a senior staffer explained.

Occasionally Republicans are brought in and a bipartisan deal is negotiated. But because of the nature of its charge, the Rules Committee is a partisan committee and true bipartisanship is rare. Even when members of the two parties work together to decide which amendments to allow, as on the DOD authorization, the relationship resembles an armed and wary truce.

Rules Committee meetings typically combine the hearing and the formal decision on the rule. The prospective majority and minority floor managers for the legislation at issue explain and justify their rule requests. Other members, whether from the committee or not, who want to offer amendments may appear and argue their cases.

Extremely close working relationships between the Rules Committee and party leaders have characterized all recent party leaderships; the extent to which the leaders have become involved in the actual crafting of rules has, however, varied somewhat depending on the Speaker. O'Neill was the least active, becoming involved only on major legislation; Wright was the most active, getting involved with most rules. Foley, members and staff agreed, was somewhere in between. According to a Rules Committee staffer, Foley was just as involved as Wright but was not so directive. "We don't micromanage," a Speaker's aide said.

Yet in attempting to meet their members' legislative expectations, all recent Speakers have involved themselves in the crafting of rules to an extent unimaginable in the prereform House. The decision on the character of the rule is so closely tied to legislative strategy that, on major legislation, the leaders cannot leave that decision solely to others. In some cases, in fact, the rule emerges out of negotiations over the substance of the legislation; conflicts are resolved by promising members floor votes on their preferred language. More generally, rules, as they have evolved over recent years, have become too powerful a tool for leaders to eschew. Members expect their leaders to use rules to save floor time, to protect them from no-win votes when possible, and to pass legislation in a form that is satisfactory to most Democrats.

Even without explicit instructions from the Speaker, the Rules Committee majority attempts to be helpful to the leadership. "The committee is extremely mindful of what the leadership wants," a senior committee staffer explained. "The purpose of Rules is to get the Democratic program through the House," a committee Democrat said. Both the method of selection and the sort of members selected produce a Democratic Rules Committee membership that tries to anticipate what the leadership wants and that generally shares the leaders' views and goals. With two members of the core leadership group on the committee and thus taking part in the committee caucus, the rest of the committee will know how the leadership sees the strategic situation and what it believes should be done.

Occasionally policy beliefs or constituents' views will make it impossible for a Rules Committee Democrat to support the party position on a committee vote. Because the Democratic leadership cannot afford to lose control of such a powerful instrument even occasionally, and yet wants to avoid when possible asking Rules Committee Democrats to cast votes that will really hurt them at home, the leaders insist on maintaining a generous party ratio on the Rules Committee. The ratio of nine Democrats to four Republicans allows one or two Democrats to defect without the majority party losing control. Rules Committee Democrats who intend to defect are expected to inform their colleagues and make sure their votes do not cause a problem.

Once in a great while, the committee does not comply with leadership requests, but when this happens miscalculation, not defiance, is the reason. In 1988, for example, unexpected absences and sloppiness about notification by Democrats intending to defect resulted in Republicans winning an initial committee vote on the rule for bringing to the floor the conference report on a major education bill. At issue was the Helms amendment—a provision banning dial-a-porn services (toll phone lines that provide pornographic messages). The provision was added to the bill in the Senate; the House had twice voted to instruct conferees to accept it; but the conferees had replaced it with a "technical fix"—a provision whereby such services would be available only to subscribers (see Morehouse 1988b). Unsatisfied with this solution, Republicans wanted a vote on the Helms language, and Republican Whip Trent Lott, a Rules Committee member, offered a rule making that possible as a substitute to the Democrats' rule. Several committee Democrats were absent, so when two Democrats voted with the Republicans, Lott's motion won. The acting chair immediately adjourned the meeting, thus blocking final action.

The two defecting Democrats were under considerable constituency pressure from the fundamentalist Christian right on the issue and, while concerned about the probable unconstitutionality of the Helms amendment, were personally strongly offended by dial-a-porn operations. Still, neither expected his vote to be decisive; one had explicitly notified his colleagues of his intentions, he said. The other had not known about the absences. Rules Committee Democrats and the leadership regrouped, and when the Rules Committee reconvened, it approved a rule allowing for a clean vote on the conference report but also for a separate vote on a new bill consisting of the Helms amendment. Dial-a-porn had, however, become too hot an issue, and the rule for the education bill was defeated. The leaders had been worried that the imbroglio might sink the education bill itself. However, the House quickly added the Helms amendment to it and the Senate easily passed the amended bill.

In another unusual case, the hearings built momentum for a type of rule the Speaker opposed, and committee members got carried away. As a participant explained:

> There was an instance last year on most-favored-nation treatment for China, and there were two proposals — the Solomon proposal, which simply denied it, and the Pelosi proposal, which made it conditional. And the Speaker had said very clearly that he wanted no amendments allowed to Pelosi, and this was a case in which it ended up that the committee went rogue. What happened is that these people came in and they asked for certain amendments and the committee was saying, "Well, that sounds reasonable" and "that sounds reasonable," so that when it came to a vote, they really kind of couldn't vote no. And I saw what was happening and told Moakley, "Maybe you had better suspend because you know it is pretty clear what is going to happen." And he said that is not going to do any good.
>
> Well, I went and talked to [a Speaker's aide] who got very upset about it. But then later, Moakley talked to Foley, and Foley asked that we kind of hold it in abeyance for a while. And then he came to talk to the Democrats in caucus up here in the Rules Committee office, and he wasn't yelling or screaming or anything like that. He was just explaining very carefully why he thought it was bad policy. And essentially Foley worked out some changes to the amendments with Pelosi. So it was handled that way and that is Foley's style.

These instances by their character as well as their infrequency demonstrate the extent to which the Rules Committee is, in fact, an arm of the leadership. As a committee Democrat summed up the relationship:

> We do what the Speaker wants. If he has a keen interest in a piece of legislation and sends us a message he wants thus and so, that's what we do. We'll go back to him sometimes and say, "Mr. Speaker, we think it should be done this way" and sometimes he'll agree with us and sometimes he won't. Of course, the Speaker doesn't take a direct interest in every piece of legislation or certainly every amendment.

The Rules Committee has lost its independence, but in return committee Democrats have gained the opportunity to become, in effect, a part of the leadership. As early as the mid-1970s, Bruce Oppenheimer, a student of the committee, reported that some members played a "field commander" role for the leadership. He quoted a senior Rules Committee Democrat:

> It's sort of like people on the Rules Committee treating themselves as if they were responsible field commanders reporting to the chief in Paris. Intelligence comes from us to the leadership. Our responsibility is to inform, advise, and execute. We're in charge of the field operation, and sometimes you have to act on your own best judgment. You can't always confer. Sometimes you need reserves like Biemiller calling up Madden. At times you make leadership decisions for the leadership. Even in a military operation it works the same way. (1977, 104)

Rules Committee Democrats act as an arm of the leadership by structuring rules so as to accomplish party legislative objectives. They may simply accede to the Speaker's specific request on the character of a rule or, when no such instructions are forthcoming, they may use their own best judgment. But the purpose is the same. "Our purpose" in designing rules, a committee Democrat explained, "is to get what the Speaker, the leadership, the Steering and Policy Committee perceive to be the Democratic program through the House."

Balancing Collective and Individualist Objectives

While House Democrats expect their leaders to use rules to save time, protect them from no-win votes, and facilitate the passage of legislation they favor, they also expect to be able to pursue their goals through individualist strategies, and doing so may dictate offering amendments on the floor. Tight rules impose constraints on individualist strategies, constraints that members may consider unacceptable. "The construction of special rules," a congressional scholar said some time ago, "has become much more an act of political and parliamentary craftsmanship" (Bach 1981, 553). Complex rules are even more powerful tools today and their construction calls for even greater political astuteness. "You have to get the balance just right," a participant explained. "You have to protect the rights of the minority, protect the rights of a variety of different coalitions within the House in order to pass the rule. And sometimes it's a delicate balance."

The requirement that every rule must be able to command a House majority limits the strategic use of rules but serves as a salutary reality check for party leaders. It lets them know quickly when they are encroaching too much on their members' freedom of action. To be sure, party cohesion is high on rule votes; increasingly, members are expected to support their party on such procedural votes. Nevertheless, if Democrats are truly dissatisfied with a rule, they will vote against it, and, since Republicans seldom support an even slightly controversial rule, high Democratic cohesion is needed to pass such rules.

In constructing rules, a party leader said, "You've got to be fair, number one, or at least be perceived as being fair. Secondly, we obviously try to protect our people from embarrassing votes, or votes that could hurt them politically by constructing a rule that would give them an option other than one that would probably prove politically damaging, so we do that as much as we can." He elaborated, "You have to be fair. If there is something of major importance to the public and the Republicans want to express their point of view, you just have to allow them to, for instance, on the death penalty . . . because if you are perceived as being unfair, you're not going to get your rule passed." A Democratic member of the Rules Committee made the same points:

> First of all you have to have 218 votes on the floor or a majority on the floor to pass the rule and so if we do anything too outrageous the rule will be defeated, and the Republicans of course are always working our more conservative members who want the opportunity to vote on some of these issues also. So that while we can protect Democrats from time to time we cannot protect Democrats if the issue is so hot that a number of Democrats want a vote on that as well as the Republicans wanting to vote on that.
>
> You can't absolutely protect members. For example, we absolutely cannot protect members from having to vote on abortion. That is very clear. The first few years that I was here, we tried to do that and we lost some rules. So we always make in order an abortion amendment if it is requested. The same thing on the drug-free workplace right now. Some members would like to be protected, but it is clear that, if we tried to protect Democrats, that enough other Democrats who would like to go on record on that subject would join

with the Republicans to defeat the rule, so there are limits on how far we can go in protecting Democrats.

When a significant number of Democrats really need a vote, the leadership will provide the opportunity. If a delicate compromise is at issue, leaders will attempt to structure the choice situation so that no damage is done to the legislation's prospects. Thus, in 1991, many liberals, including particularly members of the Black Caucus, needed to show their strong supporters that they favored a civil-rights bill much tougher than the compromise version; the leaders gave this group a vote on its own substitute. Every year at budget time the same Democratic subgroup wants the chance to vote for its preferred priorities before supporting the more realistic but less ideological congenial leadership budget resolution; every year, a liberal–Black Caucus substitute is made in order. Moderate to conservative Democrats are also accommodated when they really need to go on record. If their need is to show fiscal responsibility, for example, a cut that would otherwise be made in committee will be offered as an amendment on the floor.

By accommodating members as individuals whenever possible, especially on district-related matters, Rules Committee Democrats help the leadership maintain that delicate balance between collectively furthering members' goals through the passage of legislation on the one hand and facilitating members' individualist goal-seeking strategies on the other. "We have some quasi rules," a committee Democrat explained. "We try to help out Democratic members who may not have been able to get their amendment in committee or may need to put it on an appropriations bill because there may be a time factor. . . . We try to be fair to the minority as well, but obviously we're a little fairer to the majority." Another asserted that a part of the Rules Committee majority's job was "to take care of the needs of our membership. People come up there and they want an amendment made in order or they don't want something made in order. If it's reasonable and they have been supportive of our issues [we try to help them]. . . . I try to do the same thing with Republicans who come up there, reasonable ones."

That the committee and the party leadership usually do strike a balance members consider satisfactory is indicated by their high success rate in passing rules on the floor. To be sure, members not infrequently gripe when restrictive rules bar them from offering amendments; the whip meeting discussion of a rule for a budget resolution depicted in chapter 7 offers a vivid illustration. But, despite unusually intense complaints, that rule passed, as do most rules, with the support of the great majority of Democrats.

During the 1980s and early 1990s, the House defeated — either on passage or by defeating the motion to order the previous question — slightly more than one rule per year on average (the mean is 2.33 rules for the initial consideration of legislation per congress for the period from 1981 through 1992). As the frequency of restrictive rules has increased, defeats have not become more common. Not a single rule was lost during the 102nd Congress. Furthermore, Democrats overwhelmingly support rules on floor votes, and their level of support varies little with the restrictiveness of the rule at issue. In the 100th and 101st Congresses, there were roll calls on fifty-two rules for major legislation as defined earlier. The mean Democratic vote in favor on passage or on ordering the previous question (whichever was closer) was 93 percent. Open rules were supported by 98 percent of Democrats on average; modified open rules — those that are somewhat but not highly restrictive — by 90 percent; modified closed rules, which are considerably more restrictive, by 93 percent; and closed rules by 96 percent.[3] Thus, while occasionally the leadership and the committee miscalculate and a rule is defeated, most of the time they craft rules that the overwhelming majority of Democrats finds acceptable.

Special Rules as Strategic Tools: An Analysis of Rule Choice

The increased ideological homogeneity of the Democratic membership and the problems of legislating in the reformed House during the period of political adversity that confronted Democrats in the 1980s and early 1990s led, I have argued, to a change in members' expectations. Democrats increasingly expect their leaders to employ aggressively the tools available to them.

Rules have great strategic potential. The Democratic leaders increasingly use rules as strategic tools (see table 8.3). Since the early 1980s, items on the leadership's own agenda are almost always brought to the floor under complex and restrictive rules. Major legislation on which the leaders are active is also now usually considered under such rules, and the more centrally the leaders are involved, the greater is the likelihood that a complex restrictive rule will be used.

A systematic, quantitative analysis of the determinants of rule choice in the contemporary House lends further credence to the arguments made here. The data on the rules under which major legislation was brought to

3. The categorization of rules was done by me by examining the text of the rule and, where necessary, the debate in the *Congressional Record*. In close calls, I relied on Don Wolfensberger's judgment, and my categorization is very close to his.

Table 8.3   The Increased Strategic Use of Special Rules

	Congress				
	91st (1969–70)	94th (1975–76)	97th (1981–82)	100th (1987–88)	101st (1989–90)
% of leadership agenda considered under closed or complex rule	0	50	100	85	100
% of items with any leadership involvement considered under closed or complex rule	26	32	60	81	84
% of items with major leadership involvement considered under closed or complex rule	29	32	71	88	92

the floor in the 100th and 101st Congresses can be employed to that end. If restrictive rules are, in fact, devices the majority-party leadership uses to advance the goals of the members, one would expect that the party leaders would use restrictive rules on major legislation of importance to the party members, when the members are relatively united, and when procedural or substantive complexity or partisan opposition endangers passage of legislation in a form satisfactory to majority-party members.

For the purpose of this analysis, open and modified open rules are defined as unrestrictive, and closed and modified closed rules as restrictive. This is done because the proportion of completely open rules is so low, but it should be remembered that modified open rules also restrict amending activity, though to a lesser extent than modified closed rules. According to this definition, 48 percent of the major legislation in the 100th and 101st Congresses was brought to the floor under restrictive rules — 47 percent in the 100th and 49 percent in the 101st.

Major party leadership involvement on the measure is used as an indicator that the legislation in question is of importance to the party since the Democratic party leaders are most likely to become actively involved in the legislative process on legislation important to the members. If floor votes on the measure fall along partisan lines, reasonable agreement within the majority party and opposition from the minority party can be inferred; floor coalitions that are party coalitions are expected to be positively associated with the likelihood of restrictive rules. Opposition from the minority party is not the only threat to the floor passage of legislation

Table 8.4   Predicting Rule Choice (Logistic regression estimates)

Variable	B	t
Constant	−3.289	3.84
Major leadership involvement	2.676	3.56
Party floor coalition	1.561	2.43
Omnibus or multiply referred	1.283	2.06
Likelihood ratio statistic ($-2 \times$ LLR)	32.6	
Significance	.000	
N	71	
Percent correct	77.5	

that majority-party members want. The procedural complexities raised by multiple referral of legislation and the uncertainties of bringing legislation of very broad scope to the floor under a procedure allowing all germane amendments are also threats. Consequently, multiply referred or omnibus legislation should be more likely to be considered under restrictive rules than nonomnibus, singly referred legislation.

The hypotheses are confirmed by the data (see table 8.4). In a logistic regression, the independent variables as a group provide a highly significant improvement over the null model; all of the predictor variables' coefficients are significant and of the correct sign. Restrictive rules are more likely on legislation on which the majority-party leaders are involved in a major way, legislation that evokes partisan floor coalitions, and legislation that is multiply referred or omnibus.

The equation correctly predicts 77.5 percent of the rules — a good but far from perfect performance. Underlying the dichotomy of restrictive versus unrestrictive rules used in the analysis is a four-valued categorization. An examination of the relationship between the actual value according to that categorization and the value predicted by the equation is enlightening. The equation predicts open rules and modified closed rules very well; 83 percent of the open rules were correctly predicted by the equation to be unrestrictive rules; 84 percent of modified closed rules were correctly predicted to be restrictive rules. The equation does less well in correctly predicting that modified open rules will fall into the unrestrictive category (68 percent correct), but since modified open is a borderline type this lesser performance is to be expected. More disturbing and more interesting is the model's relatively poor performance for closed rules (67 percent correctly predicted).

Table 8.5   Partisan Conflict on Rule Votes: Major Legislation in the 100th and
101st Congresses

Rule Type	% Party Votes	N
Open	22	18
Modified open	47	19
Modified closed	72	25
Closed	33	9
Total	48	71

An examination of the legislation considered under closed rules reveals
that it is somewhat less likely than major legislation as a whole and much
less likely than legislation considered under modified closed rules to evoke
partisan coalitions on the floor or to be omnibus or multiply referred
(though it is considerably more likely than legislation considered under an
unrestrictive rule to be one or the other). Distinctively, however, on every
bill considered under a closed rule, the majority-party leaders were involved in a major way. The Rules Committee simply does not report a
closed rule unless the party leadership is actively involved in the legislative
process on the bill in question. That closed rules are infrequently used on
partisan legislation may indicate something about the limits on the use of
highly restrictive rules. Yet in a few cases, closed rules were used on contentious partisan legislation. That and even a cursory case-by-case examination of the use of restrictive rules provides a reminder that special rules,
especially as they have evolved in recent years, are powerful and flexible
tools that can be adapted to address a variety of problems.

That Democrats have become increasingly adept at using rules strategically is suggested by House Republicans' increasingly vehement response to restrictive rules. Bitter charges of heavy-handed dictatorship are
not uncommon (see Cheney 1989). And Republicans are increasingly voting against restrictive rules, especially against so-called modified open and
modified closed rules, which with their complex provisions are most likely
to be used strategically. Of rules for major legislation in the 100th and
101st Congresses, 56 percent of the open rules and 44 percent of the
closed rules were approved by voice vote on the floor, but only 16 percent
of the modified open and modified closed rules were. Conversely, modified
open rules and particularly modified closed rules were much more likely
than either open or closed rules to see a majority of Democrats voting in
support and a majority of Republicans opposed (see table 8.5). In fact, on

the average only 14 percent of House Republicans voted for the modified closed rules that elicited floor roll calls.

Structuring choices via complex rules has become a central leadership strategy. Democrats expect their leaders to use their control over the form of rules aggressively to facilitate the passage of legislation and yet to do so with sensitivity to the members' individual needs and interests. Democrats' consistent and near-unanimous voting support for the rules leaders bring to the floor — and Republicans' opposition as well — suggests that the leadership successfully meets the members' expectations in this regard.

Leaders, Committees, and the Prefloor Legislative Process

> When I first started off here . . . there wasn't much respect for the membership and what the membership needed or wanted. . . . A few barons made the decisions. And those barons had so much power the leadership could not tell them what to do. . . . [Now] because the membership has more power, the leadership has more power to get the barons to do what needs to be done. . . . If the membership and the leadership want something, the committee basically becomes the vehicle.
>
> *A House Democrat*

The formulation of policy and the crafting of legislation are primarily committee jobs in the House. The institutional and political changes of the past two decades have, however, drawn party leaders more deeply into the prefloor (and postfloor) legislative process. Legislation that a significant segment of the Democratic membership or the party collectively needs for policy or electoral reasons often now requires leadership attention well before the floor stage. To meet their members' expectations, leaders must more frequently intervene to ensure that legislation members want reaches the floor and to shape legislation so as to enhance its floor prospects. Increasingly the party leaders' role extends beyond facilitating, through coordination and mediation, House passage of legislation members want; as the range of legislative preferences broadly shared within the party has grown and as the political and policy stakes of certain House legislative decisions have risen, members have come to expect the leaders, acting as their elected agents, to step in when necessary to ensure a satisfactory outcome. That often requires party leaders to exercise policy leadership — to take a central part in fashioning such legislation.

Party and Committee Leaders: Expectations and Interactions

To enact the legislation members want, party and committee leaders must work together. They have an interest in doing so since both are agents of and ultimately responsible to the Democratic Caucus. The 1970s reforms made the autocratic committee chair who could thumb his nose at the strongly held sentiments of the Democratic rank and file a thing of the past. Moreover, committee leaders as a group are now quite representative of the Democratic party in the House, much more so than their counterparts of the early 1970s. In the 92nd Congress (1971–72), committee and subcommittee chairs were much less supportive of the party position than the typical member; the mean party-support score of full committee chairs was 47.2 percent and that of subcommittee chairs was 53.6 percent, compared with 65.6 percent for all Democrats and 74.9 percent for northern Democrats (Smith and Deering 1990, 132). Average party-unity scores rose over time for all segments of the party but, because committee leaders' scores rose even faster than those of the rank and file, the gap lessened in the postreform 1970s and disappeared in the 1980s. In the 99th Congress (1985–86), full committee chairs averaged 79.6 percent party unity and subcommittee chairs averaged 78.8 percent—which is almost identical to the 79.3 percent score for all Democrats and close to the 83.1 percent score for northern Democrats.

Despite ideological like-mindedness and a shared dependence on the caucus, bases for possible conflict between party and committee leaders also exist. For committee leaders, the committee's legislation will rank as top priority; party leaders' priorities may differ. Most of the time, the intense preferences of committee members and of interest-group constituencies will weigh more heavily with a committee leader than the less intense and perhaps still unformed preferences of the Democratic membership as a whole. The party leaders are more likely to think ahead to the reaction of the Democratic membership and beyond that to the possible reaction of broader attentive publics or even the public at large.

Decision-making authority at the committee level is vested in committee members. To influence committee decisions the party leaders must use the leverage their powers and resources give them; they must persuade and pressure committee leaders and members. Especially (but not only) if party and committee leaders disagree in their analysis of the political situation, such pressure may be resented.

Committee leaders are "a little bit ambivalent" in their expectations of the party leadership, a knowledgeable member reported. He continued:

> They expect the leadership to be helpful and to provide succor when needed to help their legislation through. At the same time they like to be left alone in

order to produce it in a form that they find acceptable. They are jealous of their prerogatives and yet when they get in trouble, they look for help, they look for the leadership to be there. But, by and large, I think they feel a responsibility to report something the membership as a whole can support. I know on the Appropriations Committee we are far more sensitive today to putting out bills that conform to the Gramm-Rudman requirements, that conform to the budget resolution, that do not present opportunities to the other party to just blow us out of the water and put our members who are increasingly sensitive to those kinds of things on the spot.

Although the seeds of possible conflict are present, by and large, party and committee leaders' expectations of each other support a reasonable working relationship. "Committee chairmen like to think that the leadership is investing in their issues and putting effort behind their initiatives," a member explained. Committee leaders talk about being part of a team. They see themselves as having a job to do and expect the party leaders to facilitate their performance in a number of routine and nonroutine ways. They expect the leadership to schedule their legislation for floor consideration efficiently and sensibly; they expect the leadership to protect existing committee jurisdictions from encroachment; and they expect the leadership to help them pass their legislation on the floor when they need assistance. As one chair explained, "We want support; we have a job to do and we want their help with committee appointments, with space, with staff, with getting legislation on the floor, and with passing legislation on the floor." Leaders of committees that seldom report controversial legislation emphasize the routine aspects, especially expectations about scheduling. One praised the leadership because "we know when our bills will be up" well ahead of time. Leaders of committees that frequently handle contentious legislation are most likely to mention leadership help at the floor stage as one of the expectations. As one said, "If it's a controversial bill, you want to make sure the leadership expends some effort on it; that makes a lot of difference. You want the Speaker to be telling people he wants that bill; the majority leader to be telling people he wants that bill."

That the leadership will protect their committees' jurisdiction from encroachment by other House committees and from threats created by the Senate's looser procedure is an expectation held by all committee chairs. This is the expectation leaders find most troublesome, the one most likely to lead them into conflict with committee chairs. The parties to a jurisdictional dispute are likely to have radically different perceptions of a fair resolution. They often place a higher priority on the jurisdictional aspects of the outcome, while the party leaders usually must be more concerned with the policy dimensions.

Although committee leaders expect the party leadership to provide them with services that make their jobs easier, they recognize that party leaders do have a broader constituency and broader responsibilities. Most consider a form of policy leadership—"providing a framework for a coherent party posture," as one chair expressed it—a legitimate and necessary part of the leadership's job. A chair talked about the relationship:

> Basically a committee chairman has to work with the party leadership, and the leadership has to work with the committee chair. It is sort of a situation where you can't have one out of sync with the other. For instance, a committee chair by himself with "his committee" can't just run out and implement policy without looking at the broader picture. The reason that leadership is there is they are the ones who are looking at the broader picture and have to put the legislative agenda together and make some sense out of the whole. . . . The leadership must understand that the committee chairman has got to develop the legislation the best that he can with his committee. You can't override that committee, even when the leadership wants to, and secondly, the committee chair has got to understand that you just can't go off willy-nilly without thinking about where the leadership is and where they want to see ultimately the policy go.

In carrying out this sort of policy leadership and in helping committees enact their legislation, party leaders sometimes must intervene in committee decision making. Committee chairs seem to accept that in general as a matter of course. "The leaders have no choice but to get involved," the chair of a major committee said, "and it is important that they get involved before things get out of hand." In a specific instance, if the committee chair's preferred course conflicts with that of the party leaders, intervention by the leaders may be perceived as unwanted pressure. However, chairs no longer expect to exercise the degree of autonomy enjoyed by the chairs of the committee government era. Too little leadership attention is as likely as too much intervention to elicit a committee chair's complaint. "It's inevitable that there will be clashes," a chair explained. "The leaders can't do everything everyone wants them to do."

Party leaders expect committee leaders to report important legislation in a timely fashion and in a form that is acceptable to most Democrats and that will pass on the House floor. Party leaders no longer expect that committee chairs will usually be able to perform these legislative tasks without help. Party leaders would like committee chairs to work out their jurisdictional disputes among themselves, but do not expect that they will do so.

Contact, direct or indirect, between committee and party leaders is almost continuous. Asked how frequently he talked with the party leaders, a chair said, "Every day, constantly." Asked the topics of conversation, he replied:

About do they want this bill or don't they want this bill. About the schedule. Telling them this bill is coming up. Asking can we bring this bill to the floor next week. It's me and the Speaker. It's me and Tom Foley. It's our staffs. Constant communication. It's essential for us to work together. Around here communication is 99 percent of the problem. Things get filtered out. It's necessary and important for chairmen and the leadership to work together and we do.

Much of the contact is at the staff level. Steering and Policy Committee staffers monitor the committees on a continuous basis; each staff aide is responsible for a number of committees and is expected to keep abreast of his or her assigned committees' activities, to understand the politics and the substance of the legislation. During the Wright speakership, the Speaker's senior legislative aide held a monthly lunch for committee staff directors. Under Foley, such meetings, although less regular, occur about as many times per year. Informal contact is much more frequent. "On any day, we probably talk with eight to ten staff directors about something," a senior Speaker's aide explained. Staffers in the majority leader's and whip's offices also are in frequent communication with committee staffers, especially those with legislation approaching floor consideration. The leaders' senior legislative aides try to be on the floor during every roll-call vote. Since most members will be there, the aides can accomplish a lot of business quickly. In addition, they are available to members, including committee leaders, who want to get a message to the leadership rapidly and perhaps somewhat informally.

Recent Speakers have held occasional meetings with all the committee chairs, most often early in the year to discuss the agenda and scheduling. Special circumstances may increase the frequency of such meetings. In the spring of 1992, the Speaker was meeting with the chairs weekly. Beset by the House bank scandal, the leaders wanted the chairs to produce legislation so attention would be diverted, they needed the chairs' input and support for internal administrative reforms, and they hoped to decrease the amount of intraparty backbiting. The Speaker attempted to use the meetings to accomplish all these purposes.

Much more usual and frequent, however, are meetings of the relevant committee leaders with the leadership to discuss some specific issue or problem. Depending on the legislative season, the leaders may have from one to half a dozen such meetings a day. Casual contact between committee and party leaders is also frequent. They see each other on the floor and, in many cases, at whip meetings and at meetings of the Steering and Policy Committee. In sum, committee leaders have considerable access to the party leaders and the leaders have multiple opportunities and sources for keeping informed of committee activities. Both are prerequisites to the sort of early involvement in the legislative process in which party leaders now often engage.

Party Leaders as Coordinators and Mediators

When party leaders involve themselves in the prefloor legislative process they usually do so to help committee Democrats produce and bring to the floor legislation that can pass, to advance the legislative aims of the Democratic membership, or, frequently, both. To meet the members' expectations of legislative outputs, congressional party leaders have probably always engaged in considerable coordination and mediation, but institutional and political developments since the early 1970s have made such tasks an increasingly large part of the job.

Helping Members and Moving Legislation

For a variety of reasons, a committee may not report in timely fashion a bill that the party membership or even its own party contingent wants for policy reasons or needs for reelection purposes. The committee's members may be unrepresentative of the membership at large; the committee may be beset with internal leadership problems; the various parties to a dispute may all believe strategic advantage is to be gained by outwaiting their adversaries. Although such problems are certainly not new, the consequences of the 1970s reforms can exacerbate them. Because committees can expect considerably less deference on the floor of the House than they were granted in the prereform era, writing a bill that will pass can be more difficult and may require compromises more unpalatable to committee Democrats.

When such a problem arises, there is now a greater expectation that the party leaders will do something about it—that they will induce the committee to act. Providing the leaders with the powers, resources, and leverage to make successful intervention in such cases a reasonable possibility was a major motive behind the reforms of the 1970s. Much leadership time is devoted to persuading members at loggerheads to compromise and prevailing on committee leaders to be responsive to the needs of significant segments of the Democratic membership or to the sentiments of the party as a whole. Most often, these efforts occur behind the scenes, but sometimes a more public forum is employed. Usually the leaders' approach is direct: they talk to, cajole, or lean on those causing the problem. Sometimes such efforts are supplemented by indirect means: others from inside or outside the chamber are enlisted to aid in the persuasion effort.

A farm-credit bill and legislation granting veterans certain rights of appeal passed by the 100th Congress illustrate the strategies leaders use to influence committees and committee leaders to act. Many midwestern Democrats had won election in 1986 by promising to do something about the farm-credit crisis, yet by the summer of 1987 the committee had still not begun marking up legislation. The Steering and Policy Committee staffer who monitored the Agriculture Committee had been periodically asking about progress since early in the year, but this form of low-intensity pressure produced no discernible effect. The Speaker held several private meetings with the committee chair, but this too failed to generate movement. In July, the Speaker called a meeting of the Democratic members of the credit subcommittee and the chair of the full committee; the chair of the Democratic Caucus and the majority whip, a member of the Agriculture Committee, also attended. The Speaker asked those members who believed it substantively important to pass credit legislation before the year was out to raise their hands; all did. Reminding his audience that many Democrats, including most of those present, had made passage of such legislation a campaign promise, he asked those who believed it to be politically important to do so to raise their hands; again all did. If legislation was not reported out before the August recess, it probably would not pass that year, the Speaker warned. Asked by the worried committee chair if he would refuse the bill floor time after the recess, the Speaker said he would schedule the bill but he believed that, unless it passed the House quickly, the Senate could not finish it this year. "I don't want you to think I'm prodding you," the Speaker concluded, to general laughter. The committee chair promised to move expeditiously and the committee reported a bill within a week. In this case, many of the Democrats who cared most about passing farm-credit legislation were on the committee. The Speaker's intervention provided them with ammunition for pressuring committee and subcommittee chairs who were dragging their feet.

For a number of years, a group of younger Democrats — some but by no means all members of the Veterans' Affairs Committee — had been attempting to change the appeals process for veterans' benefits but had been stymied by opposition from the chair of the committee. They wanted a floor vote on their proposal; he had for years managed to prevent one. After separate meetings with the two sides, the Speaker called them all to a joint meeting. By the end of a lengthy discussion during which the leaders and the younger members pressed him to promise a vote, the chair reluctantly agreed to move if the Senate did. Continued leadership pressure forced him to deliver when the Senate acted.

The chair of the Veterans' Affairs Committee had been able to avoid a floor vote in the past because that committee's legislation was generally considered under the suspension procedure, which blocks floor amendments. That the Speaker controls the suspension procedure and could force Veterans' Affairs Committee legislation to get a rule that would allow amendments was never explicitly mentioned during these meetings, but was clearly a factor in everyone's calculations.

Members are constantly asking the Speaker and, to a lesser extent, the other leaders to intervene and influence committee decisions. Party leaders can and do use their influence with committee leaders to do favors for individuals or small groups of members. A member learns that a project very important to her district is running into trouble in committee. Would the Speaker have a word with the subcommittee chair? The Speaker promises to look into the matter. A freshman member finds to his horror that a bill on the suspension calendar would wreak harm on his district. Can the Speaker do something? The Speaker takes the bill off the calendar, asks the sponsor to work out the member's problem, and has a leadership staffer help out. Two words in a conference agreement spell big trouble for a company in a member's district. The member asks the committee chair to change them, but meets resistance. Will the Speaker ask the chair? The Speaker says he will talk to the chair. A junior member's first significant legislative effort is stuck in the Senate committee and time is running out. Will the Speaker call the senator who is holding up the bill? The Speaker picks up the phone and makes the call. Such assistance is among the most valuable of the selective benefits leaders can offer. Usually, however, party leaders restrict such favors to matters about which the committee leaders are indifferent.

When party leaders ask committee leaders to do something they really would rather not do, it is almost always to benefit the membership as a whole or at least a significant subgroup of the membership. Farm-state members needed a farm-credit bill; a group of younger Democrats, many of whom were themselves Vietnam War veterans, felt strongly about changing the veterans' appeal process. The Democrats from textile-producing states who went to the Speaker in 1988 requesting his intercession with the chair of the Ways and Means Committee provide another example. Both houses had passed legislation restricting textile imports; however, if normal procedures were followed and the bill went to conference, the conference report would be filibustered in the Senate and the bill would die. The textile-state members, a sizable group, wanted the Speaker to persuade the chair of the Ways and Means Committee to accept the Senate version rather than go to conference. Because the bill was so important to these members' constituents, the Speaker undertook the task. He argued that, in this case, an obligation to these colleagues should override the chair's understandable concern about protecting his committee's influence; in response to the chair's complaint that he was tired of bailing out the Senate, the Speaker responded, "You'd be bailing out the Democratic party, not the Senate." The chair agreed to forgo a conference.

When the membership collectively needs the legislation at issue, the party leaders are most likely to get involved and have the strongest basis for doing so. In October 1991, with criticism of the House at a high and going into a presidential election year, the House Democratic party needed a solid legislative accomplishment before adjourning for the year. The big highway bill, which would benefit all parts of the country, fit the need nicely. When the chair of the Public Works Committee expressed doubt about reconciling the House and Senate versions by the Thanksgiving adjournment target date, the Speaker called him into his office. As Speaker Foley reported at an October 30 news conference, "I had a conversation with Mr. Roe last night, and we agreed the highway bill will be done by Thanksgiving" (Alston 1991b, 3178). Earlier in the year, the Speaker had prevailed on a reluctant Ways and Means Committee chair to move legislation extending unemployment benefits. Required by the budget agreement to pay for an extension with new taxes and loath to take on that fight, Rostenkowski, the chair, had resisted more gentle persuasion. However, the joint House-Senate leadership had included the extension in its publicly announced Democratic antirecession program and, particularly for Democrats from areas suffering high unemployment, this was crucial legislation. To meet the members' expectations the leaders had to get the legislation to a vote and, in fact, Speaker Foley was criticized for not moving more strongly earlier.

Multiple Committees as a Stimulus to Leadership Involvement

When more than one committee is involved in formulating legislation, committee leaders may not be capable of providing the intercommittee coordination and mediation needed to bring an acceptable bill to the floor. If the bill at issue is an important one, these tasks fall to the party leadership, which is after all the only central leadership in the chamber.

The frequency of instances in which several committees are involved in legislation has increased enormously since the early 1970s as a result of rules changes and of adaptation to the political environment. A mid-1970s rules change provided for the referral of legislation to more than one committee for the first time in the House. The adverse political environment of the 1980s often made omnibus bills — bills of enormous scope — either necessary or desirable, and sometimes both. The political climate also exacerbated conflict between the Appropriations Committee and the committees charged with authorizing programs. These developments all worked to draw the party leaders more deeply and frequently into the prefloor legislative process. Because committees are more often unable to produce legislation satisfactory to the Democratic membership without help, the leaders, in order to satisfy members' expectations, must get involved.

MULTIPLE REFERRAL

In part because it was unable to realign committee jurisdictions, the House in 1975 instituted multiple referral of legislation. The multiple-referral rule instructs the Speaker to refer a bill to all committees with jurisdiction. The Speaker can choose among three types of multiple referral: joint, in which a bill is referred to two or more committees simultaneously; split, in which various titles or sections are referred to different committees; and sequential, in which a measure is referred to several committees in sequence (see Davidson and Oleszek 1992, 131). As amended in 1977, the rule allows the Speaker to set a reporting deadline for committees under any sort of referral.

Over time, multiply referred legislation has become an increasingly prominent part of the House workload. In the 94th Congress, the first with multiple referral, 6 percent of the measures introduced were multiply referred; this increased to a little more than 10 percent in the next congress and averaged 11 percent for the four congresses between 1977 and 1983; it rose to 14 percent in the 99th Congress and averaged 18 percent in the 100th and 101st Congresses (Young and Cooper 1993, 214). Multiply referred measures now make up a considerably greater proportion of major legislation than they do of all legislation. The congressional agenda of major legislation as defined earlier included 6 percent multiply referred legislation in the 94th Congress and 11 percent in the 97th, figures very close to those for all measures. However, in the 100th Congress, 28 percent of major legislation was multiply referred and, in the 101st, 32 percent. To the extent that multiply referred legislation is likely to require leadership involvement in the prefloor legislative process, its increasing frequency among the most important legislative measures of a congress contributes to the increased activism of party leaders at the prefloor stage.

To which committees a bill should be referred is usually a routine decision and is actually made by the parliamentarian. Decisions about possible reporting deadlines are less likely to be routine. By custom, the Speaker sets reporting deadlines only on sequentially referred legislation, but he decides what type of referral to make. Whether or not deadlines are set and what they are can affect legislative outcomes. Members of the committees involved and others interested in the legislation's fate make requests and sometimes demands about referral deadlines. And the

Speaker uses his power to set deadlines as a strategic tool to advance or retard the progress of legislation.

The farm-credit legislation discussed earlier is a case in point. Because the Agriculture Committee had included as title 3 of its bill a provision establishing a secondary market in agricultural loans, the Banking Committee and the Energy and Commerce Committee, which regulates securities trading, claimed jurisdiction and demanded referral. Although the Speaker was eager to move the legislation, these committees had a valid claim, and furthermore the Agriculture Committee's version of Title 3 was badly flawed; the committee had written legislation in an area where it lacked expertise and had, in the words of a participant, "screwed up." The Speaker wanted the Banking Committee and the Energy and Commerce Committee to fix the legislation, but to do so quickly. Members of the leadership "leaned on" the committee chairs and got them to agree. The Banking Committee was given eight days; the Energy and Commerce Committee, a little more than two weeks.

This case illustrates the usefulness of the Speaker's power to set time limits, but also its limitations. Although rules give the Speaker the power to set reporting deadlines unilaterally, they are usually set through negotiation. If in the farm-credit case one of the committees had insisted the time it was given was insufficient, it could have refused to report and, while that would not block floor consideration, the committee's opposition to the legislation on the floor would likely make passage much more difficult. The Speaker's power to bring legislation to the floor without their concurrence does make committees more likely to be reasonable about the time they need. And if the legislation at issue is of great importance to a significant group of Democrats, as in this case, committees are likely to be even more amenable to leadership pressure for quick action.

As the end of a congress nears, decisions about the time limits on referral become increasingly consequential. In the fall of 1988, the Judiciary Committee was given a very short sequential referral of the veterans' appeal-board legislation, leaving enough time for that bill to complete the legislative process. After leaning on the chair of the Veterans' Affairs Committee to report a bill, the Speaker was not about to let the legislation die in the end-of-the-congress rush.

A more generous time limit—and a broadly drawn referral—for the Energy and Commerce Committee to report back banking-reform legislation contributed to that bill's demise. This legislation evoked a nasty battle between the Banking Committee and the Energy and Commerce Committee, one in which jurisdictional and policy disputes reinforced each other. The Energy and Commerce Committee reported late in the session and its language severely encroached on the Banking Committee's jurisdiction, that committee charged. The time remaining before the 100th Congress adjourned for the last time was insufficient to work out the differences between positions that were intensely held and intertwined policy and jurisdictional concerns. Had the Speaker considered the legislation top priority, he would have had to impose an earlier reporting deadline. Although he believed such legislation was needed, no great demand for it was evident in the Democratic membership, and reconciling the committees would be a difficult and perhaps costly process; consequently he decided the bill could wait until the next congress.

Banking Committee Democrats, having expended enormous time and energy to produce a bill, wanted to see it pass. They were, however, unwilling to negotiate with the Energy and Commerce Committee on its terms, which entailed conceding the committee's jurisdictional claims. Banking Committee Democrats wanted the Speaker to bring their bill to the floor under a rule that would allow the Energy and Commerce Committee to offer its language as amendments. This was a prescription for a lengthy and acrimonious floor fight. "No one has come up to me and said they really want this bill," a leader remarked pointedly to Banking Committee Democrats. "Some have said they don't." At a meeting with all the Democratic members of the Banking Committee, the Speaker refused their plea but did promise to make the legislation a priority early in the next congress.

Committee leaders often believe that their chances of passing a bill depend on their working out their disagreements before the bill reaches the floor. If they cannot do so on their own, they often turn to the party leadership. The catastrophic- health-insurance bill passed by the House in 1987 is a case in point. This bill was referred to the Energy and Commerce Committee and to the Ways and Means Committee, committees led by two of the strongest chairs in the contemporary House, John Dingell and Dan Rostenkowski, respectively. Speaker Wright, early in the process of bill development, had suggested adding a provision covering drug payments in order to put a Democratic stamp on the administration's bill. The notion was popular among Democratic-leaning groups of the elderly and was eagerly embraced by many committee Democrats, most particularly by California's Henry Waxman, the liberal chair of the Health and Environment Subcommittee of the Energy and Commerce Committee.

The bills the two committees produced, while similar in thrust, differed in a number of ways; the Energy and Commerce Committee bill was more generous. Because the administration had become increasingly hostile to the legislation, committee proponents believed that they had to resolve their differences before taking the bill to the floor. "A single bill with all the important players on board is necessary," a committee leader said. "And to get it, you, Mr. Speaker, need to be involved." "You need to take a major role," the Speaker was told. In this case, committee leaders, known as jealous guardians of their own turf, invited the Speaker's participation because without it they could not produce a bill that was likely to pass. At a meeting of the committee and subcommittee chairs, Wright brokered an agreement that resulted in one bill.

In the case of the farm-credit legislation, Tony Coelho, majority whip and a member of the Agriculture Committee, brokered an agreement between the committee chair, Kika de la Garza (D-Tex.), and the chair of the Energy and Commerce Committee, John Dingell, on the secondary-market provision. His efforts made it possible to move the legislation well before the session adjourned, as the Speaker wanted. And, given administration opposition, a bill opposed by the Energy and Commerce Committee was unlikely to have become law.

Even if no major controversies arise, coordination and mediation efforts by party leaders may be necessary to produce an acceptable bill when legislation is referred to a number of committees. The Americans with Disabilities Act, legislation outlawing discrimination against the disabled, had bipartisan support. Democratic Whip Tony Coelho was its chief sponsor; President Bush endorsed the concept during his 1988 election campaign; and support was widespread on both sides of the aisle. However, the referral of the bill to four different committees in the House and the adamant opposition of small business meant that passage was far from assured.

When Tony Coelho resigned from the House in June 1989, he asked Steny Hoyer, then vice chair of the caucus, to take over the task of shepherding the bill to passage. Foley, upon becoming Speaker, designated Hoyer the leadership's point man on the legislation. With four committees involved, the task encompassed monitoring multiple meetings of the subcommittees and full committees, encouraging action, and negotiating substance. Such coordination enhances the prospects of passage for any bill referred to a number of committees because such multiple referral entails enormous procedural and jurisdictional complexities. In this case, there were additional potential problems. A participant explained Hoyer's task and why it was crucial:

> The disability rights groups just wanted us to pass the Senate bill. But House members felt this was a major piece of legislation that really shouldn't be passed in a cavalier fashion and that the Senate bill had too much a cavalier, pasted-together character to it. It wasn't even that the chairmen were insisting on their jurisdictional rights but a feeling it needed some careful going over. And that's what Hoyer's job was — to work with the chairmen in a bipartisan

fashion and come up with deals. They went over the entire bill and came up with a much more careful piece of work. There was a major deal with Education and Labor, then one with Energy and Commerce — both bipartisan. Another with Transportation. . . . And then a smaller deal with Judiciary. If this hadn't been done we might have had a lot more trouble on the floor. There was some unease with the bill anyway. Members felt it was the kind of bill that, if no one knew what was in there, there could be some real problems. Every few years there's some kind of legislation passed that produces a major political problem. . . . People know that can happen and it makes them nervous.

In this case, then, the leadership provided coordination and quality control and worked out a lot of smaller differences among committees. A bill members wanted was brought to the floor in timely fashion and in a form that protected members from potential political problems.

That members now expect their leadership to fix the problem when legislation they want bogs down is indicated by their criticism of and pressure on leaders when they fail to get legislation moving quickly enough. During the 101st Congress, the Ways and Means Committee and the Education and Labor Committee were at loggerheads over childcare legislation; each came up with a distinct approach and refused to budge. The party leaders exhorted and pressured the committees to compromise, but to little avail. Subjected to a barrage of criticism from House Democrats, the party leaders intervened directly; Speaker Foley "personally brokered the final package," an aide explained. Because many members very much wanted the legislation and the Democratic party needed it to show that it could produce legislation addressing major problems affecting the American people, the leaders had no choice but to step in.

The party leaders are more likely to involve themselves in multiply referred than in singly referred legislation, data show. In four selected congresses since the institution of the multiple-referral rule, the leadership was active on a mean of 82.5 percent of multiply referred major measures (the mean for singly referred, nonomnibus major measures for the same four congresses was 60.5 percent; see table 4.6).

OMNIBUS LEGISLATION

Omnibus legislation — legislation of great substantive scope that often also involves, directly or indirectly, many committees — is highly likely to require leadership involvement at the prefloor stage. Because of the number and magnitude of issues and the number of political actors involved in omnibus measures, putting together and passing such legislation often requires negotiation and coordination activities beyond the capacity of committee leaders.

In the 1980s, deep policy divisions between President Reagan and House Democrats resulted in the much more frequent employment of omnibus measures. The major battles came to revolve around budget resolutions, reconciliation bills, and other omnibus measures centering on questions of basic priorities. During the 97th Congress, Reagan had used these measures as vehicles for his agenda. After the 1982 elections, in which Democrats won back twenty-six House seats, stalemate became an ever-present threat. The inability of the president and House Democrats to agree on individual appropriations bills or of either to impose its preferences on the other resulted in the frequent use of continuing resolutions (CRs), which are omnibus appropriations bills. Since CRs are must-pass legislation and thus difficult for a president to veto, they also provided Democrats with a vehicle for enacting into law provisions that Reagan would have vetoed had they been sent to him as freestanding legislation. Much the same is true of reconciliation bills: they too are major, multiprovision measures that are difficult for a president to veto and can be used to force upon the president legislation he would not otherwise accept. Reconciliation bills, however, became a prominent part of the congressional agenda because they provided the mechanism by which the unpalatable decisions necessitated by the huge deficits could be bundled; a package in which all shared the pain could be passed, if often with difficulty, while separate bills cutting popular programs and raising revenues might well have been impossible to pass. Finally, in their effort to compete with the White House for media attention and public credit, House Democrats began to package legislation on issues such as trade and drugs into high-profile omnibus measures.

As a result, omnibus measures increased as a proportion of the congressional agenda of major legislation from none in the 91st Congress to 8 percent in the 94th (all budget resolutions) to 20 percent in the 97th and 100th, the two congresses of the 1980s for which data are available. In the 101st Congress, the first of the Bush administration, the proportion decreased again to 8 percent, which included, however, massive reconciliation bills that were among the most important pieces of legislation of the congress. The party leaders were active on every omnibus measure in the selected congresses for which data are available. During this period, omnibus legislation was of a character that dictated the involvement of the majority-party leadership.

That leadership coordination and mediation are prerequisites to legislative success even on omnibus legislation that commands bipartisan support is well illustrated by the omnibus drug bill of 1988. In early May 1988, the Speaker decided the House should pass such legislation and do so on a bipartisan basis. As it was an election year, time was short. Yet a comprehensive attack on the problem of illegal drugs involved a number of complex issues — ranging from criminal-justice matters to treatment to prevention — and, consequently, a large number of committees.

The Speaker asked Majority Leader Foley to coordinate the effort and set a target date for the committees to complete their work. Foley's task and that of leadership staff aides working with him was to monitor the work of the eleven committees involved, to identify problems and try to work them out, and to push the participants to move quickly and settle their disputes expeditiously and, whenever possible, on a bipartisan basis. One of the problems, an aide explained, was that "a lot of committees did each other's work" — they invaded one another's jurisdiction. "They've been told to work it out by the deadline or we'll do it for them or work it out on the floor." Periodic meetings of the chairs were held to maintain the pressure. To keep the effort as bipartisan as possible, Foley also conferred with Minority Leader Bob Michel. When the committees were unable to reach a substantially bipartisan agreement, the issue was pushed up to Foley and Michel; which of those questions would be presented to the membership to decide on the floor was determined in negotiations between them. By the August recess, the bill was ready for floor consideration and the rule had been adopted by the House. Only the party leadership's efforts made such swift action possible.

Settling disagreements between House and Senate versions of the legislation required an even more massive and complex coordination and mediation effort and had to be accomplished within a much shorter period of time. The leadership managed the process throughout; the majority leader presided over marathon meetings in which compromises on a myriad of difficult issues involving many different actors were hammered out; both the Speaker and the majority leader were personally engaged in working out the final sticking points. The logistics were such that leadership direction was a prerequisite to legislative success.

APPROPRIATIONS VERSUS AUTHORIZING COMMITTEES

A certain level of conflict between the authorizing committees and the Appropriations Committee is endemic to the House (see Fenno 1966; Schick 1980). Most of the standing committees of the House are authorizing committees and, as such, are charged with drafting legislation that establishes or continues the legal operation of a federal program or agency or sanctions a particular type of obligation or expenditure. Authorizing committees are supposed to decide policy. The Appropriations Committee, by contrast, is supposed to fund programs that committees such as Education and Labor or Foreign Affairs have authorized; it is not supposed to legislate — that is, include policy provisions — in the appropriations bills it reports. In practice, this distinction often becomes blurred. In the 1980s and early 1990s, the conflict between the president and congressional Democrats made the passage of some reauthorization legislation extremely difficult, and in some cases impossible. In such cases, legislative provisions were often included in appropriations bills, which are must-pass legislation. Because they are difficult to veto, CRs, which bundle together a number of appropriations bills, were used to force the president to accept legislative provisions he would otherwise have vetoed. But legislating through an omnibus appropriations bill tends to cut the authorizing committees out of the process even more and thus further reduces their authority.

Conflicts between the Appropriations Committee and authorizing committees, like other intercommittee conflicts, are often brought to the Speaker for mediation. One side appeals (or both appeal) to the Speaker for help. If the conflict threatens to disrupt the legislative process, the leaders must take a hand even if not invited. In the simplest example, authorizing-committee Democrats believed the Appropriations Committee did not fund their programs generously enough. In one recent instance, Banking Committee Democrats complained that the Housing and Urban Development appropriations bill reduced funds for homeless programs and for Urban Development Action Grants too much. They wanted to sit down with the chair of the relevant subcommittee of the Appropriations Committee and work it out so as to avert a floor fight, they told the Speaker. Would he delay the granting of a rule for the bill? Always eager to avoid battles among Democrats, the Speaker agreed and asked the whip to work with the members toward a satisfactory resolution.

Often members request more substantive help; for example, a group from the Armed Services Committee and from the Appropriations Committee approached the Speaker for help in keeping the Midget Man missile alive. The Senate Appropriations Committee had "zeroed it out" (given it no funding). These members believed that the missile, because of its mobility, was much less destabilizing than the large MX missile. To keep the weapons project going, Bill Chappell (D-Fla.), chair of the Defense Appropriations Subcommittee, had to insist on about $1 billion for it in conference. The Midget Man's proponents were afraid that Chappell, a strong supporter of SDI, might be amenable to killing off the Midget Man to reduce the competition for funds. Would the Speaker talk to Chappell, they asked, and not tell Chappell it was at their instigation? The Speaker agreed but said, laughing ruefully, that all year he had been pressuring Chappell to spend less; now he would be doing the opposite.

Although it is typical for authorizing committees to get upset about the Appropriations Committee legislating in appropriations bills, sometimes this is the only way to get desired provisions enacted. In the mid- and late 1980s, arms-control proponents who were members of the Armed Services Committee, as well as those who were not, regularly prevailed upon the leadership to insist on the inclusion of arms-control amendments in the defense-appropriations bill. These provisions had passed the House as amendments to the defense-authorization bill, but Democrats could not enact that legislation over presidential opposition.

The most common authorizing-committee complaint concerns overstepping by the House or Senate Appropriations Committees. The Agriculture Committee chronically complained that Jamie Whitten, the chair of the subcommittee of the Appropriations Committee who also chaired the full committee, simply rewrote the whole farm bill if he did not like what the Agriculture Committee had done. The Public Works Committee complained bitterly that the Appropriations Committee included unauthorized projects in its bill and that this would encourage members to do end runs around the authorizing committee.

When grumbling threatens to turn into warfare, the leadership must step in. In the spring of 1988, for example, the Armed Services and Appropriations Committees were at loggerheads. Armed Services, concerned about authorizing in the appropriations bill, had included in its authorization bill a provision barring appropriated funds from being obligated until authorized. "Last year, the DOD appropriations bill was never on the floor. It was taken care of in the CR," an Armed Services Committee leader complained. "And it changed the authorization bill completely." The Armed Services Committee provision "would give us no flexibility at all. It would straightjacket us. It's line-item authorization," the chair of the Defense Appropriations Subcommittee replied. "We've worked together well. Last year was unusual with the budget summit." If the Armed Services Committee provision were to stand, "we'd have to wait for the Senate to do authorizations," an Appropriations Committee leader added. "That will slow us down and we'll have to have another CR." The chair of the Defense Appropriations Subcommittee offered to, in essence, abide by the provision if it were removed from the legislation. "We'll compromise on language," the Armed Services Committee leader replied, but not remove it altogether. "Gentlemen's agreements get forgotten in conference."

After several meetings and much informal negotiation by the leadership staff, an agreement was worked out. The Armed Services Committee would drop the offending provision; the Appropriations Committee would agree not to legislate in their bills and not to exceed authorization levels. Members of the Armed Services Committee could participate but not vote in Appropriations Committee conferences when those conditions were not met. And the Appropriations Committee would not seek waivers of points of order from the Rules Committee to protect provisions that were otherwise against the rules.

A major floor fight had been averted, but, even though the agreement was put in writing, no one expected it to provide a permanent solution. The character of the relationship between the Appropriations Committee and authorizing committees, particularly during a time when the normal legislative processes often had to be supplanted by extraordinary processes, did not lend itself to a permanent solution embodied in fixed, clearly defined roles for each committee. The best the leadership can do is work out a temporary truce that satisfies (at least minimally) the contending parties and averts a divisive battle.

When an authorizing committee's primary complaint is about the Senate Appropriations Committee, the leaders are more limited in what they can do. The House Foreign Affairs Committee had amicable relations with the relevant subcommittee of the House Appropriations Committee, but because the Senate did not pass an authorization bill for a number of years and legislated in the appropriations bill instead, the members of the Foreign Affairs Committee felt excluded from the policy process. Committee leaders would have liked the party leaders to take up their cause and make it a priority in their relations with the Senate, but understood that House leaders had other concerns that took precedence. Other House committees have also been concerned about the Senate's tendency to legislate in appropriations bills. In late 1987, for example, the chair of the House Committees on Interior and Insular Affairs and on Energy and Commerce expressed extreme unhappiness with what the Senate was doing on the nuclear-waste issue. J. Bennett Johnston (D-La.), chair of both the Senate Committee on Energy and Natural Resources and the Energy and Water Subcommittee of the Senate Appropriations Committee, was simply bypassing the authorization process altogether, they said, and doing all his legislating through the Appropriations Committee. And he was trying to shove an important provision on nuclear waste down their throats.

In response to such complaints, House party leaders can and do talk with their Senate counterparts; they may have their staff aides talk with Senate committee and leadership staff aides. They have threatened to appoint, and occasionally actually appointed, conferees from the House committees offended against. However, the differences in the legislative processes of the two chambers make such problems both inevitable and frequent. The House party leaders' capacity to influence Senate decisions is limited; they have some leverage but no authority. Because satisfying the members' legislative goals requires Senate action, the party leaders ration that limited influence, expending it in major amounts only when legislation really central to their members is at issue.

Policy Leadership

In recent years, policy leadership has become an increasingly important part of the majority-party leaders' job. The decline in Democratic ideological heterogeneity made policy leadership possible; as the range of legislative preferences shared by the Democratic membership grew, members were less likely to fear that any leadership influence on legislative substance would promote the goals of other members at their expense, and leaders gained credibility when they claimed to be speaking for their membership. Changes in the political environment made policy leadership necessary. A relatively homogeneous membership confronted by an environment hostile to its legislative aims will expect its party leaders to do what is necessary to produce the legislation members need and want, and that requires policy leadership.

As the party leaders have been drawn more deeply into the prefloor legislative process as coordinators and mediators, they have inevitably become more involved in matters of legislative substance. When the leaders broker agreements among committees, when they coordinate the work of many committees and press committee members to reach agreements among themselves, their actions affect policy. By contrast, party leaders of the committee government era, who most often restricted their involvement to passing on the floor legislation reported by autonomous committees, influenced the substance of legislation less.

Policy leadership in the current era is more than simply a by-product of the leaders' behind-the-scenes efforts to mediate conflicts and coordinate action. When the Congress legislates through bills of great substantive scope and political consequence, it is not simply the party leadership's coordinating capacities that dictate its involvement. Rather, given that every member as an individual and the membership as a collectivity has a significant stake in such legislation, members are unwilling to defer to the judgment of committee leaders, to rely solely on committee leaders to interpret their will and to protect their political and policy interests. On such legislation, only the party leadership as the elected agent of its members possesses the legitimacy to speak and make decisions for the members. In a climate of political adversity, especially when a hostile president stood ready to cast congressional Democrats' policy actions in the most negative possible light, decisions about the substance of highly salient and controversial legislation can have significant repercussions for the image of the Democratic party and thereby may affect members' electoral fate.

House Democrats need and want the legislation to pass, but in a form that is readily defensible in the public arena. When committee leaders are not sufficiently sensitive to such concerns, Democrats expect their party leaders to intervene.

Budget Politics

A central aim of the 1974 Budget Act was to provide a mechanism that would allow and, in effect, force the Congress explicitly to make a comprehensive decision about the overall level of government spending, taxing, and the deficit, and about broad priorities (Ellwood 1985; LeLoup 1977). Even in the 1970s, when the budget resolution had limited substantive effect, it was symbolically important. Passing the budget resolution is critical to maintaining the reputation of the Congress as a functioning legislature and to maintaining the majority party's reputation for competence in governing. The budget resolution can be read as a statement of priorities; because the process has always been highly partisan in the House, the press and attentive publics have taken the House resolution as an expression of Democratic priorities. "A budget document is obviously an economic document," a House Budget Committee leader explained in the late 1970s, "but it's also a political document."

In the 1980s, budget resolutions became substantively more significant (see Gilmour 1990, especially 112–15). President Reagan and his congressional supporters in 1981 used the budget process to enact a wholesale change in governmental priorities — shifting spending from domestic to military programs and drastically cutting taxes (see Sinclair 1983, 190–213). Reconciliation — a process by which the committees bring current law into accordance with the budget resolution — had been little used in the 1970s; in the 1980s, it became a regular part of the process and gave the budget resolution real bite. As the deficit grew, the decisions that had to be made in the budget process became increasingly tough. The sharp policy differences between Republican presidents and House Democrats only exacerbated the difficulties of arriving at budget decisions.

As these decisions became more central and more contentious, they also became more publicly visible. Republican presidents used that office's unparalleled ability to command media attention to hammer congressional Democrats for refusing to agree to their budgets and attempted to brand Democratic proposals as irresponsible, out of touch with the middle class, and just more examples of discredited tax-and-spend politics.

The House majority-party leadership has been deeply involved in the budget process from its inception (Ellwood and Thurber 1981; Sinclair 1992b). When the political and policy stakes of budget decisions rose enormously in the 1980s, leadership involvement increased. It became even more essential to pass budget measures (the budget resolution and reconciliation legislation) in the adversarial climate of the 1980s and 1990s, and yet doing so became more difficult. Within the constraints imposed by enormous deficits, putting together a package acceptable to a large proportion of the Democratic membership is a formidable task. In a contentious atmosphere, these measures had to be readily defensible in the public arena; they had to be crafted so as to provide a minimum of ammunition to the opposition, and to enhance the collective image of House Democrats.

The House Budget Committee was unable to meet these objectives in the adversarial climate of the 1980s and early 1990s without help. Even full leadership assistance has not guaranteed success. From its inception, the relationship between the Budget Committee and the party leaders has been different from that between the leaders and other committees. By statute, a Speaker-appointed leadership representative sits on the committee and, by custom, that representative is the majority leader. He and the minority leadership's representative are the only permanent members of the committee; the remainder of the membership rotates. A committee leader from the late 1970s commented on the relationship between the Budget Committee and the party leadership:

> The Budget Committee and the Rules Committee, in my opinion, are both and have to be very closely allied with the leadership; in fact, [we] have to be sort of arms of the leadership, because when you put together a budget document, you're putting together a position paper. The committee leadership has to have leadership support or it won't go anyplace, so, therefore, we consult frequently, and witness the fact that the majority leader is a member of the committee.

The majority leader sitting on the committee "sends an important signal," a recent Budget Committee chair explained, "because we are the only committee in the Congress where there is a leadership representative." He talked about the current relationship between the committee and the leadership:

> Budget is a leadership committee by definition. Therefore, the Budget Committee chairman is basically a part of the leadership from my point of view. . . . And I would never move anything without consulting the Speaker, the majority leader, the whip. Why? Because it is a leadership committee. There is a basic understanding and that is that the relationship between the leadership and the Budget Committee chair is a much closer one than any other committee — Ways and Means, Appropriations, Energy and Commerce. Why? Because that budget is so critical, it represents the choices and priorities of the Democratic party as a whole, not just the chairman of the committee. Now one of the things the chairman has to do with the Budget Committee is to

make sure he or she is not trying to legislate his priorities, his economic policy, but recognize at all times that they were selected by the Democratic Caucus, charged with the responsibility to establish the Democratic agenda for the Democratic party.

The close relationship manifests itself in constant communication. Leadership staff aides monitor the Budget Committee's activities. The majority leader attends meetings of committee Democrats and committee markup sessions. And the committee chair reports regularly to the Speaker. A recent chair explained:

> I made it a point once a week to talk with the Speaker all during the budget process, to bring him up to date as to where we were, what was going on, and what I thought the committee wanted to do, where I thought the obstacles and the problems were and what help I needed. So the majority leader was there to report back to the Speaker, but I also made it a point to report myself.

In the early 1980s, House Democrats and their Budget Committee confronted a serious problem in passing a budget resolution drafted by Democrats. In both 1981 and 1982, Republican resolutions prevailed in the House. Although the party's reputation and clout were at stake, Democrats individually seemed unwilling to make the compromises necessary to pass a Democratic budget resolution. Liberal Democrats balked at voting for the necessary cuts in domestic spending; more conservative Democrats were unwilling to vote for lower defense spending. Too many members seemed to believe that some sort of magic solution existed that the Budget Committee just needed to find.

After the 1982 elections, which saw Democrats pick up a net of twenty-six seats, the party and Budget Committee leaders knew they now had the potential to pass a Democratic budget resolution. However, the big freshman class of fifty-seven would have to be won over and that, the leaders decided, required first of all educating them about budget realities. Many continuing members needed educating as well. Until members learned for themselves that there were no easy and painless answers, no responsible budget resolution could pass. The leaders decided that the best way for members to learn this lesson was for them to go through a budgeting exercise and look for the easy answers. Budget Committee staff aides drew up a questionnaire that simulated the tough choices the committee would have to make. The Speaker took it upon himself to make sure members went through the exercise. At numerous meetings and in individual encounters, the Speaker cajoled and pressured members to work through the budget exercise. Members were promised that their priorities as expressed in their budget choices would influence Budget Committee deliberations.

In the end, more than two hundred Democrats filled out the questionnaire. The results provided the Budget Committee majority with some guidance about sentiments within the party and gave rank-and-file Democrats some influence over the Budget Committee's resolution. The members' perception that they had had some influence and their increased understanding of the difficult trade-offs involved in writing a budget made leadership appeals for floor support more effective, and the resolution passed handily. The combination of outreach and education is still very much a part of the budget process.

With the majority leader being a member of the committee and the committee so heavily dependent on leadership aid for floor success, the party leaders have exercised some policy direction throughout the committee's existence. Budget Committee chairs have always had to be mindful of the Speaker's interpretation of the sort of resolution needed to command the support of the Democratic membership. A Budget Committee leader from the late 1970s explained the impact of the committee's need for leadership help: "If you're going to ask for the party's help, certainly you're going to have to have the majority leadership there. Now if we had more bipartisanship, this might not be so, but in the House there's absolutely no intention of the Republicans to really buy into this process." From the mid-1980s on, with the increase in Democrats' ideological homogeneity, leadership policy direction increased (Palazzolo 1992). Speaker Wright's policy leadership in 1987, while unusually aggressive, differed in degree, not kind, from the norm.

When he became Speaker in 1987, Wright perceived an unusually favorable opportunity for the Democratic party in Congress to exercise policy leadership. President Reagan was weakened by his lame-duck status, the Iran-Contra scandal, and the loss of a Republican Senate majority. To take advantage of the opportunity, Wright announced a Democratic agenda that included a number of domestic initiatives requiring increased spending and a tax increase to pay for them and to begin reducing the deficit. For this agenda to become law, the budget resolution had to allow for the appropriate increased spending, cut spending elsewhere, and specify a tax increase.

Many, perhaps most, Democrats believed that a tax increase was necessary to reach the deficit-reduction target specified by the Gramm-Rudman law, but feared the political consequences of raising taxes; doing so would play right into the hands of Reagan and his campaign to label Democrats unreconstructed tax-and-spend politicians, they feared. Most Democrats also agreed that the programs Wright had singled out deserved priority status, but increased funding for these programs when the deficit had to be reduced would require more cuts elsewhere and so would add to the difficulty of drafting a budget resolution.

Wright's task, then, was to convince Budget Committee Democrats and the members at large that doing what they themselves regarded as making good public policy would not be political suicide. In his campaign to do so, he met repeatedly with the chair of the Budget Committee and with the committee's Democratic members; he talked with the committee chairs collectively and individually with chairs who would have special responsibilities. He used whip meetings and other such opportunities to put his case to various subgroups of the membership.

Early on, Wright had suggested a formula for the necessary deficit reduction: it should come half from new taxes and half from spending cuts, which, in turn, would be evenly split between defense and domestic programs. In part as a result of its appealing symmetry, the formula seemed eminently fair, and that made it easier to sell. Wright used his daily press conference, speeches, and other contacts with reporters and interest-group leaders to sell it. His aim was to convince such outsiders that it was the right thing to do and also a politically viable thing to do. When newspaper editorials began to reflect his views, he made sure every House Democrat received copies. When poll results substantiated his judgment, they were announced in whip meetings and then widely distributed (see Barry 1989, 123, 143–56, 169–74). The Budget Committee reported the resolution the Speaker wanted and the House passed it on a predominantly party-line vote, with only nineteen Democrats voting against it.

The budget resolution committed the House to raising taxes but did not itself enact tax legislation. To carry out the instructions in the budget resolution, the House Ways and Means Committee had to report out a bill. Unenthusiastic about doing so, the committee majority nevertheless was not prepared to defy its party and the House by ignoring the budget resolution. The Speaker, however, was not satisfied with just any tax bill that raised the specified amount of revenue. He strongly believed that the bill had to be progressive. Ronald Reagan, who had said a tax bill would become law over his dead body, would certainly mount an all-out attack, and the Speaker wanted a bill he could defend. He had, after all, promised Democrats that following his policy leadership would not result in electoral disaster.

A mixture of persuasion and pressure convinced the committee to produce a bill that met the Speaker's requirements. Jim Wright talked with the committee chair and with the Democratic members; he explained his rationale in numerous private forums to House Democrats (it was frequently discussed in the weekly whip meetings, for example); he made his position clear in innumerable public statements. A Democratic Caucus meeting on the issue showed the committee that most Democrats strongly agreed with the Speaker — the tax bill had to be progressive in nature. The

Speaker let it be known to the committee that, if the bill were not, he would let liberals offer a substitute on the floor of the House. The Ways and Means Committee reported a bill that fully satisfied the Speaker's criteria.

The opportunity the political climate offered him, his ten years' experience on the Budget Committee as majority leader, and his personal proclivity toward action all contributed to Speaker Wright's assertive leadership in the 1987 budget battles. But so too did the character of the budget process as it evolved in the 1980s. Another Speaker might have been less aggressive and less overt in his policy leadership but would also have had to provide some policy direction. Because of the magnitude of the stakes, committee leaders and committee contingents cannot make the basic decisions on their own. As Bill Gray, the chair of the Budget Committee, said in early 1987 during a meeting of committee Democrats and the party leadership, "Let me be candid. We need leadership guidance. If there won't be substantial revenues, Mr. Speaker, we need to know now. If you oppose asset sales, we need to know now" (ibid., 123). During the latter years of the Reagan administration and the Bush presidency, the basic guidelines were almost always set by summit agreements negotiated by the party leadership.

Saliency, Controversy, and Leadership Policy Direction

The highly charged, confrontational atmosphere fostered by divided control in the 1980s and early 1990s raised the stakes of legislative decisions in areas other than the budget as well. High stakes combined with an extremely complex political calculus draw the party leaders into the prefloor (and often also the postfloor) legislative process.

Legislation important to traditional Democratic constituencies in recent years provoked confrontations between congressional Democrats and the president that became highly salient, high-stakes battles. Under such circumstances a minimum-wage bill or civil-rights legislation must be drafted so as to meet three criteria. It must be satisfactory to the most concerned Democrats and the most interested constituency groups—a task easily accomplished by the relevant committees, which overrepresent strongly prolabor and strongly pro–civil rights Democrats. It must also satisfy enough other Democrats so it can pass the chamber, preferably with a large enough majority to discourage a veto. Unrepresentative committees will find this harder to accomplish; the party leaders may need to persuade committee Democrats that to pass their bill and to fulfill their obligation as agents of the Democratic membership as a whole, they must compromise. In addition, given the opposition of the president, with his enormous advantage in framing the debate, the legislation had to be readily defensible in the public arena; it had to be explainable by Democrats in terms that resonated with popular values; at minimum, it had to avoid presenting the president with ammunition for battering Democrats.

The civil-rights bill of 1991 provides an example where leadership intervention led to a bill that could pass and to damage control in the public arena. A series of adverse Supreme Court interpretations had made civil-rights forces and their House allies desperate to pass a bill returning the law to the status quo ante. President Bush vetoed such a bill in 1990, and Congress failed to override the veto. By vocally and repeatedly labeling the legislation a quota bill, Bush seized control of the debate and put Democrats on the defensive. Few Democrats are substantively or politically comfortable voting against a civil-rights bill. Yet Bush's high-saliency attack made supporting the legislation also electorally risky for some members.

The legislation reported by the liberal Judiciary Committee and the even more liberal Education and Labor Committee in March 1991 met only the first of the criteria. Speaker Foley asked Whip Bill Gray to oversee the effort to draft a leadership substitute. Working with committee Democrats, with other members, especially southerners, concerned about supporting legislation that could be labeled a quota bill, and with interest groups on both sides of the issue, Gray worked out a compromise. Among its provisions was an explicit ban on quotas. The resulting legislation satisfied, at least minimally, both the strongest civil-rights supporters and the Democratic membership as a whole—250 Democrats voted for it, only 15 against. As a result, the total vote for the bill did not drop below its total of the previous year—the minimum standard of success the press had imposed (see Biskupic 1991a, 1498)—and this despite nine Republicans switching from aye to nay. In addition, the bill as rewritten, especially in its ban on quotas, gave individual members political cover and allowed the party as a whole to cut its losses.

In late 1991, the Education and Labor Committee reported a higher-education reauthorization bill that turned the Pell Grant program into an entitlement and thereby would have shifted $62.7 billion into the mandatory-spending category over the next five years. The party leadership believed that, during a period of extreme budget stringency, the bill was probably impossible to pass and certainly impossible to defend. "I do not feel creating an entitlement is the best way to proceed," said House Speaker Foley, pointedly and publicly. Added Majority Whip Bonior: "There are a good number of people who would have problems with an entitlement in the House and the Senate" (Zuckman 1992a, 729). Under intense pressure from the leaders, the committee chair eventually gave in; he himself introduced a substitute bill that eliminated the entitlement feature.

Sometimes a measure will be so politically delicate that the party leaders are unwilling to rely on the committee process but, directly or indirectly, take over the drafting process themselves. Although this is still unusual, such instances have become more frequent in recent years.

Early in 1988, House Democrats had defeated President Reagan's package of military aid for the Nicaraguan contras. In getting the votes to do so, the leadership had promised moderate Democrats a quick vote on a package of nonlethal aid. A measure had to be produced swiftly, it had to satisfy the moderates who had voted for aid in the past and still be acceptable to liberals who had opposed all aid, and, finally, it had to conform to the strictures of the Nicaraguan peace agreement. Speaker Wright asked Chief Deputy Whip Bonior, who had been highly active on the contra-aid issue for years, to draft the plan. Bonior pulled together a group of members representing the various Democratic factions and they assembled a package. Although Bonior tried to involve them, Republicans refused to participate.

On campaign-finance legislation in 1991, Speaker Foley was unwilling to rely on the normal operation of the subcommittee selection system. Such legislation was too highly charged politically, too partisan, too complex, and too difficult to pass. To put together a package that was publicly defensible, preferably one that would put Democrats on the offensive, and that could pass the House, an especially politically adept group was needed. This was particularly so because an effort to pass a campaign-finance bill in 1990 had left some bad blood. Foley chose a chair and a task force of members from the House Administration Committee, the committee with jurisdiction. The group managed to write a bill that Common Cause endorsed and that passed the House.

The ethics–pay raise task force of 1989 was charged with an even more politically delicate task. This case illustrates the sort of circumstances that require leadership policy direction and also shows the strategy of inclusion in action at the prefloor stage. In early 1989 members of the House voted to deny themselves a pay raise that would have gone into effect automatically had no vote taken place. Intense public anger stirred up by radio talk-show hosts and media hype frightened members into forcing a vote on a pay raise that most of them wanted and needed. Members expect their leadership to help them get what they want while protecting them politically. Speaker Wright, already under an ethics cloud, had failed at both. He and the rest of the leaders—both then and after he resigned in the middle of the year—knew that passing a pay raise was important to the reestablishment of the leadership's credibility.

Shortly after the pay raise failed, Speaker Wright and Minority Leader Michel appointed a task force to put together an ethics bill. Everyone knew the package would include a pay raise but, by tacit consent, this was not discussed until late in the process. Wright chose as chair of the task force Vic Fazio, an extremely well regarded, politically adept member who, in the summer leadership shake-up, would be elected vice chair of the Democratic Caucus. The other Democratic members, all chosen by the Speaker, were Martin Frost, a politically savvy member of the Rules Committee with close ties to the Speaker, David Obey, who had chaired the commission that had last revised House ethics rules in the late 1970s, David Bonior, the chief deputy whip, Louis Stokes of Ohio, a previous chair of the House Ethics Committee, and, ex officio, the majority leader and the majority whip. The Republican members, appointed by Michel, also included as ex officio members two leadership figures — Minority Whip Newt Gingrich of Georgia and Jerry Lewis of California, the chair of the Republican Conference.

Previous experience with the politically explosive issues of pay raises and ethics reform had taught all concerned that above all bipartisanship had to be maintained and that, to make it publicly defensible and salable to members, the package had to include both a pay raise and ethics reform, which, in this case, meant abolishing honoraria. The leadership and the task force also agreed that the process should be as low in visibility as possible to minimize the opportunities offered to House members or outsiders to exploit it for political gain. However, the process needed to be open and sensitive to members' concerns and preferences.

The task force met at least once a week from late March until November, when the package was passed. In the fall the meeting schedule accelerated to twice a week, and in October to three times a week or more. Early in the process each task-force member was allowed to bring one aide to meetings, but, as negotiations became more delicate, staff was excluded.

After an intensive "education process" during which task-force members became thoroughly familiar with current rules, four public hearings were held. In a "Dear Colleague" letter, House members were invited to testify publicly or talk to the task force behind closed doors. Many did. As objections to proposals arose, adjustments were made. The task force also met with the chairs of committees with possible jurisdiction, consulting them and keeping them informed. The purpose of the extensive consultation process, a key staff aide explained, was "to give members a sense of inclusion, of participating" in the construction of the package.

Throughout the process, Vic Fazio, the task-force chair, and Lynn Martin of Illinois, his Republican counterpart, met regularly with the Speaker and the minority leader together and separately. The purpose was both to inform and to consult. As the process neared its end, items on which the task force had reached no agreement were brought to the leaders for decision.

Less than a year after a bloody donnybrook on the issue, an ethics–pay raise package became law. (For a discussion of the passage effort, see chap. 10.) The stakes for members and their leaders were very high. Another failure would not only have deprived members of a pay raise that most very much wanted, but could easily have turned into a costly disaster for members as individuals, for the majority party, and for the institution. These circumstances demanded leadership direction.

A similar case from 1992 offers confirmation. In the wake of the House bank scandal, reforming the administration of the House was essential. To repair some of the damage done to members, to the Democratic party, and to the Congress, reforms needed to be significant and, above all, swift. But because such changes could lessen the majority party's control over House operations, and because the minority party would press for changes that did, the reforms also had to be carefully made. Under these circumstances, leaving the matter to the House Administration Committee, the committee with jurisdiction, was out of the question. Speaker Foley considered bringing a Democratic leadership-drafted resolution to the floor but, in reaction to adamant Republican opposition to such a course, agreed to set up a bipartisan task force. Appointed on March 25, the task force was enjoined to bring a package of reforms to the floor on April 10. Foley appointed to the task force himself, the majority leader, the chair of the Rules and House Administration Committees, the chair and vice chair of the Democratic Caucus, the chair of OSR, the Caucus Rules Committee, and David Obey, whose reform proposal in the 1970s had called for a House administrator. Michel's appointees also included top party officials, but not Whip Newt Gingrich, who had tried to turn the bank scandal to partisan advantage.

Although in the end bipartisan agreement proved to be unattainable, Democrats largely achieved their aims. A solid package of reforms that did not undermine majority control was put together quickly and passed in the House. While enactment of management reforms did not repair the damage done by the bank scandal, it began that process. It enabled Democrats to say they had taken the problems seriously and responded in a responsible fashion.

Party Leaders as Negotiators

High-stakes legislation, especially if it is broadly encompassing, often requires leadership intervention at the prefloor stage in the House. When agreement on such measures must be reached with political actors outside the House, the involvement of the leadership is even more often necessary. The same factors that draw the leaders into the process within the House will dictate their involvement in interchamber and interbranch negotiations. Many committees may be involved, and consequently coordination may be a major task. The magnitude of the policy and political stakes may make members leery of relying solely on the judgment of committee leaders, whose perspectives and interests may differ from their own. In addition, when a bill reaches conference, differences between the chambers and with the administration must sometimes be worked out under great time pressure. "Summit" negotiations between the president and Congress—a phenomenon of recent vintage—only take place when agreement through normal processes has proven impossible.

NEGOTIATING HOUSE-SENATE DIFFERENCES

Changes in the legislative process have provided opportunities for the Speaker to influence conference proceedings more than in the past. Although House rules give the Speaker the power to appoint conferees, he traditionally deferred to the committee chair. Multiple referral of legislation has again increased the Speaker's role: he ultimately decides how many conferees each committee will have and what their range of authority will be. When conferees are appointed from more than one committee, the addition of noncommittee members becomes less of a slap at the committees of origin. The supporters of successful floor amendments sometimes press for the inclusion of one of their number among the conferees. When the Senate has added nongermane provisions to legislation that the House has passed, Democrats from the House committee with jurisdiction request and frequently receive conference representation even though the bill at issue did not go through their committee initially.

Recent Speakers have begun to take advantage of their increased opportunities for influencing conference proceedings. After the House Armed Services Committee allowed all of the arms-control amendments approved by the House to be removed in conference in 1985 (an action that contributed to the caucus challenge and near deposal of the committee's new chair, Les Aspin), Speakers regularly made use of their power to appoint special conferees so as to protect House decisions (Blechman 1990, 38–39; see also Lindsay 1991, 58–59). Doing so was necessary if the leaders were to fulfill their obligations as agents of the Democratic members, who had supported the amendments by wide margins.

In the early fall of 1987, the House and the Senate were preparing to go to conference on a debt-limit bill. A revision of the Gramm-Rudman deficit-reduction law necessitated by a Supreme Court decision declaring a part of the original law unconstitutional was included in the debt-limit bill and was the issue in controversy. Congress had given the General Accounting Office, a congressional arm, an important role in triggering automatic spending cuts. The Supreme Court, on the basis of the separation of powers, disallowed that role. Alternative triggering mechanisms, many Democratic experts feared, could easily give the administration discretion over where to cut. In addition, senators intent on tightening up the Gramm-Rudman process were discussing proposals that would, in effect, change internal House rules.

Because the matters at issue had such serious implications for the power of Congress in the political system, the Speaker believed his institutional responsibility required that he set guidelines for the agreement. After the list of conferees was drawn up but before conferees were officially appointed, the Speaker met with them as a group and asked that they commit themselves on three points: that the agreement not amend the rules of the House; that there be no provision denying a congressional pay raise (a political ploy then being discussed); and that, under the automatic spending-cut provision, the administration be granted no flexibility in which accounts to cut. "We as the legislative body should not allow them to change priorities," he said. After laying out his criteria, he asked whether anyone would have problems with any of them. Only after giving members an opportunity to respond and hearing no objections did he say, "I want you to represent me." The Speaker also appointed Tom Foley, the majority leader, a conferee and asked him to head up the House negotiating team as he had done on the original Gramm-Rudman legislation.

Although the Speaker's appointive powers within the context of multiple referral provide a new basis for leadership involvement in conference, the political factors discussed earlier provide the more important basis. Only a single House committee has jurisdiction over the budget resolution, and all conferees are appointed from one committee. Yet the magnitude of the political and policy stakes and the chair's knowledge that he will need leadership help to pass the conference report dictate that he heed the leaders' judgment. A recent Budget Committee chair explained:

> The majority leader as a member of the Budget Committee is always appointed to sit in conference. So the leadership has their special representative there. I consider myself a part of the leadership as Budget Committee chair and therefore every day at the end of the day, if there is any development at all that was new or anything that I thought that was new, or anything that was unusual, I would go and find the Speaker and report. I would come by the office and say: "Got to see the Speaker, got to tell him what was going on. Here's what is happening. What is your viewpoint?" Why? Because I always wanted to know where the Speaker was on the various decisions that had to be made. Because when you are making decisions in the conference, you want to make sure that when you come out of that conference you have a document that your leadership is going to support. The last thing that the Budget Committee chairman wants to do is go into a conference,

make a certain amount of compromise, make a lot of decisions, and then come out and find that the Speaker does not agree with you. That is not exactly the way to pass the conference report, it is not a way to win friends and influence people. So therefore one of the things that I did very purposefully was that I made a point of every day briefing the Speaker on the progress, lack of progress, or topics that came up in that day's conference. Whenever there was a major decision to be made, such as an offer from the Senate to compromise on some issue, I would never accept it until I had had a chance to talk to the leadership unless I already knew what the leadership's decision was because we had already previously talked about it.

Any chair who expects to need leadership assistance in passing his or her conference report has reason to be responsive to leadership counsel. At the conference stage, as at earlier stages, party leaders urge committee leaders to produce legislation that is acceptable to most Democrats, that can command a House majority, and that is at minimum defensible in the public arena and preferably broadly attractive.

At the conference stage, the measure's probability of becoming law looms as an immediate concern. Earlier in the legislative process, political actors certainly consider the impact of their decisions on this probability, but because there are a number of stages and of hurdles still to traverse, other concerns may take precedence. Once a bill is in conference, political actors concern themselves with producing legislation that can pass not only their own chamber but the other as well and that will not provoke a presidential veto. Since legislation that meets those criteria may sometimes be fairly distant from most Democrats' ideal and may not have much public appeal, hard choices may have to be made. Is passing some legislation essential? Is what is possible better than nothing? Or is a good issue to be preferred to weak legislation? These are the sorts of questions the party leaders have to be involved in answering.

When the deadline for passage of essential legislation draws near, as frequently occurs at the end of a session, the leaders often become the final arbiters. The leaders tend to be especially actively engaged when the legislation is broadly encompassing and thus involves large numbers of political actors and high stakes. CRs, which may fund the entire government, and reconciliation bills, which also encompass many government functions, are the quintessential examples.

During a period of budgetary stringency and divided government, the number of points in dispute among the House, the Senate, and the administration on such bills tends to be very large, and these disputed points always includes a subset on which preferences are very intense. To get an agreement, the leaders must mediate disputes and facilitate compromises and, frequently, in the end make some decisions themselves. In December

1987, Congress had to pass a CR and a reconciliation bill before adjourning for the year. The conferences on the bills, which were going on simultaneously, made quick progress at first as is typical; when the easy issues had been decided, progress slowed. It was now mid-December and members wanted to go home for Christmas. The leaders held innumerable meetings with subsets of participants; often the leaders simply pressed members to compromise. House conferees sometimes asked the leaders to help with the Senate: would the Speaker call Senate Majority Leader Robert Byrd (D-W.Va.) and have him prod senators to engage in negotiations personally? Staff-level talks were going nowhere; would the leaders talk to a specific senator? Would the Speaker tell Byrd that so long as Senator X negotiated for the Senate, no progress was possible? The leaders usually promised to try.

Sometimes they agreed with House conferees that the House should hang tough; when the Office of Management and Budget insisted that another $1 billion should be cut from Medicare, the leaders refused. Sometimes they brokered agreements: leadership staff aides helped work out House-Senate differences on another aspect of Medicare; Majority Leader Foley pressured conferees to back down from their plan to use the reconciliation bill to make significant changes in farm law and worked out a compromise on the bill's agricultural provisions.

As time went on, the leaders pressed the members harder. The entire Democratic House leadership and Majority Leader Byrd met with key House and Senate conferees in areas where disagreements remained. When, by December 19, no agreement had been reached on two issues the leaders considered of less than first importance, the two sets of conferees were told to reach agreement by the evening or the leadership would do it for them.

On two matters of more importance, the Speaker in the end had to make the unpleasant decision to give in to the administration (see Barry 1989, 567–69). The House had included in its reconciliation bill, which had passed before the budget summit, some additions to Medicaid to help especially poor pregnant women and children; the Senate provisions were much less generous and conformed to the budget summit agreement. The administration threatened a veto over the House provision. With the Senate and the administration both opposed, the leaders knew that insisting on the House position meant no bill, and they forced the deletion of most of the extra funding. The House had hoped to use the CR to write into law the fairness doctrine requiring broadcasters to air all sides of issues; President Reagan had earlier vetoed such a bill and the Congress had been unable to override the veto. When the president threatened to veto the CR, the Senate reversed itself and backed away from a confrontation with the president. The House Democratic leaders, fearing they could not even pass the conference report without some Republican votes, decided the fairness doctrine had to come out.

The most contentious issue and the one that consumed the most leadership time was that of aid to the contras. The House CR included no new aid to the contras, but the Senate version included $9 million in new nonmilitary aid through February 1988 and at least $7 million to airlift those supplies and existing military goods to the contras inside Nicaragua. The Reagan administration, which as always strongly supported contra aid, was given an additional argument when a defecting Nicaraguan major claimed the Sandinistas hoped to build an army of five hundred thousand by 1995 and to acquire highly sophisticated Soviet weapons to arm it.

The leadership decided this was not the time nor the circumstances for a showdown on contra aid. The administration position had received a boost from the defector's story, especially in the Senate. "The problem," a Democrat said at a caucus called to discuss the issue, "is not enough Senate votes and too many Ortegas." That the CR had to pass, and pass as quickly as possible since members were eager to leave town, gave the administration a substantial strategic edge. Consequently, the leaders decided the CR would have to include some contra aid.

The task was to negotiate a package the Senate and the administration would accept that did not hurt the Central American peace process and did not lose so many Democratic votes that it would endanger the CR. David Bonior, chief deputy whip and head of the task force on Nicaragua, and David Obey, chair of the Appropriations Subcommittee on Foreign Operations, were the chief negotiators for House Democrats. They met with the Speaker, majority leader, and whip to hash out the parameters of an offer; they went off to talk with representatives of the Senate and the administration; they reported back and the process started again. Sometimes other House Democratic conferees also met with the leadership, and eventually the leaders met directly with the head Senate negotiator. Over the course of a week of negotiations, various of the leaders also met with groups of Democrats to see what members would accept. In the end, a deal was worked out. Although liberal Democrats were unhappy with its provisions, on the most crucial points it did not pose a danger to the peace process. And it enabled the CR to pass.

CONGRESSIONAL-PRESIDENTIAL SUMMITS

Relatively formal negotiations between congressional leaders and high-ranking administration officials representing the president directly are recent phenomena. The president and the Congress have resorted to summits when normal processes are, for one reason or another, incapable of producing an agreement and the costs of failing to reach an agreement are very high. (For a somewhat similar argument, see Gilmour 1990.) During the 1980s and 1990s, the deficit and the budget process, especially as revised in the mid-1980s by the Gramm-Rudman automatic spending-cut provisions, often provided the sense of emergency and the statutory deadlines that made inaction politically costly. Divided control, the sharp differences in policy preferences between Republican presidents and congressional Democrats, and the tough decisions that had to be made often stalemated the usual processes.

Actually, talks similar in some respects to the summits of recent years took place in 1980 during the Carter administration. The House budget process was proceeding along its usual course when the announcement on February 22 that the consumer price index had increased at an 18 percent annual rate in January created a crisis atmosphere. Administration officials met to plan a response and decided that further spending restraints were necessary. Spending cuts would require congressional action, and the administration consulted informally with congressional leaders.

In early March an unprecedented series of joint meetings between the administration and congressional leaders took place for the purpose of discussing budget cuts. A senior Budget Committee Democrat revealed the origins of these meetings:

> They got started because there was a very real crisis, an economic crisis. It's hard to describe, but it had a threat of doom like I haven't seen since I was a child. The markets were going to hell, the bond markets, the investment markets, everything was going to hell. There was real fear in the land. The CPI was somewhere around 18, 19 percent. And the president, apparently recognizing that he had to revise his budget, initiated some talks. I think what happened is that the president spoke to Tip and Byrd at a leadership meeting along the lines of "We've got to revise our budget." So out of that original meeting came a decision to meet informally, to see what we could do.

Chaired by Senate Majority Leader Byrd, the meetings included party and committee leaders from the House and the Senate and high-ranking administration officials. The Speaker asked Majority Leader Wright to take the lead for the House. In eight days of meetings, the participants agreed on a package of spending cuts that would balance the budget and, the congressional leaders believed, could win congressional support.

Out of these meetings came what Robert Giaimo (D-Conn.), the Budget Committee chair, called his "pink sheet," which provided the guidelines for the "chairman's mark," the draft from which the committee worked. The budget resolution approved by the committee and the House closely followed the agreement reached in the joint congressional-administration meetings. Of great importance for the future of the budget process, the resolution included reconciliation instructions — the first time they were included in the first budget resolution.

In 1982, attempts at summit negotiations were made, but they proved abortive. When President Reagan submitted a budget that no one in Congress considered realistic, calls for some sort of negotiations began. The "Gang of Seventeen," a group of high-level negotiators from the House, the Senate, and the administration, held a series of meetings but was unable to come to an agreement. After this large group failed, Reagan and O'Neill attempted to reach agreement in a face-to-face meeting but did not succeed. In 1984, the impasse between the House and the Senate on the budget resolution was broken only when Speaker O'Neill and Majority Leader Howard Baker (R-Tenn.) made a deal on defense spending. In 1985, O'Neill and President Reagan at a face-to-face meeting agreed on a budget package (see Palazzolo 1992, 124–25).

In 1987, the revised Gramm-Rudman law required a deficit reduction of $23 billion in order to avoid sequestration. President Reagan and congressional Democrats appeared to be on a collision course that would lead to sequestration when, on October 19, the stock market crashed. Reagan immediately called for negotiations and Democrats, who had been advocating talks all year, agreed.

Formal negotiation sessions began on October 27. Speaker Wright asked Majority Leader Foley to take the lead role for the House. Because the president would not take part in person and his representatives could, thus, make their agreement contingent on his later approval, House Democrats believed their strategic position would be stronger if their negotiators could make the same argument with respect to the Speaker. Foley chaired the sessions. Congressional negotiators included the chairs and ranking minority members of the House and Senate Budget, Appropriations, and tax-writing committees, J. Bennett Johnston, a senior Democrat on the Senate Appropriations Committee, and Trent Lott, the House Republican whip. After the first few meetings, the Speaker asked Leon Panetta, who was expected to succeed Gray as chair of the House Budget Committee, and Pat Williams, a liberal member of that committee, to take part. Participants for the White House were Chief of Staff Howard Baker, Treasury Secretary James Baker, National Security Advisor Frank Carlucci, Office of Management and Budget Director James Miller, and William Ball, the assistant to the president for legislative affairs.

After long and difficult negotiations, an agreement to reduce the deficit by $76 billion over two years was announced on November 20. The package included new taxes, which Reagan had so adamantly resisted and which many House Republicans still strongly opposed. Democratic liberals believed it funded defense at too high a level and cut too much from social programs. The negotiators had made the sort of difficult, unpopular compromises that only peak leaders could hope to induce their members to accept.

Newly elected president George Bush called for budget negotiations in his February 9, 1989, address to Congress. Although Democrats interpreted the call as a way for Bush to avoid political responsibility for the tough choices reaching Gramm-Rudman targets would require, they had no choice but to negotiate. When the president makes the request, the opposition party in Congress cannot refuse to talk. Given the president's greater media access, congressional leaders would find it almost impossible to explain such a refusal to the American public. Furthermore, Democrats could not produce a politically viable budget resolution on their own.

On April 14, Bush and a bipartisan group of congressional leaders announced that a budget agreement had been reached. "This is not a heroic agreement," Speaker Jim Wright conceded (Rapp 1989, 804). The agreement did avert big automatic spending cuts, albeit via "smoke and mirrors."

When an agreement must be reached and the usual processes prove inadequate, summit negotiations among top congressional party leaders and high-ranking administration officials are often the only recourse. Relevant committee leaders have usually been included in summit negotiations, but the top party leaders have been clearly in charge. Only they possess the legitimacy to make such consequential decisions on behalf of their members.

Although budget summits may sometimes be necessary, members strongly dislike that mode of decision making. Because summits only occur when tough decisions must be made, the policy outcome is likely to please few members (though many may concede that the compromises made were necessary). Furthermore, the summit decision-making process is a highly centralized one that excludes most members. During the 1980s and early 1990s, being cut out of budget decision making meant being relegated to the sidelines. Given members' desires to participate fully in the legislative process, summit decision making is likely to engender dissatisfaction, even when members concede it is necessary.

The course of budget politics in 1990 illustrates the strains such decision making can create and how the party leaders have attempted to address the problem. This case shows particularly clearly how the political environment has in effect forced the party leadership to play a more central role in the legislative process.

In 1990, House Democratic leaders would have much preferred to reach budget decisions through the usual budget process. They were aware of their members' dissatisfaction with summit decision making. Yet congressional Democrats could not on their own produce and enforce a budget resolution that actually met the Gramm-Rudman targets. And when the president called for negotiations, they could not refuse to talk.

To counter dissatisfaction among committee leaders as well as the rank and file about their exclusion from the summit decision-making process, congressional party leaders appointed seventeen members — including the chairs and ranking members of the money committees — as negotiators. However, after several months of abortive talks, the negotiating group was pared down to only the top party leaders. Again, the requisites of legislative results conflicted with the dictates of the leadership's preferred strategy of inclusion.

An agreement was reached, but was defeated on the House floor when majorities of both parties voted against it. For many House Democrats, their policy preferences and their individual political interests dictated opposition; since they had again been excluded from the decision-making process, they felt no stake in its passage.

When party and committee leaders set about drafting another budget plan, they knew that the rank and file had to be brought into the process, yet time was very short. An extraordinary series of Democratic Caucus meetings provided members with information on the status of ongoing negotiations and with the opportunity to voice their views and influence the content of the package as it was being formulated. "There were eight caucus meetings in October," a leader said. "And going from a period when people were all over the map, we ended up united."

On occasion summitlike negotiations occur in areas other than the budget. The 1983 deal to reestablish the fiscal soundness of the Social Security system emerged from a process that shows some similarities to a summit. In addition, the circumstances that led to that process were similar to those that forced budget summits: a need for action and the inability of the usual processes to produce agreement. In the early 1980s, it became evident that the Social Security trust fund was headed toward financial difficulties and needed to be shored up. The issue, however, became so centrally enmeshed in partisan politics that normal processes in both the administration and the Congress were completely incapable of leading to a solution. In late 1981, President Reagan by executive order established a commission on Social Security, his aim being to distance himself from the political problem. The commission — a large if distinguished group that met in public — was not able to agree on a solution. In late December 1982, however, a much smaller subset of commission members began serious negotiations in informal, secret sessions. Crucial to the ultimate success of the process was the inclusion of negotiators who could act as agents of the principals whose agreement was essential — President Reagan and Speaker O'Neill. George Ball, a former Commissioner of Social Security, acted as lead negotiator for the Democrats, while Dick Darman and James Baker negotiated for the White House. Both sides kept in close touch with their principals. Thus, when they reached an agreement in early 1983, it was one the president and the Speaker could accept. Only a few months later, the package was enacted into law (see Gilmour 1990, 248–50).

Contra-aid agreements in 1988 and 1989 involved the House party leadership in direct negotiations with the administration. In 1988, after both President Reagan's and the Democratic leaders' aid packages had been defeated in the House and the Sandinistas and the contras had reached a cease-fire, House Democratic leaders sat down with the Republican leadership and with representatives from the White House to work out a deal. The cease-fire had removed the issue of lethal aid, and agreement on a package very similar to the Democratic leadership's initial plan was quickly reached.

In 1989, the Democratic leadership met with representatives of newly elected president Bush to work out a final agreement on aid to the contras. Although some Republicans were arguing for renewed lethal aid, they did not have enough House votes to pass such a package and President Bush decided simply to cut his losses. The Democratic leaders were willing to provide him with a face-saving way of doing so because they feared that, were Congress simply to cut off all aid, any subsequent adverse developments in Nicaragua would be blamed on them. After four weeks of intensive negotiations, Bush and congressional leaders agreed on a contra-aid package that provided some continued nonmilitary aid. Bush, in essence, abandoned the Reagan administration policy of attempting to oust the Nicaraguan Sandinistas by military force, a policy bitterly opposed by Democrats and one lacking a congressional majority. In return, Democrats gave Bush sufficient nonmilitary aid to protect him — and their own vulnerable members — against right-wing attacks that he had abandoned the "brave, freedom-fighting contras."

In the wake of the Los Angeles riots in the spring of 1992, congressional leaders and the Bush administration agreed that quick passage of an urban-aid package was essential, but sharply disagreed about what the package should include. The usual committee processes would have been unlikely to produce legislation the administration would accept. As has become increasingly routine under such circumstances, high-level negotiations ensued. Majority Leader Dick Gephardt chaired the sessions and took the lead for the Democrats. After two months of negotiations with the administration, an agreement was reached and, though many members, including Gephardt himself, judged it to be inadequate and only a first step, it was quickly enacted.

Although circumstances dictated that the leadership negotiate for the House Democrats, this was an issue on which many members wanted to participate. To give Democrats with a special constituency or policy interest in urban issues a say, the leadership established an urban task force. Its purpose, a leadership aide explained, "was to bring together people with particular interests and constituency concerns and [relevant] committee assignments to serve as a sort of advisory group." This ad hoc group was chaired by Gephardt and advised the leadership on what should be included in the package; a small subset of the group carried out the actual negotiations. Those members most concerned with the results were thus brought into the process and kept informed every step of the way. When only a minimal deal came out of the negotiations, those members knew that this truly was the best that could be achieved.

Conclusion

House party leaders are agents of their members; members expect their leaders to facilitate the passage of legislation that furthers the members' policy and reelection goals—as the grumbling when leaders fail to act quickly enough makes clear. Doing so now requires that leaders become much more involved in the substance of legislation, and that they more frequently intervene in committee processes before legislation reaches the floor and in interchamber and interbranch negotiations. When reaching a satisfactory outcome on high-stakes legislation requires leaders to act aggressively, members expect them to do so. That failure to pass such legislation often would impose an enormous cost on the Democratic membership collectively only makes leadership involvement that much more necessary.

Members also, however, expect their leaders to be sensitive to members' needs and desires to pursue their goals through individualist strategies. They expect their leaders to provide collective goods and foster collective action without imposing unacceptable constraints on members' pursuit of their goals through their own individual efforts. Adequately meeting these potentially conflicting expectations requires party leaders to engineer the passage of legislation that must be passed and of legislation their members consider good public policy without confronting their members with frequent electorally perilous decisions—floor votes, especially—and without severely restricting their members' opportunities to participate in the legislative process. The structuring of choices and inclusion are key strategies the leaders employ in their attempts to produce the policy outcomes the members want without imposing on them costs they consider unacceptable. Much leadership intervention in the prefloor legislative process is aimed at assuring that legislation members want gets to the floor in a form that will not provoke tough floor votes. By influencing the form in which legislation reaches the floor, the leaders structure members' floor choices so that most Democrats can vote for the legislation and few are faced with a choice between furthering policy and electoral goals.

The strategy of inclusion can ease the tension between the leadership policy direction necessary to produce legislative results and members' desires to participate fully in the legislative process. When the party leaders involve themselves in the prefloor legislative process in the House, their efforts tend to extend participation even if they reduce committee control. Whether by pressuring a committee chair to attend to the policy preferences of a group of more junior members or through an issue task force to draft a leadership substitute, the circle of participants is enlarged. Summit decision making, by contrast, restricts participation and thus increases the tension. The 1990 budget saga shows the problems that can result; the 1992 urban-aid negotiations illustrate how the leaders have attempted to extend the strategy of inclusion to such instances.

10

Assembling Floor Majorities

Around 11:00 A.M. on May 26, 1988, Republicans, without warning, offered an amendment to the intelligence authorization bill to lift restrictions on CIA aid to the contras. Believing passage would scuttle the peace talks between the Nicaraguan government and the contras scheduled to begin the next day, the Democratic leadership went into its "fire drill": the deputy whips were told to work the doors; a computer list of members absent for the most recent roll call was printed out and those who supported the leaders on this issue were located and asked to vote; a whip call alerting all Democrats that an important vote was imminent was sent out over the automatic phone system.

The members of the Nicaragua task force were called to the floor; each was assigned some of those fifty-one members with no hard-and-fast position whose votes would make the difference. The task force's mission was to inform and persuade. Meanwhile, the task-force chair asked the most active Republican opponent of aid to the contras to make sure the small band of like-minded Republicans was on board. The chair also persuaded an influential moderate Democrat to lobby other moderates.

As the vote approached, the leaders still lacked reliable information on sixteen members, and, because contra-aid votes generally had been close, the task force was assigned to "babysit" the sixteen. Each task-force member sat with an assignee and made sure that person was informed about the substantive and political effects of the vote. When the vote came at about 1:30 P.M., the Republican amendment was defeated 214 to 190.

★ ★

On July 13, 1988, the House passed HR 4848, the omnibus trade bill, by a vote of 376 to 45. Although a cheer from supporting members and lobbyists greeted the roll call's end, there were few other overt signs of the long, complex campaign the leaders had waged. No palpable tension filled the chamber as it had on the contra-aid vote; none of the scurrying around that signals a close vote was evident. Yet the trade bill was neither routine nor uncontroversial, and the big and unsuspenseful passage vote, far from being inevitable, was the culmination of an intense and elaborate leadership-directed effort of over a year's duration.

★ ★

As these two vignettes show, leadership floor efforts vary, from the "quick and dirty" response to an unexpected floor crisis depicted in the first to the months-long, elaborately orchestrated effort alluded to in the second. In the contemporary House, as these vignettes also suggest, party leadership involvement in and direction of mobilization efforts for floor votes is the norm.

Changes in the House and in the political environment in recent years have resulted in much more frequent demands on the leaders to become actively involved in efforts to pass legislation on the floor. To be sure, the House floor is the party leaders' traditional province, and assembling floor majorities its traditional responsibility. Yet in the prereform House, committees could usually pass their bills without much help from the party leaders. The reforms of the 1970s and the adversarial political climate of the 1980s and early 1990s combined to make floor passage much less certain. Democratic committee contingents and the Democratic members more often need their party leaders' help to pass legislation on the floor.

The contemporary party leadership becomes involved in the effort to pass an astonishing number and variety of bills during any one congress. During the 100th Congress, for example, whip task forces worked to pass the shipwreck bill, legislation concerning polygraph testing, and the Moakley refugee bill, as well as such high-visibility legislation as the clean-water bill, the trade bill, and the reconciliation bill. In recent years, the leaders have mounted organized efforts to pass legislation on the floor in about seventy instances per congress. If legislation is important to a significant segment of the Democratic membership and if passage in satisfactory form is in doubt, the leaders have little choice but to get involved. In fact, as the party leadership, responding to members' demands, became actively involved in a greater proportion of passage efforts, the scope of its discretion to pick and choose the issues on which it would become active narrowed.

The election of a Democratic president reduced that discretion still further. The members and the Washington community expect the leaders to support the president's program actively and aggressively. Problems arise when the president and a significant proportion of House Democrats are at odds — as they were on NAFTA. In that case, the leadership itself split. Party leaders in the House are agents of their own members first, but furthering their members' goals usually dictates facilitating the legislative success of a president of their own party.

Leaders continue to have discretion and, in fact, must exercise judgment about how intensive an effort to mount. They base their decision on the issue's importance, both in absolute terms and relative to other issues that require attention, and on the level of effort needed to win. In addition, party leaders can and do make the availability of their assistance contingent on a committee's responsiveness to the needs and preferences of the Democratic membership. When legislation that does not meet this test threatens to, or actually does, emerge from committee, the leaders usually will take a hand in reshaping it before floor consideration. Very occasionally, a committee will be recalcitrant and a floor confrontation between the committee and the party leaders will occur.

In April 1987, the Appropriations Committee brought to the floor a supplemental appropriations bill with funding levels well over budget ceilings. Concerned about big deficits and the integrity of the budget process, Buddy McKay, a Florida Democrat, offered an amendment to cut the bill by 21 percent. The majority leader and the whip voted for the amendment — which, as a staffer said, "sent a signal to the whole House" — and it passed handily. The vote also sent "the message to the committee that their bills had to come in under the budget ceilings," the staffer continued. To make sure the committee got that message, the leaders explicitly told committee Democrats, "If you are under budget, we will oppose more cuts; if you're over budget, you're on your own." Aware that they needed the leaders' help on the floor to protect their bills, Appropriations Committee leaders agreed to the deal; the bills they brought to the floor for the remainder of the congress scrupulously observed budget ceilings. Keeping their part of the bargain, the leaders worked with near-total success to defeat amendments that would further cut spending.

In their vote-mobilization activities, House majority-party leaders often appear to act as agents of Democratic committee contingents; the leaders work to protect from alteration and pass on the floor the legislation crafted by committee Democrats. However, as this instance suggests, party leaders see themselves preeminently as agents of the party membership as a whole; when both committee Democrats and the Democratic members generally hold intense views and they disagree, party leaders will attempt to mediate and find a compromise acceptable to both sides. But when a confrontation is unavoidable and a choice must be made, the leaders perceive their first responsibility as furthering the preferences of the membership as a whole. It is, after all, the caucus of all House Democrats on which the leaders are dependent for reelection.

The Strategic Setting

The importance of the legislation to Democratic members and the difficulty anticipated in passing the legislation determine the character and intensity of leadership efforts. High-stakes measures that also are expected to be difficult to pass in satisfactory form call for a more intense and more elaborate effort than measures that lack either of these characteristics. The leaders' resources are still limited; if leaders are to satisfy their members' expanded expectations, they must use those resources as efficiently as possible. Even with new organizational forms and processes, the leaders cannot afford to expend scarce resources — especially the scarcest of resources, their own time — on legislation that is trivial or unproblematic.

Within the boundaries set by the stakes involved and the difficulty anticipated, a number of other characteristics of the legislation and of the situation influence strategy. Must the legislation be enacted by a certain date, or is passage truly discretionary? Measures such as budget resolutions, appropriations bills, reconciliation legislation, and some other measures that must by rule or statute be enacted by a deadline present a different strategic situation than measures that can be postponed indefinitely.

Is it the leaders' aim to pass or to defeat the measure? Usually leadership efforts are geared at passing legislation the members want, though this may entail defeating alternatives offered by opposing forces. Sometimes, however, especially when the other party controls the presidency, measures the leaders oppose actually get to the floor or appear likely to do so. In recent years, constitutional amendments barring flag burning and requiring a balanced budget have been forced onto the floor over the leaders' objections. Defeating a measure, especially but not only if it is a constitutional amendment, presents a different problem than passing one.

How much lead time for planning and implementing a strategy is available? Through the clever use of parliamentary tactics, opponents can occasionally confront the leaders with a battle they have not anticipated; the contra-aid amendment vignette above gives an example. The political environment can also present issues that must be dealt with quickly; the Supreme Court's invalidation of state laws barring flag burning precipitated a political firestorm that could not be ignored. In such cases, lead time is limited and so too is the elaborateness of the possible strategies. In other cases, in contrast, leaders have a full congress in which to enact a measure and can plan their strategy accordingly.

What the leadership and other supporters can do to build support for legislation in the period immediately before floor consideration is important to the bill's chances when it reaches the floor. However, more important to the probability of floor success and a major determinant of floor strategy is the form in which the legislation reaches the floor. "The legislative deal that is struck sets the limits of how many votes you can get," an experienced whip staffer explained. "It sets an upper and a lower limit. All a whip operation can do is make sure you get the maximum."

Adept committee leaders are aware of this basic fact of legislative life. Most committees try to report out their bills in a form they believe will be acceptable to a majority of House members. According to one experienced Democrat:

> During the debates on a piece of legislation, at markup in committee, that is the constant theme: Can we get it passed on the floor? So a great deal of accommodation is done within committees external to, or free from, any pressure by the leadership. The bill that comes out of subcommittee is almost inevitably modified by the full committee. And the major modifications are in terms of how much we can accept to assure passage without doing violence to the intent of the bill.

On particularly contentious measures, committee leaders may go well beyond an attempt to anticipate the reactions of those not on the committee. A recent Budget Committee chair explained:

> So once I have a budget resolution that I think is able to pass my committee, I then go meet with small groups. I meet with the DSG executive committee, I go meet with the Conservative Caucus, meet with the Black Caucus, the Women's Caucus. I go meet with the committee chairs. And I say, "Here is where we are, here is what the budget is going to look like. Can you live with that? Can you support that?" . . . And usually I would spend a week running around feeling or testing the waters, to find out whether or not the budget can pass.
>
> And then as we recognize problems, we make the adjustments and as a result of making these adjustments, when I came to the floor with the budget, not one got rejected, because I had worked with every group within the Democratic Caucus to fine tune my budget so that everybody could be supportive.

Because the substance of the legislation sets the limits of what is possible on the floor, the party leaders monitor committee action on major bills, involve themselves early in the process when committees appear unresponsive to such concerns, and, when committees produce important legislation that is not viable, take on the crafting of a substitute that can pass.

The party leaders' aim is to pass legislation in a form satisfactory to the Democratic membership and to do so without imposing unacceptable costs on members — by, for example, asking them to cast votes too costly in reelection terms or limiting too much their legislative participation. When making strategic decisions, party leaders must balance the requisites of collective legislative success against those of members' individualist goal-promoting strategies and find means their members consider satisfactory of reconciling the two.

Timing and Scheduling

A campaign to pass major legislation consists of a number of interrelated decisions. When should the legislation be brought to the floor? Under what sort of rule? How intense a counting and vote-gathering effort is needed, and who should direct it? To what extent should interest groups be brought into the effort? Although the most important decisions, as noted above, concern the form in which the legislation will be brought to the floor, strategic choices such as these can also make the difference between success and failure.

In the attempt to enact legislation, timing can be crucial. All measures not enacted by the end of a congress die and must begin the legislative process all over again in the next congress. In the end-of-session crush, those who would delay a bill are advantaged, and delay often means death. The external political environment may provide a boost to a bill's proponents at one time and a drag on their prospects at another (see Kingdon 1984).

The leaders' aim is to schedule major legislation for floor consideration when they have the requisite votes and when the political benefits of passage are at their height. House rules and standard operating procedures give the majority-party leadership control over the floor schedule. The majority-party leaders inform their minority counterparts about scheduling decisions in a timely fashion. They may on occasion agree to requests the minority leader makes, particularly if the motive is the convenience of the members; but scheduling decisions, both routine and strategic, are decisions made by the majority leadership and do not require minority-party consent. Even so, the majority-party leaders cannot always use their scheduling powers to full strategic advantage. The leaders may have to wait for a committee to complete its consideration of the issue. Deadlines of various sorts may dictate scheduling decisions. An opposition-party president may be able to muster sufficient political pressure to force the leaders' hand. Nevertheless, the majority-party leaders' control over the floor schedule is a key resource and is often used strategically. Strategic scheduling has both long-range and short-range dimensions. In planning strategy for the major legislation of a congress, the leaders will set a target floor date months ahead; then, when the legislation is actually ready for floor consideration, the strategic situation will be reassessed and the strategy fine-tuned.

Decisions about when to bring up the top-priority items of a congress are tentatively made very early in a congress or even before. Typically, in the weeks after the elections, the Speaker meets with individuals and small groups of members to discuss the agenda for the upcoming congress. (For more on agenda setting, see chap. 11.) When the new congress convenes, a series of meetings with committee leaders usually takes place. Out of these talks emerges a list of high-priority measures with tentative target dates. If the president is of the same party, he takes a lead role in agenda discussions with the congressional leadership, and the president's priorities and preferences are given great deference by party and committee leaders.

The party leaders would ideally like some major measures reported out relatively early in a congress, the others in orderly succession, and none left to the very end. Such spacing of major legislation on the floor would allow the leaders to concentrate on a limited number of legislative battles at a time and would ensure that House Democrats received maximum public credit for their legislative accomplishments. When early in the year the floor is inactive even though the committees are at work, the press tends to criticize the Congress for idleness. And when most major legislation is passed during an end-of-the-session rush, the press concentrates on the frenzy of the process and not on the product. Committee leaders, while they share these interests, may find that internal committee dynamics or, later in the process, strategic considerations in conference make reaching the target dates a problem. A member of the core leadership explained:

> There is always some tension, some conflict between the leadership and the chairs on matters of timing and priorities. . . . The chairs always want to go late. They always want to leave things as long as possible to get the maximum of bargaining room. But if we do that, then we get ten months of stories about not having done anything and then everything happens in one month, and so we don't really get credit for what we do.

Two recent Speakers handled such problems somewhat differently. Jim Wright was much more aggressive about pushing committees and their leaders to abide by the schedule. Tom Foley was more permissive, though when delay threatened to scuttle legislation, he too put on pressure.

During the course of a congress, the priority list is likely to change at the margins. New issues may come to the fore and changes in the political environment may alter the prospects of legislative success enough to add some items and delete others. Long-range planning is difficult in any legislature, yet its lack presents problems. In one key substantive area, the Democratic leaders have made a special attempt to plan and coordinate the legislative agenda. Organized labor is a centrally important Democratic constituency; however, the conservative political climate of the 1980s made passing labor's priority legislation extremely difficult. A lack of coordination and long-range planning made a bad situation worse. A member explained: "In the past, international unions would come in in a competitive environment, each trying to get their bill through the committee and to the floor of the House first." At the beginning of the 100th Congress, the leaders appointed Pat Williams, an activist member of the Education and Labor Committee and a longtime whip, "labor whip" and asked him to "systematize the process." His task was to work with labor, the committee leaders, and the party leaders to come up with a consensus labor agenda and an agreed-upon schedule for its consideration.

Doing so required getting labor to agree to speak with one voice; Bob McGlotten, chief lobbyist for the AFL-CIO, was designated spokesperson for labor in its dealings with the Democratic leadership. In addition, in return for regular access to and consultation with the Democratic leaders, labor agreed to defer to the leaders' judgment about matters of internal congressional strategy — about which of two high-priority bills has the best chance of passage, for example. A key participant explained the system:

> Each week I meet with two of the labor representatives, Bob McGlotten and Peggy Taylor. We meet in my office at least once a week. We talk more often than that. Once a month on the average, we have a meeting between someone in the leadership, either the Speaker or the majority leader or the majority whip, and selected members of the various international unions as well as some of the leadership of the AFL-CIO to discuss the most current bills that might be moving along or that they would wish to have moving. On the labor side, I cannot speak as well about that, but they have set up a similar meeting structure for themselves. We have almost always at any given time whip task forces ongoing getting the count on potential bills that might come up to see whether or not we have a good opportunity to pass them.

When the scheduling decision at issue is of major interest to a number of other constituencies, consultation is broadened. A participant described the process:

> When we are near a decision on a contentious matter, say, deciding whether minimum wage or parental leave will first be considered by the House, the

process would be that [the labor whip] talks to a number of the international unions involved, the women's groups involved, the church groups involved, because they are all very interested in both of these bills. We get as much information as we can about who desires which bill to come first. We count the members and see where the votes are for each bill and then [Pat Williams] will take that to Chairman Hawkins [of the Education and Labor Committee]. He will review it and then we will get a meeting between Chairman Hawkins and either Mr. Kirkland or Mr. McGlotten, and they will make a tentative decision, which Gus Hawkins then takes to the Speaker.

The leaders thus get the benefit of wide consultation but reserve the final decision for themselves.

In making scheduling decisions, party leaders take into account the views of friendly interest groups. The passage of legislation important to groups that are central components of their members' constituencies is integral to satisfying their members' expectations of them. The leaders also want the groups' assistance in their efforts at passage and want the groups' efforts to be coordinated among themselves and with their own. Consultation makes that more likely. The sort of routinized consultation that occurs between the leadership and labor is unique, but leaders meet with the representatives of a broad variety of groups, and committee leaders also convey the views of affected groups to the leadership.

But while the leaders, in making legislative scheduling decisions, take into account the views of interest groups as they do the views of the most interested members, they do not in any sense delegate such decisions. A bill's strongest supporters are sometimes over-optimistic about its floor prospects and may also want a floor vote even if they know their prospects are slim. The party leaders usually oppose bringing a bill to the floor unless they have the votes to pass it. "As a general rule, I think it perverts the legislative process just to have a lot of votes for the purpose of promoting and attracting attention to different issues," a high-ranking leader said. "On highly charged, controversial issues, there's no point in members bloodying their heads against the wall of public opinion" if the bill will not pass, another top leader asserted. "This is a workplace which will be judged by its product, not just an arena for gladiators to do battle."

Groups of intensely interested members and their interest-group allies often argue strenuously against this leadership decision rule. They may contend that once the measure is scheduled, the necessary support will materialize. They always maintain that the political benefits of even a losing battle more than outweigh the costs. A proponent of legislation granting the District of Columbia statehood argued:

We have had twelve hearings and six markup sessions. We have satisfied ourselves that there is no constitutional or legal impediment to this. The [public opinion] polling has produced very encouraging results. Last year, 52 percent were for statehood and about half the rest were no opinion. Now, 66 percent are for and even a lot of Republicans are. We have got 201 members who we can count, so I think it is winnable if the leadership tells Democrats it is a matter of Democratic empowerment, that this is a good Democratic issue.

The party leaders almost always demur, promising the advocates a place on the schedule when they can show evidence that the votes are there. "We have to keep the discipline. . . . The standard the leadership has always used in making scheduling decisions is if we had the votes," a leader said. "I think it is very dangerous if we start getting into using other standards and making exceptions." The leaders are concerned about protecting the party's and their own reputation for legislative effectiveness, which floor defeats would damage. An even greater concern, however, is protecting their members from "taking a lot of difficult votes for nothing." Leaders sometimes have to ask members to take tough votes — votes that may hurt their reelection chances — in order to pass legislation the membership collectively favors. But unless the legislation has a good chance of passage in the House at least, the leaders are loath to confront the members with such votes; seldom will the collective symbolic benefit be considered worth the cost to members as individuals.

Leaders must factor into their scheduling decisions the likely fate of the legislation in the other chamber. Passing a bill in one chamber can increase the probability of its passage in the other. Because majority leaders have much more complete control of the floor schedule in the House than in the Senate and because, in recent years, the Democratic seat margin has been substantially greater in the House than in the Senate, Senate Democratic leaders often urge their House counterparts to take up controversial legislation first. Since that often makes good strategic sense, House leaders frequently agree. This strategy is, however, limited by House members' disinclination to take tough votes for nothing. If the leaders bring up a series of difficult bills that then go nowhere in the Senate, members object.

In recent years, the House and Senate Democratic leaderships have met on a regular basis, at least every other week and, since the late 1980s, usually once each week. Telephone and staff contact is considerably more frequent. The greatest proportion of the regular meetings and much of the other contact as well is devoted to conferring on and attempting to coordinate the two chambers' legislative schedules.

The two leaderships have similar objectives — to satisfy their members' expectations regarding legislative output and to enhance their party's image — and, certainly in recent years, they have been in reasonable agreement as to how to further these objectives. However, the chambers' very different rules and the consequent differences in the leaders' control over timing and scheduling can lead to conflict. These differences certainly limit the agreements that can be made and thus the strategies that can be employed. Nevertheless, some coordination is possible and, particularly late in a session, when pressure for floor time is enormous, coordination can greatly enhance the efficiency with which the limited time is used.

Even in the House, the majority-party leadership cannot always control when legislation is considered on the floor. Once in a great while, the leadership loses parliamentary control of the floor schedule. A measure can be brought to the floor over the leadership's objections by way of a discharge petition. When successful, the sponsors of the discharge petition then control the floor. A discharge petition requires the signatures of an absolute majority of the House membership and is considered a slap at both the committee and the party leadership, and thus is seldom successful. In the spring of 1992, however, proponents brought a constitutional amendment requiring a balanced federal budget to the House floor by discharge petition.

Other parliamentary tactics can occasionally be used to force to the floor matters the leaders would rather keep off the floor. In the spring of 1992, for example, a group of junior Republicans dubbed the "Gang of Seven" brought to the floor a series of resolutions ordering investigations of various aspects of House operations; this was possible because such resolutions enjoy a privileged status in parliamentary rules. The purpose was to highlight the bank and post office scandals and embarrass the majority Democrats. Although the ploy gained the Republicans a little floor time, it is limited as a means of controlling the floor schedule.

More likely to limit the majority-party leadership's discretion in the scheduling of legislation are legislative deadlines and political pressures. However, while a statutory deadline or pressure for action generated by the president may make a delay of months impossible, the leaders nevertheless retain some short-range leeway. Short-range scheduling tactics, like their long-range counterparts, have two objectives: first, passing the legislation; second, gaining maximum political benefit from doing so. Legislation likely to provoke opposition from a number of smaller constituencies — reconciliation legislation raising taxes by closing a variety of loopholes, for example — is better scheduled soon after being reported out of committee. Certainly such legislation should not be allowed to "hang out there" over a recess, during which negatively affected interests would have time to pressure members in their districts. In 1988, the leaders believed a similar argument applied to the United States–Canada trade agreement. "Don't let it cook over the recess," a leader advised in a scheduling meeting. "Somebody will come up with something they don't like about it." Bills that will confront members with difficult votes should not be considered too close together, and certainly not back to back. Thus, when the scheduling of bills on drugs and on AIDS was under discussion, spacing was an important consideration. Factors highly specific to a particular bill sometimes influence scheduling decisions. In 1988, a moderate Senate Republican who supported legislation tightening requirements that the administration report covert operations to Congress asked the House leaders to delay consideration until after the Republican convention. He did not want the bill, which the administration and most Republicans opposed, highlighted right before the convention. The most frequent short-range tactical decisions are a direct function of the whip count. If the count shows the necessary votes, the legislation will be brought up. If not, it will be delayed to allow for more work.

Sometimes the leaders' control over scheduling can be used to pressure recalcitrant key actors to come to agreement. Examples of the Speaker's threatening to bring legislation to the floor by a certain date whether or not the committees had worked out their differences were discussed in chapter 9. A particularly creative use of the scheduling power to apply pressure occurred in the 100th Congress on the farm-credit bill. Title 3 of that legislation fell under the jurisdiction of the Energy and Commerce Committee and the Banking Committee as well as the Agriculture Committee. When it appeared that those committees might drag their feet in coming to an agreement, the party leaders brought to the floor and the House completed consideration of the bill's first two titles. This split scheduling put a great deal of pressure on the committees to produce a compromise and, in fact, they did so in short order.

Political benefits also figure into short-range scheduling decisions. In choosing among bills to put on the floor right before a recess, leaders try to give members something they can brag about at home — an education bill, for example, rather than a foreign-aid bill. To the extent possible, leaders schedule major legislation attractive to the public at large when press coverage will be at a maximum and avoid dates when they know the competition will be stiff.

Designing the Rule

In the House, most major legislation is brought to the floor under a rule that specifies the conditions for its consideration. The Rules Committee usually grants a rule only a few days before the bill is scheduled to be taken up. However, party and committee leaders will have begun thinking about the rule much earlier in the legislative process. Often some tentative decisions on the character of the rule must be made before an accurate whip count becomes possible.

Rules are powerful strategic tools. But every rule must be able to command a majority vote in the House. That a particular rule might increase the probability of the leadership's preferred outcome prevailing on the floor is of little relevance if the rule cannot be passed. If a majority of the House judges a rule too restrictive or otherwise unacceptable, it can vote the rule down. When a rule is defeated, the Rules Committee can simply report a revised rule for the legislation; the majority party does not lose control of the floor (as does occur if the motion to order the previous question on the rule loses). Since defeating a rule does not have horrendous parliamentary consequences, majority-party members can vote against a rule to show their dissatisfaction without incurring heavy costs.

Because, on politically difficult issues, commanding a majority among their members is frequently easier on procedural than on substantive roll calls, the leaders often do prefer that the key vote come on the rule rather than on a major amendment, for example. And, while losing a rule is extremely embarrassing, it may well represent less of a setback than the adoption of a killer amendment would. The leaders must, however, guard against arousing dissatisfaction sufficient to induce a majority of the House to defeat the motion to order the previous question on the rule. If that occurs, the successful opponents of the motion and the rule may then propose their own rule, thus placing this powerful tool in the hands of the leaders' adversaries. (This happened in 1981 in the fight over the Reagan economic program; see chap. 8.)

In some cases, the major contours of a rule emerge out of negotiations on the legislation. Recent drug bills have been bipartisan in the sense that the majority and minority leaders cooperated in bringing them to the floor. However, a significant number of the myriad issues involved in these bills split Democrats from Republicans (as well as, in some cases, dividing the parties internally). Which amendments to allow on the floor was central to interparty negotiations at the leadership level. Liberal Democrats would have preferred rules that disallowed Republican amendments on "hot-button" issues such as the death penalty and the exclusionary rule. However, the price of Republican cooperation was allowing votes on some such amendments, and the Democratic leaders knew that, in any case, they could not pass a rule that barred such votes. Thus, on the 1988 drug bill, Tom Foley, negotiating for the Democrats, agreed to allow the Republicans' top-priority amendments in return for their limiting the number of such amendments they would offer.

Party and committee leaders' diagnosis of the nature of the problem the bill is likely to confront on the floor shapes the rule. How much protection does the legislation need? Does a particular amendment or a barrage of unanticipatable amendments pose the primary danger? Are there special circumstances that require specially tailored provisions? The more important the measure and the more complex and nonroutine the strategic situation, the greater the role of party leaders in making these decisions.

Sometimes a measure is so politically delicate that it requires the maximum protection that a closed rule affords. The 1989 ethics–pay raise package provides a quintessential example. Had amendments been allowed, some members would undoubtedly have succumbed to the temptation to make political points and confronted their colleagues with killer amendments against which it would be impossible to vote. An amendment to delete the pay raise would surely have been offered and would have placed many members in a politically untenable position. The closed rule gave members who wanted the pay raise but feared its reelection consequences cover; they could explain and justify their vote for the pay raise as a vote for ethics reform. The rule prevented members from pursuing their goals through individualist strategies that would impose severe costs on their colleagues.

In some cases, a rule is designed to guard against a particular amendment that presents serious problems. In the spring of 1992, President Bush sent Congress ninety-nine requests to rescind $5.662 billion in already-approved budget authority. The Budget and Impoundment Control Act requires congressional approval for such rescissions to go into effect but also allows one-fifth of the House membership to force a vote on a rescission request. As part of his reelection campaign, Bush intended to force Democrats to cast a series of painful votes and to excoriate Congress for any spending cuts it failed to approve. With the House already under intense criticism for the bank scandal and other internal management problems, the party and the Appropriations Committee leaders decided Democrats had to match Bush's spending cuts, but that Congress, not the president, should decide where the cuts should come.

The Appropriations Committee went to work and reported out a measure that slightly exceeded Bush's total in savings. Even though committee Republicans had participated fully in deciding where to make the cuts, Republicans wanted to offer a floor amendment adding Bush's cuts to those the committee had made. Republicans hoped to force Democrats to choose between voting for cuts that they believed to be bad public policy (in part, undoubtedly, because some of them would be harmful to their districts) and casting a hard-to-explain vote. The committee and the leaders worried that, given the highly charged political atmosphere, their members' reelection fears would dictate a vote for the additional cuts. They therefore structured the rule so that members would choose between the committee's package of cuts and the package recommended by Bush. Republicans fought the rule but the previous question was ordered on a

257 to 160 vote and the rule approved on a 240 to 178 vote. Only one Democrat defected on the previous question vote and only twenty-four opposed the rule, a clear indication that the leaders had rightly judged the members' expectations.

The welfare-reform bill in 1988 and the civil-rights bill in 1991 were both endangered by specific amendments as well, as discussed in chapter 8. In the former case, the rule barring the draconian Carper amendment but allowing the less severe Andrews amendment made it possible to hold together a majority in support of the bill. On the civil-rights bill, had an amendment to remove the cap on women's discrimination suits been allowed, many Democrats would have felt they had to vote for it, it likely would have passed (thereby undoing the carefully crafted compromise), and any chance of amassing enough votes to override an expected veto would have died. Legislation enacting the Democratic version of the five-year budget summit agreement in 1990 offers still another example. Democrats brought the Omnibus Budget Reconciliation Act to the floor under a rule that barred the offering of the Republican substitute. The president and congressional leaders had agreed the package should contain $500 billion in deficit reduction. House Republicans, however, refused to go along with any tax increase, and their substitute did not meet the target. The failure of the package to meet the target, Democratic leaders believed, justified denying Republicans a vote on their plan — which, with its lack of new taxes, would have been tough for many Democrats to oppose.

In many cases no specific amendment but a possible barrage of amendments poses a threat to the legislation. Considering certain kinds of measures under an open rule allowing all germane amendments produces a highly unpredictable floor process. Legislation that is very broad, that incorporates a delicate compromise on a politically charged subject, or both can too easily be confronted on the floor with potentially disastrous amendments for which the bill's supporters have had no opportunity to prepare. It is now standard operating procedure for the Rules Committee to require members to submit to the committee the amendments they would like to offer, and, usually, only certain of these amendments will be made in order. Bringing broad measures like the budget resolution, a continuing (appropriations) resolution, or a reconciliation bill to the floor under an open rule is never considered. Almost any conceivable amendment would be germane, and opponents would likely be able to come up with some amendment that would unravel the bill's carefully constructed compromises and certainly with amendments that would put majority members on the spot, making floor strategy impossible to plan.

On other sorts of legislation, whether to use an open rule and, if not, how much to restrict amendments is still a question, but increasingly the answer is to protect legislation and members through a rule that restricts amendments. When, in 1990, the Democratic leadership brought a bill concerning campaign-finance reform to the floor, it did so under a tight rule. This is a highly partisan issue; Republicans hoped to derail the bill so it would never get to the president's desk and, in the process, force Democrats to take a series of tough votes. For example, amendments to restrict labor-union participation in politics but presented in the guise of reform of political action committees would certainly have been offered. By giving the Republicans a substitute but not allowing them to offer a series of amendments, the leaders precluded that tactic.

Rules that allow a vote on a Republican substitute but bar the offering of a number of narrower amendments further several leadership aims simultaneously and thus are increasingly used. They save time and reduce uncertainty; they are perceived as fair by the Democratic members but, because they cast the choice in partisan terms, they tend to maximize the party vote; they focus debate on the big choices and thereby highlight the message the Democratic party is attempting to convey.

In the spring of 1992, the leaders made the unusual decision to limit amendments to a general appropriations bill. During that period of intense media scrutiny and attack, the legislative appropriations bill that funds Congress was too attractive a target for the Republican Gang of Seven and others wishing to score political points at the expense of the institution, the party and committee leaders believed. The Appropriations Committee had already cut Congress's budget by 5.7 percent. Nevertheless, amendments doing real damage to the institution were likely to be offered and Democrats, to protect the institution, would have to cast votes difficult to explain in the Congress-bashing climate. The Rules Committee required that amendments be submitted to it, chose from among those, and reported a rule making about a dozen amendments in order. The rule did not and could not protect the bill against all change; its aim was to provide the bill's supporters with the predictability of knowing which amendments would be offered and to block the most irresponsible, politically motivated amendments.

When a decision to employ a restrictive rule has been made, questions about which amendments to allow and how to structure floor consideration remain. The leaders' aim is to craft a rule that allows the House to make the big choices and that therefore they and the members consider fair but that also structures choices so as to advantage the outcome Democrats favor. Some new devices, combined with restrictions, have made highly creative answers to this strategic puzzle possible. The rule for consideration of the 1989 minimum-wage bill offers an example. The Bush administration proposal was made in order first under the king-of-the-hill procedure, followed by the leadership-crafted compromise. Since the leadership compromise, as the last alternative to be voted on, only required a majority to prevail, members could, if they wished, vote for both without endangering the Democratic bill, and in fact five Republicans and twenty Democrats did so. An amendment by Republican Thomas Petri of Wisconsin to increase the earned-income tax credit as an alternative to increasing the minimum wage represented a possible threat to the legislation had it been allowed. However, since the amendment was not germane, barring it presented no real problem.

Strategy sometimes dictates making an amendment in order to make a political point. In February 1992, when the Democratic leadership brought its tax-cut package to the floor, the rule specified a vote on Bush's tax plan. The president had proposed an economic plan and, amid great fanfare, challenged Congress to pass it within a hundred days. On close examination, Bush's proposal proved to have a variety of defects and, when Democrats forced a floor vote over Republican objections, only one House member voted for it. In the past, Democrats used similar rules to force votes on Reagan's and Bush's budgets. By demonstrating that the president's budget could command only a handful of votes, Democrats hoped to substantiate their argument that these were not serious budget proposals.

Even a rule that makes in order a large number of amendments can structure debate and confer strategic advantage. The rule for the annual Department of Defense authorization bill is a case in point. Because the committee is unrepresentatively pro-Pentagon, its bill cannot be brought to the floor under a severely restrictive rule. In fact, during the 1980s the party leadership was regularly involved in altering the bill on the floor by passing a selected number of amendments related to arms control that Democrats strongly favored. In addition, the leaders had an interest in an orderly process and in helping the chair, a leadership ally, pass a sensible bill that could command broad support among the Democratic membership.

The rule for consideration of the defense-authorization bill in the spring of 1987 illustrates how these objectives can be attained even when many amendments are allowed. After the Armed Services Committee reported the bill, about four hundred floor amendments were proposed. If the Rules Committee had granted a simple open rule allowing all germane amendments, floor consideration would have gone on for weeks, with totally unpredictable legislative results. The rule allowed about two hundred amendments, set time limits for various amendments, and specified, or gave the committee chair the discretion to specify, the order in which amendments were to be considered. The decisions on order provided important strategic opportunities to structure choices. "The House doesn't want to go on one tack for too long," committee chair and bill manager Les Aspin explained. "If it hits a couple of votes going left, the boys are then looking to tack back and go to the right. The rhythm of the place is important. You will want to structure a debate so you catch the wave. It's like surfing" (Greenhouse 1987). The rule contained several king-of-the-hill provisions and gave the chair authority to roll a number of relatively minor amendments into one en bloc amendment. Because the chair can demand changes in amendments as the price of inclusion, this gave the chair added bargaining power.

Rules can sometimes solve or at least ameliorate special problems that arise during an effort to pass legislation. In the spring of 1988, Reagan's plan for more military aid for the contras was defeated by a very close vote. The Democratic leaders, who had orchestrated the campaign against more lethal aid, had promised the members a vote on a humanitarian-aid package. Republicans wanted to offer Reagan's lethal-aid package again. Under the usual parliamentary procedure, the Reagan plan would be made in order as a substitute to the Democratic proposal. The Reagan plan would be voted on first, and only if it was defeated would there be a vote on the Democratic proposal. Those Democrats — mostly moderate southerners — who had provided the leadership's margin of victory opposed the usual procedure; they objected to having to vote against Reagan's plan again, arguing that doing so would hurt them with their constituents. They had voted it down once; could the leadership make it possible for them to vote for the Democratic plan without having to vote against the president? The leaders did so; the rule designated the Reagan plan as the base bill and made the Democratic proposal in order as a substitute, thus reversing the order of the votes.

In late 1987, Democrats had come up with a deficit-reduction package containing in equal amounts spending cuts and tax increases. Skittish about voting for tax increases, many Democrats balked when the reconciliation bill, which increased taxes, was brought to the floor before the appropriations bill that contained some of the matching spending cuts. Assurance from the leaders that the bill making the remainder of the cuts would be on the floor soon was not sufficient; nervous Democrats wanted something included in the reconciliation bill itself. Through a self-executing provision, the rule, upon adoption, added to the reconciliation bill language stating that Congress committed itself to enacting legislation reducing the deficit by the full amount agreed to and in a manner consistent with the policies set forth in the budget resolution.

In September 1986, the House had passed a major antidrug bill, having first added a death-penalty amendment on the floor. Opponents of capital punishment in the Senate kept such a provision out of the Senate bill by threatening to filibuster, and they were equally determined to block any House-Senate compromise version if it contained the death penalty. House sponsors of that provision were just as determined; they refused to send the Senate a compromise bill without the death-penalty amendment.

Drugs were a highly salient issue, a congressional election was fast approaching, and many members had worked hard putting the legislation together. The House Democratic leaders did not want to see it die. An "altogether unprecedented" rule provided a solution to the problem (see Rovner 1986; see also Sinclair 1989, 185–87). Under the rule, a single House vote would send to the Senate two measures: the compromise bill without the death-penalty provision and a resolution mandating that the capital punishment language be added to the bill. This satisfied House death-penalty advocates; as they had insisted, the death-penalty provision was sent to the Senate. The Senate leaders, to avoid a filibuster, called up the bill, which was approved, and ignored the resolution.

Mobilizing the Vote

The process of engineering passage of major legislation consists of a number of highly interdependent and often simultaneous activities; a decision made at one point in the process may have to be reconsidered because of information gleaned later in the process. Thus a neat chronological description risks depicting a complex, varied, and sometimes frenetic process as cut-and-dried.

Counting Votes

The counting of votes usually starts well before the Rules Committee grants a rule. However, a good count requires knowing what the key votes will be, so a tentative decision on the character of the rule has to be made before a formal count. Conversely, information from the count may cause the leaders to alter their preliminary decision on the rule.

Party and committee leaders discuss what the difficult floor votes are likely to be and decide which to ask about in the whip poll. If the projected rule is highly restrictive, the vote on the rule will almost certainly have to be counted. In addition, a substitute amendment or other particular amendments may pose the primary danger. Since only a severely limited number of questions can be asked in a whip poll—three at most, and preferably two—making the correct choices is crucial, and the varied sources of information committee and party leaders bring to the effort increases the probability of their together coming to the right decision. If the legislation is of less than primary importance or the strategic situation is routine, these decisions are made by senior staff aides, though the principals always review and sign off on them.

An experienced staffer in the whip's office writes the questions. To provide useful data, the questions must be unambiguous and neutrally stated; as in opinion polling, loaded questions produce tainted results. To serve as a signal to members of the vote the leadership wants, the questions are always worded so that the "correct" answer is yes.

The questions (along with brief explanatory material) are conveyed to the zone whips; they conduct the count and report their results back to the whip's office within the time specified, usually around twenty-four hours. The result of the zone-whip count is a division of Democrats into support categories: yes, leaning yes, undecided, leaning no, no, absent, and not contacted. The whip's staffers enter the results into a computer as they come in.

Forming the Task Force

If they have not already done so, the leaders now set up a task force. Their key decision is the choice of task-force chairs. "You need people who understand the bill, you need people who are willing and able to sell the bill to the people who need to be persuaded," a senior whip's staffer explained. To that end, one of the cochairs is almost always from the committee. As a recent whip said, "We try to use somebody from the committee so that they know the issue and know the members, and what went on, and what was debated and what was not debated in committee and so forth, and then somebody from the whip operation, and I give every deputy whip a chance to head up a task force." Representativeness and the inclusion of someone with ties to those segments of the party that need to be persuaded are also important. "We try for balance. We may try for an unexpected supporter," the senior staffer said. "Obviously if you put a group together like that, you want diversity," a task-force chair said. "It doesn't do you any good to get together a group of people that think alike, that belongs to the same clique of members." He continued: "[The leadership] likes to have me in the forefront because I am from the South, and it gives comfort to others in that area to have somebody local out front on issues like that. So having me there is a way of saying, okay, we have got the South represented by somebody that some members of the South tend to listen to."

The choice of the chairs for a task force does send a message to House Democrats, the leaders believe, and choices are made with that in mind. A senior whip's staffer explained:

On the Central American refugee-aid bill, we had Kostsmeyer, who has always been a contra-aid opponent, and Larry Smith, who has always been a supporter of contra aid, cochairing that task force, and the point in that was to give the clear message that this bill is not about contra aid; this bill is about refugee aid, and, in fact, we got Duarte [the president of El Salvador] to support the bill, which also helps. So, we are becoming more and more, we hope, politically creative in the use of task forces. Another example is Flippo chairing the debt-limit task force. That sends several kinds of important signals. It means that they are not going to come up with something that is not okay with the South. Flippo won't let those kinds of decisions be made, and, of course, Flippo can go talk to the southerners, which is important. The other signal it sends is that since Flippo is close to the chairman of the committee, this is not an issue on which you have the leadership and the chairman split, but rather they are working together on that.

In their appointment of task-force chairs and especially in their continuing effort to expand the number and variety of people involved, the leaders have in mind aims beyond winning the immediate legislative battle. A recent whip said:

I have gone out of the whip system [in choosing chairs]. To broaden, to bring in a group in the caucus that may not be there with us a lot and to bring them in more to the caucus. Members will come to me and say, "I want to get used more, I don't feel like I am being used, I would like to be helpful, I would like you to get me involved." So what I'll do is I'll put him on a task force, see how they operate on a general task force, and if they operate well, then I'll put them in charge of a task force after a couple.

During the 100th Congress, forty Democrats—approximately 15 percent of the party membership—chaired at least one task force; twelve of the forty were southerners.

The members who enjoy chairing task forces and do it well, according to a whip, are "issue-driven people, people who like being involved in the action, who like to put things together, real players." They are, in other words, activists skillful at politics as well as knowledgeable about substance. Thus they are just the sort of members that the leadership particularly wants to draw into its orbit; their help is invaluable, their opposition would be troublesome.

Typically after the task-force chairs have been chosen, a notice of the first meeting is sent by mail to all the whips and to committee Democrats. Whatever members appear for the meeting make up the task-force membership. If the chairs have been carefully chosen, this method of self-selection usually works adequately; friends of the chairs and other members from the same segment of the party are likely to participate. Sometimes, however, a more active effort to include members with ties to those who most need to be persuaded must be made. A frequent task-force chair explained:

> I will seek out some people who I know are particularly good. One of the problems that we have on defense issues — and I think it crops up in some other areas — is that those areas of the country that are particularly likely to have a problem on these things, for example, the South on defense issues, you just do not get a good turnout of members from that region. Either they personally have not made up their minds and do not feel strongly or they do not feel strongly enough that they want to lean on their friends or, knowing how their friends feel, they do not intend to be rubbing them the wrong way. So you know one of the problems that I have discovered and one of the ones that I have worked to mitigate is to get regional distribution, get friends of the people who we are going to have problems with to be on the task force. So that is where I will recruit.

Recruitment, as another task-force chair made clear, is done on an informal basis:

> Once you get the self-selection and you find that there is an area, a region, a philosophy, no blacks, no women, no Hispanics, or whatever, yes, there is consciously an effort to say, well, let's involve Mickey Leland or Bill Richardson or Pat Schroeder or Barbara Boxer, or this or that or the other, or somebody from the South, somebody from Georgia or somebody from this state or that state, to make sure that you have the ability to touch the right members.

Refining the Count

The task force's first job is to refine the count. All Democrats not reached or listed as undecided in the initial count must be polled. The staff-to-staff character of the zone count "doesn't turn out to actually create huge accuracy problems for you," a whip staffer explained. "Because what happens is that those [staff] people don't feel comfortable saying yes or no because they don't feel like they've got authority to do that. So the problem that creates for you is you just end up with lots of people with no response or leaning that are clearly yeses or noes. And you have to go and clean them off." The whip's office adamantly insists that every such member be checked, no matter how "obvious" his or her position is. A senior whip's aide elaborated:

> Nobody is a yes until they tell us they are a yes. And that's just the rule we impose on them. It's a silly rule in some sense. We do an arms-control count and Les AuCoin on the sheet is not yes because the staff is asleep. Members look at you and say "Why do you have to ask? We all know Les is OK." But what we do is we say we're not going to get into that conversation because if

we get into that conversation then we have to start making tough decisions. And you are not a yes until you have told somebody you are a yes. That's just a work rule we imposed at the beginning.

Democrats reported as supporting the leadership position whose support is inconsistent with past behavior are also rechecked. A knowledgeable senior staffer used to examine the initial count for reported voting intentions that "looked funny." Now the zone whips' reports are checked against similar previous votes on the computer. A whip's aide outlined the procedure:

> We always code the people that come back as yeses against previous votes. We create what we call a recheck list, which we sometimes give out orally but most of the time we type onto cards and hand out. And those are people who told the zone whips they are yes but voted against on the same issue or similar issue before. And they get rechecked, even though they told us they are a yes.

Because most issues are recurrent, the initial count seldom produces major surprises. "Most of your votes are pretty firm, pretty automatic, and you run a whip count just to make sure there isn't anything out there you don't know about. Because there might be something somewhere you don't know about because it's a big House," a whip staffer explained. Because it involves member-to-member contact, the process of refining the count is more likely to produce new information. To be sure, it also often consists of determining that members do intend to vote the way in which any informed observer would have predicted. Skillfully done, it can produce information that allows for better strategic decisions. A frequent task-force chair explained:

> Without personal contact, you do not have enough impact or feedback. It is a two-way street. You don't know what their problems are and they do not know how badly the leadership wants them. There is a sort of a subtle relationship; sometimes people hide out from you which is a bad sign because they do not want to tell you what they know you are not going to want to hear. What you really have got to do is develop rapport with people to the point where they will talk to you, even if they are going to tell you something negative. You can learn from that. Maybe you can make adjustments in the amendments that are going to be offered, you can learn perhaps that it is not worth taking the time to make that effort and that you ought to go back and try something else, or that you should pull a bill or that this is much ado about nothing, this is going to fly, put your efforts somewhere else. You need to be able to have that rapport.

Adjusting the Strategy

If the count indicates trouble, the strategy will have to be reassessed. Sometimes intimations of trouble are sufficiently strong even before a count, that reassessment precedes the initial count. The party leadership, the committee leaders, and the task-force chair must decide whether the legislation simply needs to be "worked harder," that is, the persuasion effort needs to be intensified, or a change in parliamentary strategy is required, or the legislation must be altered in substance so as to pick up sufficient support.

The chairs of the Ways and Means and Education and Labor Committees, the committees of origin, strenuously argued for bringing the welfare-reform bill to the House floor under a closed rule in 1987. When the whip count demonstrated that such a rule would not pass, strategy had to be rethought. Party leaders hoped a compromise between committee sponsors and Tom Carper, the leading Democratic critic of the bill, could be worked out, and pressed the principals to negotiate. Those talks bore no fruit; the two sides were too far apart. The bill's strong proponents, faced with incontrovertible evidence that their bill if uncut would face serious trouble on the floor, then agreed to accept a moderate amendment proposed by Mike Andrews, a Ways and Means Committee Democrat. A rule allowing a vote on the Andrews amendment would pass, a whip count showed, and since passing the rule had throughout the process been considered the major barrier, the shift in strategy solved that problem.

A whip count showed that the campaign-finance bill as initially crafted by a special task force in 1991 did not command sufficient votes from southern Democrats to pass, given a united Republican opposition. Provisions relating to public financing were the problem, and only a substantive change in the legislation was likely to provide the needed votes. The task-force chair and the chair of the House Administration Committee worked out changes in the legislation with a group of southerners. When the compromise was brought to the floor a few days later, all but twelve Democrats supported it (Alston 1991a, 3509–10).

In 1989, the Education and Labor Committee reported legislation raising the minimum wage considerably more than President Bush wanted and did not include the subminimum or training wage he had demanded, even though Bush had insisted earlier that he would veto any bill that did not closely conform to his proposal. Although the whip count indicated that the committee bill might well pass, political circumstances dictated that the measure be moderated. As a leadership staffer explained, "We might actually have passed the bill but it would have been a very tough narrow victory. . . . We would have looked like we were pushing everyone to the wall for something that couldn't be held. Everyone knows that a compromise with the administration will eventually be required." In addition, as another staffer explained, "We needed as big a vote as possible to send a strong signal to the administration."

In this case, the whip's office took the lead in working out a compromise. Initially a southern member was asked to "inventory" the South — to talk to all the southern Democrats for whom supporting the legislation presented the greatest constituency problem — and come up with a bill they could vote for. Although his effort was successful, the resulting legislation was unacceptable to the members of the liberal Education and Labor Committee and to other Democratic liberals. The leadership next turned to Arkansas Democrat Tommy Robinson, who, with Republican Tom Ridge of Pennsylvania, was sponsoring an alternative bill. The compromise amendment to be offered as a substitute on the floor was worked out in negotiations among selected committee Democrats, whip Tony Coelho and his staff, Robinson and Ridge, and the AFL-CIO. It cut the size of the increase and included a two-month training wage but was still distant from Bush's proposal. Another whip count showed the changes had picked up a significant number of votes and, importantly, had made it a much easier vote for southern Democrats.

The Task Force at Work

The importance of the legislation, the amount of time available, and the anticipated difficulty of floor passage all influence the character of the task-force effort. When the whip system is not overburdened with work, it will help pass legislation of secondary importance but the effort will be a "quick and dirty one." As a senior whip's staffer explained:

> There really are two different types [of task-force efforts]. There are what I call the quick and dirties; these are the task forces that work for only twenty-four to forty-eight hours. We found that in that time period we can have an impact. Basically in that kind of time period you cannot do a really very tremendously accurate count. You can't be 97 percent accurate in that kind of thing, but what you can do is get information out to members, generate a good deal of energy, and reduce certainly the accidental vote. Basically, you don't want people coming in to vote not knowing what it is they are voting on and voting "no" and then later finding out that this is really Joe Moakley's bill and Joe has helped you out several times on Rules and, gee, if you had known, you would have gone with him. So, that is an example — on Moakley's bill. He came to us; the last time he had won by only one vote and he was concerned and he felt he needed help, and so on that one we did one of these quick and dirties, and, in fact, we picked up something like sixty-five votes. Now, this sort of task force is the kind where neither the Speaker nor the majority leader probably called anybody. It's not one of the major elements of the Speaker's agenda or anything of that sort. But it's one where some difference can be made. The second type are the longer-range ones where we'll start usually certainly a few weeks before we get to the floor.

Sometimes a lack of sufficient lead time will force an abbreviated effort. Increasingly, when time is very short, no zone count will be done because, as a whip's aide explained, "for a zone-whip count you really need twenty-four hours to turn that around." Instead of assembling a task force through a mailed notice to all whips and committee Democrats, the whip's office will call the people on that list or, if time does not allow even that, simply get together the group of people who are most often active on the issue. The whip's office keeps computerized records of who participated on which task forces and how actively; thus a list of Democrats who have been especially active in any particular issue area can be generated at a moment's notice.

The task force thus assembled will work from "the books," booklets listing all House Democrats by state, or (increasingly often) from similar past votes. When the task force works from the books in such a time-pressured situation, its members have to reach every Democrat in a very short period of time. According to a deeply involved staffer, "It's amazing when you have committed people and a lot of votes on the floor, you can do things very fast." The floor votes bring Democrats to the House floor where task-force members can talk to them quickly and efficiently. Using similar past votes as a baseline to generate a "swing list" of members to reach is a more efficient use of scarce time so long as comparable past votes exist and the choices are skillfully made. Generally the swing list is defined as all Democrats who are not consistent supporters of the party's position on the issue; even firm opponents will be approached by a task-force member.

Occasionally a task force will begin without a zone-whip count for reasons other than time constraints. In rare cases, legislation will be considered so politically delicate that the leaders believe all informational and persuasive contacts should be member-to-member — that the staff-to-staff character of zone counts would make the results misleading and the process might well be counterproductive. These circumstances also may dictate a rare invitation-only task force.

When the independent-counsel legislation was up for reauthorization in 1988, Republicans planned to offer an amendment to subject members of Congress to an independent counsel. This was one of those "exceptionally sensitive" matters on which the leadership decided "it should be member-to-member from the very beginning." The arguments against the amendment were complex, as a staffer pointed out: "We thought that the arguments were so complicated. The Justice Department can subject members of Congress to independent counsel on the motion of the attorney general right now if he wants to, so it was a purely political amendment, and we felt the only way we could get that communicated was member-to-member." What was needed was an educational effort rather than an initial count. And because of the political sensitivity of the issue, a thorough effort was crucial. The staffer continued:

> And you needed to do everybody. You couldn't leave anybody to chance, because when they come to the floor and they get to the door, the inclination to vote safely is overwhelming. They have got to know that the majority of the House is not doing that; that people like ___ and ___, really solid people, moderates from the Judiciary Committee, were opposed to the amendment.

By far the most common type of task-force effort involves a general-invitation task force, begins its work several weeks before the bill is scheduled for consideration on the floor, and works from a zone-whip count. The task force's job is to refine the count and, if need be, persuade enough members to support the party position so as to assure success on the floor. Depending on the circumstances, success may be defined as mustering a bare majority, a substantial majority, or even a two-thirds vote so as to discourage a veto. Typically such an effort will involve three or four meetings.

The initial task-force meeting will begin with a briefing on the substance and politics of the legislation at issue. To be effective counters and persuaders, task-force members must be conversant with the bill; since interest in the legislation attracted most of the people to the task force, few begin their service without some background knowledge. Nevertheless, the task-force chairs and other committee Democrats may well be able to provide additional needed information.

The assignment of names for counting and persuasion constitutes the task-force meeting's major business. The names of those Democrats who need to be reached are read out and task-force members volunteer to talk to them. Asked which names they usually took, two frequent task-force members explained. "Mostly freshmen and those I'm close to, which means mostly members from [my region]. But not all. I think I now know all the Democrats by their first name," a freshman replied. A senior member said, "First, I talk to the people from [my state]. Second, people who came with me in the same class. Third, those who serve on the same committee with me." Another Democrat gave much the same answer but elaborated on the underlying factors at play:

> What I find is I will take people on my committee. Most of us know the people on our committees better. Or I'll just take people that I know. All this is networking. . . . My networks are largely predictable. My committees, my state, my class, the class I came in with. You end up getting to know people you got elected with. You spend a lot of time together as a new member.

But not all his networks are so predictable. He continued:

I play on the baseball team, and there are about twenty Democrats who play baseball together for two months of the year. We know each other. That is where I get to know some conservative Democrats. And they are my pals, and I'll vote with them once in a while on a close call if I can, and they will vote with me once in a while on a close call. That is sort of an unusual network, but it is just as good as a committee network really.

"Even before geography and committee is a personal relationship," a frequent task-force chair explained. "Do I know ___ well enough to talk to her about this issue?" Especially when the aim is persuasion, "it needs to be somebody who has some credibility with her." But beyond a member's closest friends (who often are also from the same state or committee), the sort of relationships that make effective persuasion possible do most often develop on geographical, committee, and class bases simply because people met on those terms are the people with whom a member is likely to spend time. The frequent task-force chair continued:

[After a close personal relationship] the next cut is "Look, I'll take all the people in [my state]." I may not be particularly close to ___ philosophically but we are in the same delegation and I know her well, I've known her for a long time, and I'll talk to her. And then [my committee]. For instance, I take Whitten a lot, not because I am particularly close buddies with him, but because I am on his committee and I have an ongoing relationship with him and I feel at ease talking to him and he feels at ease I think talking to me. So if you are on the committee with somebody you have a greater ongoing relationship with them, so I think there is a real personal basis. . . . [So the criteria are] who do I know best, secondly, my state or geographic region, and then thirdly who do I serve with on committees and work with. And that almost has the facet that if you are on the committee with somebody, normally you will ask them to help you from time to time and therefore them coming to you to ask for help would be expected in the future.

Asked about the sorts of arguments he used in his persuasion efforts, a frequent task-force participant said, "About the only generic argument is the leadership argument, that the leadership needs a united front on this; otherwise, the argument depends upon the issue." He added with a smile, "Some members don't want an argument; they just want to know what the leadership position is. You always want those [i.e., as your assignees] because they're very fast. The task force gives you arguments to use." The number of Democrats who just want to know the leadership position is small and declining, all the members questioned agreed. A persuasive argument requires both an appeal on policy substance and a sensitivity to the political dimensions of the vote. "In this day and age you have got to be able to convince members of the correctness of your position on substance; it has to be an intellectual appeal," a leader explained. "And further, you have to be able to convince them that there is a way that they can explain their position to their constituents." A zone whip with considerable task-force experience said much the same thing:

You have got to make a good case on the merits; you need to know the merits and you need to make that case. What I try to do is work the case on the merits and make sure someone is covered on the politics so that they don't do something that is going to hurt them. That varies depending upon the member. But the essence of your argument is on the merits. Now you will vary that argument a little depending on where you know someone is coming from philosophically, but basically you need to be able to make a case on the merits that is going to be compelling to the person you are talking to.

Because substance is important, the persuasion effort is frequently an educational effort. A member deeply involved in the arms-control fights of the late 1980s labeled the efforts "educational more than disciplinarian." Illustrating the complexity of the issues involved, he spoke about two amendments and their fate on the floor:

Logically if you voted for the Schroeder-Markey-Downey test-ban limitation, you should vote for the other Markey amendment, which was less onerous because . . . [he explained what the two amendments did]. Anybody who understood that and anybody who voted for the test ban should have voted for Markey. Instead, the test ban passed by a good margin. Markey's amendment failed. Now, number one, it says the members were not following debate; number two, the arms-control communities were not working the issue, the new issue; number three, the whip system did not whip it. So that's a classic illustration of where whipping an issue like this really pays off.

An educational effort is sometimes needed to overcome members' political fears as well as their substantive ignorance. In combating an amendment to a housing bill that would, in effect, have sanctioned discrimination against people with AIDS, such an educational effort was essential. The task-force chair explained:

What we wanted to do was to make sure that first of all everybody understood the issue. That voting against it was not in fact giving an imprimatur to homosexual behavior or drug abuse or at-risk conduct, which people are nervous about doing, because they don't want to be perceived as sanctioning adverse conduct. That's political. So that was the first strategy to show them that this is a question of discrimination. And also show them that discriminating against victims of AIDS will diminish the ability to identify victims of AIDS and therefore also diminish the ability to intervene in trying to assist and also to change behavior.

Special circumstances may call for special arguments. In whipping the leadership tax package in 1992, the task force made a strong and unabashed appeal on the basis of party loyalty. "What we argued was that it was the defining issue for the party," a participant explained. "That even for people who did not think it was good policy, that Bush had really forced us into it, and that we had to take him on on this."

When, in 1988, Republicans attempted to send the omnibus trade bill back to conference over the issue of plant-closing notification, the leaders made sure that supporters of the repeal of the windfall-profits tax, which was included in the trade bill, understood the likely implications of their vote. If the bill went back to conference any part of it could be changed; a number of powerful Senate Democrats opposed the repeal of the windfall-profits tax; and, the implication was, the House leaders would not exert themselves to help members who had brought the problem upon themselves by voting against the leadership and the committee.

Occasionally help in persuasion will come from an unexpected source. During a heated debate on the floor, a young representative got a call from his mother strongly urging him to vote for the leadership position. She had been watching C-SPAN and decided that the Speaker, a member of her church, needed her help.

The limits of legitimate persuasion are, in general at least, clear and well understood. You do not press someone to cast a vote that will seriously hurt his or her reelection chances, experienced persuaders say. And you do not ask members to vote against their own deeply held principles. A frequent task-force chair spoke about the effort to persuade and how it is limited by these precepts:

> For the most part, there are, I guess, really two kinds of issues: one are those kinds of issues that are of personal philosophic importance to the member, that is, they feel philosophically about a decision. The second kind of issues are issues that are of political consequence. And then third, of course, are ones which are of really no philosophical or political consequence, and the member tries to do the right thing. And, of course, they are the most easily influenced, because at that level if it's a question of "Well, I'm not sure, but if you think it's a good thing to do, okay, good, I'll vote for it. If [the Speaker] wants it, that's fine."
>
> If he has got a political problem, or she has a political problem, then you have to rationalize with them as to why politically they can explain their vote and why politically that is not as disadvantageous as they may think. Now, the best whip is the whip who knows ___ can't vote for this and I'm not going to ask for her to vote for this. It's not so much wasting energy; it's a question of in ___'s best interest, ___ is my friend, and ___ is going to be voting for me nine more times after this one. On this one she needs a bye because in her district, if she votes with us, it's poison. And a good whip needs to do that; you need to tell ___ that sometimes, ___, you can't be with us on this one. Because that gives me greater credibility with ___ the next time around when I say, "Look,

——, I think you can vote with us on this one, I don't think you have a risk." And there are a lot of members who respect the opinion of a Tony Coelho. He's perceived as having a very keen political sense. Tony says, "Look, I think you in your district, you have no problem at all." Well, he probably knows about as much about their district as they do, so that lends some support, psychological support for them to do something that they may want to do anyway.

The last, the philosophical, very few times do you have a member vote against their philosophical beliefs. Right-to-life, that's not really a whippable issue. . . . You do not recommend to somebody that they ought to vote for right-to-life or pro-choice. That's something they have got to do because their gut tells them.

Under special circumstances, this member continued, whips and the leaders will vigorously urge members to support legislation that contravenes their strongly held beliefs about good public policy. But only when the House's and the majority party's basic institutional and governmental responsibilities are at stake will members be pressured to cast such a vote. In recent years, fiscally minor but philosophically important provisions in must-pass legislation such as the continuing resolutions that are needed to keep the government functioning have presented this problem. In some such cases, aid to the contras was the issue that raised deeply held philosophical concerns for liberal Democrats. "This is the vehicle to fund the government and we have got to move forward," the frequent task-force chair explained. "So there are times when you get to the point where, okay, fight the issue, if you lose on the amendment and it goes in the bill, and you don't like the amendment, well, that's the process but the bill has got to pass, so you vote for it." But this is the relatively rare sort of circumstance under which members can be persuaded to vote against their own deeply held policy beliefs. He continued:

And [it is] probably the only time you should prevail. If somebody really feels in their gut on an issue, then they ought to stick with it. And I think my experience in politics over twenty-four years or so is that, generally speaking, you can't play that game very long of trying to prevail on someone over their philosophical convictions because, if you do that too often, they pretty soon get to the point where you are perceived as not caring about them; they are just somebody you are delivering, and once the personal trust is breached, you are not very effective [in the] long term.

While asking members to vote against their own strongly held convictions is seldom considered legitimate or wise, task-force members and leaders often do press Democrats to accept half a loaf. Furthermore, the big deficits of the 1980s and 1990s have often confronted Democrats with extremely unpalatable choices and leaders have frequently had to ask their members to support legislation far from the ideal because the alternatives were worse.

The Role of Interest Groups

On most legislation of some importance, affected interest groups are involved in the legislative process from its inception, monitoring it and attempting to influence its provisions in committee. Committee members have longstanding, ongoing relationships with representatives of groups that are interested in the committee's legislation on a continuing basis; those groups that generally support committee Democrats' legislation become trusted allies.

Supportive groups continue their efforts after a bill leaves the committee, working with committee members and, if they are actively involved, with the party leaders. Informal coordination between outside groups and the party leadership has long been standard operating procedure. The leaders provide allied groups with the information on schedule and procedure necessary for an effective group effort; to some extent, they steer groups to those members who need persuasion, though actual sharing of whip information has always been a delicate matter. The groups provide the leadership with another source of information on members' voting intentions; to the extent that the groups have constituency ties to undecided members, they can be powerful persuaders.

In recent years, the party leaders have worked toward greater coordination and organization of the joint effort. In each of three recent whips' offices, a senior staffer has been charged with the task. This staffer's job is to organize and oversee the efforts of outside groups. In many instances, the groups would be lobbying on the issue in any case, but the staffer's efforts can make that lobbying more effective, as a recent occupant of that position explained:

> I can direct them a little bit better. I know where the problems are. Sometimes they don't know where the members have problems. I happen to know where the members have problems. I happen to know what the strategies are. A lot of the groups, let's face it, 90 percent of the groups are based on volunteers, or grass-roots membership out in the field, they don't understand the issues. . . . I can say, "Listen, by next week, I would like to have these twenty members checked; I would like to find out where they are, what their problems are." So it forces them to be accountable to us instead of their just saying, "We're working." . . . So a lot of the groups have their own operations, but what we do is force it to be more concise, more focused, instead of working all the Democrats, they should be concentrating on their strengths. I know which groups have the ability to work more than one thing at a time.

The task-force chairs, committee leaders, and members of the party leadership and their staffers will meet with the group representatives to brief them. The group representatives also meet periodically, usually just with staffers, to share information among themselves — on the overall count, on where individual members stand, and on what or who might influence a particular undecided member. For example, a labor lobbyist's conversations with a member may have convinced him or her that the president of a college in the member's district might be able to influence the member on the issue in question. The representative of a higher-education group might be able to arrange the approach.

Although the leaders consider the information supplied by groups regarding members' voting intentions useful as a double-check, they do not rely on the information. A leader explained:

> What we do is we bring in groups but we never count on their votes. If the group tells me that so and so is with us, we say fine. We put them on the prospect list, and we have members go and check. Because you never know why a member says something to an outside group, or exactly what he says. So we always have the outside group's information checked by members, and so it's always filtered through the members.

To get a good count, another leader said, "You need experienced vote-counters who can really listen." Experienced members, according to the consensus, are better counters than even the best lobbyist.

Groups can be extremely useful allies in persuasion efforts. The energies of a group are most efficiently used if they are targeted on those members who need to be worked, yet the sharing of whip-count results with outside groups is an action of borderline legitimacy. Members who honestly respond to a whip poll do not want as a result to have a multitude of interest groups descend on them. Selectively sharing such information with sophisticated, experienced lobbyists is not a big problem, but inexperienced groups are another matter. The whip's staffers attempt to circumvent this problem by sharing the information in an oblique fashion — not giving out the member's response to the poll but just suggesting that the member needs to be talked to — and by educating less experienced group representatives about the norms of Capitol Hill. A whip's staffer elucidated:

> I always start all my meetings by saying, "Listen, I want your help. I need your help and assistance, but I'm not telling you these people are right or wrong. I'm just telling you these people need to be talked to. . . . So whatever you do, don't go to them and say, 'The whip's office tells me you are wrong on this issue.' Just find out where they are and if you can answer any of their

questions, please answer them. If there is a problem, let us know about it so we can try to figure it out."

Another way around the problem of sharing whip-poll information is to teach less experienced groups how to identify on their own the members who need to be approached. "So if you teach groups how to do vote analysis, you don't have to tell them [i.e., share vote counts]. They know," a whip's staffer explained. He illustrated:

> So if a group does a vote analysis, if you look at contra-aid votes in the 99th Congress, and you pick the right four votes, and you look at how members voted, you will end up with a swing list. And then all you have got to do is figure out the freshmen. And the freshmen are pretty easy to figure out because you've had a moratorium vote.

The leaders' efforts to involve more groups in their endeavors require that they educate those groups in the ways of Capitol Hill. A staffer talked about the difficulties:

> It's hard to explain to someone that you want them to go talk to the member about supporting the rule. If it's a new group, they may not understand what a rule is, they may not understand what the procedural process is, and even under the best intentions, the message can get bogged down and get diluted and you can have some problems. . . .
>
> I think that you have got to be very careful in whom you ask to do what, and make sure they do not construe it wrong, because members can get very offended if someone comes up to them and says, "You got to vote like this," or "We can cause you a lot of problems back home if you don't vote like this." That happens. Their intentions are good but they don't know how to go about it.

Heavy-handed approaches are especially disastrous if they seem to have leadership sanction. The staffer continued:

> Every time we have a meeting, I say, "Listen, I do not want you to go to that member and say, 'The Whip's office tells us you're wrong on this issue.'" It happens. That's the price you have to pay sometimes. Because people will go out and say, "Tony Coelho tells me you're wrong on this issue. Why are you wrong on this issue?" That does us a lot of good, right!

The educational effort ranges from explaining procedure to inculcating the lessons of effective persuasion to making sure neophyte lobbyists know that "people like to be thanked."

The effort to educate new groups and to coordinate the work of all supportive groups is worthwhile, the leaders believe, because joint efforts are more effective and because the inexperienced groups' undirected lobbying might well be counterproductive. The arms-control and contra-aid battles of the 1980s convinced the leadership of the need to educate and work with the inexperienced groups that formed the bulk of their supporters. In both cases, the groups over time learned how to become effective players in the legislative process. A whip staffer described the leadership's evolving relationship with the peace groups on the contra-aid issue:

> We brought them into the leadership process. We gave them inside and early information on what the leadership was doing, and in return for that, we made certain demands on them. I think that the top people here at leadership offices are much better, they are more professional at this kind of thing than are even the top paid lobbyists. So what we did was to exert a kind of pressure for professionalization on them. We asked of them that they integrate their media effort with us, that they inform us when they had something; and we were willing to help them; so, for example, if they had difficulty getting a member of Congress to come to their media event, we would help them get someone. This would open up their ability to get a room on the Hill to hold their event, which would make it much easier to get press coverage because it means that the media people here don't have to go downtown; it is right on the Hill. So, we made sure that was, in fact, integrated with our media calendars. We asked that they become much more sophisticated in terms of their approach to members, both that they become more sophisticated in counting and that when they made us promises in terms of who they would approach and the like, that they actually deliver. Third, we asked that they become much more sophisticated procedurally.

The intensity of the peace groups' views made compromise and procedural maneuvering difficult for them; a strategic compromise that the leaders knew was needed to avoid complete defeat was too easily seen as an unprincipled sellout–by the grass roots if not by the Washington representatives. Yet over time, the groups did become more sophisticated and, when the leadership needed liberal votes for a humanitarian-aid package in order to defeat lethal aid, some of the groups provided the cover liberals needed. A member of the Nicaragua task force explained, "Liberals have been afraid to do what they felt was the responsible thing to do unless they had political cover from their left in their districts. And some of the liberals were candid enough to say, we think it is the right thing to do but we can't do it politically. But the outside groups made it doable."

Often, experienced groups are involved. Economic interest groups with long-established Washington operations do not need to be educated. Coordination of efforts can still be extremely useful. And the leaders can also stimulate to action some groups that would otherwise be quiescent. Many groups had a direct economic interest in the massive highway bill passed in early 1987 and would have worked to override Reagan's veto. With leadership prodding and organization, almost five hundred lobbyists attended the meeting to coordinate group efforts to override. "Lobbyists from every conceivable industry and union, from state governments, from city governments, from government unions, from suppliers of materials attended: the National Governors' Association, the American Public Transit Association, the American Road and Transport Builders' Association, individual representatives for each of dozens of cities, the limestone lobbyists, cement lobbyists, gravel lobbyists" (Barry 1989, 190). The message they heard, as paraphrased by an observer, was "If you want this bill, go out and work it. Get your membership back home excited, get them to call the members — and the senators, don't forget the senators" (ibid.).

As that message suggests, the most effective lobbyists are those with ties to the member's district and the most effective lobbying technique is the activation of the grass roots. House members who hear from their constituents in significant numbers may not alter firmly held positions, but they certainly will listen. And if constituent sentiment reinforces the leadership's message, the member is likely to go along.

Information from across the Aisle

Traditionally, Democrats have relied on interest groups to provide information on the voting intentions of Republicans. When Tony Coelho became whip, he began an organized effort to count Republicans through the whip system. At first, the outside groups' count was used as the starting point. The swing list provided by that count was then carefully assigned to task-force members who knew the Republicans well. Coelho also, an aide explained, "got the staff to make a careful quantitative study of Republican voting patterns, using a variety of the voting studies, like from CQ, as well as how Republicans voted on selected important leadership issues in '85–'86, and from that study, we have identified the patterns."

Identifying swing votes by computer has become standard procedure: "If it's a recurring issue, based on previous votes, and if it's a nonrecurring issue, based on similar previous votes," a staffer explained. Information from the groups is still welcomed, but, especially on recurring issues, computer analysis quickly provides an accurate swing list of Republicans who are possible supporters.

A whip's staffer described the current procedure for counting Republicans' votes: "We count Republicans on the inside in two ways. We try to identify Republicans who are prepared to be what we call leaders on their side, that is, who actually go out and talk to members and count for us. And that is the most effective way — Republican to Republican." Finding such a Republican leader is much easier on a continuing than on a new or one-time issue, he explained, and consequently counting votes on such issues is easier:

> It's easier to build an accurate system to count a recurring issue, because like on contra aid, you have Republicans who have a history of opposition to contra aid, always going to be against contra aid, and you can talk to them, and they can talk to you about what other people are doing, so you know where to go. But when a new issue comes up, who do you talk to? Who is the Republican leader? Who's going to take it on? If it's not a recurring issue, is it worth some Republican's time to piss off their leadership to talk to you, given that the issue is not recurring so there's no recurring constituency, so there's no recurring benefit for him? So, we feel very good about it on the recurring issues.

But whether or not a Republican leader can be found, Democrats now routinely count Republicans—though with great care. The aide continued:

> And then the other thing we do is the task forces count Republicans. And we ask members to only count members that they know personally, normally members who they are on the committee with, the delegation with. But there are all sorts of funny things, like maybe they live next to each other or maybe their offices are next to each other or maybe their lockers in the gym are next to each other. . . . And when we count Republicans, we say, don't take more than two. That's another way of making sure that they only take people they are very close to, so we can get a reliable count, an honest count from them. And that has worked for us.

Even though friendships in the House tend to form along partisan lines, there are enough cross-party relationships to make such counting possible. A junior Democrat who frequently served on task forces talked about counting Republicans' votes: "I served with two of the three [same-state] Republicans in the general assembly so I know them quite well and the third is more moderate. And I have some Republican friends from my committees. Now I won't usually call a Republican; it will be a more informal sort of contact; the gym is a good place for that." A more senior member said he would occasionally count Republicans' votes, usually a member from his state "or somebody I worked with recently, like ___ and I worked together closely on defeating the ___ amendment and I would not feel at all reticent about going to ask [him] about something now. We get along well and work well together."

On most highly controversial, closely fought legislation, Democrats cannot expect to pick up many Republican votes; if they could, an elaborate effort would be unnecessary. Attempts to override vetoes, where the required majority is two-thirds of the vote, are the exception (see the Grove City example in chap. 11). Ordinarily, however, the counting of Republicans' votes constitutes, certainly in terms of time expended, a modest part of the overall effort. As a staffer commented, "You don't waste time on most Republicans because your home run success is like twenty-three votes, right. So you're not going to count 177 Republicans. Besides, you'd get lynched."

More consistently important is information on the opposition's plans. What amendments do opponents intend to offer? What procedural moves do they plan to attempt? The better informed the bill's supporters are, the more effectively they can plan their strategy. Communication between the majority- and minority-party leaderships on matters of this sort takes place routinely at the senior staff level. A leadership aide explained:

> ____ and ____ [the senior floor aides of the Speaker and the majority leader] really handle the communications with the other side. And there is kind of a pretty straightforward rule: If you don't tell us, we're not going to tell you. And since we're the majority, if we start not telling you, it's going to be a lot harder on you than it is on us. And so, for example, when they didn't tell us [that they would offer a motion to instruct conferees on a major Democratic bill] till that morning, ____ and ____ didn't tell them a couple of things the next week. And they lose on it, so they can't afford to play that game. As long as ____ and ____ stay tough and insist, they have to tell us. So they make a big thing out of that, actually because it's a losing game for them to not tell; so they sort of say as a matter of ethics and pride and institutional honesty, we'll tell you. But it's also self-serving, and then they try and sort of guilt us into telling them.

Although the Republican party leadership seldom attempted to blindside its Democratic counterpart in the 1980s, it did not control the activities of all the Republican members. A substantial number of House Republicans were less pragmatic and more intent on embarrassing the majority and making a political point than was then Minority Leader Bob Michel. With the election of Newt Gingrich as Republican whip and his choice of Bob Walker as assistant whip, these members gained a foothold in the leadership itself. The "bomb throwers" or "crazies," as these members are often referred to, are much more likely to engage in surprise attacks, to use parliamentary procedure for guerrilla warfare.

Nevertheless, the Democratic leaders will often be forewarned. Committees are frequently good sources of information. Committee Republicans, especially senior ones, may have an interest in the legislation at issue and frequently have an interest in preserving a good working relationship with their Democratic counterparts. "The committees usually know," a whip staffer said, "because the minority members won't necessarily agree with the crazies and/or they'll have a relationship with the chair." In addition, "the parliamentarians tend to hear things" and information comes to the leaders from Democrats approached by the opposition. As a senior leadership staffer said, "We hear a lot of things. To win they have to pull off some of our people, and that means that they talk to our people, and that means that that often comes back to us." And, as another senior aide succinctly stated, "People blab."

The leaders, therefore, are seldom caught completely unaware. Still, especially if a group of Republicans unconnected with either the Republican party or committee leaders is the instigator, Democrats may not have much knowledge of the details before the fact. Consequently, no matter how meticulous the planning, the leaders must always be alert to problems developing on the floor.

Making the Final "Go/No Go" Decision

As the projected floor date approaches, a final "go/no go" decision must be made. If the task force's count shows a solid majority, all proceeds as planned; but if, after everything that could be done to pick up votes has been done, the count is still marginal, a decision must be made. Usually the decision is not to bring the legislation to the floor; "generally we don't bring the bill to the floor until we have 219 or 220 committed votes," a leader said. During the 100th Congress, legislation to raise the minimum wage never came to the floor. The whip count never showed a majority and the leadership had no intention of making vulnerable members "walk the plank" if the bill could not pass.

Sometimes, however, the decision will be to go ahead. In 1987, the Speaker strongly believed the reconciliation bill had to be passed quickly so as to give Democrats a good bargaining position in budget summit talks with the administration. The bill contained welfare reform and the count showed that the rule for its consideration might not pass. However, if welfare reform were taken out before the bill came to the floor, liberals might well desert the leadership on the rule or the legislation. Since this appeared to be a "damned if you do and damned if you don't" situation, the Speaker decided to go ahead as planned despite the iffy count.

On must-pass legislation there is no real option, especially as the deadline approaches. In the fall of 1990, the whip count on the original budget-summit deal gave the party leadership little hope that the legislation would pass, but there was no alternative to bringing it to a vote.

Top-Leadership Persuasion

As the date for consideration of the legislation on the House floor approaches, the effort becomes more and more intensive. The top leaders devote increasing amounts of their own time to the effort, sometimes meeting with major interest-group representatives and usually working closely with the committee leaders. As a committee chair said, "When you go to the floor, it just becomes more and more of an intense relationship. You almost end up living with the Speaker and the whip."

When the task force has done all it can to mobilize the needed vote and yet has fallen short, the top leaders become involved in one-on-one persuasion. Current procedure, in which the task force carries out the bulk of the personal contact and persuasion, is highly efficient in that it preserves the top leaders' time and influence. They can concentrate their limited resources on the tough issues and the tough members. A frequent task-force chair described the situation after the task force had gone through several rounds of persuasion: "Then from that point on, it sort of escalates on up, as the number is reduced, then the focus of the leadership can come on the ten or fifteen or twenty swing votes, the Speaker, the majority leader, majority whip, others in the leadership, the committee chairman, Rostenkowski on a tax bill."

It is usually to a top leader that a member will promise an "if-you-really-need-me" vote. Members make such promises when a proleadership vote is difficult for them, usually for constituency reasons, but they do not want to be responsible for the party's defeat. If a member is to cast such a tough vote, he or she wants to get maximum credit, and this means making the promise to a top leader directly.

In the final days before and also during consideration of a bill on the floor, party leaders engage in efforts to sell the legislation to their members using standard forums. At whip meetings, the leaders exhort their members to work and vote for the bill at issue; they extol it substantively and bring to their members' attention polls or favorable newspaper editorials that make support more politically attractive. The Speaker often uses his daily press conference to promote the legislation substantively and politically, knowing that the media's portrayal of the bill can make it easy or hard for members to support it. A meeting of the entire Democratic Caucus to brief—and persuade—members may be called. The Steering and Policy Committee may be asked to endorse the legislation. The party and committee leaders may jointly send out a "Dear Colleague" letter to all their members urging support.

The Floor Campaign

The floor campaign may begin with an organized series of one-minute speeches on the legislation. At the beginning of each legislative day, House members may speak for one minute on any subject and, in the days before the bill is scheduled, a leadership-orchestrated series of such speeches may set the stage for floor consideration. The aim is to draw favorable media attention to the legislation, to attempt to frame the debate in terms most favorable for proponents, and to provide members with explanations for a pro vote.

The whip system no longer relies simply on members' reports of their expected whereabouts to gauge attendance. If an important vote is expected during the day, an early roll call — usually on approving the journal — is called to check attendance. As a staffer explained, the whip "is insistent that there is, in fact, a vote on approval of the journal in the morning before an important vote, and that the whip count is then adjusted for the results of that. He wants to know not what people said several days ago as to where they would be, but actually where they are on this given date."

Floor consideration begins with a Democratic member of the Rules Committee managing the rule — explaining and defending it in debate and parceling out debate time to other members who want to speak; when the rule has been approved and the House has resolved itself into the Committee of the Whole, a senior committee Democrat, usually the committee or subcommittee chair, takes over, managing the debate and the amending process. The task-force chairs' job at this point is to assist in holding together the majority that has been assembled, and to respond to attempts to disrupt it with the necessary countermeasures. A frequent task-force chair summarized his responsibilities once the legislation is on the floor:

> Spending a good deal of time on the floor during the debate, participating in debate perhaps, and then working the doors and organizing people to do that on the floor so that each possible entrance to the chamber is covered by somebody who can make the right pitch. And I take my responsibility very seriously at that point where I feel that I have got to be the closest person, the handholder so to speak, for those people who had the most difficult time in making up their minds. And I would be aware of those who would have other problems but perhaps are willing to give us a vote if we need one but not necessarily are desirous of doing so if they can avoid it.

The whip's staff works closely with the committee to produce flyers or information sheets for use on the floor of the House when the character of an issue seems to demand it. On matters that are both complex and potentially politically sensitive, oral floor arguments and the written material sent out before floor consideration may need to be backed up by a concise written summary that can be handed out on the floor. Much legislation is multifaceted as well as complex, and proponents may not always be able to predict what facet will cause confusion, if not trouble. A senior whip's staffer explained that one member of the whip's staff spends most of his time on the floor, in part to respond to such circumstances: "One of the things that he will do is figure out if there is some confusion on some element of a bill, and then we can put out an information sheet immediately, just respond and then hand it out at the door to take care of any confusion."

On an important vote, the members of the task force, the whips, and sometimes other committee and party leaders "work the door" — that is, they stand at all the doors leading into the chamber and inform members of the desired vote. "You are informing members of what the party position is *and* that [the vote] is important" an aide explained. Usually the members who work the door are knowledgeable about the legislation at issue and can provide succinct information on the substantive meaning and political implications of amendments to their colleagues.

In recent congresses, the door work of members of the AIDS task force has been especially important in combating punitive and draconian amendments, which have often been offered by right-wing Republican Bill Dannemeyer of California. Because of the potential political cost of opposing amendments that play on people's fear of AIDS, defeating them depends on the effective deployment of members who can authoritatively explain the amendment's negative impact on controlling and treating AIDS.

Even when no task force is operating, the whip's office can cover the doors if that seems necessary. "A door project consists of having the caucus chairman and vice chairman and the deputy whips on all the doors," an aide explained. "You have a door project when the votes are very close or it comes up at the last moment or you think the committee's okay but maybe they are nervous and you want to help them out, but you don't want to commit your full resources when you are pretty sure it is not necessary."

Sensitive to the signal that having whips on the doors sends, the leadership, however, avoids working the door when doing so is unnecessary to success. The aide continued:

> You only need 218 votes and it's not that hard to get that when you have 267 [Democrats]. When you only need 218 you don't want to press members all the time because if you are asking them to vote with you all the time, you are going to overload, you're going to wear out your welcome. If in fact you have whips on the door all the time, there would be a sense of asking for too much. I mean by implication it's asking for votes.

On a really tough issue, it is sometimes possible to manage the voting process so as to advantage the outcome desired. The AIDS task force working to defeat a series of Dannemeyer amendments used the lateness of the hour to its advantage. It is much easier to defeat such amendments on a nonrecorded vote. A task-force member explained:

> It was late at night, [the strategy was] having enough members on the floor so you didn't have to have [recorded] votes. In other words, if you had a quorum, then [the amendment's supporters] had to get the requisite number to stand for a roll call, and on three different occasions, we had everybody sit down. So that strategy worked.

Occasionally getting a big vote up early will increase the probability of ultimate success. The whip system has developed an elaborate process for getting its committed members to the floor and recorded within the first several minutes of the fifteen-minute voting period. The process "makes a lot of use of member resources and you don't want to do that too often," a senior aide said, but on certain types of issues — the pay raise, the constitutional amendment banning flag burning — it can be important. He explained:

> Now you do this when you have the votes but it's close. It's not going to work if you don't have the votes because at some point you get your people up early but it's going to stall. . . . In essence, a lot of these are issues on which you have gotten members to agree to jump off the cliff together and you never want it to look like not everybody is sticking with the agreement to jump off the cliff. So with ethics, as people came in, there were lots of names up there. It never looked like there was going to be reneging.

If, as the roll call nears its end, the party position is a few votes shy, pocket votes will be called in. The leaders have before them "the wait list" of members who have promised to vote with the leadership if their vote is absolutely necessary. Sometimes task-force members are assigned to keep track of these Democrats so they can be easily located if their votes are needed. However, whips' staffers report that, by and large, this is not necessary. "Members understand that if they tell you they are going to wait, they have to stay," a senior aide explained. "You might say, I need you to hang around. But that's sort of the deal: if they tell you they are going to, that means they will stay and they all do."

Finally, if at the very end a few votes are still needed, proponents attempt to get the requisite votes through feverish last-minute persuasion on the floor of the House. At this point, top party and committee leaders play the greatest role; other proponents have already done what they could. The 205 to 203 vote to approve the conference report on the 1991 crime bill required such an effort. "I decided right there on the floor," a junior representative from Texas recounted. Fellow Texan and the chair of the

Judiciary Committee Jack Brooks "did a real comprehensive job" of persuasion, he added (Biskupic 1991b, 3530).

If the proponents' aim is to discourage a presidential veto or if they believe there is safety in numbers, they will attempt to amass a large majority and will try to dissuade members from changing their votes. Ordinarily, however, the leaders simply want to win, and as cheaply as possible. Members for whom the vote is difficult will be subjected to an intense persuasion effort only if their votes are considered necessary. One aide said: "You don't want to hurt your friends. And also if you ask them once and it does hurt them, then it is harder to ask them again. So you don't want to use that if you don't need to, but in this case we just could not be sure, so we wanted them as extra insurance."

Once a victory is assured, members whose votes are not needed are released from their commitment when this is logistically possible. In late 1987, it was essential to pass a continuing resolution to keep the government functioning; the CR, however, included some aid for the contras and thus was very difficult for some Democrats to support. A whip's staffer described the vote:

> It was like four in the morning or something, and [the whip] was up in the front and people were voting. At the end there were some Republicans who were prepared to vote yes but wanted to vote no, and there were some Democrats who were prepared to vote yes who wanted to vote no, and they were being released in a methodical fashion, producing a 209–208 victory.

In this particular case, the Democratic leaders not only wanted to protect their members from having to cast a difficult vote unnecessarily, but also wanted a close vote to show the administration and congressional Republicans the extent of the sentiment against aid to the contras among House Democrats.

Responding to Emergencies

Restrictive rules and careful preparation have reduced uncertainty on the floor. "You don't have to be that clever because you have the Rules Committee," a high-ranking staffer said. "The leadership is allowing fewer and fewer bills under an open rule, so it's a little hard to get surprised." Even so, floor emergencies do occur; not all possible surprise tactics can be foreclosed by rules. Furthermore, as the level of partisan animosity has increased in recent years, Republicans have become more willing to violate norms of advance notice even if they ultimately lose by doing so. During the 102nd Congress, for example, the Gang of Seven repeatedly offered, without warning, resolutions intended to embarrass the majority

Democrats; most highlighted the bank or post office scandals then plaguing the House and, because they held privileged status, their consideration could not be blocked (see, for example, Kuntz 1992). The complexity of the legislative process offers a bill's opponents various opportunities to make mischief, even when the bill is brought to the floor under a tight rule; sometimes totally unexpected troubles can emerge at the last moment.

Having the ability to respond quickly to an emergency is essential. The initial responsibility for handling a floor emergency rests with the whip's office. A senior aide talked about the process when an instantaneous response is necessary: "You have the three chief deputy whips and usually two task-force chairmen, and David [Bonior, the whip] makes six. And, say, each can pull in a couple more—that's a lot of people working in an emergency." Usually, the leaders have sufficient time to mount a more extensive effort. Because the Speaker is the House's presiding officer, he can almost always delay a vote for a few hours at least. If a task force is in operation, its members can be activated quickly and the heavy guns of the top leadership can be brought into play if need be.

If the problem is a surprise amendment or an unanticipated motion to instruct conferees or to recommit a conference report, no task force may be active. However, the whip system, from its records of previous task-force participants, can quickly locate a group of Democrats interested in and willing to work on the issue in question. Within half an hour an organized effort can be underway. The response to the contra-aid amendment unexpectedly offered to an intelligence authorization bill described at the beginning of this chapter provides an example of how the process works. Republican attempts to instruct the conferees on the trade bill to drop the Gephardt amendment provide another illustration. The leaders learned one morning that Republicans intended to make a motion to instruct that day. A whip's office staffer recounted what ensued:

> What we did was we just got out the lists of the people who [had been] involved in the task force on the Gephardt amendment. So that gives us a list of about thirty to thirty-five members who have already expressed interest in it. So we called all of those and we asked them to come to a meeting on like forty-five minutes' notice. So then we got like fifteen of those who came, and then we took a whip sheet from the Gephardt fight where the yeses were about 156 or 160, it was sort of a midterm whip count. Most of the Northeast and Midwest people who were automatically yeses were in the yes column. Those people are automatically going to vote against the motion to instruct. So we weren't wasting our time on those people. And almost all the people who turned out to be the problem votes for us when we counted the Gephardt amendment [initially] were still on the sheet, so it was a good list, eighty or ninety names. Everyone took some of those ninety names and we did a count

on that immediately, reporting to Bonior on the floor. He sort of ran that effort for us. And then when we came back very strong, we then got extremely ambitious, we took the Democrats who voted against Gephardt, and we started to talk to them about voting with us on a motion to instruct, which is a procedural vote. And we went on the offensive and we just sat on the floor — and at that time we were down to like six people, Bonior and Steny Hoyer, and I'm trying to remember who else. We have the alpha list of members who voted against Gephardt, Democrats who voted against Gephardt, and we'd sit there and Bonior would take the first and Hoyer would take the second, and ____ the third, and ____ the fourth. There were about five of them. They'd go to the phone and make those calls and they'd come back with a report and we'd reassign the next five, and they'd go to the cloak room and they'd call. And we went through the fifty and got almost everybody because it was a procedural vote. . . . The Republicans shouldn't have declared war. . . . We had started the long morning just figuring while we had won Gephardt by two votes, we can do better on this, so you win this by fifteen or twenty, let's go after our swings. And then what we discovered is that because it was considered abusive, a kind of procedural abuse, we could get everybody, so we shot for everybody.

The defeat of the rule for the 1987 reconciliation bill required a more complex response. Upset by the inclusion in the bill of an expensive welfare-reform program at a time when fiscal austerity seemed called for, enough Democrats defected to defeat the rule on the floor. Because the leadership considered it so important to pass the reconciliation bill quickly, the top leaders themselves immediately swung into action, personally calling moderates who had voted against the rule.

The leadership was confronted with a procedural difficulty: getting the Rules Committee to report immediately a new rule excluding welfare reform was no problem, but waiving the twenty-four-hour layover requirement before the rule could be considered on the floor necessitated a two-thirds vote — an impossibility given Republican opposition. Yet waiting twenty-four hours would require a Friday session, and members already had plans to leave town Thursday night. In addition to inconveniencing members, the delay would weaken Democrats as they prepared to enter budget talks with the administration. A senior aide to the Speaker remembered a procedural maneuver that solved the problem; as had been done occasionally in the past, the House could formally adjourn and then immediately reconvene, thus creating, for parliamentary purposes, a new legislative day.

The Speaker, the majority leader, the whip, and the chairs of the Budget and Ways and Means Committees met with the moderates. The Speaker told them that welfare reform would be taken out, as they had wanted, and explained the procedure that would be employed. Although their tone was low-key and conciliatory, the leaders emphasized how important they considered passage of the bill. Most of the members present promised their support.

A little later, the leaders met with strong supporters of welfare reform—liberals, members of the Ways and Means Committee, and members of the Black Caucus. The leaders wanted to be sure that these members' disappointment did not translate into a vote against the new rule or the reconciliation bill. The Speaker promised them he would schedule a vote on the welfare-reform bill soon and tried to reassure them about another element of the reconciliation bill on which they had doubts. Meanwhile, the task force was hard at work. When the leaders finished their meetings, each took a list of names and began making calls.

The first rule had been voted down at a little after noon; at 2:40, the majority leader took the floor to begin the procedural maneuvering leading to a vote on the second rule. At 4:45, the House voted 238 to 182 to approve that rule, with only thirteen Democrats (and one Republican) defecting. The leadership and the task force continued to work the final passage vote, first making phone calls and then buttonholing members on the floor.

Even so, when the fifteen-minute minimum time for a roll call ran out, the vote stood at 205 to 206. As the Speaker held the vote open, proponents scurried around seeking a Democrat willing to switch. Finally the whip and a senior Speaker's aide prevailed on a junior representative from Texas for whom the Speaker had done many favors. That vote made the difference and the bill passed.

The contretemps over immigration-reform legislation in late 1990 illustrates that, during the end-of-the-session crush, problems that otherwise could be handled relatively easily can become life-threatening; like the reconciliation example, it shows how procedural control, creatively employed, can make the difference. The conference report on the immigration bill had passed the Senate easily and House proponents expected no trouble. "Everyone was overconfident, including myself," the bill's floor manager admitted afterward. "We didn't whip it" (Biskupic 1990b). Latino members were, however, upset by one minor provision, a pilot program to create a forgery-proof driver's license that employers could use to screen out illegal workers. They worked the vote and defeated the rule. A Rules Committee staffer explained: "Basically, the Black and Hispanic Caucuses joined hands and that is a picket line that most liberals are not willing to cross. The rule went down. And Judiciary Committee staffers were crying and it was close to the end of the year." The Democrats who voted against the rule did not want to kill the bill, but with time very short, the usual legislative options were not available. The staffer continued: "There was a lot of scurrying around and somebody came up with this notion of using a concurrent resolution to correct the enrollment of the bill, which essentially changes the bill. . . . We used the rule to do that and that was a particular instance of what can be done with rules."

The rule specified that, by adopting the rule, the House also adopted a resolution removing the driver's-license provision from the bill; further, it stipulated that when the Senate had adopted a similar resolution, the conference report would be in order on the House floor. This expedited the process sufficiently to make final action on the bill possible even though only one day remained in the session.

Variations

A major leadership floor effort is typically partisan, most often focuses on passing a bill as shaped by the committee (perhaps as modified by a leadership-negotiated compromise), and is usually successful. There are, however, exceptions to each of these tendencies, and examining such atypical cases illuminates dimensions of the process less visible in the more usual cases.

In recent years, most of the big legislative battles have pitted Democrats against Republicans. Even when Democrats needed and expected to get an appreciable number of Republican votes—on a veto override, for example—the Republican leadership led the opposition. An exception was the struggle in 1989 to enact an ethics–pay raise package. From its inception in the wake of the pay-raise debacle in early 1989, the effort was thoroughly bipartisan. (See chap. 9 for a discussion of the prefloor effort.) As much as most members wanted the pay raise and expected their leaders to orchestrate its enactment, even the support of both party leaderships did not ensure passage. Members are extremely skittish about voting for a pay raise, and the success of the measure depended on minimizing the electoral risks of a pro vote. Tying the pay raise to ethics reform was a key element of the strategy; it allowed proponents to argue that opposing the bill was a vote against ethics reform and thus also had its dangers. The closest possible bipartisanship was the second key element of strategy. By drawing in—in effect, by implicating—as many major actors as possible, proponents hoped to limit the future use of this vote against members.

Once the leadership-appointed task force had put together a package and the top leaders had signed off on it, the bipartisan House leadership and the task-force leaders met to map strategy. Speaker Foley and Minority Leader Michel sought and received a letter of endorsement from the president. The drafting task force held a series of meetings with members "to educate and inform." For example, the task force briefed Democrats at a meeting of the Caucus Committee on Party Effectiveness and Republicans at various special meetings. A bipartisan whip task force was put together to work the vote; membership was by invitation only. Democratic Whip Bill Gray and Republican Whip Newt Gingrich served as cochairs. In a joint letter, the chairs of the Republican and Democratic National Committees and of the two congressional campaign committees promised to oppose the use of the vote as an election issue. The Democratic leadership appeared before a Republican party caucus and the Republican leadership attended a meeting of the Democratic Caucus "to signify we were all in it together, to show good faith." The whip task force operated in a fully bipartisan fashion, sharing even the most sensitive information. A participating staffer said "We shared numbers and even names where appropriate. Often where there were problems, they were delegation problems—people didn't want to be alone—so where that would make a difference, we shared names."

"We knew it would pass when we took it to the floor," another staffer said. Yet, because of the nature of the issue—one that provokes "visceral fear," a member claimed—the whip system carefully managed the vote so as to insure against anything going wrong. A whip's staffer explained:

> What we did was very simple but very important. We called everyone who was against and asked them to vote late and called everyone who was for and asked them to vote early. So we got a great big pro vote up there early, so the vote was never in question. That meant that a lot of members who wanted to go with it, could; those who needed a lot of company—they would see they weren't alone in terms of their own state delegation. So having a big vote up there was important. This was a case where there were dangers voting either way: for pay or against ethics.

The informal agreement between the two leaderships specified that a majority of each party's members would vote for the package, thus providing bipartisan cover for the other. However, Speaker Foley had made passage of a pay raise a high priority and the Democratic leadership did not want to see it fail for want of a handful of Republican votes. Good intelligence and vote management helped prevent such an outcome. The whip's staffer explained:

> It was also important for us to know what [the Republican] count was because there were a lot of Democrats who felt Republicans had to get over 50 percent of their members before they would vote "for." The Republicans thought they would make it but we saw pretty clearly that, while they would come close, they probably wouldn't make it. And that made it all that much more important for us to get that big vote up there early so that we wouldn't get a lot of Democrats holding out and waiting for that 50 percent on the Republican side. As I remember it, they fell one vote short of 50 percent but that didn't blow things up.

The ethics–pay raise package passed 254 to 174, with Republicans splitting 84 to 89 and Democrats 156 to 85. The leaders had delivered on their promise without pressuring marginal Democrats into casting a risky vote; of the twenty-one Democrats elected in 1988 by 55 percent of the vote or less, only three voted for the measure, and few junior members, whether marginal or not, supported it. The story was the same on the other side of the aisle. Vulnerable members were given a bye (see Bragdon 1989).

In a typical leadership floor effort, the task is to ward off a limited number of destructive amendments and pass the legislation at issue. Restrictive rules and, in some cases, the character of the issue keep down the number of amendments offered. However, some legislation that attracts multitudes of amendments is still considered under essentially open rules. The foreign-aid and State Department authorization bills and the bill to reauthorize legal services are recent examples. Such bills have traditionally been considered under open rules and, while significant, they are not important enough to the leaders to make a partisan fight over a tight rule worthwhile. (By contrast, the foreign-aid appropriations bill has recently been considered under a less than totally open rule.) When many amendments are expected, some tough strategic decisions must be made. On bills of this sort, the whip system will help the committee defeat those amendments it considers most destructive but will not even attempt to mobilize the vote against every amendment offered. A whip staffer explained:

> [The whip] is absolutely rigorous about what the whip organization will do and that the whip organization won't commit to working to oppose individually every amendment on the bill. . . . So what [the whip] says to the chairman is, "You have to pick, you have to give me priorities, and we'll go out and win your priorities." But it can be a very important part of the process of winning your priorities to almost sometimes even set it up for members to vote the other way during the consideration of the bill. That's always an education because the chairman's reaction is to do everything, bring the committee bill to the floor and have the committee bill come off the floor without having lost anything. That's what they want the whip system to do—Department of State bill with seventy-five amendments or a foreign-assistance bill with one hundred plus.

The annual defense-authorization bill also attracts multitudes of amendments, but otherwise illustrates an unusual strategic situation. From the mid-1980s through the early 1990s, the Democratic leadership was regularly active in efforts to amend the bill on the floor in a manner opposed by a majority of the members of the Armed Services Committee. When the Democratic membership and the committee have intense and conflicting legislative preferences and the leaders must choose, they now act as the agents of the membership.

The early Reagan administration's rhetoric about the "evil empire" and the survivability of nuclear war raised concerns among many congressional Democrats and among segments of the public as well. The latter coalesced into a strong grass-roots movement that advocated a nuclear freeze and pressured Congress to pass a profreeze resolution (Blechman 1990, 84–87). When, on a contentious issue, a substantial Democratic consensus exists or the issue is of great importance to a significant segment of Democrats, members expect help from the leadership. With the Democratic leadership fully engaged in the effort, the freeze resolution passed the House in 1983, but in watered-down form.

Arms-control advocates then shifted their attention away from the freeze and to attempts to require the administration to abide by various treaties, signed and unsigned (ABM and SALT II), to restrict the development and deployment of SDI, and to place a moratorium on tests of antisatellite weapons. Instead of a freestanding bill or resolution, they used as their legislative vehicles the Department of Defense authorization and appropriations bills. Their strategy was heavily dependent on aid from the leadership. The conservative Armed Services Committee would not include arms-control provisions in its bill; consequently, they would have to be added as amendments on the floor, and to do so, the leadership's vote-mobilization operation and its control over the Rules Committee were crucial.

As this was a recurrent legislative battle, a standard procedure evolved. An ongoing arms-control strategy group consisting of those Democrats most dedicated to the cause began meeting each year at least a month before the bill was slated for floor consideration. These members also met regularly with representatives of the outside groups for whom this was a major issue. Senior leadership staffers and sometimes some of the leaders attended these meetings.

The key decision that emerged out of this series of meetings was which amendments to work. Again the leaders insisted that the number be kept reasonable. In 1988, for example, the whip system worked seven amendments. Asked how that decision was made, a senior staffer explained:

> It starts early in the year. We met with the outside groups. . . . You see the arms-control community is one of those communities that has got lists this long. The message to them is that we can only do so much, that there is a system-overload problem, and we have to address it. . . . Our position was that if you want us to do new stuff, you are going to have to not do old stuff. . . . [The whip] met with the arms-control groups months ago and started talking to them about this. . . . And there were like two or three different meetings of

what we call the arms-control strategy group, which is about twenty-six members. And we were saying to them there is a systems constraint.

The system-overload problem, as the leaders see it, is not limited to the danger of overtaxing the whip system but extends to asking too much of members. As a senior staffer expressed it:

> We are not going to count a dozen amendments not only because of the mechanical burden on the system but because if you go to the members and tell them they have to line up ten times — let's pick the defense-authorization bill, a classic example — that they have to line up ten times on arms-control amendments, then the members start to revolt because they all feel that some way or another they have got to do a prostrength vote.

The leaders insisted also that the amendments chosen be ones that commanded widespread support among Democrats. A participant talked about the standards used to choose the amendments: "One part was we can only take on so much. And the other part was this sort of standard we developed in all these conversations, which is we are only taking it on if there is a coalition, which means liberals and moderates in the House and the groups." He gave an example: "So on SDI what happened was that the only amendment that the moderates would support on SDI this year was so weak that the groups didn't care about it. So they weren't united. So we're not going to work it, forget it." An agreement was later worked out, as a result perhaps of the leaders' hard line.

Once the decision on amendments had been made, task forces to work each amendment were constituted. The arms-control strategy group supplied the chairs and the core membership of the task forces, but many other Democrats also became involved at this stage. A member who frequently chaired task forces on arms-control issues talked about the process:

> It often takes two to three weeks to pass that bill. So you work in other people's armies before you enlist them in yours and, as time goes by, you shift emphasis from one issue to another. We may cover five or six. Usually if we get more than that, we tend to lose our edge and not do as good a job, so we have to pick our spots. And I'll begin by having a meeting on the subject alone or sometimes with another task force, depending on how closely bunched the votes are going to be, going through the details of the situation we are in. We may have five related amendments, some going higher than the committee, some going lower, some close on either side. [We] get into the politics and the strategy as well as the merits and the details on the proposals, and then normally begin the process of handing out responsibilities to each of the people in attendance, looking for consistent attendance because it probably will take three meetings before we are finally at a point where we think that we

know where we can concentrate our efforts. So, at the point where we are ready to go to the floor, hopefully we are down to about twenty to twenty-five people who are the "don't know, up in the air, undecided" people, who often seem to be similar from one issue to another, but you know in each case unique situations are created.

Both the substantive and the political-strategic complexity of arms-control issues complicated the task of persuasion. The amendments involved highly technical issues; in addition, members realized that the House's decisions were not the final ones but constituted a basis for bargaining with the Senate and the administration. A task-force chair talked about the process of persuasion on an SDI amendment:

> The SDI task-force issues are difficult for a number of members because they know the public is strongly in support of SDI, they have district interests — universities, defense contractors — that are inclined to support it. They have concerns about the budget on the other hand, and the fact that many of the peace groups have made it a cause célèbre has made them rather goosey about the difficulty of the issue. And yet it gets defined in very narrow terms: are you going to spend three billion or four billion or 3.9 or 4.1? . . . It is very complicated and a lot of members get caught up in this dance back and forth about where shall I draw the line? What is the right level? And it becomes a negotiating posture as well, vis-à-vis the Senate and the president. So it takes an awful lot of explaining to the degree that they understand what it is we really are asking them to do, what is a defensible position, and we have been successful because I think we have found that for them.

The peace and church groups that worked on these issues became increasingly sophisticated and effective, members and staffers agreed. The small locally and regionally based groups increasingly worked in concert with experienced groups such as Common Cause, the League of Women Voters, the Council for a Livable World, and SANE. These groups can have their greatest impact by mounting a grass-roots campaign at the correct time and, as a frequent task-force chair explained, they became increasingly adept at doing so:

> For those [groups] who are really involved in this town, who have communications as a result of lobbyists who are here, they are getting better and better at bringing up the visibility of some of these issues at the crucial time back home where people can be visited on a trip to the district in advance of the vote and that sort of thing.

By the late 1980s, this organized effort was paying off in success on the House floor. In 1988, for example, six of the seven amendments the whip system worked passed in the House.

Sometimes a seemingly well crafted strategy simply does not work. When the Senate added the Helms amendment banning dial-a-porn services to a major education bill, Speaker Wright told Democratic House conferees they could not simply drop it in conference; if they did so, the conference report would not pass. Conferees came up with a technical fix, a provision whereby such services would be available only to subscribers, and the leaders believed the problem had been solved. That this represented a misreading of the situation was suggested by the Rules Committee's difficulties; when the committee first attempted to report the rule the leadership wanted, the Democrats were defeated. The leaders, realizing they had underestimated the political impact of the issue but still hoping to keep the almost certainly unconstitutional Helms amendment off the education bill, shifted strategy. The new rule allowed a clean vote on the conference report and a separate vote on a new bill that consisted of the Helms ban.

The next day when floor action began, the situation looked dicey, so the leadership decided to take up the Helms ban first; it passed easily on a 380 to 22 vote. Yet it did not serve its intended purpose of providing cover for members. Supporters of the Helms provision argued vehemently that the Senate would kill the freestanding bill and that only by attaching it to the education bill could a member demonstrate his or her true opposition to dial-a-porn. The motion to order the previous question on the rule was defeated 131 to 272; in the final moments of the vote, when the leadership's impending defeat became clear, forty-three Democrats and two Republicans changed their votes from yea to nay (Morehouse 1988a). Under such circumstances, the leaders release members from any commitments they have made; neither leaders nor members have an interest in members casting possibly costly votes when they do not make a difference.

The House then proceeded to attach the Helms amendment to the education bill and send it back to conference. Despite the fears of committee Democrats and the party leaders, the Senate swiftly approved that change and made no others, and the bill became law.

Why did the leadership lose and why did the leaders misjudge the situation so badly? Why were they always one step behind? This was a case in which the whip count never really caught up with the quickly worsening situation. A staffer said:

> The first count we did was very positive, one of the strongest first counts we had gotten ever. Like 150 people were "yes." And it was like one of those things. There are things out there that we don't control that happen, that sweep through the floor, and you sort of have to intuit them before they happen if you're real smart, and we weren't.

The approaching election and the recent tough vote on overriding the president's veto of the Grove City civil-rights bill underlay the situation, the staffer believed.

> So, then along comes dial-a-porn, [and members think] wait a second, this is election time, why should I do this? The second big factor we have is the Grove City override. . . . We didn't lose because all these guys did a real courageous thing. They were all getting slammed in their districts. They are still getting slammed in their districts. When you get two thousand contacts and it takes your office three to four to six weeks just to clear those out — they're still signing those goddamned letters — and then along comes dial-a-porn, and they said, "Wait a second. I just took it for being for the gays and now you want me to be for the pornographers. You guys got to be dreaming."
>
> So, as I said, we screwed up. . . . We were not sensitive enough to know how bad Grove City still hurt these people. Because from a leadership perspective, you have that win, you go on and you are not necessarily in contact with the fact that for the members that win did not disappear like it does for you. By next week for you, it's old news; nobody wants to talk to you about it, right. But, for the members, it's not old news; it's a continuing thing, and we weren't sensitive enough to that.

When, despite the multitude of contacts they have with their members, leaders are not sensitive enough, those members have available effective means for making their sentiments clear. The impressive array of tools leaders now have for assembling floor majorities are heavily dependent on at least the acquiescence, and more often the active cooperation, of the members whose agents the leaders are.

Setting the Agenda and Shaping Debate

In order to do what you want to do, . . . you've got to be able to communicate it so that people understand it, and [so] you can build support in a democracy for the policies that you think the country should be following. You can't do it in a vacuum; you can't just escape to the Capitol and do the good things that you feel strongly about and believe in and be able to ultimately succeed. Because you have to have popular support for what you are trying to do — they have to understand, they have to be for it, they have to vote for your candidates, they have to give you the ability to do it.

Majority Leader Dick Gephardt

Substance is crucial but has no political effect without an outside strategy.

David Obey

We want our leaders to be able to use the Congress as a pulpit to explain issues to the American public, we want our leadership promoting issues, explaining needs, enlisting support. We want them doing it publicly.

An activist, midseniority Democrat

Agenda setting and public communication make up a prominent part of the contemporary party leadership's job. House Democrats have come to expect their party leaders to function as outward-oriented public leaders as well as inward-oriented institutional leaders because effectively furthering members' goals requires it. Members now expect their party leaders, acting as their agents, to take an active part in setting the congressional agenda of major items. Agenda setting involves singling out, focusing attention on, and attempting to build pressure toward action on a problem, issue, or policy proposal, and members expect their leaders to employ their institutional powers and resources and their media access to that end. During the long period of divided control, House Democrats also came to expect their party leaders to participate effectively in national political discourse, to attempt to influence the terms of the debate so as to further Democrats' immediate legislative goals, and to protect and enhance the party's image — in Majority Leader Gephardt's words, "to try to articulate to the outside world what Democrats are fighting for, what Democrats are doing" (Madison 1990, 2906).

Origins of the Public Speakership

"Sam Rayburn could have walked down the streets of Spokane, Washington, without anybody noticing him," Majority Whip Tom Foley said in 1986. "Tip O'Neill couldn't do that. And it's very unlikely that any future Speaker will be anonymous to the country. The Speaker is going to join the vice president, the chief justice, and a few cabinet members in the forefront of public recognition," remarked the man who would himself become such a highly visible Speaker (Ehrenhalt 1986, 2133).

House party leaders were much more frequently mentioned on the network evening news in the 1980s than in the previous decade. They received almost 30 percent of the total number of mentions of House members on these broadcasts, and were considerably more prominent relative to other House members in the 1980s than in the 1970s (Cook 1989, 62). Certainly to a reasonably conscientious news watcher during the Bush administration, Speaker Foley was a familiar figure, often responding to the president's foreign initiatives or challenging him, though politely, on domestic policy. From 1989 through 1992, he appeared on or was mentioned by the evening network news an average of seventy-one times a year (Baumer 1992, 330; Vanderbilt Television News Archive). A regular watcher of the television news talk shows would likely regard him as an old acquaintance; during 1991, for example, Foley appeared thirty-seven times on shows such as *Meet the Press* and *This Week with David Brinkley* (Browning n.d.).

The Speaker's increased public visibility is largely a result of contemporary leaders' more active role in setting the congressional agenda and serving as party spokespeople. Divided control shaped the expectations of members in response to which the leadership assumed these functions. When the same party controls the presidency and Congress, the president serves as the party's primary agenda setter and public spokesperson. When control is divided, the House party until recently lacked a high-profile leader to perform these functions. During the period of committee government, the agenda consisted of whatever emerged from autonomous committees; the Speaker lacked the tools and the mandate from his members to direct the process. Neither he nor anyone else assessed whether the bills produced by the committees collectively made either substantive or political sense. No highly visible leader publicly promoted the party's agenda, explained its positions, or countered presidential criticism.

The lack of a party agenda or real party positions was one of the reformers' major complaints. They objected to the dominance of the agenda-setting process by often unrepresentative committees and to the lack of any coordination or collective responsibility. A number of the rules changes — the establishment of a Steering and Policy Committee with the Speaker as chair, most obviously — were aimed at remedying these problems. During the 94th Congress (1975–76), liberal Democrats pressured Speaker Albert to take advantage of his new tools and of seemingly favorable political circumstances to set an ambitious agenda for the House. Albert complied but splits within the Democratic party hindered its enactment.

In the early 1980s Ronald Reagan taught House Democrats a lesson about the uses of the media that altered their expectations of their own leaders. Reagan's media skills and a favorable political climate allowed him to dominate public debate and thereby dictate the policy agenda and propagate a highly negative image of the Democratic party. At the same time, in the aftermath of the Republican takeover of the Senate, the press anointed Speaker O'Neill as chief Democratic spokesperson, thus enhancing the party leadership's already considerable access to the national media.

Democrats came to understand that the president's great media access gave him an enormous advantage in political and policy struggles and that they as individuals could never compete with the president in the realm of public opinion. They needed spokespeople to counter the president. House Democrats came to expect their leaders to use their access to the media to promote the party's policy agenda and to protect and enhance the party's image.

House Democrats made some attempt to counter Reagan with their own agenda even during the first Congress of his presidency, when he was politically strongest. Although O'Neill in his speech accepting election as Speaker in 1981 simply pledged cooperation, in April he announced a Democratic economic program that had been drafted by a task force chaired by Dick Gephardt. During the first half of 1981, the political tides were running too strongly in Reagan's favor and this agenda-setting attempt sank without a trace; it produced neither legislation nor good publicity. In 1982, however, House Democrats, helped by the developing recession, were a little more successful. A task force appointed by the leadership and chaired by Jim Wright drafted an economic program consisting mostly of various sorts of jobs programs that did become an important part of the congressional agenda. Of the forty-five measures that constituted the congressional agenda in the 97th Congress, 44 percent were from the president's agenda; 9 percent were items on the Democratic leadership agenda. Thus, while a politically potent president dominated the agenda-setting process in the 97th Congress, the Democratic House leaders played a greater role than their counterparts had in the 91st when agenda setting by the Democratic leadership was negligible. And this was so even though conditions were less favorable for Democrats in 1981–82 than in 1969–70. By the last congress of Reagan's presidency, when conditions were much more favorable, the Democratic leadership had become the single most prominent agenda setter.

Asked what members expect of their leaders, a highly regarded southern moderate talked about members wanting efficient and effective management of the internal legislative process, but also wanting a leadership that sets the agenda — "we are looking for leadership who says, okay, we need to pass ___ and we need to do it now, and this is what we want to do and this is why" — and leaders who are effective spokespeople for their members. We want, he said, "leadership in the sense that when we do something in the House, [the majority leader] and [the Speaker] can defend it to the country and do it eloquently and well, putting the best possible face on it for us." Every House Democrat questioned about members' expectations of the leadership mentioned in one form or another this more public role. Contemporary House party leaders can no longer be just inside players, as their predecessors were. Effectively furthering their members' policy and reelection goals requires that the leaders go public (see Kernell 1986).

Going Public: Structures and Routines

As members' expectations have increased, the party leaders have developed a variety of mechanisms to enhance their capacity to play the role of spokespeople effectively.

Resources and Routines

Each of the leaders employs one or more staffers whose primary charge is press relations. Before they moved into the top ranks of the leadership, the party leaders dealt with the press, as all members do. Those in the top three positions soon learn, however, that the aide who handles the district press cannot possibly also take on the leadership-related press work. The increase in volume and the change in character of media relationships that accompany ascending to a top leadership position requires a staffer who is engaged primarily with the national media.

A considerable part of these press aides' time is devoted to providing information to reporters in a straightforward way. Asked to describe his job, one said: "It is to provide the press with the substantive side of what the Speaker and the House are doing, to provide them with information on what bills are up, on what the leadership position is, on our strategy, on what the agenda is. It is to make the press understand our position and what we are trying to do." Another leader's national press person described this aspect of the job:

> There is an established set of questions: What's happening on the schedule? Is the leadership going to be meeting at two o'clock on contras? If so, can we show up, can we attend, participate, ask questions, will there be a stakeout? All the rudimentary questions. Second, there are process questions. What was the evolution of a decision that was made? Third, there are "for background" or "on any basis that you can get it" questions. What happened at a particular meeting? Who disagreed with the Speaker? Where was Foley? Why did Coelho leave the room smiling? That kind of thing.

Sensitive to the members' expectation that leaders take a more active media role, these staffers see their jobs as helping their bosses to do so. And that requires a proactive rather than a reactive posture. "You could spend all your time [reacting to press inquiries] if you are undisciplined and without compass, because there are certainly enough calls to respond to," an aide explained. "We meet with [his boss] every Monday morning to plot a week, a month, six months."

Leadership staffers thus are not only available to reporters but actively seek them out. After the Speaker's daily press conference, in the Speaker's lobby right off the House floor, and by phone, leadership press aides attempt to influence reporters' agendas and interpretations. "We initiate a lot of calls," a top-level press secretary said. "We initiate calls to reporters to point out issues, to point them in directions. I mean, they have to be willing to go. You are not manipulating them. They know what they are doing. But it all helps. We have a number of good issues that are not derivative from the administration, things like health care, and we want to get some attention on them." Such contacts are not restricted to Capitol Hill reporters. "I do try to talk to the White House TV people fairly regularly," a senior press staffer reported. "Sometimes the White House will say things that are just off the wall. If you can catch it in time, you can present the real case."

During the long period of divided control, the leadership's long-range media strategy was aimed at portraying the Democratic party as competent and compassionate, as a potential governing party. A staffer explained:

> Well, the most important thing that we're trying to accomplish is to demonstrate the capacity of Democrats to govern. . . . Congress is what defines the identity of the Democratic party. [That involves] getting reporters to tell our story, and in a way that gets beyond the institution. Rather than having them just write the Congress passed a bill that does X, we want them to write a richer story about how we are responding to the public, about how we are taking the country in path-breaking directions, and to the extent that we can get them to write that story, then I feel that I've accomplished what I am supposed to do.

Party leaders have available a variety of forums that provide opportunities for getting their message out. Every day that the House is in session, the Speaker holds a ten- or fifteen-minute press conference. Although press corps attendance varies, generally at least twenty and often many more reporters show up. When the Speaker leaves to convene the House, the other top leaders and senior leadership staffers stay behind to answer more press questions one-on-one.

The leaders sometimes hold special press conferences in the TV/radio gallery on the third floor of the Capitol or occasionally in the more commodious Rayburn Room near the Speaker's office. Reporters always attend, but getting the wide coverage that is the objective requires a "news peg," and thus can be tricky. In the spring of 1991, a news conference held to unveil an ambitious Democratic antirecession program was largely ignored by the media; it had been pegged to an expected rise in the unemployment rate that did not materialize. In contrast, when in 1987 Speaker Wright was deeply involved in the Central American peace process, his special press conferences made news and thus received extensive coverage (see Barry 1989).

The leaders hold occasional luncheons with selected reporters; the format allows for either an in-depth examination of a specific issue or for a wide-ranging and more informal discussion than a press conference does. All the leaders grant numerous one-on-one interview requests, not only with reporters from the national press but with those from specialty publications or media — the American Association of Retired Persons' *Modern Maturity* or *BizNews*, for example — and even with those from foreign publications. "There's infinite informal contact with the leadership," according to a Capitol Hill reporter. In addition to press conferences and prearranged interviews, reporters can often catch a leader in the halls of the Capitol, which are open to the press.

The Varied Aims of Going Public

Their many press contacts give party leaders opportunities to further a variety of ends. Leaders highlight issues and accomplishments. Throughout 1987 and 1988, for example, Speaker Wright constantly called attention to the legislation that constituted the Democratic agenda. Whenever an item cleared a legislative hurdle — being reported out of a subcommittee or full committee, floor passage in each chamber, conference agreement — Wright reported on the progress at his daily news conference and often in other forums as well, thereby attempting to keep the issue in the media spotlight and to ensure that Democrats received credit for their legislative accomplishments.

Leaders also try to frame debate on major issues, interpreting and explaining them in a way that casts the party's position and the party itself in a favorable light. Responding to President Reagan's claim that the trade-bill provision requiring that companies give their workers advance notice of an intention to close a plant served "the special interests and not the national interest," Speaker Wright argued:

> workers and young people and the unemployed [are] not special interests; they're American interests. They're people who were thrown out of their jobs without notice by a company only to have that company open up another plant overseas. They're not a special interest to be spurned. They're American citizens who are victims of our trade policy. (Speaker's press conference, May 2, 1988)

Defeat of the debt-limit increase "would create the first public default in the history of the United States . . . it would raise interest rates immediately . . . throw the country back into a deeper recession . . . and create an international monetary crisis . . . and bond-market chaos," Speaker Foley argued during his press conference on March 10, 1993. "[To vote against the measure] is the most irresponsible 'no' vote ever cast by members of Congress. . . . It is a question of whether, if we are in debt, we pay our obligations." Voting no would be like running up a big American Express bill and then refusing to pay on the basis the one had reached one's personal debt limit, the Speaker pointed out.

When leaders seek to frame debate, they are also providing their members with rationales and explanations for a vote supporting the party position and attempting to put pressure on opponents. Speaker Wright was trying to deter President Reagan from vetoing the trade bill by making a veto as politically expensive as possible. At another press conference during the height of the battle, he pointed out that South Korean workers were guaranteed prior notice of plant closings.

Often during the long period of divided control, the party leaders attempted to use the media to pressure presidents with whom they had limited direct contact and less influence. While at a major disadvantage in media access vis-à-vis the president, leaders could at least sometimes get the press to ask pointed questions of the president. In the jockeying before and during the 1990 budget talks, the Democratic leaders made good use of the media to pressure Bush publicly to answer questions about the possible contours of a package, questions he would have preferred to avoid (Sinclair 1991).

Not infrequently, the targets of leaders' attempts to apply pressure through public statements are their own members. Whenever a leader highlights a bill, the result is some pressure to move the legislation on those responsible for doing so; certainly such a statement increases the likelihood that they will be asked about the legislation's progress and that slowness will be interpreted as defiance of the leadership. When Speaker Foley, responding to a question at a press conference about whether the House would pass legislation instituting enhanced rescission, said "Oh, yes. I'm absolutely certain. . . . I'm absolutely satisfied there will be action," he put Democrats less than happy with the change in an awkward position (Speaker's press conference, March 10, 1993). They had to decide whether they really wanted to make their leader look bad.

Occasionally the pressure is considerably more overt. Asked at a press conference on June 4, 1987, if the Ways and Means Committee would come up with the tax increase he wanted, Speaker Wright replied:

> If that is what is called for in the budget resolution, they surely will. The Ways and Means Committee is not uncooperative. They are part of the leadership of the House. They are elected by their colleagues and it is a very much coveted position to serve on Ways and Means. It is a servant of the Democratic Caucus. I think they have always lived up to their responsibilities. They will do so with full faith and confidence.

Press contacts by no means always result in coverage, and not all coverage is equally valuable. Television evening news is the big prize but also a relatively elusive one. "Television has a terrific power of setting issues, in terms of, say, how they treat the administration, how they treat the Democrats," a top-level press aide said. "You try but you get little coverage. There isn't much coverage of the Congress and it's frustrating." The morning TV news shows offer an opportunity to reach a wide audience and more time than a congressional leader is ever likely to get on the evening news. Consequently, despite the early hour, invitations to appear are almost always accepted. The Sunday interview shows such as *Meet the Press* and the nightly *MacNeil-Lehrer Newshour* reach a smaller audience but an important one; the Washington political community and attentive publics around the country watch these programs. Along with the *New York Times* and the *Washington Post,* they influence the judgment of network news and of the local press about what stories are important and who the key actors are. Speaker Foley, who was very good in that format, appeared frequently.

In addition to influencing the news judgments of the other media and thereby influencing public opinion, the major national newspapers — the *New York Times,* the *Washington Post,* and the *Wall Street Journal* — are read by members of the Washington political community, including members of Congress, and are a means of communicating with them. A leader's statement made publicly and carried by the press communicates a level of commitment that the same statement made privately cannot convey. A leader's explanation of a party position, if treated sympathetically in one of these newspapers, is likely to reassure members more effectively than the same explanation offered behind closed doors.

Op-Ed pieces in the national press, as leaders see it, serve similar objectives. When they succeed in getting an Op-Ed piece accepted, which is not an easily accomplished feat, leaders hope it will be picked up by other newspapers around the country; they hope also to influence the broad Washington political community. In addition, they see it as an opportunity to provide their members with information, rationales, and explanations in a respected forum. As a press aide commented, "You reach a small, select audience. It may be useful internally in influencing members, depending on the newspaper it appears in. Members tend to believe what's in the newspaper, so if it appears in the *New York Times,* they may figure, well, if it appears there, it must be true."

The House party leaders have a great deal of contact with the press and some access to a number of media forums that are, to varying degrees, available to them for putting forth their message. Yet compared with the president, who under conditions of divided control is the leadership's primary competitor, the Democratic leaders are at a severe disadvantage. The president's media access is incomparably greater than their own; much of what he says and does is considered news in a way that their words and actions are not. Because the media consider the president the central character in the Washington political drama, they tend to cover the congressional leadership in response to the president — "below the fold," in the vernacular. The president's action, proposal, or position is usually the lead in newspaper and television stories, with the congressional leaders being quoted about their reactions to the president's move, not about their own initiatives. Commenting on television news routines, a leadership press aide said: "There is a tendency for the White House to be the main story. The reporter at the White House is the one who has the main story, and what the people say from here on the Hill, feeds into it. And that can result in a problem with the Congress's position not being presented as fairly as it might be." The president's standing as head of state when combined with his greater media access gives him an enormous advantage in getting his message across, in defining the agenda, and in having his interpretation, especially of complex and abstruse matters, accepted by the public over that of his congressional opponents.

New Structures and Techniques

The congressional party's problem in competing with an opposition-party president in the public arena does not, however, stem only from the greater media coverage the president receives. Although members want their leaders to act as spokespeople, they do not thereby take a vow of silence. The problem of getting everyone "to sing from the same hymnbook" is a perpetual one. The clear message the leadership would like to convey may get garbled in a cacophony of different voices. And with the expansion of leadership positions, the conscious coordination of messages even within the leadership circle has become more necessary.

In the last few years, a formal attempt to "harmonize the various communications operations . . . of the various leaders and the caucus" has been instituted, a staffer involved with this effort explained. "If nothing is done, Democrats' worst instincts come out. You get people talking about the Democrats in disarray. . . . You certainly miss opportunities for presenting a unified front."

Every morning that the House is in session, a group of about eighteen members — leaders and "midlevel activists who understand the media" — meet in the majority leader's office. The Message Group, as it is called, has been in formal operation since July 1989, shortly after Gephardt became majority leader. In addition to Gephardt, Majority Whip David Bonior, Caucus Chair Steny Hoyer, and Vic Fazio, the caucus vice chair and chair of the DCCC, are members and attend almost every morning. In general terms, the group's aim "is to harmonize the themes and points of view being expressed by the leadership and by Democratic members," a staffer explained, and to plan a strategy for getting a "coherent message out."

More concretely, the aim most frequently is to link the major item on the week's legislative schedule — "the anchor" — to broader themes that reflect favorably on the Democratic party. The unified theme that emerges if the process is successful is then conveyed to other members and to the media through a variety of means. The staffer in charge gave an example of a relatively elaborate effort:

Last week's anchor was parental leave. We did the rule on Wednesday, passage on Thursday. We did one-minutes all week; we had a press conference on Tuesday in which we had [two victims of the lack of parental leave] tell their stories. We got on two network news shows on Tuesday and the other on Wednesday. Our press conference defined the coverage [as a family and a fairness issue], it made us look good and the president the bad buy. . . . You want to define yourself and the other guy. That's what the struggle is all about.

A coordinated series of one-minute speeches on the House floor at the beginning of business is a favorite technique for conveying the message. Somewhat less frequently, Special Orders speeches after the House has finished its regular business are used; during this period, members can speak longer but because they occur late in the day and are longer, such speeches are less likely to be picked up by the media.

To deliver these speeches, the small strategy group relies on a pool of ninety to one hundred members known as the Message Board. A staffer explained the procedure:

We have six team captains. Two each are in charge of Tuesday, Wednesday, and Thursday. And so, for instance, ____ is the person who organizes the one-minutes on Wednesday, and there will be people who are signed up who are part of the Message Board to speak on Wednesdays and he takes the message that has been decided upon in the message meeting and calls these people and gets them to do a one-minute on that topic.

In the 100th Congress, before such an elaborate structure had been developed, Steny Hoyer, then a deputy whip, organized twenty-eight one-minute efforts. Many were in support of Democratic agenda items — the trade bill, welfare reform, and plant-closing notification, for example; others justified and urged support for the party position on Central America; still others criticized the Reagan administration and its policies or the Republican presidential ticket. Over the course of the Congress, one hundred Democrats — 38 percent of the membership — participated in one or more of these organized one-minute campaigns. These efforts are televised by C-SPAN, but real success is defined as getting coverage in newspapers or, even better, on network television.

Over time, the leaders have learned from more-experienced media players a variety of techniques for getting coverage. The press conference with participants especially appealing to the media — celebrities or those with human-interest stories illustrating the need for a particular bill — are part of the leadership repertoire. So too is the media event; the "Grate American Sleep Out," in which members of Congress slept on the streets of Washington for a night to call attention to the plight of the homeless, received substantial media attention. "Counterprogramming" to take advantage of the media's routines was a not-infrequent strategy during the Reagan and Bush administrations. On any day on which the president was known to be addressing a major issue, some event that highlighted the congressional Democrats' opposing views was planned. Media norms of fairness dictated coverage of the event.

To the extent that Democrats in House and Senate can coordinate their messages, they will enhance their impact. The payoffs of coordination are especially great during periods of divided control. During recent years, the leaderships in the two chambers have tried to achieve such coordination, with mixed success. There is extensive contact between the Speaker's and the Senate majority leader's press secretaries; the other press people are also frequently in touch; and the floor staffers talk daily. The leaders of the chambers themselves are in regular contact. Thus information exchange is extensive, and this makes informal coordination possible. Formal joint actions — policy statements or press conferences — are sometimes undertaken, but they present more difficulties. The chambers are different and so the problems the leaders confront are different. An attempt to get agreement on a policy statement or agenda between the chambers multiplies the number of people who must agree and the political problems that must be overcome. Describing an attempt to come up with an economic-policy agenda in 1991, a senior press aide said, "After a great deal of agony we did work out a joint listing of legislative proposals, but there was no agreement across the chambers on just what was really doable and what was not. So it was a very mixed list and it got lousy press. It didn't have any credibility with the press."

The Democratic leaders employ these various forums and techniques with short-range and long-range objectives in mind. The aim may be to increase the probability of a specific bill passing tomorrow; it may be to enhance the image of the Democratic party that voters take into the election booth several years hence; it may be both. But so long as the president was the party leaders' adversary rather than an ally in these endeavors, even the most adept use of the media strategies available to them was unlikely to bring frequent clear-cut success. The occasional victories were, however, important in meeting at least minimally their members' expectations.

Agenda Setting

In December 1986, immediately after being chosen the Democrats' nominee for Speaker, Jim Wright outlined a policy agenda for the majority party and the House: deficit reduction achieved in part through a tax increase, clean-water legislation, a highway bill, trade legislation, welfare reform, and a farm bill were included. In his acceptance speech after being elected Speaker on January 6, 1987, and in his televised reply to Reagan's State of the Union address on January 31, Wright further specified and publicized the agenda, adding aid to education, aid to the homeless, and insurance against catastrophic illness. Leadership agenda items accounted for 33 percent of the 1987–88 congressional agenda; the president's agenda accounted for only 23 percent.

Members' Expectations and the Character of Leadership Agenda Setting

Special political conditions facilitated the Speaker's aggressive agenda setting. President Reagan had been weakened by the Iran-Contra scandal, the loss of a Senate majority, and his lame-duck status. House Democrats believed that they finally had the opportunity to pass legislation stymied during six years of the Reagan administration — if they were disciplined enough to exploit the opportunity. House Democrats wanted policy leadership.

The members' expectations to which Speaker Wright responded, although intensified by these special circumstances, were not created by them. Since the mid-1970s, Democrats had increasingly come to expect their party leaders to take an active role in setting the congressional agenda. Speaker Albert in the 94th Congress (1975–76) and Speaker O'Neill in the 97th (1981–82), under pressure from their members, engaged in some agenda-setting activities. During the Bush administration, Speaker Foley was substantially more involved in agenda setting than Albert and O'Neill ever were, yet to the extent that he pursued that course less aggressively than Wright, he was subject to considerable criticism from members.

When Republicans control the White House, congressional Democrats will usually be dissatisfied with the president's agenda. Yet even when his party is a minority in Congress, the president has great advantages in the struggle to define the national and the congressional agenda; to get their preferred issues on the agenda, House Democrats need leadership aid. One third-term House Democrat put it this way:

> The party leadership has an obligation to be out front taking the lead on controversial policy decisions which are important to the issues the Democrats care about, whether it is a humane way to balance the budget including raising taxes in a progressive fashion, whether it is getting us out of Central America, whether it is fashioning a general legislative policy. And when I say take the lead on substantive issues I mean both in the House and in the media.

In agenda setting as in their other key leadership activities, House party leaders are agents of their members, and their objective in assembling an agenda is to further the goals of their members. More concretely, leaders try to include some legislation that is really important to every member, avoid to the extent possible any that will seriously hurt an appreciable segment of the membership, and assemble a package of bills that reflects favorably on the Democratic party. Like the president, the leaders may find problems forced on them by events outside their control. Accomplishing their objectives may require that they respond effectively to emergencies; thus, in the spring of 1992, the Los Angeles riots thrust urban policy to the center of attention. The House Democratic leadership had to make passage of an urban-aid package a top priority both to satisfy urban members and to show the Democratic party as competent and compassionate.

The Democratic agenda put together by Speaker Jim Wright in the 100th Congress illustrates the variety of objectives leaders pursue. Farm legislation and aid to the homeless were very important to particular segments of the party membership. Clean-water legislation and the highway bill benefited the districts of almost all House members and, most Democrats believed, the country as a whole. In addition, because both had passed by large margins in the previous congress, the two bills could be moved quickly and thus provide early legislative victories. Trade and welfare reform were nationally important issues that many Democrats, including the leaders, believed a responsible Congress had to tackle. Dealing with these issues successfully would also, they believed, demonstrate that Democrats could govern, and thereby enhance the party's image. None of these bills presented any appreciable group of members with serious reelection problems. Only in proposing tax increases to help reduce the deficit did Speaker Wright clearly step outside the area of consensus; many members feared any talk of a tax increase would hurt them and the Democratic party electorally. Most did, however, agree that a tax increase was good public policy — necessary for deficit reduction and required to make possible some badly needed increases in social spending.

Foley became Speaker under circumstances that militated against aggressive agenda setting. He took over in midsession when Wright was forced to resign. He faced a newly elected president, who, he believed, had to be given a chance to lead. Like all recent Democratic leaders, Foley believed that the American public expects Congress to give a new president that chance and will punish the opposition party if it does not do so. By 1991, it had become clear that Bush did not, in fact, intend to provide much domestic-policy leadership but his willingness to use the veto made enacting legislation over his opposition very difficult. Also, during much of the first half of 1992, the House was engulfed by the bank scandal.

Yet despite all these barriers and his own innate caution, Speaker Foley and his leadership team did engage in considerable agenda-setting activity.

When Foley succeeded Wright in June 1989, he inherited an agenda consisting of legislation concerning the minimum wage, childcare, clean air, ethics reform, and campaign-finance reform — an agenda that, as majority leader, he had participated in formulating. Foley pursued that agenda, he gave added emphasis to a combined pay raise–ethics package, and he added legislation covering medical and family leave to the list of top-priority items. The Democratic agenda that emerged early in the 102nd Congress encompassed legislation regarding energy policy, antirecession programs (including legislation promoting infrastructure renewal and the extension of unemployment insurance), health-care reform, and again campaign-finance reform and family leave. In May 1991, the party leadership explicitly added a tax cut for the middle class to the agenda.

Yet despite a level of agenda setting far surpassing those of the speakers before Wright, Foley was subjected to considerable criticism for not being aggressive enough. House Democrats called openly for a more clearly delineated agenda. "The leadership needs to get the major actors together, the committee chairmen, the activists in the party who are influential, to have a significant discussion with full give-and-take so a coherent agenda can be laid out," Les AuCoin (D-Ore.) said publicly early in the 102nd Congress (*Riverside [Calif.] Press-Enterprise*, March 17, 1991).

During the 1989–92 period of Tom Foley's speakership, the process of setting the agenda was more evolutionary and even more participatory than under his predecessor. Foley was also less aggressive and less single-minded than Wright had been in keeping press attention on the agenda. As a result, the Democratic agenda was less clearly defined and this produced criticism. Agenda setting, like most leadership functions, requires striking a satisfactory balance between members' desires for participation and autonomy and their desire for policy leadership. As an activist Democrat phrased it, "The party leadership has an obligation to do two things on policy: one is to be out front taking the lead on controversial policy decisions. . . . Secondly, to involve the membership in that process." As he recognized, "That's tricky."

In-House and External Agenda-Setting Strategies

Agenda setting can be pursued through in-House activities intended to influence the legislative process directly and through external activities aimed at favorably shaping the environment in which legislative decision making takes place. The leaders can single out, highlight, and generate pressure for action on a policy proposal by using their influence over the legislative process in the House; by, for example, assigning the legislation a symbolically important low number, putting a tight deadline on committees for reporting the legislation, or using their floor-scheduling powers.

The leaders can also use their access to the media to bring such attention to a policy proposal, mentioning it repeatedly in press conferences, TV appearances, and speeches.

It is the leaders' capacity to affect the House legislative process directly that allows them to compete at all with the president in setting the agenda and that, to a considerable extent, accounts for the media access they do have. The media do not consider the congressional leadership intrinsically newsworthy, as they do the president. To receive coverage, the leaders must make news, and they can do so by reporting newsworthy decisions ex post or by credibly predicting them ex ante. The leaders' credibility in predicting that, for example, the House will pass particular legislation in the upcoming session rests, to a considerable extent, on the leaders' capacity to influence that outcome. That is, their ability to make things happen internally gives them credibility with the media externally. The in-House aspects of agenda setting undergird the external aspects. The stronger the leadership is perceived to be internally, the greater the leaders' media access.

Analytically, the in-House aspect of agenda setting can be divided into the process of formulating a party agenda and the process of promoting it within the House, but in practice the two phases are not neatly distinguishable. In the process of putting together an agenda, the leaders formally or informally involve a large proportion of their membership. They hold formal meetings with members, especially with committee leaders and with other members known to be particularly interested in and active on a certain issue. For example, in November and December 1988, after the elections, the Speaker held a series of meetings on possible agenda items in preparation for the 101st Congress. On the issue of campaign-finance reform, several meetings led to the Speaker designating the chair of the appropriate subcommittee the "lead horse" to coordinate the effort. A number of activists who did not serve on the committee of jurisdiction were drawn in. A package of bills—some alternatives and some complementary—would be drafted and ready for introduction on the first day of the congress, it was agreed. When the legislation was ready as planned, the Speaker gave the bills numbers eleven through twenty, as promised. In putting an agenda together, the leaders consult among themselves and with the Senate Democratic leadership. And, in making their judgments, they draw on information gleaned from the multitude of contacts they have with their members.

The in-House promotion phase of agenda setting includes leadership monitoring of committee deliberations and, if necessary, the use of a variety of direct means to pressure committees toward action. It also includes the leaders using forums such as whip meetings, caucus meetings, and other encounters with groups of members to keep the spotlight on the legislation. Often under the guise of reporting on a bill's progress, the party leaders highlight the legislation, emphasize its importance to Democrats, and pressure the committee or committees to move expeditiously.

The cooperation of the committee or committees with jurisdiction over the legislation and of their leaders is vital to successful agenda setting. A high-ranking staffer talked about the relationship between the Speaker and the chairs:

> Generally, the chairmen are very deferential to the Speaker. They try hard to do whatever he wants them to do, and if they think the Speaker represents the will of the caucus that is even more so. But it is a two-way street. It is important that the Speaker be responsive to the committee chairmen; if the Speaker wants something that they do not want to do, and he pressures them, they may do it, but they can essentially sabotage it in all kinds of ways by talking to the press and saying that this is really crummy legislation, or a lot of different things. So, you really have to persuade them, not coerce them.

While committee leaders may not like the pressure to move legislation on schedule that goes with agenda status, they usually do want the special leadership attention and assistance that also accompanies it. "Committee chairmen or other people identified with causes like to think that the leadership is investing in their issues and putting efforts behind their initiatives," an activist Democrat explained.

During the Reagan and Bush administrations, party leaders periodically found themselves at odds with the Ways and Means Committee. In 1987, the party leadership put a progressive tax increase high on the party's agenda. In the early 1990s, periodic extensions of special unemployment-insurance benefits and a tax cut for the middle class were near the top of the leadership's priority list. In each case the committee was unenthusiastic and dragged its feet, but in each case, when the Democratic membership made its wishes clear, the committee complied.

As important as these in-House activities are, agenda setting as defined by members includes an important component of promotion external to the House. Outside strategies can increase the probability of inside legislative success and are essential in assuring that House Democrats receive some credit for their legislative accomplishments. The party leaders have available a number of forums for publicizing the party agenda. The Speaker's speech upon being elected to his position at the beginning of a congress and the party's reply to the president's State of the Union address are especially good forums for enunciating the party's agenda. The opening session of a congress is broadly covered by the media, with the three major TV networks and almost every daily newspaper carrying a story. The reply to the State of the Union address is nationally televised and thus offers to party leaders, who now always speak for the party, a rare and valuable opportunity to speak directly to a large national audience.

The leaders can call a special news conference for agenda-setting purposes. The advantage of using a special news conference is that the leaders control the timing; the disadvantage is the greater burden on the leaders to provide the media with real news. When the leaders call such a news conference, reporters will come but media coverage will result only if reporters perceive the leaders' message as hard news. When, in the wake of the Los Angeles riots, the House and Senate Democratic leaders held a press conference to announce their urban-aid package, favorable and abundant coverage resulted. The riots made urban problems highly salient and made legislative action highly likely; when, in addition, the White House reacted favorably to the Democratic proposals, the press treated them as real news. Several other special leadership press conferences in 1992 were less successful. "How many times can you go out there and announce that the Democratic leadership has made health care the top priority for the remainder of the Congress when you do not have anything legislatively new to report?" a leadership press aide asked rhetorically. Such press conferences "really have no credibility with the media," he pointed out.

External promotion activities, skillfully directed, can have an internal impact. The daily news conference, appearances on the Sunday talk shows, one-on-one interviews with reporters, press luncheons with groups of reporters, and speeches to interested groups provide leaders with frequent opportunities to talk about various agenda items — about the problem, about the character of the proposed solution, about its legislative progress. To the extent that the leaders succeed in keeping an agenda item in the spotlight, they place considerable pressure on other actors, especially other party members, in decisive positions to move the legislation in an expeditious fashion. A lot of publicity creates the perception of a public demand for action, which affects all the elected actors. Members of the same party are especially pressured because, by refusing to act, they make their leaders look bad, which is something they usually want to avoid.

The party leaders publicize the party's agenda through the media for a second and at least equally important reason: to garner credit for the party and the House. Members want their preferred legislation to pass and they also want to receive credit from the public for its passage. The leaders themselves have an interest in the House as an institution looking good since public perceptions of them are influenced by the institution's public image. In the late 1980s and early 1990s, House Republicans under Minority Whip Newt Gingrich worked assiduously to persuade the public that institutional performance was the majority party's responsibility, arguing that the Democratic majority should be blamed for the internal bank and post office scandals and for policy gridlock. Whatever its success with the public, the effort did persuade most Democrats that House performance might well influence their electoral fates.

If passing the items on the party's agenda brings credit, then presumably failing to do so will yield blame. A concern about likely media criticism if the leadership were unable to deliver on an ambitious agenda contributed to Speaker Foley's relatively cautious approach to agenda setting. Worried about overpromising (and determined to practice the strategy of inclusion in formulating a set of priorities), Foley did not announce an agenda at the beginning of the 102nd Congress; rather, the agenda evolved and emerged from a process of consultation and reaction to events. The criticism to which Foley was subjected as a result substantiates the consensus from interviews: while not unmindful of the danger of overpromising, most Democrats believe that, under conditions of divided control, the congressional majority party does not get credit for the legislation it does produce unless it has a clear, publicly enunciated agenda.

Agenda Setting and Agenda Success: A Quantitative Summary

Since the president is acknowledged as the premier agenda setter in the American political system, the congressional party leadership's role can only be assessed relative to that of the president. In fact, presidents tend to dominate agenda setting in the first congress of their presidencies, but are much less prominent in the last congress of an eight-year administration (see table 4.2).[1] Conversely, the party leadership is most active when the president is least so.

In addition to the cyclical pattern, congressional party-leadership agenda setting shows a strong secular trend as well. When congresses at the same stage in a presidency are compared, a clear increase in agenda-setting activity over time is evident. Thus, during the last congress of the Nixon-Ford presidency, 17 percent of the items on the congressional agenda of major items consisted of leadership measures; during the last congress of the Reagan administration, this figure had almost doubled, to 33 percent. During Nixon's first congress, leadership measures accounted for only 2 percent of the agenda; during Reagan's first, for 9 percent; and during Bush's first, for 12 percent.

Announcing an agenda is one thing; enacting the items on it is another.

1. The data in table 4.2 reveal one clear deviation from the expected pattern. President Bush did not dominate the agenda during his first congress, as Nixon and Reagan had. Bush's meager role in setting the agenda of the 101st Congress reflects his unusual political weakness for a newly elected president (see Sinclair 1991).

Table 11.1   Leadership Success on the Democratic Party Agenda (% of items)

	Congress			
	94th (1975–76)	97th (1981–82)	100th (1987–88)	101st (1989–90)
Floor				
Won	50	100	85	83
Lost	13	0	0	0
Final disposition				
Won	50	50	92	50
Lost	50	50	0	33

Unless a considerable number of the items pass in the House, agenda setting is a hollow exercise and the leadership and the party lose credibility.

In the mid-1970s, the leadership's tenuous internal control resulted in a less-than-stellar win-loss record on the House floor; on only half of the agenda items did the leaders have an unambiguous win, passing their measure without change on the floor, and on 13 percent, they suffered a complete loss (see table 11.1). By contrast, in the 1980s and early 1990s, the strengthened leadership clearly prevailed on the floor on a high proportion of its measures and was never defeated.

The House majority-party leaders have less control over the final disposition of legislation; they may be able to engineer passage in the House, but the Senate and the president are more difficult for them to influence. In fact, even though the criterion of winning on balance on final disposition is less strict than the clear-win criterion used for judging floor success, final outcomes are usually less satisfactory than floor outcomes. The obvious exception is the 100th Congress, in which the leaders won on 92 percent of their agenda items — even though in many cases the president was clearly opposed to their position. Although paling in comparison, the record of the 101st Congress is quite good when matched against any of the other congresses, especially when the size of the agenda is taken into account.

Despite substantial activity and considerable success, majority-party-leadership agenda setting during the Bush administration did not keep pace with members' expectations. To prod their leaders to be more aggressive and to make their expectations of full cooperation clear to committee chairs, Democrats in late 1992 established the new Speaker's Working Group on Policy Development. By caucus rules, the working group is charged with helping the party set an agenda and follow through on it, but with the election of a Democratic president, what it should and can do became unclear. Clinton, like all modern presidents, has assumed the position of primary agenda setter for his party.

Shaping Debate and Claiming Credit

"Sometimes to pass a bill," Tom Foley has said, "you have to change the attitude of the country" (Ehrenhalt 1986, 2134). To the extent that leaders can shape debate, to the extent that they can influence the way in which issues are defined, they can ease their task of passing legislation that furthers their members' policy and reelection goals. How the choice is defined often determines the electoral risks inherent in a particular vote. In the controversy over funding for the National Endowment for the Arts, for example, opponents of content restrictions attempted to define the issue as one of artistic freedom and opposition to censorship; those who favored restrictions, in contrast, cast the choice as favoring or opposing federal funding of pornographic art. Since how the issue is defined determines how easy or hard casting a given vote is, it strongly affects the opposing sides' probability of legislative success. In addition, specific legislative battles and broader controversies may leave residues on party images. Which party ultimately benefits and which loses in the court of public opinion, which gets the credit or which bears the blame is largely determined by how the issue in controversy has been defined.

Shaping Debate to Pass Legislation

Sometimes getting the necessary House votes depends on a successful campaign to influence the public climate. On certain difficult issues, if the battle in the press is lost, the members will not go along, a top leader explained. "You've got to convince the press it's the right thing to do." The fight to override President Reagan's 1988 veto of the Civil Rights Restoration Act—popularly known as Grove City—is a case in point; the media campaign was an essential and central element of the effort to build a winning coalition.

On January 28, 1988, the Senate passed the Grove City bill by a 75 to 14 vote. To no one's surprise, President Reagan announced on March 1 that he intended to veto the bill. Nevertheless, the House on March 2 approved the bill by a vote of 315 to 98. Everyone knew the Reagan administration would focus on the House in trying to sustain the veto. A staffer explained:

> That was one where we were the target; almost always the Senate is the target; we have a sort of history of doing better in the House. But on that bill the

House was the target. They knew they could not win in the Senate but they thought they had a chance to win in the House, so the administration's strategy from the beginning was to try and win in the House.

The overwhelming vote in favor of passage boded well, but overriding a president's veto in the face of determined opposition is never easy.

On March 7, the Reverend Jerry Falwell transformed the battle. He sent out a "Special Memorandum to Pastors" in which he claimed:

> Because of the pressure brought on by the homosexual movement in this country, Congress has caved in to this pressure and passed a law that, combined with present court cases, would qualify drug addicts, alcoholics, active homosexuals, transvestites, among others, for federal protection as handicapped....
>
> What this means to you and me is this: Our churches and religious leaders could be forced to hire a practicing active homosexual drug addict with AIDS to be a teacher or youth pastor, etc. Your preaching and moral values would be dictated by the government with federal intervention if you didn't obey.

He exhorted the pastors to action:

> Please call your Congressman today and urge him to sustain the veto....
> It is also imperative that you encourage members of your congregation to do the same. This is not a drill. OUR RELIGIOUS FREEDOM IS ABOUT TO BE DESTROYED!
>   MAKE AN ANNOUNCEMENT THIS SUNDAY, PUT IT IN YOUR BULLETIN OR NEWSLETTER, BUT PLEASE, PLEASE GET THE WORD OUT!

Many responded to Falwell's call to action and House members — especially southerners — were deluged with letters and phone calls. David Price, a North Carolina Democrat, reported "thousands of letters and calls ... that kept the phones in all my offices tied up for two weeks. Grove City," he continued, "is still talked about with considerable awe among my staff, and it has become the high-water mark against which all future floods of calls about flag-burning, gun control, congressional pay raises, and the like are to be measured" (1992, 116).

The Democratic leaders quickly realized that if Falwell were not countered promptly, their big margin could slip away. And the only effective way to counter him was through a media campaign to influence opinion. Because the problem that the members faced was from the grass roots, the media that needed to be reached were the local newspapers. A leadership staffer explained:

> Members wanted to do the right thing but they were being slammed. Five hundred calls a day in some offices. And they needed cover, which means that they needed their editorial communities to step in and interpret what is

happening to their constituents, so it wasn't just them against Jerry Falwell, it was them plus local community, editorial opinion, against Jerry Falwell.

The leadership responded quickly. The staffer recounted the first response:

> [The whip's office] did a mailing to every newspaper in the South and in the border states. What we did was we sent a copy of Jerry Falwell's mailing and we took that sentence that we made famous, "practicing, active, homosexual, drug addict with AIDS," and we put that up big in front of the letter . . . and in a two-week period — because that was about what we had — we tried to make that sentence into sort of the classic example of hysteria. And it worked.

Coelho's letter, which was released to the Washington press as well, asked the editorial writers to "consider whether your newspaper will add its voice in support of [the] legislation."

The whip's office also coordinated the efforts of supportive outside groups so as to obtain maximum publicity. "We put together a coalition of handicapped, First Amendment groups, blacks, church people, people across the spectrum who had an interest in Grove City," a staffer explained. The support of church groups was repeatedly highlighted. In his letter to the editors, Whip Tony Coelho wrote:

> Read the fact sheet and ask yourself whether the American Baptist Churches, the Church of the Brethren, the U.S. Catholic Conference of Bishops, or the Union of American Hebrew Congregations would endorse this legislation if Falwell's reckless charges were accurate. The sad truth is that Rev. Falwell has broken the Commandment against bearing false witness in order to defeat a civil rights bill.

A press conference in which representatives of church groups reiterated their support and condemned Falwell's statement was organized. The staffer responsible said: "It was beautiful. It set the stage and tone. . . . We set up the press conference, we got them here. They all wanted to do it, we didn't have to convince them. But it's hard to get all the groups talking to each other. So we had a big meeting. We decided a press conference was going to happen, and it happened." People for the American Way, one of the groups working with the leaders, ran full-page newspaper ads and did a one-hundred-thousand-piece mailing on the issue. In these communications, the group used the first of the two strategies on which the leaders had decided: making Jerry Falwell the issue. By his outrageous claims, Falwell had made it both necessary and relatively easy to discredit him, the leaders believed.

As the publicity campaign was going on, the task force that had worked for passage of the Grove City legislation continued its effort. "We just kept the same effort going, essentially without a break," a participant explained. A recount was done; a special effort to count Republicans was undertaken. On the day of the override vote, the leadership's second strategy was put into effect. A whip's staffer said: "The second piece of the campaign was to shift the terms of the debate, and that involved our project today to fill the Capitol with disabled individuals and to turn it from a women's/black vote into a disability vote. So we worked with the disability groups to literally fill the Capitol with people in wheelchairs." The staffer in charge of the effort elaborated:

> We sent handicapped people to see members, we headquartered in 324 [a large room in the Capitol] from which we sent people out all day long. And we sent five or ten or fifteen people out to a member of the Congress, to sit in their office and wait. We knew who was weak and undecided and we sent those people out [to see them].

A final tactic relied on the order in which the two chambers voted. When, on March 22, the Senate overrode the veto by a vote of 73 to 24, House proponents used the big vote to good effect, letting House members — especially southern Democrats and Republicans who could be swayed — know when senators from their states had voted to override. A participant explained, "We immediately took the Senate vote and then we contacted the people from the delegation to say, boom, the Senate did this. And so, you know, when Sam Nunn votes for it, why should the Georgia guys [vote against it]?" When the House voted later the same day, it overrode the veto by a 292 to 133 vote: Democrats voted 240 to 10 to override; 52 Republicans joined the Democrats. The leadership's aggressive media campaign countering Falwell made it possible for most Democrats to vote their policy beliefs, not their reelection fears.

The effort to prevent passage of a constitutional amendment outlawing flag burning was in many ways similar to the Grove City battle except that it extended over a period of months, not days. In that case as well, changing the opinion of attentive publics in members' constituencies was a prerequisite to success on the House floor; without some local support, a vote that could be depicted as favoring flag burning would have been too dangerous for many members to cast.

When, on June 29, 1989, the Supreme Court struck down a Texas statute outlawing defilement of the flag, a firestorm of outrage broke out. Individuals and groups — especially veterans' groups — called for a constitutional amendment to overturn the decision; public-opinion polls showed strong support for such a course of action. President Bush joined the clamor. Members of Congress, pressured by calls and letters from constituents, and in some cases themselves outraged, agitated for quick legislative action.

Senior Democrats on the Judiciary Committee and the party leaders believed a constitutional amendment was unwise and would set a dangerous precedent. Given the pressure from members, however, they could not simply block action. They decided to bring legislation barring flag defilement to the floor and, for the time being, prevent a constitutional amendment from coming to a vote. The bill would give members the opportunity they demanded to go on record against flag burning. For the many Democrats who agreed that amending the Constitution was too drastic a response, it provided the cover they needed to oppose bringing an amendment to the floor in accordance with their notions of good public policy. The bill might actually take care of the problem, but if it too were declared unconstitutional, as many on both sides believed likely, it would buy time for opponents of a constitutional amendment.

Opponents of the amendment were forced to agree to a provision for expedited Supreme Court review of the statute, so the showdown was not postponed indefinitely. To be ready, a task force began work months before the ruling was expected early in the summer of 1990. Chaired by Don Edwards (D-Calif.), who was the chair of the Judiciary Subcommittee on Civil and Constitutional Rights, and Chief Deputy Whip David Bonior, the task force began a public-education campaign. It met with grass-roots groups and wrote to newspaper editors around the country, arguing that such an amendment would, in order to bar isolated acts, do irremediable damage to the Bill of Rights (Biskupic 1990a). As soon as the Court handed down its decision on June 11, task-force members held a news conference and appeared on talk shows making the same argument. At least partly as a result, newspaper coverage, editorial opinion, and constituents' views changed. "This year you could hardly find a hometown paper that was editorializing for the amendment," Don Edwards reported (ibid., 1963). And, although polls still showed majorities favoring an amendment, the tenor of calls and letters from constituents changed. "Last year, the theme was that this [court decision] is such a disgrace and that no one should be allowed to burn the flag. This year, they [constituents] were saying, 'Don't tamper with the Constitution,'" an aide to a Republican supporter of a constitutional amendment said (ibid.).

The task force also mounted an in-House effort; it began talking to members one-on-one in May, well before the decision came down. The leadership made use of its internal tools as well. The task force's work gave opponents of an amendment a head start over supporters. When the Court struck down the federal statute, the leadership scheduled a vote on the constitutional amendment quickly and refused to heed Republican demands for delay, taking considerable pleasure in pointing out that Republicans had pushed for quick action and had, in the past, severely criticized the Democratic leadership for not moving fast enough. The Rules Committee, under leadership direction, refused to allow floor amendments that might make the constitutional amendment more palatable. Speaker Foley personally called members, asking them to oppose the amendment; he spoke on the floor, closing debate for opponents; and, in an unusual move, he voted—something the Speaker does ordinarily only to break a tie. Foley thus showed members that he himself was willing to cast the dangerous vote he was asking them to cast.

On June 21, the constitutional amendment was defeated 254 to 177— 34 votes short of the two-thirds needed; 160 Democrats and 17 Republicans opposed the amendment. In-House strategies, while important, would not by themselves have been sufficient. By changing the terms of public debate, the leadership made it possible for those 177 members to cast what, a year earlier, would have been for many an unexplainable and potentially fatal vote.

Managing Issues

Contemporary party leaders have the know-how, though not often the time, to "manage issues"; on a few particularly contentious and important issues, the leaders employ a comprehensive long-range strategy to attempt to influence public debate. The first full-fledged instance of such issue management occurred in the mid-1980s on aid to the contras. The president's advantage in the struggle to define issues is at its greatest on matters of foreign and defense policy. His standing as commander in chief, as premier foreign-policy maker, and as symbol of the nation make challenging him a formidable and politically dangerous enterprise. Simply getting coverage of an opposing viewpoint can be difficult.

A large group of House Democrats profoundly disagreed with President Reagan on his policy of supporting the contras in their attempt to overthrow the Sandinista government of Nicaragua. Given all the president's advantages, opponents of contra aid knew a purely in-House campaign would not be sufficient. The Nicaragua task force, set up in early 1985 with David Bonior as chair, set out not just to round up votes against aid to the contras but also to get the opponents' message out, to ensure that their views were covered by the press. To this purpose, a systematic long-range series of events was worked out for the press to cover. Hearings by the appropriate subcommittee of the Foreign Affairs Committee, an allied group's report on human-rights abuses, a trip to Central America by a congressional delegation, and a protest against aid to the contras by church groups were some of the events.

A staffer who worked with the task force talked about the development of a several-pronged strategy:

There were a couple of things that we did with the Nicaragua–contra aid task force that were very important. One, we developed a media strategy. We, in effect, developed a calendar of events that was geared to the congressional events that were going on with respect to the contra-aid issue that would allow us to get media attention to this issue. Second, we became much more aggressive in bringing in outside groups. . . . We asked of them that they integrate their media effort with us, that they inform us when they had something; and we were willing to help them. . . .. So, we made sure that was, in fact, integrated with our media calendars.

The task force was always prepared with an event on any day the president dealt publicly with Central America. The staffer explained why such counterprogramming is an effective means of increasing the visibility of opponents' points of view:

When there is a big issue coming up, the president has a set of events that he is going to use to direct media attention to the issue and the position that he supports; so what you can do is counterprogram. You simply have events on the same day that the president has his, and the media people's sense of fairness requires that these be covered, so you will get coverage. Now, you may not get the spin you would like on an issue, but, in fact, you will get coverage.

This effort became, the aide said, "a model for later ones"; it illustrated methods for "the leadership to manage issues on a much more sustained basis."

Ensuring Credit

Much more often, a media strategy is not essential to passing the legislation at issue; rather, its aim is to ensure that House Democrats get credit for their legislative efforts and, during a period of divided control, to pressure the president to accept the legislation. "It just does not do us any good to vote right and do what's right, you have to market what you are doing," a leader asserted. "If you don't market it, it doesn't do you any good [politically]."

Legislation mandating family and medical leave would pass handily when it came to the floor in 1991, the leaders knew, but not by enough votes to override a veto. By raising the visibility of the popular bill, the leaders hoped to discourage Bush from vetoing it or at least make him pay a political price for doing so. To that end, the leaders staged a press conference featuring victims with human-interest stories appealing to the press. A campaign of one-minute speeches was mounted in the days before the vote. The strategy paid off. All three evening network news programs ran stories that week and defined the issue as the Democrats had cast it: as a matter of family values and of fairness.

To raise the visibility of a bill, a dramatic event designed to get media coverage can sometimes be created. The "Grate American Sleep Out" was designed to highlight the plight of the homeless just before an aid bill was scheduled for a vote on the House floor. About a dozen members of Congress, including Majority Whip Tony Coelho, a group of movie stars, and some advocates for the homeless spent the night of March 3, 1987, sleeping on steam grates not far from the U.S. Capitol (Blakely 1987, 422). As intended, the event was highly publicized. The president, who had expressed opposition to the legislation, in the end signed it into law.

In 1988, when the Democratic party leadership was attempting to enact plant-closing-notification legislation, a carefully orchestrated daylong series of events featuring workers thrown out of work without any notice received extensive media coverage. Strong public support for the notification requirement eventually persuaded Reagan, who had adamantly opposed the provision, to let the legislation become law without his signature. By making the issue highly visible, Democrats had made an election-year veto too politically expensive for the president.

In late October 1991, Democrats staged an all-night House debate on the suffering of the nation's jobless. Carried live on C-SPAN, the vigil was aimed at keeping the pressure on President Bush to agree to an extension of unemployment benefits. The campaign of which it was part contributed to Bush's ultimate acceptance of legislation he had initially opposed.

In all these instances, the media campaign was at least moderately successful: coverage ranged from respectable to extensive in amount; its tone was by and large favorable to the Democrats' policy goals; the president was put under pressure. In three of the four cases, the president signed legislation that he had initially opposed. The effort did not deter Bush from vetoing the family-leave bill, but even in this instance, Democrats believed they had scored a partial success; the president, they believed, paid a price with the public for that veto.

Media campaigns are not always successful. Minimum-wage legislation in 1989 is a case in point. In the mid- and late 1980s, the raising of the minimum wage was a top legislative priority of organized labor, a major Democratic constituency. President Reagan's adamant opposition retarded congressional action, even during the 100th Congress, when Democrats controlled both chambers. Bush's support for a modest increase encouraged the Democratic leadership to put the proposal high on its agenda in 1989. Speaker Wright cited the legislation as a top priority in his speeches in late 1988 and early 1989, including it in his reply to Bush's first address to Congress; he assigned the bill the symbolic low number HR 2.

In keeping with the high priority that Democrats placed on the issue, the House passed a bill on March 23, 1989. Although a moderate com-

288 LEGISLATORS, LEADERS, AND LAWMAKING

promise measure, it still raised the minimum wage more that Bush wanted, and the training-wage provision it included was distant from Bush's proposal. Democrats had hoped that Bush would be willing to negotiate, but when he showed no sign of flexibility, the Senate passed a bill similar to the House version. The bill was sent to Bush, who immediately vetoed it.

During the 1988 presidential race and continuing during the months in which the legislation worked its way through the House and Senate, Democrats had attempted to publicize the minimum-wage increase, hoping to make it a major issue and to frame it as a fairness issue, thereby pressuring Bush to approve a more generous increase than the one in his initial proposal. Congressional leaders made innumerable public statements; they contrasted Bush's stinginess toward low-wage workers with his support for a capital-gains tax cut that would benefit primarily the rich; they signaled their willingness to compromise and called on him to talk. A coalition of labor, civil-rights, and women's groups ran radio ads urging the president to sign HR 2 and coordinated a letter-writing protest by low-wage workers.

The effort was unsuccessful. Even after Bush vetoed the bill, no public indignation was evident. "Nobody has hassled the president over this veto," an aide to the subcommittee chair, Austin Murphy (D-Pa.), said. "Nobody" (CQA 1989, 334). The House failed to override.

Given their disadvantage vis-à-vis the president in media access, the congressional majority-party leaders are highly dependent, in their efforts to pressure the president, on the ways in which the media decide to play stories. The press defined the minimum-wage increase as a labor issue; proponents could never persuade the media to cast it as a fairness issue. After the vote, when the media emphasized presidential decisiveness rather than the Democrats' preferred line—presidential insensitivity to workers—there was little the leadership could do.

Despite the Democrats' failure, many congressional Republicans were "uneasy" about Bush's hard line and did not "want to go to the wall a second time" (ibid., 333); they pressured the administration to talk. Democrats, aware they would not be able to override a veto, were also willing to make more-extensive compromises. Late in 1989, talks among administration officials, the AFL-CIO, and congressional leaders produced a compromise somewhat closer to the Democrats' position than to Bush's initial one.

The leadership's capacity for orchestrating the process inside the House and for producing substantial House majorities was sufficient to enact a bill that Democrats preferred to no legislation at all. To enact the strong bill they really wanted and to reap significant political benefit from the confrontation would have required success in the public-relations battle, and that the leadership could not deliver.

Promoting the Party's Image

"The message is not something that is delivered overnight," a high-ranking Democratic staffer said. "It is the filling in of a mosaic, and it has to be assembled over a long period of time" (*Los Angeles Times,* October 4, 1992). To have more than an ephemeral impact, the leaders' media strategies need to be designed for the long haul. If they are to have a significant effect on how a complex issue is perceived or on how the Democratic party is evaluated by the public, media efforts must have a longer-range focus than simply winning a particular vote. Despite the leaders' considerable access to the media, they lag far behind the president in their ability to get their message out. Consequently, especially if the congressional leaders are competing with the president, a consistent, coordinated campaign is crucial. Given the time pressure under which the leadership works, the number of leaders, and the leaders' inability to enforce a consistent message on their members, it is also difficult to achieve.

Leaders attempt to promote their party's image through carefully thought out and sustained media campaigns. "If you don't have [a media strategy], you are unilaterally disarming yourself against people who don't share your interests who have those strategies," a leadership press aide said.

> The White House has them, right. They think strategically. They think in yearlong, six-month, month, two-week, week, daylong blocks. . . . If public opinion is shaped by the print and electronic media and you are unilaterally disarming yourself and not participating in that shaping of opinion, opinion may well be turned against you.

The development and conveyance of broad themes that reflect favorably on the Democratic party are seen as the keys to a successful strategy. The forums to which leaders have access should be used not simply to provide information to the press or to promote specific legislation but to convey a broader message. Campaigns to pass particular bills should present and justify the specific legislation in terms of these broad themes. Demonstrating that Democrats could govern was a major theme — especially from 1987, when Democrats won back the Senate, to the end of the Bush administration. During this period, leaders consistently sought to cast legislative accomplishments as evidence that "Democrats have the capacity to govern." Whether in the daily Speaker's press conference, on *This Week with David Brinkley,* or in a one-on-one interview with a *Wall Street Journal* reporter, the leaders would reiterate this motif.

At year's end, particularly elaborate efforts are made: a special press conference is held; a major push to place the top leaders on the prestigious interview shows is made; talking points are distributed to "key 'talkers' in Washington — the people to whom reporters will turn for comment on the year-end wrap-up stories" and to the Democratic membership as a whole. A staffer discussed the end-of-the-year effort in 1987, which because of special circumstances offered special opportunities for extensive coverage:

> In late October, we began to see reporters making inquiries that led us to the inescapable conclusion they were working on profiles of Jim Wright. We also knew because of the calendar that Jim Wright was concluding his first year in office as Speaker, that meant year-end profiles, year-end wrap-ups on Congress as a whole, on what were we able to accomplish this year. So [the whip] and I worked on a memo that got circulated on the second floor that resulted in a meeting in early November where we tried to figure out what the story line should be and what we should be talking about and how we should move aggressively to set up interviews with CQ, *National Journal, Washington Post, New York Times, L.A. Times,* and others, to affirmatively and aggressively get the story out: "Jim Wright is breaking new ground as Speaker. He identified legislative priorities and they are all getting realized. Subtext, the Democratic Caucus is lined up behind Jim Wright. Subtext, subtext, the Democratic party's capacity to govern." . . . Coelho and Foley sat down with all the CQ reporters and all the *National Journal* reporters for lunches on successive days and got that story out. It was in the *New York Times* profile. The print press was replete with examples of how they wrote that story our way.

During the Bush administration, the Democratic leadership also sought to develop a set of themes that one aide summed up as "Democrats want to rebuild the economy and are on the side of working Americans." Legislation as diverse as the family-leave bill, the big transportation reauthorization, a middle-class tax cut, and a program to make student loans easier to get were linked to these themes of growth and fairness.

As a particularly media-savvy aide pointed out, defining yourself is only half the game; defining your opponent is also critically important. In 1989, and to some extent in 1990, many Democrats criticized Foley and Senate Majority Leader Mitchell for not taking Bush on aggressively enough. "We clearly have not defined ourselves as a party or contrasted ourselves with the President," complained David Nagel, a party loyalist (*Los Angeles Times,* October 8, 1989). "It's time to sharpen our message," Vic Fazio, vice chair of the Democratic Caucus, said. "A growing number of members are no longer willing to pull their punches" (ibid., February 3,

1990). Foley believes that sharply attacking a president early in his presidency and attacking him gratuitously at any time will hurt rather than help the party's image. "I don't think it's my daily task to try to embarrass the president," Foley responded when asked about Democratic criticism of his reticence.

Over time, Bush's partisan attacks on Congress and his lack of a domestic agenda diminished Foley's reluctance. Asked about the Speaker's frequent appearances on the Sunday interview shows, a Speaker's aide said:

> When Foley and Gephardt are asked, they [say yes] for important reasons. We have a president that has done very well on foreign affairs, but does not have much of a domestic agenda. You are in a period where the media are kind of writing the Democrats off in the next presidential election. You have a Congress that has more of a domestic agenda than the president has and a good way of conveying that to the public, and the only way we have, is through the media. So certainly we say yes when we are asked, and in fact we are likely to increase it rather than anything else. We have people who are good on television. It is very hard to compete with the president, but by taking every opportunity you at least lessen the odds.

In 1991 and 1992, with the recession lingering, Bush by his actions and by his inaction in the domestic realm provided Democrats with a series of opportunities to define him in negative terms. A top leadership press aide explained:

> The big issues that we have worked on in this Congress, the two biggest were unemployment compensation and the tax cut. Unemployment compensation was really terrific for us almost completely. That was an almost continuous story from July to November of 1991. It highlighted a number of arguments against Bush that have been very effective: that he doesn't stand for anything and just vetoes things, his foreign travel, that he only cares about the rich and not about the middle class. And it really has allowed us to divide Republicans to a certain extent, and it provides a sequence of votes that we hope some of our challengers can use. The tax cut has been almost as good.

Media routines are such that the congressional leaders' opportunities for coverage tend to be greatest when they are responding to the president. Using those opportunities well is central to an effective media strategy. A textbook example of a well-coordinated response occurred in June 1991. In a March 6 address to a joint session of Congress, Bush had challenged Congress to pass transportation and crime legislation in one hundred days. "If our forces could win the ground war [in the Persian Gulf] in a hundred hours, then surely the Congress can pass this legislation in a hundred days," the president said. Congress was working on legislation in both areas and making good progress, but would not finish within the stipulated one hundred days. As the deadline approached, rumors began circulating that Bush intended to criticize the Congress harshly for failing to meet his deadline. An aide described the leadership's response:

> A couple of weeks ago word got out that Bush intended to really bash the Democrats in Congress as do-nothing, etc. And the moment we found that out, we immediately started mobilizing. We had a meeting with Mitchell right away, and we got out a document explaining what we had done, and we just overall mobilized quickly and thoroughly and made a massive effort to hit first and to hit hard.

Senate Majority Leader George Mitchell charged that the president's tactics represented "a new low in political cynicism," and Speaker Foley labeled it the beginning of a reelection campaign centered on "Congress-bashing" (*Los Angeles Times,* June 12, 1991). In his daily press conference, Foley called the president's proposals on crime and transportation "woefully inadequate and insufficient. We'll send him much better legislation than he sent us," Foley added. Asked if the president has a domestic agenda, Foley, in a much-reported reply, snapped, "Not that I can determine" (ibid.). Majority Leader Gephardt, in a press release, labeled Bush's the "Polaroid presidency." "This is a President who prefers rhetoric to action, symbols to substance, vetoes to progress, and campaigning to governing," Gephardt charged. "It worked very well," the aide concluded. "Our story got out and it got lots of play. And from what we know, the president's attack then was a whole lot less strident then he had initially intended it to be."

In contrast, Democrats' attempt to counter Bush's claim that their civil-rights bill was a "quota bill" was universally acknowledged to have been ineffective—"a disaster," in the words of several. It began much too late, it was not well organized, and it was badly targeted, various members and staffers said. One commented:

> We were led by two chairmen who are from the pretelevision era and do not understand the media, and the quota issue was just handled much too late, and badly. What we needed was a full-court press very early on. We knew that this was an issue months and months ago. We should have put in [the bill] a quota division in the Department of Justice with some sort of assistant attorney general in charge of making sure that WASP males did not get discriminated against.

Democratic party and committee leaders did explain over and over again the bill's provisions and why it did not encourage hiring quotas—in written material prepared for the media, in press conferences, and, when given the opportunity, in television interviews. Majority Leader Gephardt in a floor speech accused the president of "practicing racial division" and, on *Meet the Press,* charged that Bush wanted a campaign issue, not a solution to the problem — comments widely quoted in the press. A provision explicitly barring quotas was included in the legislation. None of this, however, had much impact on the public at large. Eventually circumstances induced Bush to compromise; Democrats' efforts were not capable of doing so. On this highly inflammatory issue, the president's clear, simple interpretation — repeated often and amplified by his unparalleled media access — easily dominated his congressional opposition's more complex and nuanced interpretation, which, in this case, was not even presented in a well-orchestrated fashion.

One final example demonstrates that, when circumstances are especially favorable, a presidential attack can provide an opportunity for Democrats in turn to go on the offensive. The enhanced media access a presidential attack brings the party leaders can occasionally be employed to turn the tables on the president. Doing so requires a sophisticated strategic response.

On November 26, 1991, as Congress was frantically finishing its legislative business for the year, President Bush unexpectedly endorsed a tax-cut proposal that conservative House Republicans were pushing. "I want to see the package passed and I want to see it done fast," he told the press (Alston 1991a, 3506). The statement was a surprise because most in the administration had opposed any immediate tax cut and, in any case, the House Republican package was hastily crafted legislation that had not been subjected to careful scrutiny. In fact, the president's endorsement appeared to represent not true support but rather an attempt to solve several political problems. Democrats had been criticizing the president for his lack of an economic-recovery program. Their concerted attack was receiving increasing media attention and was probably contributing to Bush's falling popularity in the polls. By endorsing the conservative Republicans package, Bush would put Democrats on the defensive and satisfy House Republicans, who wanted their president's support. Only hours away from the planned adjournment, there appeared to be little danger of that bill or any other tax cut actually passing.

The Democratic leadership responded quickly. "It was unbelievably irresponsible for the president to suggest that he would like us to vote today on a proposal that wasn't even a legislative proposal until last night and has been costestimated at $23 billion," Speaker Tom Foley told the press. "It is totally irresponsible" (*Los Angeles Times,* November 27, 1991). In an unusual speech on the House floor, the Speaker called for "an end to the gamesmanship"; he challenged Bush to phone him and ask for

Congress to return in December if Bush really wanted a tax bill (Alston 1991a, 3506).

At a caucus of House Democrats late in the evening of November 26, the leaders outlined their strategy. The House would not formally adjourn when it finished its business, so that the leadership could easily recall members should Bush decide to bash Congress for not passing a tax cut. In December, the Ways and Means Committee would hold hearings to highlight the troubled economy, expose problems with the conservative Republican plan, and begin to build support for a Democratic alternative.

The media found this high-stakes confrontation riveting, and devoted extensive coverage to the leaders' adept response to the president's political ploy. That the Democrats had called Bush's bluff and come out well ahead was the consensus view. The interest created by this imbroglio probably increased media coverage of the December Ways and Means Committee hearings. Carefully orchestrated to showcase the difference between Democratic proposals for middle-class tax relief and Republican plans to cut the capital-gains tax, which would benefit the rich, the hearings clearly put the Democrats on the offensive and the president on the defensive.

With Congress out of town, the president had expected to monopolize the spotlight, using that media attention to repair some of the damage done to his popularity by the bad economy and Democrats' effective exploitation of the issue. He had hoped, in fact, to turn the tables on his political opponents, blaming the country's economic woes on congressional Democrats. In this instance, the House Democratic leaders, by their adept response to the threat, not only protected their members and the party's image but actually transformed the situation into an opportunity to promote the party's image and its policies.

With a Democratic president, the party leadership need not fear that the full power of the White House publicity apparatus will be used to make House Democrats and their policy preferences look bad. Usually the congressional party leaders and the president are working toward the same objectives, and White House media efforts further House Democrats' goals. But even with a Democratic president, House members still expect their leaders to continue their outward-directed party-promoting activities. Their interests and those of the White House are not always identical, and even though they are usually similar, the magnitude of the task confronting Democrats requires that congressional leaders continue their efforts. The fate of Clinton's presidency and of congressional Democrats is tied to the fate of an ambitious agenda and, in an era of constricting deficits and antigovernment sentiment, success depends on winning the battle to shape the debate.

Pursuing Policy and Reelection in a Media Age

House members have learned that, in contemporary politics, the successful pursuit of policy and reelection often requires that one go public — that one get one's message out through the media that are now so pervasive a part of the American political process. In the 1970s many members believed that they could as individuals effectively exploit the new opportunities the media age offered. With the weakening of the party as an organization and of party identification in the electorate, members were able to further their goals through individualist entrepreneurial strategies — building more heavily personal rather than primarily party-based electoral coalitions, and using outward-directed agenda-setting and promotion activities and the new participation opportunities the reforms created internally to advance their policy goals.

In the 1980s Democrats discovered the negative side of media-dominated politics in an era of weak parties. For an adept president, the media are powerful tools for furthering his goals. And, given the weakening of party identification in the electorate, the party vote, the parties' images, and party identification itself are not so stable as they were in the past, which gives a skillful president a real chance to influence them to his advantage. Ronald Reagan used the media to paint a highly negative image of the Democratic party and of its policy preferences. Polls showed the public holding less favorable views of the Democratic party than they had before, and party identification shifted in a pro-Republican direction. House Democrats found that all their goals were being threatened and, given the magnitude and source of the threat, few believed that they could respond effectively as individuals.

Thus, Reagan taught House Democrats that they needed collective media strategies, and they of necessity looked to their party leadership to take on that task. Now, working to get the Democratic message out and to shape debate to the benefit of the party's policy agenda and its image with the public are routine parts of the leadership's job.

Does Activist Leadership Make a Difference?

Legislative Success and the Lawmaking Process
in the Postreform House

A brief description of the House Democratic leadership's role in the passage of President Clinton's economic program began this book. The majority leader brokered a compromise that assured the support of more-conservative Democrats; at the leaders' direction, the bill was considered under a restrictive rule that protected it from being picked apart and shielded vulnerable Democrats from having to cast a series of tough votes. The leaders orchestrated an elaborate and comprehensive vote-mobilization process and passed the bill on the floor of the House. Contrast the party leadership's activism and consequentiality in this and in many other cases described above with the much less central and effective role available to the Democratic party leadership in the prereform era and in the immediate postreform years. The 1975 debacle on a major energy bill described in chapter 3 provides a good example. The Democratic membership wanted legislation but no one proved capable of putting together a broadly supported package. Even though the bill that emerged from committee was clearly in trouble, the top leaders made no attempt to broker a compromise. Unprotected by a restrictive rule because Democrats were unwilling to so constrain themselves, the bill was decimated by amendments on the floor. There was little the party leadership could do.

The House majority-party leadership's role in the legislative process has changed substantially since the mid-1970s; it has become more active, more central, and more consequential. The leadership puzzle raised at the beginning of the book is real: despite the weakening of the parties' grip on the electorate, party leadership in the House is stronger now than at any time since the revolt against Speaker Cannon.

The considerable alterations in the legislative process in the House during this period are both a cause and an effect of the change in how the leadership functions. Internal reforms and a transformed political environment altered the legislative process, making difficult the passage of legislation Democrats needed to advance their policy and reelection goals. House Democrats turned to their party leaders for help. More active party leadership was, in effect, the Democratic members' solution to the problems created by changes in the legislative process in the 1970s and early 1980s, altering that process to the advantage of the majority party. The solution to the leadership puzzle lies, as I will elaborate below, in the cost-benefit calculations of majority-party members of the House.

To conclude this study, I consider the impact of the leadership's expanded role. Does it increase the majority party's legislative success? Does it make a difference in how the House carries out its core task of lawmaking? If so, what are its effects? In particular, does stronger leadership enhance the House's lawmaking capacity? After all, our interest in party leadership stems primarily from its potential for enabling the Congress to perform that core function. How stable is the current set of arrangements? How likely is this approximation of party government to endure?

The Impact of Leadership Involvement on Legislative Success

Leadership strength was earlier defined in terms of activity and impact on legislative outcomes. One leadership can be said to be stronger than another if it is more active in the legislative process and if this activity has an impact on legislative outcomes. The increase in activity or involvement was systematically demonstrated in chapter 4; it now becomes necessary to show systematically that leadership involvement does, in fact, increase the likelihood of legislative success. Doing so will complete the demonstration that the House majority-party leadership has become stronger over the period under study. It will also lend further credence to the explanation that has been offered. The benefits of strong leadership to members, which are an important component of my explanation, obviously exist only if leadership help in the legislative process makes a difference in outcomes.

Because the members' need for help is a major determinant of leadership involvement, the party leaders get involved in the tough legislative battles; if there is no controversy or if victory is assured, there is no need for the leaders to get involved. Consequently, to compare success rates on measures that evoked leadership involvement with success rates on measures that did not is to compare success rates on tough issues with those on easy issues. Considering only measures that might be expected to face some difficulty in the legislative process makes for a more meaningful

Table 12.1 The Impact of Leadership Involvement on Committee Success when President and Committee Disagree

	Congress				
	91st (1969–70)	94th (1975–76)	97th (1981–82)	100th (1987–88)	101st (1989–90)
Floor: Committee won					
% of all measures	46	60	59	73	68
% when leadership involved	50	68	50	81	67
% when leadership not involved	43	46	83	25	75
Final disposition: Committee won on balance					
% of all measures	47	52	22	65	46
% when leadership involved	83	60	18	67	50
% when leadership not involved	22	36	33	50	25

Table 12.2 The Impact of Leadership Involvement on House Democrats' Success on Measures Pitting the President against Two-thirds or More of House Democrats

	Congress				
	91st (1969–70)	94th (1975–76)	97th (1981–82)	100th (1987–88)	101st (1989–90)
Floor: Democrats won					
% of all measures	75	83	61	91	83
% when leadership involved	83	92	54	96	83
% when leadership not involved	50	60	80	—[a]	75
Final disposition: Democrats won on balance					
% of all measures	38	44	28	78	48
% when leadership involved	50	54	23	77	50
% when leadership not involved	0	20	40	—[a]	40

[a]N = 1.

comparison. Presidential opposition is used as an indicator that the measure confronted some significant opposition. One must remember, however, that even these measures varied enormously in how controversial they were, in the strength of opponents other than the president, and in how much effort the president expended in opposing them, and, consequently, in how difficult they were to pass. By and large, the more difficult the battle expected, the more Democrats needed their leaders' help and the more likely the leaders were to get involved.

Committee win rates generally are higher when the leaders are active than when they stay on the sidelines; leadership involvement does appear to increase committees' probability of legislative success on the floor and on final disposition (see table 12.1). On those measures pitting House Democrats against the president, Democrats were more successful on the House floor and in terms of final disposition of the legislation when the party leaders were active than when they stayed out of the battle (see table 12.2).

In the 97th Congress, however, the relationship was reversed, a result, it appears, of the very tough issues on which the leadership attempted to build coalitions in opposition to President Reagan. The leaders were active on all of the measures on Reagan's core agenda and, in 1981, lost a series of major battles to the popular president (Sinclair 1983). Clearly, while leadership involvement can increase the probability of legislative success, it cannot ensure it regardless of other conditions. The very low success rate on final disposition in the 97th Congress reflects Republican control of the Senate.

Leadership involvement had a significant impact on the success of committees on the floor (see table 12.3). Clearly the difficulty of the battle — represented here by whether the president opposed the committee's position — affected the chances of winning. So too, and more strongly, did the

Table 12.3 The Relationships among Leadership Involvement, Presidential Position, and Committee Floor Success

Leadership Involvement	President/ Committee	Committee Win Rate
Major	Agree	84.6
Minor	Agree	73.3
Major	Disagree	67.5
Minor	Disagree	61.9
None	Agree	57.9
None	Disagree	55.0

involvement of the leadership. When the committee and the president disagreed and the leaders stayed out of the battle, the committee clearly won on the floor only a little over half the time (55%); major involvement by the leaders raised that win rate to two-thirds of the time (67.5%).

Probit analysis shows that even after the character of the floor coalition is taken into account, leadership involvement in interaction with presidential position significantly influenced the success of committees on the House floor.[1] A committee is more likely to win on the floor if floor coalitions are partisan rather than ones that split Democrats along regional lines. The success of committees on the House floor is also positively and significantly related to the extent of leadership involvement and whether the president and the committee agree or disagree, with the probability of success being highest when the leaders are involved and the committee and the president agree, next highest when the leaders are involved in a major way and the committee and the president disagree, and lowest when the leaders are not involved. Activist leadership does make a difference; by getting involved, party leaders can facilitate significantly the passage of legislation their members need and want.

The Leadership Puzzle Solved

Because contemporary American political parties are weak by historical standards, strong congressional party leadership should not be possible. So most scholars would have argued until recently, at least (see, for example, Crotty 1984). Scholars have believed congressional party-leadership strength to be a function of the strength of the political parties external to the legislature; vigorous parties with distinctive constituency bases that command the loyalty of most voters, ones that play an important role in the recruitment and election of candidates, make strong legislative leader-

---

1. The interaction variable is coded as follows:

Leadership Involvement	Pres./Comm.	Code
Major	Agree	5
Minor	Agree	4
Major	Disagree	3
Minor	Disagree	2
None	Agree	1
None	Disagree	0

"Disagree" here includes partial as well as complete disagreement. The results are highly similar if the mixed cases are excluded.
Floor coalition is coded 1 for partisan, −1 for North/South split, and 0 for other.
The probit coefficients and standard errors are:
Leadership involvement/Pres. position interaction .129 (.06)
Floor coalition .253 (.13)

ship possible. The relative weakness of contemporary parties in the electorate would seem to preclude strong party leadership. Yet that is exactly what I have established to be the case.

An answer to the leadership puzzle emerges from a consideration of the rationale underlying the relationship between external party strength and congressional party-leadership strength. Strong parties external to the legislature ensure that, for most majority-party members of Congress, the benefits of strong party leadership outweigh the costs because strong parties make likely a high degree of intraparty consensus on the legislation members need to meet their reelection and policy goals. It is not external party strength per se but how it affects the costs and benefits to members of strong internal leadership that is key. Consequently, changes in internal leadership strength may result from factors other than external party strength that influence those costs and benefits. And that is what I have found.

To meet their reelection and policy goals, members need legislation. When majority-party members found that the extant legislative process was no longer producing the legislation they needed, the costs of maintaining the institutional status quo became very high. Contemporaneously, the costs of change in the direction of stronger leadership declined as the party membership became less ideologically heterogeneous.

Are the character of internal party leadership and the state of parties external to the legislature not linked? To the contrary, the character of the contemporary party and electoral system does affect the exercise of House party leadership. The story is just more complex than conventional wisdom or the new scholarship would have it. On the one hand, the conventional wisdom often overstates the weakness of contemporary parties (see Baer 1992–93 for a corrective). Party organization at the national and state levels has become more rather than less vigorous in recent years (Cotter et al. 1984). To be sure, party identification has weakened and appears less stable than it used to be, and split-ticket voting is very high (Wattenberg 1986). Nevertheless, the core of most members' electoral coalitions still consists of voters who identify with the member's party. And with the change in southern voting habits, the parties in the House have become more distinct in their constituency bases.

Furthermore, the greater malleability of party images, of the vote, and even of party identification itself presents dangers and opportunities that did not exist to the same extent when they were highly stable. In such an environment members derive a real benefit from a party leadership strong enough to engineer activities and outcomes that promote a favorable party image and, perhaps more crucially, to forestall the sort of activities and outcomes that would severely harm the party's image.

Yet the weakness of party identification in the electorate, the basic underpinning for strong external parties, does constrain party leadership. House Democrats' constituencies, while less heterogeneous than in the past, are still far from uniformly homogeneous. With party identification more lightly held than in the past, constituents' perceptions of the candidates as individuals play a more important role in their voting decisions (Jacobson 1992b). As a result, members continue to insist on considerable autonomy to fashion individualist reelection strategies suited to their constituencies, thus limiting and influencing the character of party leadership and thereby the character of the legislative process in the House.

Leadership Strategies and the Evolution of the Legislative Process in the House

Majority-party members of the House, I have argued, expect their leadership to advance members' goals of reelection, policy, and influence by fostering the collective action prerequisite to lawmaking, but to do so without imposing unacceptable constraints on members' pursuit of their goals through individualist strategies. What members consider the optimal balance between these two concerns will vary over time as a function of the costs and benefits to members of assertive versus restrained central leadership. In the 1980s Democrats' optimal balance shifted and made the more active, more consequential leadership of the contemporary period possible.

The shift in members' expectations was by no means sufficient to allow for a highly directive, command style of leadership. By the late 1970s, members of the House had become accustomed to exercising great autonomy in the pursuit of their reelection and policy goals. In subsequent years, members came to realize that passage of the legislation they needed and wanted required a willingness to live with more constraint. Yet the candidate-centered electoral context within which they sought reelection necessitated, members believed, considerable autonomy to tailor reelection strategies to their individual constituencies. Democrats became willing to allow their leaders to use their tools aggressively when the securing of satisfactory legislative outcomes required it, but they certainly issued no blank checks. The effective use of the leadership's most potent tools is contingent on member acquiescence and often on explicit consent.

The House Democratic leadership responded with considerable creativity in developing strategies to meet the members' complex and potentially conflicting expectations. The strategy of inclusion gave members the access to their leaders and the opportunity to participate broadly in the legislative process that they wanted and provided the leaders with the assistance in carrying out a range of leadership functions that they needed. Members can, and in fact are expected to, pick and choose the party legislative battles in which to enlist; when reelection needs or policy preferences (or simple time constraints) dictate sitting out a battle, a member can do so without incurring a significant cost. Certainly choosing not to participate in one instance does not preclude future participation. Because the entire Democratic membership constitutes the base from which those active on a particular legislative battle are drawn and a large proportion choose to be active at least occasionally, the leaders usually find themselves with an adequate number of genuinely willing workers.

For junior members who have not yet attained positions of committee influence, the strategy of inclusion in its various manifestations offers especially welcome opportunities for them to participate meaningfully in the legislative process. However, members of middle and high seniority also value access to an increasingly consequential leadership and the information and shot at influencing party strategy that such access yields, as well as opportunities to participate on issues of interest to them outside their committees' jurisdiction. The strategy of inclusion permeates the organization and functioning of the contemporary House Democratic party and its leadership. Without it, the party leadership could not be active on nearly so much legislation as it is, nor (probably) would the members countenance so much involvement on the part of the leadership.

The structuring of choices through procedure is the second linchpin of contemporary leadership strategy. Leaders use procedure, particularly special rules, to structure choices so as to advantage the party's position. This strategy constrains members in the pursuit of their goals through individualist strategies, most frequently by limiting or barring them from offering amendments that might advance their reelection or policy goals. Democrats consent most of the time because the leadership constructs rules that, on balance, advance members' goals. Frequently, rules are designed so as to allow members to vote their policy preferences rather than their reelection fears. Democrats also consent because the strategy of inclusion ensures that they have some input, direct or indirect, on decisions about rules.

The legislative process in the House of Representatives is, within the majority party at least, participatory and inclusive; it is a considerably more democratic process than it was in the prereform days. At the same time, some of the virtues of central leadership are evident. Majority-party leaders do provide some central direction, a collective-interest perspective, and considerable coordination. The chamber's agenda and schedule are to a greater extent the result of explicit decisions informed by a view of what is in the interest of country, institution, and party, and less simply the unplanned result of the activities of a number of autonomous committees. Similarly, both substance and strategy on major legislation are more likely to be shaped by a perspective that is sensitive to the collective interests of the membership.

To be sure, in acting to advance collective interests, leaders are limited by what their members will allow; in an electoral context that is candidate-centered rather than party-centered, those limits are very real. Furthermore, leaders have a clear interest in the reelection of their members and only rarely would want to further the party's collective interest at the expense of any appreciable segment's individual reelection prospects. Finally, most of the routine legislative business of the House is still handled by committees without any significant leadership involvement or oversight.

Nevertheless, despite these caveats, the legislative process in the House has changed significantly. It is a process that offers majority-party members multiple opportunities for participation and yet one characterized by stronger internal central leadership than at any time since early in the century. Since these stronger, more-active central leaders are party leaders, party influence in the legislative process has been enhanced. Republicans complain bitterly that their opportunities to participate meaningfully in the legislative process have been curtailed. To be sure, their vocal protests contain a considerable component of partisan posturing. On much legislation, the House still functions in a relatively bipartisan way, and in committee, Republicans have the opportunity to take part in the shaping of legislation. Yet major legislation increasingly splits the membership along partisan lines and meaningful participation in shaping the legislation and amassing support takes place within the majority party. So long as Democrats remain reasonably unified and willing to allow their leadership to use its tools aggressively, the minority party is irrelevant. A commentator has called Republicans' complaints the "shrieks of the eunuchs." The price for more party influence in the legislative process appears to be considerable partisan rancor and nastiness.

The benefits are, however, considerable. The contemporary legislative process allows members of the majority party to pursue their collective interests much more effectively than was possible during the committee government era or the immediate postreform years, and to do so without sacrificing their individual needs.

As a result of the increased importance of party, major House decisions are now most frequently made by a stable, organized majority, not by ephemeral majorities that form on a particular issue today and quickly dissolve to be replaced by a different and equally transitory majority when a different issue takes center stage tomorrow. A stable, organized majority is more likely to produce coherent policy. Perhaps even more important, a stable, organized majority can be held accountable by the voters for its actions and inaction. Citizens can judge the majority's overall record and make their voting decisions accordingly. With one party controlling both Congress and the presidency, the conditions for accountability are especially favorable. Without accountability, true democracy does not exist.

Since the mid-1970s, the legislative process in the House of Representatives has become much more flexible and varied. The old "bill becomes a law" diagram accurately describes the process for fewer and fewer major bills. The bill reported by a single committee and considered on the floor under a simple open rule still exists, but it is not likely to be major legislation. Bills that are referred to a number of committees and broadly encompassing omnibus legislation—some, but not all, related to the budget process—now make up a substantial part of the congressional agenda. The shaping or fine-tuning of legislation by way of extracommittee or postcommittee processes in the House is no longer an unusual event. Occasionally committees are bypassed altogether; more frequently task forces under leadership auspices, or the leaders themselves, work out substantive changes in committee-reported legislation to enhance its prospects of enactment. Much legislation is passed under suspension of the rules, a process controlled by the Speaker. Most major legislation is brought to the floor under complex and often restrictive rules, frequently ones fashioned to deal with problems specific to the particular bills at issue. Even summits at which congressional party leaders and top-ranking administration officials negotiate agreements on major policy issues are no longer extraordinary events.

Particularly when it hits the headlines, lawmaking through these newer processes is often not neat and not pretty. Used on highly salient and contentious issues, these processes often provoke screams of outrage from members who believe their rightful role has been usurped. Yet these new processes and the stronger, more activist leadership on which the successful functioning of many of the new processes depends have made it possible for the House to legislate in an environment of severe legislative constraint. Divided control and huge deficits made stalemate a constant threat. The more flexible and varied legislative process in the contemporary House has made it possible for the majority-party leadership to tailor the process to the problem at hand and keep the House operating.

During the long period of divided control, the House transformed itself into a much more formidable competitor to the president. The House's majority party as an entity can now challenge an opposition-party president on the setting of the agenda and on the shaping of legislation with a greater prospect of success. Most consequential in the long run, however, the altered legislative process enables the House to function under extraordinarily difficult circumstances and thereby to fend off pressures to make changes that would permanently reduce its power in the American political system. Republican presidents vigorously advocated the line-item veto, a constitutional amendment requiring a balanced budget, and various other "reforms" that would fundamentally alter the interbranch balance of power at the national level. Although the battles between Congress and the president took a severe toll on both institutions' standing with the public, Congress withstood the pressure to make structural changes that would permanently damage the institution. Without a strengthened leadership to stand up against the temptation to follow the expedient course and, even more crucially, to keep the House functioning legislatively, the president and other Congress bashers most likely would have prevailed.

Never popular, Congress has been subject to unrelenting criticism in recent years; gridlock is the central problem plaguing American government, according to conventional wisdom, and Congress is at fault. In fact, the political context of huge deficits and, until 1993, divided control has made legislating extraordinarily difficult. Deficits make all the choices difficult ones; divided control made it necessary to overcome deep policy differences between the president and congressional majorities in making the tough choices. Yet, despite this context, the House has continued to perform its legislative functions and, during the most difficult of these times, has managed to protect and even enhance its role in the American political system. The development of a stronger central leadership along with the constellation of changes in the legislative process here described made this possible.

The House, the Democratic Party, and Its Leadership: What Lies Ahead?

The House of the early 1990s functions quite differently not just from the prereform House but also from the House of the early postreform years. The way in which tasks, powers, and resources are distributed has been significantly altered; the legislative process has become more flexible, and new variations and paths have developed. How stable are these new arrangements? What lies ahead?

The hallmark of the new legislative process is flexibility and variety—in effect, a lack of stability. The use of many of the newer variants depends on circumstances created by the political environment, and that is likely to remain true in the future. Much of the omnibus legislation and all of the summits have been responses to particular problems, and their future use is likely to depend on such problems arising again.

The major changes wrought by the reforms of the 1970s are a stable element; they are not likely to be reversed. Powerful, autonomous committees capable of passing their legislation without help are a phenomenon of the increasingly distant past. Consequently, an active, broadly involved majority-party leadership able to use its tools aggressively is essential for the House to function. The continued existence of such a leadership is dependent on members' expectations, on how the members of the majority party weigh the costs and benefits of assertive versus more restrained leadership.

The increase in Democrats' ideological homogeneity is, in significant part, a result of long-term changes in the supportive constituencies of southern Democrats, and those changes are not likely to be reversed. However, Democrats' constituency-based cohesion, while sufficient to make assertive leadership a possibility, does not ensure it. Democrats are certainly not ideologically monolithic; the issues at the center of conflict and how they are framed will influence the extent to which Democrats will find it "natural" to vote as a party.

Most of the evolution here depicted occurred under divided control, and certainly much of the change was a response to the problems divided control created for House Democrats. The election of a Democratic president changed the political context. What are its implications for stability or change in House functioning, for members' continued willingness to countenance assertive leadership?

Before the fact, and considering the problem abstractly, one might have predicted that united control would confront Democrats with two related temptations that could pose a danger to the party's legislative performance. First, members on the left of their party's spectrum might see the election of a Democratic president as an opportunity to place on the agenda scores of expensive new social programs. That form of massive agenda expansion would likely create dissension and reduce cohesion. Second, members from all parts of the spectrum might reassess the costs and benefits of the structuring of choices by party leaders. In a seemingly more favorable political climate, many Democrats might find irresistible the attractions of the freelance variety of policy entrepreneurship prevalent in the 1970s, and thus be less willing to acquiesce in restrictive rules, for example.

In fact, the budget deficit has served as an enormous constraint; neither the adoption of grandiose new social programs nor the development of a freelance entrepreneurial style appears realistic, despite the change in the presidency. House Democrats' realization that the conditions for accountability are optimal and that they are very likely to be judged collectively at election time has also served to keep them from succumbing to these temptations.

Over the longer run, the continuation of the current set of arrangements, with its activist, assertive party leadership, depends on whether the collective benefits it delivers outweigh the costs of the constraints it imposes on members' individualist strategies. If Congress and President Clinton are able to enact into law a significant legislative program that furthers most Democrats' policy goals and if Democrats fare well in the elections, members will perceive current arrangements as meeting their needs. On the other hand, if policy or reelection results are seriously disappointing, members are likely to reassess the adequacy of those arrangements, with an insistence on greater autonomy to pursue their goals through individualist strategies the likely result.

The House of Representatives has transformed itself in such a way that it can function as a moderately effective legislature in a very difficult environment. An active, assertive majority-party leadership supported by a reasonably cohesive party membership is the key component of that transformation. Yet because that stronger internal party leadership and its members' cohesiveness are not based on a strong party external to the Congress, the current arrangements appear relatively fragile. Internal party strength requires that the members of the congressional party see their individual interests as coinciding to a significant extent and, without strong parties in the electorate, the perception of coinciding interests is highly vulnerable to erosion by short-term forces in the political environment.

Given the chamber's postreform institutional structure and the current and foreseeable political environment, a weakening of the majority-party leadership would reduce the House's lawmaking capacity enormously. Perhaps that cost as well as the flexibility inherent in leadership strategies will forestall such incapacitating change.

Afterword, 1998

With shocking unexpectedness, Republicans for the first time in forty years won a House majority in the 1994 elections. Newt Gingrich's phenomenal success in engineering the win and then in steering the Contract with America and a balanced budget through the House had journalists and political commentators hailing him as a reincarnation of the legendary powerful Speakers of the past and as a successful revolutionary leader beside. Is Gingrich a different sort of leader? Does Republican party leadership in the 104th and 105th Congresses show continuity or discontinuity with that of its Democratic predecessors, and why?

Gingrich's success at majority building as perceived and interpreted by his members explains much of what differentiates his leadership in the 104th from the preceding Democratic leaderships and from his own in the 105th as well. The extraordinary political context of the 104th and how it shaped members' expectations were the key determinants of Gingrich's relationships with his members and with the committees and their chairs—relationships that were unusual for the modern Congress. Even so, Republican leadership strategies show considerable continuity with the past. Little that Gingrich did was unprecedented in kind; however, the political context allowed him to push the envelope, to exploit leadership tools more aggressively than any of his postreform predecessors. When the context changed in the 105th so perforce did Gingrich's leadership.

The new Republican majority that the 1994 elections produced was unusually ideologically homogeneous and believed itself to be mandated to make far-reaching policy change. The huge freshman class—seventy-three strong—consisted largely of true believers, deeply committed to cutting the size and scope of government and to balancing the budget; with the sophomores, who were similar in outlook, they made up over half of the Republican House membership. Many more senior Republican conservatives had been waiting for such an opportunity for years. Even moderate Republicans strongly agreed that, since Republicans had run on the Contract, they would have to deliver on their promises to maintain their majority.

Gingrich, in the eyes of most Republicans and the media, was responsible for the unexpected Republican victory. He had worked to build a majority for years; he had recruited many of the challengers who won and had helped them with fund raising and campaign advice; the Contract with America was Gingrich's idea and he had orchestrated its realization. As a result members did feel grateful to him. More important for the power and discretion they allowed him to exercise, members regarded Gingrich as a world-class, once-in-a-century political genius, an opinion reinforced in the early months by the media. Since they were convinced that Gingrich shared their policy and electoral goals, Republican members, many of whom were very junior, gave Gingrich, the miracle maker, broad latitude.

Understanding his opportunity as well as the magnitude of the task ahead, Gingrich aggressively exploited his discretion. In the days after the elections, he exercised power well beyond that specified in Republican Conference rules. He designated Republicans to serve as committee chairs, bypassing seniority in several instances. Gingrich also engineered a rules change to increase the party leadership's voice on the committee on committees and used that new influence to reward junior Republicans, his strongest supporters, with choice assignments.

Gingrich and the rest of the new Republican majority party leadership in the 104th Congress were highly active on the legislation that made up the congressional agenda of major measures, but not unprecedentedly so. They were at least somewhat involved in 80 percent of the measures and, for 63 percent, their involvement was major—a rate of activity almost identical to that of the Wright leadership in the 100th Congress.

The Republican leadership's role in agenda setting in the 104th stands out as uniquely high. The Contract with America was an innovation; although previous congressional leaders had developed agendas to guide legislative action and to enhance the credit their party could claim from legislative productivity, no leader before had made an agenda the centerpiece of a nationalized congressional campaign. With the Contract and then the balanced budget legislation, the Gingrich leadership dominated the agenda to nearly the same extent that presidents do at the beginning of their administrations, and he almost completely eclipsed President Clinton; 41 percent of the congressional agenda consisted of leadership agenda items, only 4 percent were presidential agenda items. In the previous congress, by contrast, Clinton's agenda items had accounted for 46 percent of the congressional agenda.

Although the Democratic party leadership in the 1980s and early 1990s had been actively involved in all stages of the legislative process, sometimes intervening in committee, not infrequently brokering compromises after a bill was reported and occasionally bypassing committee altogether, the relationship between party and committee leaders was different in the 104th Congress; committee leaders were clearly subordinate to party leaders. The party set the agenda; party leaders held the committees to a tight schedule and exerted a strong influence on the substance of legislation.

When a committee was incapable of mustering a majority for legislation that the party leadership and the membership wanted, the leadership stepped in and bypassed the committee; for example, when the Agriculture Committee refused to report the "Freedom to Farm" bill, which made cuts in farm programs as required by the budget resolution, the leadership inserted the language directly into the reconciliation bill. When the legislation a committee reported was unacceptable to a majority of the Republican membership, as on the term limits constitutional amendment, the leadership altered the language substantially after it had been reported and before it went to the floor. On Medicare, one of the most politically sensitive issues the Republicans took on, Gingrich himself headed the "design group" that made the major substantive decisions; that group also included the Republican leaders of the committees and subcommittees with jurisdiction.

The Republican leadership could act so assertively because much of the membership was ideologically committed to passing the legislation at issue and almost all were convinced that the party's fate depended on delivering on their promises. When, at the beginning of the Congress, Republicans revised House and party rules, they on balance strengthened the party leadership a bit vis-à-vis committee chairs, especially by imposing a three-term limit on committee chairs. A Conference rule on leadership issues, although not new, took on added importance; it reads, "the Speaker may designate certain issues as 'Leadership Issues.' Those issues will require early and ongoing cooperation between the relevant committees and the Leadership as the issue evolves." It was, however, the Republican membership's commitment to passing the Contract and Gingrich's prestige, not new rules, that allowed Gingrich to exercise such clout. With the leaders acting as agents of an intense and determined membership, the committees had little choice but to go along.

The leaders could not ignore such membership sentiment, either; they occasionally found themselves forced by their members into a course of action they would have preferred to avoid. The Republican leadership brought to the floor the gift ban, lobbying reform and campaign finance legislation only because of pressure from a determined group of mostly junior members.

Although the political context of the 104th differed in some important respects from that in which Democratic leaders had operated, in other ways it was similar, as were Gingrich's leadership strategies. Like his predecessors, Gingrich relied on a strategy of inclusion. Long before he moved into the leadership, Gingrich had sought to involve others in his majority building efforts, to get them to "buy in." As whip he continued that effort, reaching out to members with whom he had little in common ideologically.

The putting together of the Contract exemplifies the strategy. In late 1993, Gingrich began to talk about holding a Capitol steps event during the 1994 election campaign. At the House Republicans' retreat in February 1994, members held intensive discussions in small groups and took the first steps toward identifying the common principles and core beliefs that would guide the drafting of the Contract. Republican incumbents and challengers were surveyed about what should be included. The leaders decided to exclude measures that were divisive within the party. When the items to be included had been determined, working groups of members and leadership staff put together the actual bills. Any member who wanted to could participate, but younger activists were likelier to do so than senior committee leaders. Still, a large number of members did have a hand in shaping the Contract and so felt some pride of authorship.

Once in the majority, Gingrich and the Republican leadership team continued the "buy-in" strategy. Gingrich established numerous task forces to carry out a great variety of jobs. Some were charged with expediting action on Contract legislation, others with devising broad-based compromises on divisive issues, others with outreach beyond Congress, and still others had an electoral purpose. Inclusion—especially of junior members—was clearly an important goal, and freshmen were very heavily represented on task forces. "Newt uses task forces to get people involved who have a common interest on something," a moderate Republican explained. "He wants to let everybody do their own thing, pursue their own interests."

The Conference meets weekly, as does a large leadership group of about twenty, which includes a cross-section of the party membership. Gingrich also makes it a point to consult and stay in regular contact with the various party subgroups. During the 104th Congress, when the Republican leadership was engaged in budget talks with the Clinton administration, Gingrich sought to keep his troops informed on a daily basis, even recording a briefing that members could access by phone when the sessions ran late. Summits cut most members out of the decision making process and this breeds resentment; aware of this problem,

Gingrich worked to counter it by at least keeping members informed.

The weight Gingrich puts on shaping the terms of the political debate leads logically to the centrality of message to his leadership strategies. Much more than for his Democratic predecessors, message became strategy.

Gingrich's prespeakership majority-building activities were based largely on message. He pioneered the use of C-SPAN to disseminate messages. Gingrich's attack on Speaker Wright was very much a media-based effort. Through tapes and speeches, Gingrich coached Republicans in the language to use; for example, recommending that they label Democrats as *pathetic, sick,* and, of course, *corrupt;* words such as *change, moral,* and *family* were to be associated with Republicans.

When Gingrich became whip, he continued to concentrate on majority building, much of it through message-disseminating activities. When, in 1990, he opposed the budget deal negotiated by President Bush and the bipartisan congressional leadership, it was to protect the party's message he had worked to shape. Only by maintaining a sharp difference between the parties and preserving the Republicans' best issue—lower taxes—could the Republicans hope to win a congressional majority, Gingrich believed. When the House "bank" scandal broke in 1991, Gingrich encouraged the junior Republicans who took to the floor and the airwaves to demand the release of members' names; the bigger a story the scandals became the more effective they were as a vehicle for disseminating Gingrich's message about the "corrupt Democratic Congress."

The Contract with America was itself an elaborate effort to disseminate a bundle of messages about the Republican party: messages about the policies the party supported but also the message that the party, unlike the majority Democrats, was dedicated to cleaning up the "corrupt" Congress and prepared to stake its future on fulfilling its promises. Thus, the first plank dealt with congressional reform; it was called a contract to give it an aura of legal weight, and Republicans explicitly invited voters to throw them out of office if they did not fulfill their promises. The language used to name the bills in the Contract was tested through polling and focus groups; welfare reform was named the "Personal Responsibility Act," and a cut in the capital gains tax and changes in the regulatory process aimed especially at weakening environmental regulations made up most of the "Job Creation and Wage Enhancement Act."

Message continued its primacy when Gingrich became Speaker. His media access was, however, much greater—a not unalloyed benefit, it turned out. Not only did Gingrich take advantage of the press's interest by granting innumerable interviews and appearing on myriad talk shows, he opened the Speaker's daily press conference to television coverage. (When reporters began to concentrate on ethics charges against him, Gingrich canceled daily press conferences altogether.) The Republican leadership insisted that each of the committees hire a press secretary and coordinate message strategy with the beefed-up leadership press operation. The Republican "theme teams," members organized to use the one-minute speeches at the beginning of a day's session to promulgate the message of the day, continued to operate. The Conference produces a "blizzard" of information, much of it aimed at advising members about how best to talk about issues.

Although members would later bitterly criticize the leadership for not being sufficiently effective at communication, immense effort went into attempts to shape public perceptions of Republicans' policy proposals. Special task forces put together media kits for use by Republican leaders and rank and file on each of the major issues. On Medicare, Republicans mounted a massive campaign. Much of the most intense effort was aimed at shifting the terms of the debate—from cutting the program to saving it by slowing the rate of increase.

The Democratic leadership in the postreform years refined the quintessential legislative strategy of using its control over procedure to structure the choices members confront. When Republicans were in the minority they complained bitterly about Democrats' use of procedure and especially their use of restrictive rules to structure choices. When Republicans became the majority in the 104th Congress, this history complicated their calculus on the design of rules. In the mid-1980s, House Republicans had given their leader the authority to appoint Republican members of the Rules Committee as the Democrats had a decade earlier; thus, under Republican control as well, the committee is an arm of the majority party leadership. Republicans kept the outsized majority margin on the committee (nine majority to four minority) when they took over.

The new Republican majority in the 104th Congress had promised to deliver on an ambitious agenda, much of it in the first one hundred days. When Republicans brought one of the early Contract items to the floor under an open rule, Democrats behaved just as the minority Republicans had when given the opportunity by an open rule: they offered multitudes of amendments, many designed to force vulnerable Republicans to cast difficult votes. In response and despite their promise, Republicans began to bring most major legislation to the floor under complex and restrictive rules. The proportion of all rules that were restrictive did go down from 70 percent in the 103rd Congress to 55 percent in the 104th, though Democrats claimed Republicans manipulated the figures by considering under open rules some noncontroversial legislation that should have been considered under the suspension procedure. Furthermore, rules were used not just to prevent obstructionism but also to structure choices; 77 percent of rules for the consideration of major measures were restrictive in the 104th—compared to 82 percent in the 103rd and 72 percent in both the 100th and 101st Congresses—and, according to the Republican Rules Committee's own classification, 63 percent of those rules were either modified closed or closed.

In sum, Gingrich's leadership strategies as Speaker show considerable continuity with those of recent Democratic leaderships. The "buy-in" strategy is the Republican version of the strategy of inclusion, an attempt to involve a large proportion of the membership in leadership efforts and thereby give them a stake in their success. Democrats had recognized the importance of participating effectively in national political discourse and had moved to increase their capabilities in the battle for public opinion; message is even more important to Gingrich's leadership. Although when they were in the minority Republicans vowed to eschew the strategy of structuring choices through the use of procedure, especially through special rules, the Republican leadership has, in fact, resorted to that strategy on a regular basis, as did their Democratic predecessors.

The political context changed drastically from the 104th to the 105th Congress. The extraordinary context of the 104th Congress and the way it shaped members' expectations and perceptions proved to be a two-edged sword. Gingrich found it impossible to persuade the bulk of his membership, especially the big freshman class, that flexibility and compromise were necessary, and a lengthy government shutdown, which the public blamed on the Republicans, resulted. Republicans held onto their House majority in the 1996 elections, but the margin was reduced and the sense of mandate generated by the 1994 elections had completely dissipated. There was no consensus within the party on strategy for the new Congress; many members were themselves uncertain, and few had the confidence in their leaders that they had had two years earlier.

The Republican leadership faced a much more difficult job in the 105th than it did in the 104th. The party leaders responded by exercising less aggressive leadership. They proposed no ambitious agenda and committees were subject to less direction from the leadership. Without the credibility with its membership that it had enjoyed in the 104th, the leadership had less leeway to be innovative in strategy and aggressive in using its resources. Trusting their leaders' judgment less, members were more likely to second guess their strategic decisions, to bicker among themselves about strategy and policy, and to go their own way when they disagreed with leadership decisions. Thus, the leadership had to work harder at keeping its members together even on the less tough issues. It needed to engage in more piecemeal bargaining and in a great deal more hand-holding. Constant communication with the membership and the inclusion of members in leadership efforts take on even more importance in this context.

Although less dominant and less successful than it was in the 104th, the House Republican leadership remained an activist, engaged leadership. Members still needed an activist leadership to advance their goals; for example, no budget deal would have been possible without it. Given the context, the Republican leaders are unlikely to be able to meet their members' expectations fully, yet their attempts to do the best they can entail the exercise of activist leadership—as has been the case for all majority party leaderships since the 1980s.

References

Albert, Carl. 1990. *Little Giant*. Norman: University of Oklahoma Press.

Alston, Chuck. 1991a. "First Session Winds Down after Tax-Cut Dither." *Congressional Quarterly Weekly Report*, November 30: 3506–10.

———. 1991b. "The Speaker and the Chairmen: A Taoist Approach to Power." *Congressional Quarterly Weekly Report*, November 2: 3178–80.

Arnold, R. Douglas. 1990. *The Logic of Congressional Action*. New Haven: Yale University Press.

Bach, Stanley. 1981. "The Structure of Choice in the House of Representatives: The Impact of Complex Special Rules." *Harvard Journal on Legislation* 18: 553–602.

Bach, Stanley, and Steven S. Smith. 1988. *Managing Uncertainty in the House of Representatives*. Washington, D.C.: Brookings Institution.

Baer, Denise. 1992–93. "Who Has the Body? Party Institutionalization and Theories of Party Organization." *Midsouth Political Science Journal* (Winter): 49–64.

Baker, Ross. 1983. "A Short History of the House Democratic Caucus." Manuscript.

Barry, John. 1989. *The Ambition and the Power*. New York: Viking.

Baumer, Donald. 1992. "Senate Democratic Leadership in the 100th Congress." In *The Atomistic Congress*, edited by Ronald Peters and Allen Herzke. Armonk, N.Y.: M. E. Sharpe.

Biskupic, Joan. 1990a. "For Critics of Flag Measure, Advance Work Pays Off." *Congressional Quarterly Weekly Report*, June 23: 1962–64.

———. 1990b. "Immigration Overhaul Cleared after Last-Minute Flap." *Congressional Quarterly Weekly Report*, November 3: 3743.

———. 1991a. "Bill Passes House, Not Muster; Next Chance Is in Senate." *Congressional Quarterly Weekly Report*, June 8: 1498–1503.

——. 1991b. "Crime Measure Is a Casualty of Partisan Skirmishing." *Congressional Quarterly Weekly Report,* June 8: 3528–30.

Blakely, Steve. 1987. "House Approves $725 Million for Homeless." *Congressional Quarterly Weekly Report,* March 7: 422–23.

Blechman, Barry. 1990. *The Politics of National Security.* New York: Oxford University Press.

Bolling, Richard. 1965. *House Out of Order.* New York: Dutton.

Brady, David, and Barbara Sinclair. 1984. "Building Majorities for Policy Change in the House of Representatives." *Journal of Politics* 46 (November): 1033–60.

Bragdon, Peter. 1989. "Though Pay Will Be a '90 Issue, Most Members Have Cover." *Congressional Quarterly Weekly Report,* December 2: 3324–26.

Browning, Robert X. N.d. "Television Talk-shows and U.S. Representatives." Manuscript.

Brown, Lynne P., and Robert L. Peabody. 1987. "Patterns of Succession in House Democratic Leadership: The Choices of Wright, Foley, Coelho, 1986." Paper presented at the annual meeting of the American Political Science Association, Chicago.

——. 1992. "Patterns of Succession in House Democratic Leadership: Foley, Gephardt, and Gray, 1989." In *New Perspectives on the House of Representatives,* 4th ed., edited by Robert L. Peabody and Nelson W. Polsby. Baltimore: Johns Hopkins University Press.

Calmes, Jacqueline. 1987. "Aspin Makes Comeback at Armed Services." *Congressional Quarterly Weekly Report,* January 24: 139–42.

Cheney, Richard B. 1989. "An Unruly House." *Public Opinion* 11:41–44.

Collie, Melissa P., and Joseph Cooper. 1989. "Multiple Referral and the 'New' Committee System in the House of Representatives." In *Congress Reconsidered,* 4th ed., edited by Lawrence C. Dodd and Bruce I. Oppenheimer. Washington D.C.: Congressional Quarterly Press.

Congressional Quarterly's Guide to the Congress of the United States. 1971. Washington, D.C.: Congressional Quarterly Press.

Cook, Timothy. 1989. *Making Laws and Making News.* Washington, D.C.: Brookings Institution.

Cooper, Joseph. 1977. "Congress in Organizational Perspective." In *Congress Reconsidered,* edited by Lawrence C. Dodd and Bruce I. Oppenheimer. New York: Praeger.

Cooper, Joseph, and David W. Brady. 1981. "Institutional Context and Leadership Style: The House from Cannon to Rayburn." *American Political Science Review* 75:411–25.

Cotter, Cornelius, James Gibson, John Bibby, and Robert Huckshorn. 1984. *Party Organizations in American Politics.* New York: Praeger.

Cox, Gary, and Mathew McCubbins. 1993. *Legislative Leviathan: Party Government in the House.* Berkeley: University of California Press.

Crotty, William. 1984. *American Parties in Decline.* 2d ed. Boston: Little, Brown.

Cummings, Milton C., and Robert L. Peabody. 1969. "The Decision to Enlarge the Committee on Rules: An Analysis of the 1961 Vote." In *New Perspectives on the House of Representatives,* 2d ed., edited by Robert L. Peabody and Nelson W. Polsby. Chicago: Rand McNally.

Davidson, Roger. 1988. "The New Centralization on Capitol Hill." *Review of Politics* 49 (Summer): 345–64.

Davidson, Roger, and Walter Oleszek. 1992. "From Monopoly to Management: Changing Patterns of Committee Deliberation." In *The Postreform Congress,* edited by Roger H. Davidson. New York: St. Martin's Press.

Dirksen Congressional Center. 1991. *Newsletter.* Fall.

Dodd, Lawrence C. 1979. "The Expanded Roles of the House Democratic Whip System: The 93rd and 94th Congresses." *Congressional Studies* 7 (Spring): 27–56.

Dodd, Lawrence C., and Bruce I. Oppenheimer, eds. 1977. *Congress Reconsidered.* New York: Praeger.

———. 1981, 1985, 1989, 1993. *Congress Reconsidered.* 2d, 3d, 4th, 5th eds. Washington, D.C.: Congressional Quarterly Press.

Eaton, William J., and Douglas Jehl. 1991. "Democrats Plan Vote on Tax Cut." *Los Angeles Times,* November 30.

Ehrenhalt, Alan. 1986. "Media, Power Shifts Dominate O'Neill's House." *Congressional Quarterly Weekly Report,* September 13: 2131–38.

Ellwood, John W. 1985. "The Great Exception: The Congressional Budget Process in an Age of Decentralization." In *Congress Reconsidered,* 3d ed., edited by Lawrence C. Dodd and Bruce I. Oppenheimer. Washington, D.C.: Congressional Quarterly Press.

Ellwood, John W., and James A. Thurber. 1981. "The Politics of the Congressional Budget Process Re-examined." In *Congress Reconsidered,* 2d ed., edited by Lawrence C. Dodd and Bruce I. Oppenheimer. Washington, D.C.: Congressional Quarterly Press.

Fenno, Richard F. 1965. "The Internal Distribution of Influence: The House." In *The Congress and America's Future,* edited by David B. Truman. Englewood Cliffs, N.J.: Prentice-Hall.

———. 1966. *The Power of the Purse.* Boston: Little Brown.

———. 1973. *Congressmen in Committees.* Boston: Little Brown.

———. 1978. *Home Style.* Boston: Little, Brown.

Ferber, Mark. 1964. "The Democratic Study Group: A Study of Intra-Party Organization in the House of Representatives." Ph.D. diss., University of California, Los Angeles.

Fiorina, Morris, and Kenneth Shepsle. 1989. "Formal Theories of Leadership: Agents, Agenda-Setters, and Entrepreneurs." In *Leadership and Politics,* edited by Bryan D. Jones. Lawrence: University of Kansas Press.

Follett, Mary Parker. 1974. *The Speaker of the House of Representatives.* 1896. Reprint, New York: Bert Franklin Reprints.

Fox, Harrison, and Susan Webb Hammond. 1977. *Congressional Staffs.* New York: Free Press.

Galloway, George B. 1961. *History of the House of Representatives.* New York: Thomas Y. Crowell.

Garand, James C., and Kathleen M. Clayton. 1986. "Socialization to Partisanship in the U.S. House: The Speaker's Task Force." *Legislative Studies Quarterly* 11 (August): 409–28.

Gertzog, Irwin N. 1976. "The Routinization of Committee Assignments in the U.S. House." *American Journal of Political Science* 29 (November): 693–712.

Gilmour, John B. 1990. *Reconcilable Differences?* Berkeley: University of California Press.

Greenhouse, Linda. 1987. "A Military Bill Like None Other." *New York Times*, May 13.

Hager, George, and David S. Cloud. 1993. "Democrats Pull Off Squeaker in Approving Clinton Plan." *Congressional Quarterly Weekly Report*, May 29: 1341.

Hall, Richard L. 1987. "Participation and Purpose in Committee Decision Making." *American Political Science Review* 81:105–27.

Hardin, Russell. 1982. *Collective Action*. Baltimore: Johns Hopkins University Press.

Herrnson, Paul. 1988. *Party Campaigning in the 1980s*. Cambridge, Mass.: Harvard University Press.

History of the Committee on Rules. 1983. Washington, D.C.: U.S. Government Printing Office.

Hook, Janet. 1990a. "Foley Leaves Mark on Panels as Coveted Seats Are Filled." *Congressional Quarterly Weekly Report*, December 8: 4066.

———. 1990b. "Younger Members Flex Muscle in Revolt against Chairmen." *Congressional Quarterly Weekly Report*, December 8: 4059–61.

Jacobson, Gary. 1992a. "Deficit Politics and the 1990 Elections." Paper presented at the annual meeting of the American Political Science Association, Chicago.

———. 1992b. *The Politics of Congressional Elections*. 3d ed. Boston: Little, Brown.

Jones, Charles O. 1964. *Party and Policy-Making: The House Republican Policy Committee*. New Brunswick, N.J.: Rutgers University Press.

Kernell, Samuel. 1986. *Going Public: New Strategies of Presidential Leadership*. Washington, D.C.: Congressional Quarterly Press.

Kiewiet, Roderick, and Mathew McCubbins. 1991. *The Logic of Delegation: Congressional Parties and the Appropriations Process*. Chicago: University of Chicago Press.

Kingdon, John W. 1973. *Congressmen's Voting Decisions*. New York: Harper and Row.

———. 1984. *Agendas, Alternatives, and Public Policies*. Boston: Little, Brown.

Kofmehl, Kenneth. 1964. "The Institutionalization of a Voting Bloc." *Western Political Quarterly* 17 (June): 256–72.

Krehbiel, Keith. 1988. "Spatial Models of Legislative Choice." *Legislative Studies Quarterly* 13 (August): 259–320.

———. 1991. *Information and Legislative Organization*. Ann Arbor: University of Michigan Press.

Kuntz, Phil. 1992. "Probes Continue to Embarrass as Feuding in House Grows." *Congressional Quarterly Weekly Report,* April 11: 933–34.

LeLoup, Lance T. 1977. *Budgetary Politics.* Brunswick, Ohio: Kings Court Press.

Light, Paul. 1982. *The President's Agenda: Domestic Policy Choice from Kennedy to Reagan.* Baltimore: Johns Hopkins University Press.

Lindsay, James M. 1991. *Congress and Nuclear Weapons.* Baltimore: Johns Hopkins University Press.

Loomis, Burdett. 1988. *The New American Politician.* New York: Basic Books.

MacNeil, Neil. 1963. *Forge of Democracy: The House of Representatives.* New York: McKay.

Madison, Christopher. 1990. "Message Bearer." *National Journal,* December 1: 2904–8.

Maisel, L. Sandy, ed. 1990. *The Parties Respond.* Boulder: Westview Press.

Malbin, Michael J. 1977. "House Democrats Are Playing with a Strong Leadership Lineup." *National Journal,* June 18: 940–46.

———. 1981. "Remember the Caucus." *National Journal,* September 12: 1642.

Masters, Nicholas. 1963. "Committee Assignments in the House of Representatives." In *New Perspectives on the House of Representatives,* edited by Robert L. Peabody and Nelson W. Polsby. Chicago: Rand McNally.

Mayhew, David. 1974. *Congress: The Electoral Connection.* New Haven: Yale University Press.

Morehouse, Macon. 1988a. "Dial-a-Porn Ban Approved as Rider to Big Education Bill." *Congressional Quarterly Weekly Report,* April 23: 1078.

———. 1988b. "Dial-a-Porn Dispute Delays Education Bill." *Congressional Quarterly Weekly Report,* April 16: 1033.

Murray, Hyde. 1990. "House of Representatives in Changing Times: House Parliamentary Procedure." Paper presented at Georgetown University Law Center, December 1.

Oleszek, Walter J. 1984. *Congressional Procedures and the Policy Process.* 2d ed. Washington: Congressional Quarterly Press.

Olson, Mancur. 1965. *The Logic of Collective Action.* Cambridge, Mass.: Harvard University Press.

Oppenheimer, Bruce I. 1977. "The Rules Committee: New Arm of Leadership in a Decentralized House." In *Congress Reconsidered,* edited by Lawrence C. Dodd and Bruce I. Oppenheimer. New York: Praeger.

———. 1981a. "The Changing Relationship between House Leadership and the Committee on Rules." In *Understanding Congressional Leadership,* edited by Frank H. Mackaman. Washington, D.C.: Congressional Quarterly Press.

———. 1981b. "Congress and the New Obstructionism: Developing an Energy Program." In *Congress Reconsidered,* 2d ed., edited by Lawrence C. Dodd and Bruce I. Oppenheimer. Washington, D.C.: Congressional Quarterly Press.

Oppenheimer, Bruce I., and Robert Peabody. 1977. "How the Race for Majority Leader Was Won—By One Vote." *Washington Monthly* (November): 47–56.

Ornstein, Norman J., ed. 1975. *Congress in Change.* New York: Praeger.

Ornstein, Norman J., Thomas E. Mann, and Michael J. Malbin. 1990. *Vital Statistics on Congress, 1989–90.* Washington, D.C.: American Enterprise Institute.

Orren, Gary, and William Mayer. 1990. "The Press, Political Parties, and the Public-Private Balance in Elections." In *The Parties Respond,* edited by L. Sandy Maisel. Boulder: Westview Press.

Palazzolo, Daniel J. 1992. "From Decentralization to Centralization: Members' Changing Expectations for House Leaders." In *The Postreform Congress,* edited by Roger H. Davidson. New York: St. Martin's Press.

Peabody, Robert L. 1976. *Leadership in Congress: Stability, Succession, and Change.* Boston: Little, Brown.

Peterson, Mark. 1990. *Legislating Together.* Cambridge, Mass.: Harvard University Press.

Phillips, Don. 1989. "Being Nice on His Way up the Ladder." *Washington Post National Edition,* October 23–29: 13–14.

Pitney, John. 1988. "The War on the Floor: Partisan Conflict in the U.S. House of Representatives." Paper presented at the annual meeting of the American Political Science Association, Washington, D.C.

Polsby, Nelson W. 1968. "The Institutionalization of the U.S. House of Representatives." *American Political Science Review* 62:144–68.

Powell, Lynda. 1991. "Changes in Liberalism-Conservatism in the U.S. House of Representatives: 1978–1988." Paper presented at the annual meeting of the American Political Science Association, Washington, D.C.

Price, David E. 1989. "From Outsider to Insider." In *Congress Reconsidered,* 4th ed., edited by Lawrence C. Dodd and Bruce I. Oppenheimer. Washington, D.C.: Congressional Quarterly Press.

———. 1992. *The Congressional Experience.* Boulder: Westview Press.

Rapp, David. 1989. "Negotiators Agree on Outlines of Fiscal 1990 Plan." *Congressional Quarterly Weekly Report,* April 15: 804–5.

Ripley, Randall B. 1964. "The Party Whip Organization in the United States House of Representatives." *American Political Science Review* 58:561–76.

———. 1967. *Party Leaders in the House of Representatives.* Washington, D.C.: Brookings Institution.

———. 1969. *Majority Party Leadership in Congress.* Boston: Little, Brown.

Robinson, James A. 1963. *The House Rules Committee.* Indianapolis: Bobbs-Merrill.

Rohde, David. 1988. "Variations in Partisanship in the House of Representatives: Southern Democrats, Realignment, and Agenda Change." Paper presented at the annual meeting of the American Political Science Association, Washington, D.C.

———. 1991. *Parties and Leaders in the Postreform House.* Chicago: University of Chicago Press.

Rohde, David, and Kenneth A. Shepsle. 1987. "Leaders and Followers in the House of Representatives: Reflections on Woodrow Wilson's 'Congressional Government.'" *Congress and the Presidency* 14:111–33.

Rovner, Julie. 1986. "With Death Penalty Removed, Anti-Drug Measure Is Cleared." *Congressional Quarterly Weekly Report,* October 18: 2594.

Schick, Allen. 1980. *Congress and Money.* Washington, D.C.: Urban Institute.

Scholzman, Kay Lehman, and John T. Tierney. 1986. *Organized Interests and American Democracy.* New York: Harper and Row.

Sheppard, Burton. 1985. *Rethinking Congressional Reform.* Cambridge, Mass.: Shenkman.

Shepsle, Kenneth. 1978. *The Giant Jigsaw Puzzle: Democratic Committee Assignments in the Modern House.* Chicago: University of Chicago Press.

——. 1989. "The Changing Textbook Congress." In *Can the Government Govern?* edited by John H. Chubb and Paul Peterson. Washington, D.C.: Brookings Institution.

Sinclair, Barbara. 1982. *Congressional Realignment.* Austin: University of Texas Press.

——. 1983. *Majority Leadership in the U.S. House.* Baltimore: Johns Hopkins University Press.

——. 1985. "Agenda Control and Policy Success: The Case of Ronald Reagan and the 97th House." *Legislative Studies Quarterly* 20 (August): 291–314.

——. 1988. "Majority Party Leadership in the House of Representatives: A Reassessment." Paper presented at the annual meeting of the American Political Science Association, Washington, D.C.

——. 1989. *The Transformation of the U.S. Senate.* Baltimore: Johns Hopkins University Press.

——. 1990. "The Congressional Party: Evolving Organizational, Agenda-Setting, and Policy Roles." In *The Parties Respond,* edited by L. Sandy Maisel. Boulder: Westview Press.

——. 1991. "Governing Unheroically (and Sometimes Unappetizingly): Bush and the 101st Congress." In *The Bush Presidency: First Appraisals,* edited by Colin Campbell and Bert Rockman. Chatham, N.J.: Chatham House.

——. 1992a. "The Emergence of Strong Leadership in the 1980s House of Representatives." *Journal of Politics* 54 (August): 658–84.

——. 1992b. "Strong Party Leadership in a Weak Party Era — The Evolution of Party Leadership in the Modern House." In *The Atomistic Congress,* edited by Ronald Peters and Allen Herzke. Armonk, N.Y.: M. E. Sharpe.

Smith, Hedrick. 1988. *The Power Game.* New York: Ballantine Books.

Smith, Steven. 1989. *Call to Order: Floor Politics in the House and Senate.* Washington, D.C.: Brookings Institution.

Smith, Steven S., and Christopher J. Deering. 1990. *Committees in Congress.* 2d ed. Washington, D.C.: Congressional Quarterly Press.

Vanderbilt Television News Archive. 1972–. *Television News Index and Abstracts.* Nashville, Tenn.

Waldman, Sidney. 1978. "Majority Party Leadership in the Contemporary House: The 94th and 95th Congresses." Manuscript.

——. 1980. "Majority Leadership in the House of Representatives." *Political Science Quarterly* 95 (Fall): 373–93.

Wattenberg, Martin. 1986. *The Decline of American Political Parties: 1952–1984.* Cambridge, Mass.: Harvard University Press.

Wayne, Stephen J. 1978. *The Legislative Presidency.* New York: Harper and Row.

Wolfensberger, Don. 1992. "Comparative Data on the U.S. House of Representatives." Compiled by the Republican staff of the House Rules Committee. November 10.

Young, Gary, and Joseph Cooper. 1993. "Multiple Referral and the Transformation of House Decision Making." In *Congress Reconsidered,* 5th ed., edited by Lawrence C. Dodd and Bruce I. Oppenheimer. Washington, D.C.: Congressional Quarterly Press.

Zuckman, Jill. 1992a. "Ford Drops Pell 'Entitlement' from College Loan Bill." *Congressional Quarterly Weekly Report,* March 21: 729–31.

———. 1992b. "Most House Chairmen Hold On; Freshmen Win Choice Posts." *Congressional Quarterly Weekly Report,* December 12: 3785–88.

Index

LIBRARY OF CONGRESS CATALOGING-IN-PUBLICATION DATA

Sinclair, Barbara, 1940–
  Legislators, leaders, and lawmaking : the U.S. House of Representatives in the
postreform era/Barbara Sinclair.
      p.   cm.
  Includes bibliographical references and index.
  ISBN 0-8018-4955-1 (alk. paper)
    1. United States. Congress. House—Leadership.   2. Democratic Party (U.S.)
3. Legislators—United States.   4. Political leadership—United States.   I. Title.
JK 1411.S55   1995
328.73´0762—dc20
                                                                        94-33953

ISBN 0-8018-5712-0 (pbk.)